CRITICAL

HISTORY AND DEFENCE

OF THE

OLD TESTAMENT CANON.

BY

MOSES STUART,

PROFESSOR OF SAC. LITERATURE IN THE THEOL. SEMINARY,
ANDOVER, MASS.

WITH AN INTRODUCTION AND NOTES,

BY SAMUEL DAVIDSON, D. D.

OF THE UNIVERSITY OF HALLE.

Wipf and Stock Publishers
EUGENE, OREGON

Wipf and Stock Publishers
199 West 8th Avenue, Suite 3
Eugene, Oregon 97401

Critical History and Defence of the Old Testament Canon
By Stuart, Moses and Davidson, Samuel
ISBN: 1-59244-372-9
Publication date 10/1/2003
Previously published by George Routledge & Co., 1849

CONTENTS

Sect.		Page
I.	Introductory Remarks	1
II.	Definition of the word *Canon*	22
III.	Commencement of the Canon	29
IV.	State of Literature and Instruction among the Hebrews	56
V.	Continued History of the Canon; books of known authors	124
VI.	Continued History .... Books anonymous	132
VII.	Lost books of the Hebrews	168
VIII.	Manner of preserving the Sacred Books	180
IX.	Genuineness; general considerations	199
X.	Completion of the Canon	206
XI.	Ancient divisions of the Canon	227
XII.	Sameness of the Jewish Canon ever since its completion	238
XIII.	General Results	272
XIV.	Canon of the Egyptian Jews	276
XV.	How were the Scriptures estimated by the Jews?	279
XVI.	Summary of testimony by Sirach, Philo, and Josephus	290
XVII.	Nature and importance of New Testament testimony	291
XVIII.	Appeals by the New Testament to the Old	296
XIX.	Result	321
XX.	Conclusion	323
XXI.	Remarks on doubts respecting some of the Old Test. books	326
XXII.	Use of the Old Testament	360

APPENDIX.

No.		PAGE
I. Testimony of the Son of Sirach		395
II. — — of Philo Judæus		399
III. — — of Josephus		401
IV. — — of Melito		403
V. — — of Origen		404
VI. — — of the Council of Laodicea		407
VII. — — of Cyrill of Jerusalem		408
VIII. — — of Gregory Nazianzen		409
IX. — — of Athanasius		411
X. — — of Synopsis of Scripture		413
XI. — — of Epiphanius		415
XII. — — of the Council of Hippo		417
XIII. — — of the Council of Carthage		418
XIV. — — of Jerome		ib.
XV. — — of Hilary		421
XVI. — — of Rufinus		422

INTRODUCTORY ESSAY.

FEW intelligent theologians, and fewer Biblical scholars, can entertain a doubt of the necessity of a new treatise on the Canon of the Old Testament. If the Canon of the New Testament demands investigation at the present day, as it assuredly does, that of the Old Testament does so more imperatively. There is an obscurity about the whole subject which needs to be dissipated as far as it may be by the aid of the most recent light. Considerable difficulty will probably still remain to baffle the skill of the learned; but after due allowance has been made, it will appear that much *can* be done towards an explanation of the topic in question.

Four points connected with it naturally suggest themselves to the mind. *First,* By what principle or principles were certain writings regarded as sacred and authoritative by the Jewish nation at large, while others were looked on as of mere human origin? *Secondly,* Are Christians bound to follow the Jews in this respect, and so to regard the same writings as Divine? *Thirdly,* When and by whom was the Canon completed or closed? *Fourthly,* Were any changes made at this time in the books, either in the way of addition, or of rectifying errors which had crept in from the time they were first written? A full examination of these questions would embrace all that could be said on the subject of the Canon. A *full and impartial* examination I mean. But this cannot be expected very soon. It will probably be a long time ere such a work make its appearance in the

English language. Not many possess the learning and judgment adequate to its production. Large and varied attainments, such as seldom fall to the lot of one person, are required for its due performance. Qualifications natural and acquired are demanded for it. A philosophical spirit, capable of wielding and guiding multifarious learning, is eminently needed. Calm judgment, acute discrimination, freedom from the slavery of current opinions, fearlessness in following out investigations to their legitimate results, and in enunciating those results to the public—all this, combined with a deep reverence for whatever is sacred and divine, must belong to the right-minded and successful inquirer into this department of theological learning. The Germans possess some of these qualifications; but in others they are lamentably wanting. So also with regard to English theologians. The man who would write conclusively on the whole subject, settling it as far as it is capable of such settlement, should unite in himself the best qualifications of German and English scholarship—the varied learning of the former with the practical common sense of the latter—the liberty of thought exemplified by the Germans with the conservative tendency of the English mind.

The reader of the following treatise will perceive, that it throws considerable light on the *first two* questions. On the *last two*, especially on the fourth, little is advanced. The work indeed is rather *an apology* for the present Canon, than a full and impartial history of it. It bears *the apologetic* air throughout. Perhaps it is too like the writing of a man who sets out determined by all means to uphold the existing and commonly received books. Hence, serious difficulties are occasionally kept in the back-ground, or altogether unmentioned. There is no *complete* statement of objections to the opinions advocated by the writer. Formidable hinderances to his sentiments are not every where fairly brought out. Hence the treatise is not *exhaustive*. It is therefore less satisfactory. Indeed it is not fitted to afford entire satisfaction on many points of importance and interest. The learned author has not *settled* every thing about the Canon. The subject still requires a *comprehensive* treatment. In particular, the separation of the so-called *apocryphal* books from the inspired books of the Old Testament needs further explanation. In proof of these remarks, the reader is requested to compare the observations made by Mr. Stuart on Origen's testimony respecting the Canon with the following passages in the works of that learned father. In his treatise *De Princip.* ii. 1, he writes thus: "Ut ex Scripturarum auctoritate hoc ita se habere credamus, audi quoque in Maccabæorum libris." Here he speaks of the books of the Maccabees as *authoritative Scripture.* Again, in his treatise against Celsus, (viii. 50,) he refers to Ecclesiasticus as $\theta \varepsilon \tilde{\imath} o \varsigma$ $\lambda \acute{o} \gamma o \varsigma$, *a divine treatise;* and in another place the same expression is applied to the book of Wisdom. To Tobit he applies the distinctive term $\gamma \rho \alpha \phi \acute{\eta}$, *scripture.* Like observations occur in Irenæus, Clement of Alexandria, Cyprian, and other fathers. Thus Irenæus writes, (Adv. Hæres. v. 35,) " Significavit Jeremias propheta," where the apocryphal book of Baruch is meant. Clement of Alexandria refers to the third chapter of Baruch when he writes, $\dot{\eta}$ $\theta \varepsilon \acute{\imath} \alpha$ $\pi o \upsilon$ $\lambda \acute{\varepsilon} \gamma \varepsilon \iota$ $\gamma \rho \alpha \phi \grave{\eta}$, *Divine Scripture says in a certain place* (Pædagog. II.). Cyprian has, " Scriptura divina instruit," where Tobit is meant (De Orat. Domin.). These few particulars will serve to justify the correctness of our observations respecting difficulties unnoticed by Prof. Stuart—difficulties which a *comprehensive* treatise could not fail to notice.

But though the work is not an *exhaustive* treatise on the Canon; though it even fails to settle in a satisfactory manner various matters more or less fully introduced, yet it has its value. The esteemed author probably did not intend it to be a *complete* critical history and defence of the Canon— so complete as to omit nothing of consequence. His work is essentially a *contribution* to the history of the Old Testament Canon. And a very valuable contribution it is. It deserves an honourable place in the Biblical literature of the present day, and must be of great service to future inquirers. No work in the English language occupies the same position or possesses the same excellence in reference to the important subject of which it treats. I am persuaded, therefore, that it will be most welcome to many thoughtful minds. It is pervaded by a spirit of candour not very common in modern times. Proceeding as it does from one imbued with reverence for the Divine oracles, who has been conversant during a long life with the interpretation of them, and who is well acquainted with recent theological literature, the treatise will be acceptable to a large and happily increasing class. It breathes a healthy spirit of investigation. The author is not very anxious to evade difficulties when he is aware of their existence. He is not afraid to think; and to avow his opinions even when they may be adverse to the great majority of the so-called orthodox. He gives due credit to his opponents, without indulging in violent invectives against them. He looks their assertions calmly in the face, dealing in argument rather than vituperation. Hence it is pleasant to be in company with the writer. Quite refreshing is it to hold communion with one, who in the midst of an evil-speaking generation is no slave to current opinions in theology, *simply because they are current.*

I have said, that the propriety of reprinting this American work cannot be questioned for a moment; for the book of Mr. Norton which gave rise to it has been also republished in England. If therefore it be desirable that the antidote should go after the poison in one country, it is equally desirable in another. And it is needless to blind our eyes to the fact, that scepticism in various forms is freely circulated in this island, at the present day. The New Testament history has been impugned in different ways. How then can the Old Testament escape? It has *not* escaped the fiery test. External evidence in favour of the canonical books has been depreciated of late. *Intuitions, feelings, pure reason, the divine* or *spiritual* in man, phrases which mean the same thing, are now exalted to undue prominence—so much so as to set aside, by their arbitrary authority, strong historical testimony. A vague, mystical, spiritual *something* within, sits in judgment on the sacred writings, dealing with them in a very summary method, and rejecting whatever does not meet its approval. This is the sort of scepticism which the truth has to encounter. It matters little whether it consist in *reason*, or *philosophy*, or *intuitional faculties*. Names vary, but the *thing itself* remains the same. I am well aware, that the Bible in all its parts must be consonant with right reason and sound philosophy. It addresses itself to the understanding as well as to the heart of mankind. If it contradict the true light which God has implanted within, it cannot be received as a book containing messages from Heaven. The judgment must be satisfied of its truth. But it is quite possible, at the same time, to uphold as *pure reason*, or *right intuition*, or *sound philosophy*, or *internal consciousness*, that which has no good claim to the honourable appellations in question. And not only is this possible, but it has been exemplified in cases not a few. The thing is notorious. The error—and it is a grievous one—is committed every day. Individuals set up *their own* reason as the ultimate standard by which they try the Divine authority of the Bible. This is taking a one-sided view of the subject. It wants generalization and is therefore unphilosophical.

If it were necessary to adduce an additional reason for reprinting the present treatise, I should point to the work entitled "A History of the Hebrew Monarchy from the Administration of Samuel to the Babylonish Captivity." London, 8vo, 1847. Here is a book conceived and executed in the worst spirit of German Anti-supranaturalism. It is quite worthy of a Paulus, as the following extracts will serve to show.

"Their [the prophets'] characteristic emblem was some musical instrument, and their highest function to compose and sing solemn psalms of religious worship or instruction. The Hebrew prophets were not free from various tinges of fanaticism, which generated also affectation. That they often worked themselves into a religious frenzy (as in the wild Asiatic ceremonies which the Greeks called *Orgies*) may be inferred from the same verb in Hebrew meaning to prophesy and to be mad. . . . . Even later prophets are recorded to have walked naked and barefoot, or to have lain upon one side sometimes for years, like the religious madmen of the East; and some proceedings yet more ambiguous are ascribed to them. . . . . Their mode of seeking for a Divine reply was not ceremonial or superstitious, however tinged with a high enthusiasm. The prophet either played on the lyre himself or (oftener perhaps) called for a minstrel to do so, and wrapt himself in pious meditation on the subject of inquiry; until, gaining an insight into its moral bearings, and kindled by the melody, he delivered a response in a high-wrought and generally poetical strain."

Such, according to the writer, is the best general idea we can get of the position and agency of the prophets; p. 31—37.

"The book of Chronicles is not an honest and trustworthy narrative, and must be used with great caution as an authority, where any thing is involved which affects Levitical influence;" p. 146.

"To inveigh against Omri is absurd and monstrous in writers (the compilers of the Chronicles) who cannot spare a word of censure for Solomon's gratuitous heathen marriages and heathen abominations;" p. 177.

"The crisis called forth two great prophets in succession, Elijah and Elisha; whose adventures and exploits have come down to us in such a halo of romance, not unmingled with poetry of a high genius, that it is impossible to disentangle the truth. The account of these occupies twice as much space as the history of the kings of Judah and Israel together, from the death of Solomon to the accession of Ahab; but as their deeds are nearly all prodigies, attested to us only by a writing compiled three centuries after the facts, and having no bearing that can be traced on the real course of the history, we are forced to pass them over very slightly. The ascription, however, of miraculous powers to these prophets is a notable circumstance, as being altogether new in Jewish history. To find any thing analogous we must run back to the legendary days of Moses. One general inference may be drawn,—that the danger and importance of the struggle worked up the minds of Jehovah's worshippers into a high enthusiasm and intense belief of his present energy to aid his prophets. The after-tale also shows, that here, as elsewhere, persecution made its victims bigoted, undiscriminating, and ruthless in their turn;" p. 180.

"It is unpleasing to find the prophet Isaiah (ch. xxiii.) exult in the dangers which came upon this noble city, (Tyre,) while standing in the foreground for freedom, and really shielding Jerusalem from the common oppressor. We here see the evil element of exclusive patriotism, which, when imbibed by those who had not Isaiah's other great qualities, made the Jew to be regarded as *a hater of mankind.* In the ode itself there is no indication that Tyre was regarded as hostile to Jerusalem: the slave trade is not named, nor the alliance with Philistia or Syria. But here, as elsewhere, the Hebrew prophets show a narrow-minded abhorrence of worldly art, skill, and science, as producing merely wealth, pomp, luxury, and pride;" p. 286.

"We have no evidence against this king (Jehoiakim) better than the vague words of the man whom he pursued as a political offender;" p. 353.

"Jeremiah's memory failed of reproducing accurately the utterances of years long past;" p. 352, note.

"The writing (of *the younger Isaiah,* ch. xl.—lxii.) is obviously that of a Jew in Babylonia during the exile; and his great subject is, the approaching restoration to their own land;" p. 366.

"Had the announcements of Jeremiah and Ezekiel (respecting the conquest of Egypt by the Babylonians) proved true, we should inevitably have learned of it from Herodotus," p. 364.

I trust that the readers into whose hands this dangerous book may fall, will not be seduced by its flippant statements. I do not deny that it evinces much learning and acuteness; but it wants the calmness and impartiality of true philosophy. The writer evidently sets out with the denial of miracles and prophecy. In this respect, he goes beyond some of the Germans, whose learning he makes use of, and whose conclusions he implicitly adopts wherever they serve his purpose. It would be easy to show, that there is much unfairness in many of his reasonings. He repeats arguments which have been answered. He fathers conclusions which have been successfully combated, without hinting at the names of the scholars who have stood forth in defence of the truth. Should any be unhappily led astray by this work, the present treatise will help to set them right, or suggest at least another view of various questions. As an example, I refer to the observations respecting Manasseh in both works. The anonymous writer denies that Manasseh had been guilty of so grave an offence as that of persecuting the sacred book, "when it has not been charged on him." If he did so act, it is thought he must have failed, "because numerous copies must have been in the priests' hands;" pp. 330, 331. Here the dogmatic *must* plays an important part. Compare Mr. Stuart's observations on the same point, and a much better idea of the matter will be obtained. So with regard to other matters. It is to be hoped, however, that comparatively few have arrived at the height of wisdom to which this writer has attained. There is enough of good sense, not to say religion, in the land, to turn away with abhorrence from the notion dogmatically propounded: "it must not be assumed, that these 'false prophets' were not fully equal in moral worth to Jeremiah, and as sincerely convinced that Jehovah spoke by them, as he was in his own case;" p. 357. But enough of this author, and of his "History of the Hebrew Monarchy," which would require a much larger book than itself to refute.

The fundamental mistake committed by Mr. Norton and the anonymous writer in question, consists in a transference of the full light of the Christian dispensation to the dimness of the Jewish. They have not carefully or calmly considered the genius of the one as compared with the other. The first was very imperfect and dark when placed by the side of the second. It was meant to prepare the way for the latter, and must therefore have been inferior in many respects. In regard to the nature of the Old Testament dispensation itself it might be shown, that the entire arrangement was adapted to the period of the world during which it continued, the rude notions of the people whom God singled out from among the other peoples of the earth, the degree of civilization then existing in Asia, and the temporary character of the dispensation itself. When it is remembered, that the old economy was merely a shadow of good things to come, not the substance—that it typified the sacrifice of Christ—that it was limited to one nation, not universal like Christianity—that the revelations of Heaven to men must be accommodated in a good degree to their prevailing conceptions and imperfect culture—it will be seen, that the Jews were taught in the only way in which they could have been instructed consistently as well with the nature of humanity and their peculiar national character as with the design which they were chosen to answer in the history of God's dealings with the inhabitants of the earth. Things were permitted then, which Christianity cannot allow. The times of ignorance then, God winked at. Matters were commanded then, which are not commanded now.

Bloodshed was far more common then than now. God spake then in diverse ways. He speaks otherwise now. Different agencies were employed, which could not now be employed consistently with the purposes of Deity. The darkness is past, and the true light now shineth. Hence a different tuition is necessary. But there is still a pure and elevated morality directly sanctioned by God under all dispensations. The character and attributes of Jehovah are the same, though presented in various aspects. Sin is ever an object of the Divine displeasure. The character of man and the character of God are *essentially* the same as described under the two dispensations. God's *dealings* are different, but his nature is one and the same. He dealt with the Jews in a manner consistent with the great purpose which that people were selected to fulfil in the history of humanity; and it would be very difficult, if not impossible, to point out any other course of proceeding which he could have pursued towards them, equally worthy of *himself* and adapted to all the circumstances in which *they* were placed.

These general observations may suffice to show the unfairness of judging of a former economy by the light of another which succeeded, and then condemning many things connected with it, because they do not come up to the full standard of Christianity. And yet this is what is done by Mr. Norton and others. Having their minds fully possessed with the pure principles and exalted ideas of Christianity, they go back to the Old Testament; and, failing to find the same elevation there, they criticise, discredit, or discard what appears to be unworthy of the Deity as He is revealed by the Son.

To return to the work of Mr. Stuart. I have no intention on the present occasion to *review* the different parts of which it consists. While I agree with the great majority of the statements made, I do not assent to them all. Some topics are ably, others imperfectly discussed. In this respect there is considerable diversity. Thus the eighteenth section, in which the appeals of the New. Testament to the Old are considered, does not exhibit much cogency of argument. The writer deals too much in general assertions, even where quoting particular passages. Nor is the twenty-first section satisfactory. Here indeed the learned author had to grapple with serious difficulties. The books of Esther, Ecclesiastes, and Song of Songs, present perplexing anomalies which have never been cleared away. Manfully has he endeavoured to solve them. But that he has been successful, will scarcely be maintained by such as are fully aware of those anomalies in all their extent and magnitude. It will be perceived at a glance that the apologetic tone is far too prominent in this section. On the other hand, the twenty-second section is able and conclusive, though partaking of the diffuse character which belongs to the entire book.

Those who know what *Introduction* as used by the Germans embraces will see, that many topics examined but partially in the present volume belong to *it*. An Introduction to the Old Testament professedly takes up by far the largest proportion of the matters here introduced. The writer has accordingly made good use of the recent German Introductions. In one part, however, he has unaccountably neglected that of Hävernick. But De Wette's, with all its faults—and they are most serious ones—is the only work of this kind which is entirely up to the present state of knowledge; and with it the author seems fully conversant. He should have made more use of Herbst's, which is very able in some respects, though the work of a Roman Catholic. It is surprising that Mr. Stuart should have overlooked some other treatises, such as *Koester's* book on the prophets, which is very much superior to *Knobel's* dull and flat production. Strange too it is, that none of the articles in Kitto's Cyclopædia should have been consulted. It is superfluous to specify others which Mr. Stuart ought to have read. For this neglect, however, I am far from blaming him. Rather am I astonished that he has read and consulted most of the recent German literature bearing on his subject. At his age, and with his very precarious state of health, it is marvellous that he has kept pace with the rapidly accumulating materials issuing yearly from the press. Add to this, his style, though very diffuse and full of repetitions, has the fresh vigour of youth about it. It betokens the sprightly temperament of a young man.

I have subjoined a very few notes here and there, which are distinguished by the letter D. The text itself has been altered in no more than two or three words; but several erroneous references to chapters and verses have been rectified. The only retrenchment worth mentioning, which I have ventured to make, is the omission of the greater part of page 397 in the American edition, where the author digresses into an apostrophe to the Free Church of Scotland, that had just then seceded from the Establishment. The apostrophe has nothing to do with a work on the Canon, and may be well spared; especially as a periodical bearing the name of the "Free Church," has been latterly filling its pages with abuse of Mr. Stuart himself, and of others who do not happen to agree with the type of orthodoxy ignorantly maintained by it.

S. D.

Lancashire Independent College,
  Manchester, June 8th, 1849.

CRITICAL HISTORY

AND DEFENCE OF THE

CANON OF THE OLD TESTAMENT.

SECTION I.

INTRODUCTORY REMARKS.

THE time has been, when few, if any, who admitted the Divine origin and authority of the Christian religion, deemed it consistent or decorous to deny the sacred authority of the Old Testament Scriptures. But that time has passed away, and we have come to witness new developments of sceptical feelings, at which our ancestors would have stood astounded. I do not mean to aver, that there has not, for ages past, been a class of men in all Christian countries, who doubted the Divine authority of the Christian and Jewish religion, and of course the Divine origin and authority of the sacred books in general. But the professed reception of the Christian religion as Divine, with the admission that the New Testament contains at least a credible and authentic account of it; the admission at the same time, that the Jewish religion had some proper and real claim to be considered as having been approved and established by God, while the Old Testament is regarded in the main as a work of sciolists and impostors; is a phenomenon that has rarely occurred, I believe, in any country, but which we of the present day are called upon, perhaps for the first time, to witness.

Past experience and *a priori* reasoning from the nature of the case would probably have led most persons to conclude, that such a development would not take place on the part of any well-informed and consistent man; yet Mr. Norton, in a work replete in many respects with learning and valuable matter—a work which he entitles *Evidences of the Genuineness of the Gospels*—has taken the unusual position which I have been describing. In a Note appended to Vol. II. of this work, extending from p. 402 to 512, in which he has brought under review "the Jewish dispensation, the Pentateuch, and the other Books of the Old Testament," he has developed his opinions at length on these subjects, and actually and earnestly laboured to show, that in order to maintain the Divine origin of the Jewish religion, as founded by Moses, it becomes necessary to show that he did *not* write the Pentateuch; and in like manner, in order to show that the Jewish prophets and others who laboured to promote the observance of the Jewish religion, were the true disciples of a true religion, it becomes necessary to show, that most of the Old Testament books are filled with incredible, or trivial, or superstitious narrations and notions, and that the best we can do, even with the prophets, is to select here and there a passage that accords with reason and sound judgment, to which we may give our assent as being worthy of the ancient dispensation, while the rest is to be placed under the same category as the fictions and extravagant accounts of all other nations, respecting their origin and their history in ages too remote to have been consigned to writing.

It is not my design, in the present work, to review at length and controvert all the positions of Mr. Norton. It will be seen, in the brief account that I shall give of them in the sequel, that a great proportion of them belong rather to the department of Christian *theology*, especially of apologetic and polemic theology, than to the department of sacred literature. I leave to others what properly belongs to them, not doubting in the least that there is the ability and the will, among some of the theologians of our country, to put on their armour and advance to the contest, when the attempt is made to take our citadel by storm. My intention is to confine myself, in the main, within the limits of *a critical and historical view of the Jewish Canon of Scripture in the days of Christ and the apostles, and to show that this Canon, as received by the Jews at that time, was declared by our Saviour and his apostles to be of Divine origin and authority, and was treated by them as entitled to these claims.* If it can be shown that Christ and the apostles, as the commissioned messengers of God to establish Christianity, did receive, regard, and treat the Scriptures of the Jews as obligatory and of Divine authority, and also that these Scriptures were the same books which belong to our present Old Testament, then two consequences must follow from the establishment of these propositions. The first is, that whatever doubts or difficulties any one may have about the critical history or origin of particular books in the Old Testament, still he must now acknowledge that they have received the sanction of an authority from which there is no appeal. Universal scepticism alone can make exceptions to them, on the ground of credibility and authenticity. The second is, that the man who admits the Divine origin and authority of the Christian religion, and that the New Testament contains a credible and authentic account or development of it by Christ and by the apostles, must be altogether inconsistent with himself and inconsequent in his reasonings, if he rejects the Divine origin and authority of the Old Testament Scriptures.

If I succeed in proving in a historico-critical way what I design to prove, the *nucleus* of the question, as to the authority and claims of the Old Testament, would seem to be reached. I shall not endeavour therefore to invest myself, on the present occasion, with the panoply of the merely apologetic and polemic theologian. Let those use it, who have long worn it, and are *semper parati* for contest. The simple sling and stone of historical criticism are all that I essay to use. And if I miss my aim, I must leave it for others to defend our common citadel in a more effectual manner; for defence would seem to be needed. The contest has become one *pro aris et focis*.

Mr Norton's work consists of three volumes, and is printed in a splendid manner. The size of the work, and the consequent price of it, will doubtless prevent a widely extended circulation of the book.* On this account, and because of what I have already said respecting it, I have thought it

---

* It has been reprinted in London in two volumes octavo, and at less than half the price of the American edition. The references have been adapted accordingly to the pages of the English reprint. D.

would appear desirable to most of my readers to learn something of the nature of the attack which he has made upon the Old Testament, through the medium of some brief communication. In as summary a manner as possible, I will therefore now present them with a *coup d' oeil*, or table of contents, of that portion of his work which I have specially in view on this occasion.

He commences with the concession, that the Jewish *religion* is Divine, and that Christianity is built upon it. But this, he says, does not make Christianity in the least degree responsible for the *books* of the Old Testament. The Jewish religion itself, he avers, is no more responsible for the books of the Old Testament, than Christianity is responsible for the writings of the fathers from the second century to the eleventh ; p. 402, seq.

The character ascribed by most Christians to the Old Testament Scriptures, he goes on to say, brings them into collision with rational criticism in the interpretation of language, with the moral and religious conceptions of enlightened men, and with the progress of the physical sciences. They are contradicted by geology ; p. 404. The philosopher must reject their [the scriptural] views of the Godhead ; the enlightened Christian and moralist must reject the cruelties which they often enjoin, as appropriate only to a dark and barbarous age ; the careful inquirer will be revolted by their contradictions and discrepancies. The explanations and defence of these things have been unsatisfactory, and built on false principles and assumed facts ; so that one can hardly believe that the men who have offered them have been sincere in so doing ; p. 405, seq.

In expressing these views, he says that he merely gives form and voice to the ideas and feelings that exist in the minds of a large portion of intelligent believers ; p. 405. To separate all these things from Christianity, so that it shall not be responsible for them, is the duty of every friend to this religion ; p. 406.

To maintain that Moses was a minister of God, is one thing ; to maintain that he was the author of the Pentateuch, is another. So far is the truth of either proposition from being involved in the other, that, in order to render it evident that the mission of Moses was from God, it may be necessary to prove that the books, which profess to contain a history of his ministry, were *not* written by him, and do not afford an authentic account of it; p. 416.

The Pentateuch puts forward no claims to be considered as the work of Moses. The fact that the Law, in the time of Ezra, was ascribed to Moses, does not prove that the authorship of the Pentateuch was at the same time ascribed to him. In the reign of Josiah, a short time before the captivity, the Jews were ignorant of any written copy of their national laws, as is evident from the discovery as represented of a copy of the Law in the temple. Such a book was before unknown to Josiah, a pious king, to the secretary Shaphan, and to the high priest Hilkiah. " The story of its being accidentally found in the temple, may be thought to have been what was considered a justifiable artifice, to account for the appearance of a book hitherto unknown;" pp. 418, 428, 429.

The Canon of the Old Testament, after the captivity, comprised all the books of the Hebrews then extant. This Canon was formed upon no principle of selection, but comprised *all* the remains of ancient literature. There is little doubt that compositions were ascribed to some of the prophets, particularly to Isaiah, of which they were not the authors; p. 419, seq.

The tradition that Ezra revised and re-edited the books of the Old Testament, is obviously fabulous. There exists no historical evidence that Moses was the author of the Pentateuch. In the other books of the Old Testament, there is indeed reference to various narratives and laws now found in the Pentateuch; but these references are in fact to traditions and national laws that existed before the Pentateuch; and by the aid of these the Pentateuch was afterwards compiled; p. 420, seq.

No such book as a Pentateuch by Moses is mentioned in the books of Samuel, or Kings, or in those of the prophets who were the public teachers of religion; p. 426, seq. The Pentateuch could not have been the national code of the Jews; for its ordinances were not observed during the long period of the monarchies, and many things were often done which the Pentateuch forbids; or neglected which it enjoins; p. 431, seq.

The Pentateuch was not written until some time after the return of the Jews from the captivity; and then, traditionary stories, laws, customs, ritual observances, &c., were inserted, and all these were attributed to Moses, in order to give greater weight and authority to the compilation; p. 436, seq.

The art of writing was not in use in the time of Moses; and consequently the writing of the Pentateuch by him was impossible; p. 439, seq. The style of Moses could not possibly have been so much like the style of the later writers. A period so long, without more change of language, is incredible and contrary to all experience; p. 441, seq. The Pentateuch contains narrations of events *later* than the time of Moses, and if it had been really his work interpolations of this kind could never have taken place; p. 443, seq.

The Pentateuch does not make claim to Moses as its author. It always speaks of him in the *third* person, and not in the first. Such a semblance of modesty would have been wholly unsuitable for him in his official character; p. 444.

The *facts* related in the Pentateuch show that it is full of inaccuracies. The number of fighting men, (600,000,) when the Israelites left Egypt, is incredible and impossible. Their original number and time of sojourning in Egypt were utterly inadequate to have brought into existence such a number. The genealogy of Moses proves that the Israelites could not have been in Egypt more than 215 years at the most, instead of the 430 as commonly reckoned, and 215 years could have done but little toward producing such a number; p. 446, seq.

The account of the flight from Egypt, and of the journey through the wilderness, is replete with difficulties, incredibilities, and impossibilities. How could two and a half millions of men be put in motion in one night? Whence all their flocks, and herds, and wealth? How could they all quench their thirst at Marah, or at Horeb? p. 449, seq.

Before the birth of Moses, Pharaoh is represented as saying, that the Israelites had become stronger than the Egyptians, and therefore the male children must be destroyed. The thing is impossible. The command is incredible. How could Pharaoh wish to lessen the number of his slaves?

How could he suppose it possible, that the Jews would submit to his cruel orders and obey him? p. 450, seq.

Moreover, how could such a multitude find food and drink in the Arabian waste? The water was supplied miraculously but twice. What became of their flocks and herds? They must have all perished in such circumstances; and hence their state of starvation, i. e. by reason of losing them. And yet, before they quitted Mount Sinai, they appear to have had an abundance of cattle for sacrifices, lambs for the passover, and all manner of spices, flour, oil, wine, &c.; p. 451, seq.

Whence came all their skill in the different arts? How could brick-making slaves understand architecture, engraving, and the manufacture of splendid furniture and garments? How could they transport all these through the desert, when they had no camels? p. 452, seq.

The Israelites are forbidden to destroy all the people of the land of Canaan, lest wild beasts should overrun the country. Were not two and a half millions of people more than enough to keep in due subjection the wild beasts of a country, which was only 200 miles in length and 100 in breadth? p. 454, seq.

On the supposition that all the wonderful events took place which are narrated in the Pentateuch, how is it possible to believe that the Jews would have been so stupid, ungrateful, and rebellious as their history represents them to be; p. 455, seq. There is indeed sublimity in the description of the creation, and lofty conception as to the true nature of religion in the precept, that men should love God with all the heart and their neighbour as themselves. But "in coming to the Pentateuch we have entered only the precincts of true religion, while grotesque shapes are around us, and the heavens are obscured by clouds from which the thunder is rolling;" p. 456, seq.

The conceptions of God, in Genesis, are very rude ones. In Ex. iv. the account of Jehovah's meeting Moses and seeking to slay him, is strange indeed. Ex. xxiv. is not less so. The marvellous theophany related there, and all its tremendous solemnity of preparation, ends in the command to the Israelites to bring silver and gold and rams' skins and goats' hair and aromatics, &c., and make and furnish a tabernacle for Jehovah to dwell in. Many other directions in the sequel are equally trivial; p. 458, seq.

God is represented in a most unbecoming manner throughout the Pentateuch. The command to punish the Egyptian nation because of Pharaoh's haughtiness and cruelty; the injunction to extirpate the Midianites, but to keep the virgin females for their own use (which at least did but sanction and perpetuate the barbarism of the age); the command of utter excision in respect to the Canaanites; are inconsistent with the justice or the mercy of God. Why should the innocent suffer with the guilty, as an oriental despot exterminates a family for the offences of its head? The effect of making the Jews executioners of the Divine indignation against the idolatrous Canaanites, must have been to convert them into a horde of ferocious and brutal barbarians; p. 459, seq.

The distinguishing rite of the Jews was painful, and the thought of it disgusting. Nothing can render it probable, that the laws respecting slaves were from God. And what shall we say of the command to destroy witches? What of such commands as forbid the eating of particular birds and beasts, some of which no one would ever think of eating, except in case of actual starvation? On many laws, moreover, which the Pentateuch contains, delicacy forbids one even to comment; p. 461, seq.

On the whole, it is altogether evident, that the original institutions of Moses had been greatly corrupted and changed by superstition, and by hankering after ritual observances, before the Pentateuch could have been written as it now is; p. 463.

The spirit of the prophets is wholly different from that of the Law, and often in opposition to it. They put no faith in sacrifices or ritual observances; p. 464, seq. The Pentateuch, in declaring that God visits the iniquity of the fathers upon the children, stands in direct opposition to Ezekiel, who declares that the son shall not bear the iniquity of the father, nor the father the iniquity of the son, Ezek. xviii. This same Ezekiel is full of unseemly representations of the Godhead. His work is repulsive for other reasons. The last nine chapters show him to have been a stickler for mere rites and ceremonies; p. 464, seq.

Malachi shows how the Jews reasoned and felt, after the full ritual of the Pentateuch was introduced. What he says is directly in opposition to Ps. l.; p. 470, seq. The Son of Sirach, Philo, Josephus, the Essenes, all thought but little of the ritual ordinances of the Pentateuch; p. 472, seq.

Our Saviour every where shows how little he regarded the Jewish ritual ordinances. "It is an unquestionable fact, that his words are not always reported to us with correctness." Sometimes, also, he employed Jewish modes of expression that were common, in order to avoid the exciting of prejudice among his hearers. Both these things are to be kept steadily in view, in the interpretation of what he may seem to have said about the ancient Scriptures; and nearly every difficulty can be removed by the aid of these two considerations. E. g. where he is reported as saying, "Moses *wrote* concerning me," it is evident that the evangelist, through default of memory or want of reflection, used the word *wrote* instead of the word spoke. So, instead of receiving, in its simple and obvious sense, the declaration of Christ as reported by John, (John v. 46,) viz. "Had ye believed Moses, ye would have believed me; for he wrote concerning me," we are to adopt the following substitute as expressive of Christ's real meaning, viz. "Had ye believed Moses, ye would have believed me; for the books which, *as you suppose*, Moses wrote, concern me;" p. 475, seq.

The Jewish Law was *civil* as well as ecclesiastical. It was on this ground merely that the Saviour and his apostles obeyed it, and required others to do so, while it continued; p. 470, seq. Sometimes, indeed, Jesus violated it; e. g. in order to do good on the sabbath, and to inculcate the duties of kindness and humanity. This was intended to lead the Jews to reflect on the folly of their attachment to ritual observances; p. 486, seq. Occasionally Christ directly taught the vanity and groundlessness of the Jewish laws; e. g. by what he says about eating that which is unclean (Matt. xv.); by what he says in respect to the matter of divorces (Matt. xix. and v.); p. 491, seq. The conversation with the Samaritan woman (John iv.) shows, how little value Jesus put upon the whole Jewish ritual; p. 496.

Thus much for the Pentateuch. Now for the other books of the Old Testament.

In the books of Joshua and Judges there is a great mixture of fabulous traditions, such as are found in the early history of all other nations; p. 498. No one who puts aside the notion of the Divine authority of all the Hebrew books, can doubt that extravagant fables and false prodigies are found in all those which relate the Jewish history antecedent to the time of Samuel; and there seems to be no good reason why the books of Samuel and Kings should be regarded as exceptions to this mixture; p. 500. But still we may admit real miracles, in cases where an important and evident moral design is in view; p. 501, seq.

The *prophets* were moral preachers. Some of their number may have been occasionally employed as the special ministers of God. Jesus never appeals to them for evidence of his Divine mission. Our Saviour did not accomplish any express prophecy relating to him; but he came in conformity to an expectation, which the whole tenor of God's providence had taught the Jews to entertain; p. 503, seq.

The error committed in representing the Old Testament as of Divine origin, has, beyond question, been a most serious hinderance to all rational belief of the fact, that God has miraculously revealed himself to man; p. 510.

I have now given a compressed view of the arguments employed by Mr. Norton, in order to overthrow the claims of the Old Testament to be considered as a book of Divine origin and authority. I have in no case made, by any design or effort on my part, the representation stronger than he has made it. It is not my wish to paint in more vivid colours than those which he has employed. In most cases, I have employed his own language; and where I have not, I have changed the diction merely for the sake of abridgment, and not from a design to employ any stronger colouring.

Mr. Norton himself declares, (p. 405,) that "in expressing his opinions he is only giving form and voice to the ideas and feelings that exist in the minds of a large portion of intelligent believers;" and also, that "there is nothing in them of *novelty* or of *boldness*." It is indeed most obviously true, that there is nothing special in them of novelty. For substance they have been before the world for some sixteen centuries. Porphyry and Celsus knew well how to manage weapons of this sort. But as to *boldness*, I think his modesty should not have shrunk from a claim to this. It certainly did require some boldness for one who had been a preacher of the gospel and a teacher in a theological seminary professedly Christian, to make before the whole world declarations such as he has made. No one indeed who knows him well, can fail to regard him as an independent thinker and reasoner; and after what he has recently published to the world, he may not very unreasonably be denominated somewhat of a *free thinker*. His objections to the Old Testament are, it is true, nearly all of a date somewhat ancient. But I do not regard him, on this account, as merely copying and retailing the opinions of others. It is manifest enough, through his whole work, that he has thought and reasoned for himself, even when he has employed material which others had collected and which he found in a manner ready to his hand.

I have already said, that it is no part of my design to examine in detail all the objections of Mr. N. to the Old Testament. Most of them plainly belong to the province of polemic and apologetic theology ; and I shall therefore leave them to those whose proper business it is to act in this department. Why they have not sooner begun to act in defence of one of the citadels of revelation, I know not. I have not unfrequently heard the remark made, that 'had the question been one of *metaphysical* theology, which concerned points where even evangelical Christians may and do disagree, and have for centuries disagreed, there would not have been wanting a goodly number of defenders, especially against an attack made either by one side or the other upon points mooted by New School and Old School. But now, (they have the boldness to add,) the theologians stand off at wary distance, as the camp of Israel did when Goliath came out to bid defiance to them.' But I am reluctant to accede to such an intimation. I know indeed full well, and I regret, the excessive zeal that is abroad about points of mere speculation in theology, which are never likely to be settled; but I must still believe, that there are not many Christian ministers in the evangelical ranks, who would not relax, and recede from the boundaries that sect and party names have set up, when it becomes necessary to unite in order to defend and save the citadel of all religion. Time will show whether I am not in the right.

I cannot resist the impression made on me by the reading of Mr. N.'s *critique* on the Old Testament, that the estimation in which he has for many years held it, has prevented him from devoting much of his time to the study of it. He tells us, (p. 412,) that his remarks on the Old Testament were committed to writing more than ten years before he put them to the press. If he had named a period thrice as long, I could easily have believed his declaration to be true. He has surely made some *faux pas* in matters of Old Testament criticism, which, had he read more widely, and kept up at all with the times in their development of historical criticism pertaining to the Hebrew Scriptures, he could not well have made. I do not say this *ad invidiam*, nor in order to wound his feelings. I say it from a full persuasion, that more enlarged views would have given quite a different direction to some parts of his *critique*, and spared him the labour of defending some things, which he must now find, on a more extended examination, to be indefensible.

My present design forbids me to go into detail at all, in order to justify these assertions. I can only glance at one or two matters, as explanatory of what I mean.

Mr. N. asserts, that there is no satisfactory evidence that *alphabetical* writing was known in the time of Moses. Should he not have known, that the recent paleographic examinations in Egypt, Phenicia, Persia, and Assyria, make entirely against this, even if he sets aside the abundant evidence of the Greek writers, that their alphabet is as old as the time of Cadmus? Gesenius, most of his life a strenuous assertor of the *late* origin of the Pentateuch, was compelled by his Phenician and Egyptian investigations to say, that "alphabetic writing must have been in use among the Egyptians at least 2000 years before the Christian era;" and that 'their neighbours, the Phenicians, in all probability, must have employed this method of writing as early as the reign of the shepherd-kings in Egypt.' Ges. Heb. Gramm. edit. 13. Exc. I. p. 290. The preëminent paleographer, then, from whose decision it is not very safe to appeal as to such matters, places the art of alphabetical writing long enough before the time of Moses, to give it a wide sweep in Egypt and Phenicia, and indeed in the neighbouring countries. And if Moses was "learned in all the wisdom of the Egyptians, and was mighty in words and deeds," as the martyr Stephen asserts, (Acts vii. 22,) cannot one venture to attribute to him the knowledge of alphabetic writing?

Again, when Mr. N. avers, (p. 441, seq.,) that the Hebrew of the Pentateuch and of the later Hebrew books is of the same stamp, and that we cannot possibly suppose, that an interval of 900 or 1000 years would not have made a greater change in the Hebrew language than is developed by these Jewish writings, I must think that he has not paid very strict attention to the history of languages. Is it not a fact, that the Peshito or old Syriac version of the New Testament, made during the second century, is altogether of the same linguistic tenor as the Syriac Chronicon of Bar Hebræus, written about one thousand years later? Is it not a fact, that the Arabic of the Coran, and of the Arabian writers just before and after the time of Mohammed, differs but slightly from that of the Arabian writers from the tenth down to the eighteenth century? And yet another fact. The late Dr. Marshman, a missionary in Hindoostan, translated into English the great work of Confucius, the celebrated Chinese philosopher and teacher, who lived more than five centuries before the Christian era. The same gentleman diligently consulted the principal commentators on the work of Confucius, and he assures us, that commentaries written 1500 and more years after the time of Confucius are altogether of the same type of language which is exhibited in the work of that philosopher. Facts like these, now, need no comment. They place the matter beyond fair appeal. Indeed the nature of the case speaks for itself. The Jews were neither a literary nor a commercial people. They saw little of strangers abroad, and very few foreigners resided among them. They knew little of the arts and sciences, and certainly made no advances in them. What was there then to operate in the way of producing many and important changes in their language? There was nothing like to that which produces changes of this nature at the present day, among the nations of the West. Their case was, in respect to intercourse, like to that of the Chinese. The effect of such a state of things upon language, was the same in Palestine and in China.

Yet even in any state of a nation, however uniform, we cannot but suppose that a long time will make some variations in language. It did so among the Hebrews. The assertion of Mr. N. is by no means correct, that there are no diversities of language between the Pentateuch and later books of the Hebrew. Jahn, that well known and highly respected theologian and critic at Vienna, just before his death, published a series of Essays in Bengel's *Archiv*, which demonstrate the point in question beyond appeal. *Archaisms*, or whatever Mr. N. may call them, abound to some extent in the Pentateuch; and the ἅπαξ λεγόμενα of the Pentateuch, Jahn has shown to be quite a large number.

Once more; but in respect to a case of a different tenor. Mr. N. thinks, that the use of the *third* person in the narrations of the Pentateuch, shows that Moses was not the author. There was no reason, he avers, for his adopting such a method of writing. It was Moses' business to speak with authority, and to place himself directly before the people.

The histories of Cæsar and Clarendon, which employ the third person, are no justification, in his view, of the usage in question. Yet Mr. N. maintains that the Gospels of Matthew and of John are worthy of credit. But where, I ask, have these writers spoken of themselves in the *first* person?

Mr. N. says, that the Pentateuch does not claim to be the work of Moses, i. e. he has not affixed his name to it as the author, and therefore, there is no certainty that the work is his. He will permit me to ask him, how he could write three volumes to show the *Genuineness of the Gospels*, when not a single one of them has the name of its author affixed to it, or contains an explicit declaration as to who was its author? Every sciolist in criticism knows, that the titles now affixed to the Gospels, are the work of critics quite remote from the times of the apostles.*

But I must withdraw my hand. I have said enough to illustrate and confirm the representation which I have made above; and this is all that can now be done.

* See Chrysostom, Homil. I. in Matt.; also Hug. Einl. ins N. Testament, § 47.

Mr. N. appears to cherish strong feelings of disapprobation toward that branch of the so-called Liberal Party, who have discarded the authority of both the Old Testament and the New; who doubt the personality of the Godhead; and who flatly deny the possibility of miracles. He speaks of their system as a "shallow philosophy," and appears to be much in earnest when defending the miraculous power of Christ; but rather less so, perhaps, when defending that of the apostles. Yet most of the reasons of any considerable weight, which Mr. N. has brought forward against the claims of the Old Testament, either flow from, or are connected with, his unwillingness to believe in the miraculous interpositions of the Godhead as there declared. Was there not as much need of these interpositions in the ancient times of darkness and ignorance, as there was at a later period when the New Testament was written? He allows, indeed, a few cases in which he thinks that a miracle may be deemed probable; e. g. such a case as that of fire falling from heaven to consume the sacrifice which Elijah had prepared, in order to put to the test the claims of Jehovah and of Baal to Divine honours. But he erases from the list of credibles every case of alleged miraculous interposition, where he cannot perceive the moral purpose accomplished by it. A *subjective* line of separation between the true and the false, he has probably drawn for himself. A copy of the drawing, it may be, is impressed upon his own mind. But what the *objective* rule for testing the credible and incredible is, by which others, who are of different modes of thinking and who view religious matters in a different light, may be guided, and may thus possibly come to an agreement with him, he has not told us. There are men, who at least would be greatly offended at having either their learning, or their logic, or their piety called in question, and who in fact regard religion as a matter of very grave import, and yet have avowed themselves unable to discover the great *moral* end of converting the water at a wedding feast into a large quantity of wine; who are not quite satisfied with the moral bearing of Christ's permission to the demons to enter an immense herd of swine and drown them in the sea; who hang in suspense concerning the great moral design manifested by cursing and withering the fig-tree. Now what has Mr. N. to say, to satisfy these doubters? Whatever it may be, it will at least be as easy to say the like things, in order to satisfy our minds respecting many miracles related in the Old Testament which he rejects with scorn.

Some persons, in a state of mind quite different from that of Mr. N., or of those who are filled with doubts about the miracles of Christ mentioned above, still hesitate to decide at once on the matters under consideration, and therefore inquire, and cautiously and candidly examine. It is quite possible to suppose, that there are men who, after having done all this, are not entirely satisfied with the reasons alleged for defending the reality of these miracles, (I mean so far as their *intellectual* judgment is concerned,) while at the same time, they remove all real stumbling-blocks from their way, by the consideration, that there may have been ends accomplished, or may be ends to be accomplished, by some miracles, of which they are not aware. They are conscious that their knowledge is imperfect, and that to decide with confidence against the truth of such narrations as relate the miracles in question, while all around is admitted to be credible and true, would be like to deciding that the black spots which have recently appeared in such numbers upon the face of the sun, do not in reality belong to that body, because, as they apprehend, it can be nothing but a uniform blaze of glory.

To me this state of mind, however undesirable, presents a much more cheering aspect than that of Mr. N., or of his bolder liberal brethren. My experience has taught me something in relation to such subjects. In the early part of my biblical studies, some thirty to thirty-five years ago, when I first began the critical investigation of the Scriptures, doubts and difficulties started up on every side, like the armed men whom Cadmus is fabled to have raised up. Time, patience, continued study, a better acquaintance with the original scriptural languages, and the countries where the sacred books were written, have scattered to the winds nearly all these doubts. I meet indeed with difficulties still, which I cannot solve at once; with some, where even repeated efforts have not solved them. But I quiet myself by calling to mind, that hosts of other difficulties, once apparently to me as formidable as these, have been removed, and have disappeared from the circle of my troubled vision. Why may I not hope, then, as to the difficulties that remain? Every year is now casting some new light on the Bible, and making plain some things which aforetime were either not understood, or were misunderstood. Why may not my difficulties be reached by some future progressive increase of light? At least, in the revolution of the sun, the dark spots will sooner or later disappear. And, what is more than all considerations of this kind — speedily the whole will be known. In the light of heaven no darkness is intermingled. Soon the anxious and devoted inquirer after truth will, if a true Christian, enjoy the opportunity of asking the writers themselves of the books of Scripture, what they intended, and what they designed to teach. It is good, I do believe, both to hope and patiently wait for the light of eternal day, if, after all our efforts to clear up a few difficulties in Scripture that remain, we do not succeed to our utmost wishes.

Mr. N. evidently regards those who discard all revelation, as unbelievers. He speaks apparently with much feeling concerning them. I believe that he has given them an appropriate place in the category of religious names. The most liberal party, (who seem hardly to have acquired a distinctive name yet, but probably would not dislike that of *Rationalists*,) begin with a very simple process in the way of reasoning. I have it before me, in a letter from one of the first philologists and antiquarians that Germany has produced. It is this : 'The laws of nature are merely developments of the Godhead. God cannot contradict, or be inconsistent with, himself. But inasmuch as a miracle is a contradiction of the laws of nature, or at the least an inconsistency with them, therefore a miracle is impossible.'

Now this is very short, and simple, and intelligible. At least we know what the writer means who says this. But how it can be *proved*, that the God who constituted the laws of nature as the usual way and method of his operations, is not at liberty to depart from these, for the sake of ends which he judges important ; or how it can be proved that he has not done so ; is what I am not able to show or explain.

Mr. N. calls all such reasoning *shallow philosophy*. I assent. But what is the philosophy, which leaves us to select according to the measure of our light, our own personal feelings, and our wishes, a part of the miracles of the Old Testament and of the New, and reject all the rest? In other words, Is a revelation to prescribe to us, or we to the revelation? This is the simple question, divested of all the drapery thrown around it in order to conceal its real form and lineaments. Such is evidently the position of Mr. Norton. I would not speak with any disrespect or unkindness; but I cannot help the feeling, that Mr. N. never travels on Scripture ground without furnishing himself, like some careful surgeons, with weapons adapted to probing and excision. He is ever ready to employ them, and prepared to sever a limb supposed to be withered, or a seeming excrescence, from the sacred body of the Scriptures, old or new.

Does not Mr. N., moreover, give up, yea strenuously oppose the doctrine of future punishment, or certainly, at least, of eternal punishment? Now if this position of his is true, of what great consequence can he deem it, whether the New Testament is believed or disbelieved? For, in the first place, who, on his ground, can draw the line in all cases between what we are to believe, and what we are to reject? Then, in the second place, if the doctrine of all future punishment of sin is rejected, no wise man can deem it of importance to give himself any solicitude about religion.

It would surely be a curious phenomenon in the religious world, and a matter of no small importance to the uninitiated, should Mr. N. publish an *expurgated* edition of the Scriptures both New and Old, and let the public know what true and reasonable Christianity (as estimated by him) demands and expects of us. Or if he would even republish selections from some Catechism, say the Racovian, with additions and alterations suited to these enlightened days, might he not do a great service to the cause of liberal Christianity? To me, however, at present it seems, that Mr. N. has a very brief creed, which might be expressed in a single sentence, namely: "I do *not* believe what the Christian churches in general *do* believe."

As to his *more liberal* opponents among the class of Liberals, I have but a word to say. I commend their honest and open-hearted course. They openly and avowedly discard all that is of a miraculous nature, and by consequence all the books of Scripture, which either assert things of a miraculous nature, or are built upon that foundation. As the popular saying is, They go for the whole. For my own part I like this. We know where they are, and where we have to meet them. But in controversy with Mr. N., we never know on what ground we are treading. We refer, for example, to facts or declarations recorded in the Scripture, in order to illustrate or confirm any position that we have taken. But Mr. N. meets us at once with the avowal, that he does not regard that fact or those declarations, appealed to, as entitled to any credit. So, we have, in our efforts to oppose him, all the while been merely sowing to the wind, and at last must of course reap—no very promising harvest.

Some of the high Liberals, as it seems to me, would be *Straussites* to the full extent, if they well knew what Strauss or Hegel in all cases really maintains.* Alas! there are few heads, among us, from which spring the prominences appropriate to making such a discovery. Thus much, however, these Liberals seem to themselves to understand, and thus much they maintain, viz. that God is an *impersonal* being, the τὸ πᾶν of the universe; and that he developes personality only in rational beings, and for a little season at a time. In the mean while the argument against miracles, which has been stated above, is fully admitted by them, and the Scriptures are brought before its tribunal. But here I must demur. If the Godhead is an impersonal and unconscious being, as they assert, then how can it be impossible that the laws of nature should change? If there be no *mind*, and no almighty power to direct and secure the natural order of things, what hinders these things from developing themselves in different ways? Why may they not assume every shape, and go one way as well as another? What is it which renders secure and constant the uniformity of things?

But I must desist, or I shall intrench upon the main object of my book. I cannot conclude these introductory re-

---

* Here there is an awkward combination of Strauss and Hegel. The one is a theologian; the other a philosopher merely. The one has written on the New Testament; the other on metaphysics. It is exceedingly easy to understand what Strauss means and maintains. He writes most transparently. Hegel, however, is often unintelligible because of his shadowy philosophy, which is essentially Pantheistic. It is true that Strauss holds the philosophy of Hegel; but it has not obscured his meaning. D.

marks, however, without saying, that so far as I know, all who sympathize with me in their theological views, feel much better satisfied with the honest and open avowal of the high Liberals, than with the ambiguous, reserved, non-committal creed of the more moderate class of Liberalists. The High Liberals or Rationalists are willing to stand before the world in the character which they really sustain. I do not think the same can be said with truth of their shrinking and non-committal brethren.

In canvassing the subject of the ancient Jewish Canon of Scripture, it is not my design to exhibit a mere skeleton of the subject. It is not with the view of answering merely what Mr. Norton has said respecting the Jewish Canon, that I have been induced to take up my pen. I feel as one may be naturally supposed to feel, who has spent his life in the instruction of youth, i. e. I feel a strong desire to communicate something on this important subject, if it be in my power, which may aid young theologians in forming more satisfactory and well-grounded opinions about the extent and authority and obligation of the Old Testament Scriptures. I desire to speak of the labours of others before me, in regard to this matter, with all proper respect and deference; but is it too much to say, that we have in English no book on this subject, which is sufficiently historico-critical to answer in a satisfactory manner all the present demands on sacred literature? If there be such a one, it is unknown to me. At least I know thus much, viz. that for years I wandered in the dark in relation to this matter, not being satisfied with the evidence before me, and not knowing where to go for better views. If I do not wholly mistake the true state of the case, there is a great number of pastors in our country in the same predicament. All young students in theology must of course be somewhat in the same predicament. It is an unpleasant one. The mind hesitates not only as to what kind of reliance to place on certain books, at least, of the Old Testament, but also as to what relation the whole bears to the New Testament, in regard to authority and obligation. The use which should be made of much of the Old Testament must, in this state of the mind, necessarily become a matter of doubt and perplexity.

My present object is, to aid, if it be within my power, in

the removal of a part at least of these difficulties. I design to produce the evidence that may be gathered from antiquity, as to the extent of that Canon of Scripture which our Saviour and his apostles regarded and appealed to as Divine and obligatory. If this was the Canon of the Hebrew Scriptures, as then received by the Jews in general; and if it can be shown that this Canon was the same which is now comprised in the Hebrew Scriptures; then the doubts and difficulties which many entertain in regard to the Old Testament, or in respect to some parts of it, may be removed. The authority of Christ and his apostles to determine such a matter, should not be called in question; I would even say, cannot be consistently called in question, by any one who professes to be a *Christian*.

Some things have been presented to my notice, in the course of the reading and reflection through which I have passed in order to prepare for writing the present treatise, which do not seem to me to have been adequately, or in some respects correctly, developed in the pages of the leading writers on the subject of the Old Testament Canon. Things absolutely new, I do not promise to bring before the reader. But there are some things, that have been noticed by even the more thorough investigators, which ought in justice to be placed in a new attitude, in order that they should be seen in their true light. Something of the task of doing this, I would hope to perform. One thing at least will be achieved by the present work, if it does not miss its mark; and this is, the presenting in a body, and regularly disposed, the evidence extant respecting the Old Testament Canon, accompanied by a historico-critical examination of the same. The reader, if this shall be done, will at least have the material before him, out of which he can make up his own opinion.

I shall not advance to the consideration of this subject by taking the attitude of one who assumes the point to be proved, and then pours forth monitions or comminations upon all who may even seem to doubt. For the present, I take my leave not only of Calvinists and Unitarians, but of all the sects in Christendom, yea even of theology itself, in its technical sense, and aim to act merely the part of a historical inquirer, who applies to the appropriate sources of information, and endeavours in this way to find out what he ought to believe. This is the first step. The demands of intellect and reason must be met, in order to satisfy a reasonable being. Then comes, in proper order, the application of results thus won to the conscience and to the heart.

SECT. II. *Definition of Canon.*

THE meaning of this Greek word, (for such it is, viz. κανών,) as now employed by our churches in reference to the Scriptures, hardly needs an explanation. It is employed as designating that list or collection of books, either of the Old Testament or of the New, which we are accustomed to regard as sacred or inspired, or of Divine authority. But it was not always so employed, in ages that are past; and the inquirer needs to be put on his guard, with respect to the various uses of this word in ancient times.

In classical Greek, the original meaning of κανών is *straight stick* or *rod, staff, measuring-rod* or *pole, beam of a balance,* &c. Hence tropically, *rule, norma;* thence *law, prescription, fundamental* or *guiding principle.* Among the Alexandrine Greek grammarians, κανών was employed to denote a list or collection of ancient Greek authors, who would serve as *models* or *exemplars* for other writers. It meant what we should call *classical* writers.

One sees very readily, how this succession of derivate meanings sprang from the original sense of the word. The literal idea of *rod, measuring-rod, measure,* was applied tropically to whatever was a rule, guide, model, or exemplar, of conduct or of actions, of art or of science. The Alexandrine grammarians employed the word in a sense so kindred to that which we now give it, that the mind of every one must be struck by the resemblance. Those books which are the rule, measure, law, exemplar, of a moral and pious life, are the *canonical* books of the Scriptures, according to the present usage of this word.

Among the Christian fathers the word *canon* obtained an enlarged and sometimes a technical sense. It was sometimes used to designate a list or catalogue of the clergy or of other persons belonging to a church; a list of psalms and hymns appropriate for public worship; and even a list of furniture belonging to a church, &c. Very naturally it came to be employed to designate *a list of the scriptural books* which were publicly read in the churches. It was not, however, until the third century that these usages of the word commenced, or at least became common.

Readers of the present day, in perusing the testimony of many of the ancient fathers and councils respecting the *canon* of Scripture, often make great mistakes as to the meaning and force of the testimony. It is a fact which lies on the face of ancient church history, that in the latter part of the second century, and more in the third and fourth, other books besides those which were regarded as properly inspired, were read more or less in the churches. With the Septuagint version of the Old Testament, which the Oriental and African churches every where made use of, was early intermingled more or less of the books which we now name *apocryphal*, and which for the most part were written in Greek, and not long before the commencement of the Christian era. The leading reasons for mixing these recent productions with the books of the Hebrews, seem to have been the following; first, they were mostly written by Jews, as the tenor of them demonstrates; secondly, they were of a religious cast, and parts of them were adapted to useful instruction, while other parts communicated narratives of some interest, whether considered in the light of history or of allegory. But be this as it may, the Christian churches, at least many of them, in the third century and onward, admitted a number of the apocryphal books to be publicly read along with the Jewish Scriptures. Now when the word *canonical* was applied in such a sense as to designate merely the books which were publicly read, *the canonical books of the Old Testament*, for example, would mean not only the Jewish Scriptures, but also such of the apocryphal books as were combined with them in the Septuagint Version, and were publicly read. But to say that a book was *canonical*, and to say that it was *inspired*, at that period and when this usage prevailed, was saying two very different things. There might be (and were) *inspired* books which were not publicly read; e. g. such as the Apocalypse of the New Testament, and the Canticles of the Old Testament. On the other hand, several books not inspired were included in the *reading* canon of the day, i. e. in the list of books publicly readable; e. g. 1 Maccabees, 2 Maccabees, Sirach, Wisdom of Solomon, Tobit, Judith, the Shepherd of Hermas, the Epistle of Clemens Romanus, the Revelation of Peter, &c. In regard to this matter, viz. the extent of the canon or list of books to be publicly read for profit, there was, for a long time, no fixed rule among the churches. Each seems to have done what was right in its own eyes. It was not until the fourth century, that councils interfered, and limited the number of books to be read in the churches. And these decided differently, as any one may see by reading the accounts of the Council at Laodicea, at Hippo, at Carthage, at Rome under Gelasius, and elsewhere, as given by Mansi, in his great work *Sanctorum Conciliorum nov. et ampliss. Collectio*, particularly in Tom. I. III. VIII. Indeed, in order to read these records of ancient times intelligibly, one must keep in mind what Jerome says, at the end of his enumeration of the books of the Hebrew canon, in his Prologus Galeatus. After naming the books in the Hebrew Scriptures, (the same which we now reckon as belonging to them,) he goes on to say, "Whatever is not included among these, is to be placed among the apocryphal books," [i. e. in his idiom, *among the uninspired books*]. After particularizing various apocryphal works, he adds, "One reads them in the church, but he does not receive them among the *canonical* Scriptures. . . . *They may be read to the edification of the people, but not for the purpose of establishing ecclesiastical doctrines.*" Jerome here plainly employs *canonical* in the sense of inspired; contrary to the common usage of the preceding century. And from what he says, it is plain that books for *edification* were read in the churches, for which no claims of inspiration were made, and which could not establish any religious doctrine.

We often see quotations made from the fathers and from the decrees of councils, in order to show, that there was no prevailing and fixed belief in the ancient churches respecting the definite number of books which are to be considered as belonging to the Scriptures. How easy to commit important errors in relation to this subject, if one does not know the various uses of the word *canon!* To show that a book belongs to the canon, i. e. was publicly readable, is not to show that it was even regarded as inspired; less still will it show that it was in fact inspired; on the other hand, to show that any book was omitted or excluded from the canon, i. e. was not publicly read, is showing nothing to disprove its inspiration.

As this is a matter of high importance, I would not deal in assertions without adequate proof. What Jerome says, goes directly to show that many books were publicly read, which were not at all regarded by the churches as sources of appeal in cases where doctrines were to be established. On the other hand, the case of Philastrius of Brixia, the intimate friend of Ambrose, near the close of the fourth century, illustrates and confirms what I have said concerning books not publicly read, and yet admitted to be inspired. In his book *De Hæresibus*, c. 88, he exhibits a catalogue of *canonical* books, i. e. books which, as he says, ought to be read in the church, in which is found neither the Epistle to the Hebrews, nor the Apocalypse. Yet in c. 60 he says, that "they are heretics who do not receive the Apocalypse, and that they have no understanding of the excellence and dignity of this writing." In c. 88 the same writer speaks of *Scripturæ adsconditæ*, [i. e. *Scriptures apocryphal*, in his sense of the word, viz. not to be publicly produced,] "which," he says, "ought to be read for moral improvement by the perfect, [i. e. full-grown Christians,] but not to be read by all." In the same way Gregory Nazianzen, (Opp. II. p. 44,) says, "I heard John the evangelist enigmatically saying to such ἐν ἀποκρύφαις, [q. d. in the *apocryphal writings*, i. e. private ones, such as were not publicly read,] I would thou wert either hot or cold," &c. Yet the same writer (Life of Ephrem, III. p. 601) calls the Apocalypse ἡ τελευταία τῆς χάριτος βίβλος, i. e. the last book of grace, or, (in other words,) of the New Testament dispensation. Now this same Gregory, (Opp. II. p. 98,) in some verses reciting the books of Scripture, omits the Apocalypse at the end, and concludes his verses by saying, "πάσας ἔχεις· εἴ τι δὲ τούτων ἐκτός, οὐκ ἐν γνησίοις, i. e. Thou hast all; if there be any besides these, they belong not to the genuine." There is only one way to solve this apparent inconsistency, and that is by applying to his case the same considerations as those which belong to that of Philastrius. Gregory, in his verses, included the canonical, i. e. publicly readable, books only; in the other passages he gives his private opinion respecting the true character of the Apocalypse.

Nothing is plainer, than that the words *canonical* and *apocryphal* bear quite a different sense, in the works of different fathers and councils, in different ages and countries. Athanasius distributes the so-called Scriptures into three classes of books, viz. canonical = inspired, apocryphal = spurious or deserving rejection, and books permitted to be read in the churches; Epist. ad Rufin. Tom. II. p. 39, seq. Rufinus himself, a contemporary with Jerome, follows the same classification; see in Opp. Cypriani, p. 575. After specifying the books belonging to the present Protestant canon, which he calls *canonical*=inspired, he names several of the books belonging to our present Apocrypha together with the Shepherd of Hermas and the Judgment of Peter, and says of them, that they are called *ecclesiastical*, and " are to be read in the churches, (whence their name,) but not to be produced as authority in matters of faith—non tamen proferri ad auctoritatem ex his fidei confirmandam." Other books which have respect to religion, but are not to be read in the churches, he names *apocryphal*.

Jerome makes use of phraseology a little different from this. In the famous passage of his, in his *Prologus Galeatus*, he specifies the same Old and New Testament books which are now in the Protestant canon, and then adds, that 'the books *extra hos*, i. e. not included in these, are to be ranked among the *apocryphal*, and are not in the *canon*.' Then, after mentioning several of the books in our present Apocrypha, he adds, respecting some of them, " The church indeed reads them [in public], but does not receive them among the canonical [inspired] Scriptures. . . . . [reads them] for the edification of the people, not to determine matters of faith."

Thus it is perfectly apparent, that no one can read the ecclesiastical fathers or the decrees of ancient councils, on the subject of the canonical Scriptures, and rightly understand and appreciate them, without narrowly watching the use of

DEFINITION OF CANON.

the technical terms employed in describing their classification. *Canonical* at one time means *publicly readable*; at another, it is the equivalent of *inspired*. *Apocryphal*, at one time, means *not publicly readable*; at another, it is the equivalent of *uninspired, destitute of binding authority*.

Nor does this different usage belong exclusively to any one age. We find Origen dividing the religious books of his day into *canonical*=inspired, and apocryphal=uninspired and (with him) unworthy of credit. Afterwards we find Eusebius dividing religious books, in relation to the New Testament, into (*a*) Ὁμολογούμενοι, i. e. the genuine and acknowledged writings of the evangelists and apostles. (*b*) Ἀντιλεγόμενοι, books whose genuineness was doubted or was unsettled. (*c*) Νόθοι, books which were *spurious*, i. e. were not written by inspired men. Besides these he mentions books ἄτοπα καὶ δυσσεβῆ, *stolid and impious*.

The result of this investigation is plain. We can understand ancient writers only by watching with the closest scrutiny how they employ the words *canonical, apocryphal, ecclesiastical,* and the like, and for want of so doing, many a glaring error has crept into the works of some even recent writers on the subject of the *canon*. Another consequence is also deducible from our premises, viz. that, if we mean to be rightly understood, we must define and uniformly adhere to the meaning which we give to the words *canon* and *canonical*.

We dismiss the subject of the New Testament canon, of course; for to canvass that, is not our present business. In respect to the Old Testament, what meaning shall we assign to the phrase, *Canon of the Old Testament?*

Shall we attach to the word *canon* the meaning of *a list of books that were publicly read in the Jewish synagogue, in the time of Christ and his apostles?*

Before the Babylonish exile the Jews had no synagogues. Previous to that time, only the Law of Moses, i. e. the Pentateuch, appears to have been read once a year in the temple. After the return from exile, and the erection of synagogues, the Law of Moses was read in them, being distributed into fifty-two *Parashoth* or sections, so that each sabbath in the year might have its due proportion. When Antiochus Epiphanes (171 — 164, B. C.) invaded Judea, abolished the worship of the temple, and commanded all the copies of Moses' Law which could be found, to be burned, the Jewish synagogue, according to the Rabbies, made selections from the *prophets*, corresponding to the *Parashoth* of the Pentateuch, which they called *Haphtaroth*, (i. e. *dis missions*, because when the reading of these was finished the people were *dismissed* to their homes, see פטר, *to dismiss*,) and which were read in the room of the Law.* After the death of Antiochus, the Jews reintroduced the Law with its Parashoth, and also continued the reading of the prophetical Haphtaroth; which is still practised by them. At the feast of Purim, once in a year, the book of Esther is also read. If we should extend, therefore, the Jewish canon only to the books which the Rabbies suppose to have been publicly read, our list would comprise but a moderate portion of the books which were regarded as of Divine authority. Some books of Scripture, e. g. Canticles, and the first and last eight chapters of Ezekiel, the Jews did not permit any person to read, even in private, before he had attained the age of thirty years. Yet they did not deny the Divine original authority of these ἀπόκρυφα. We cannot use the word *canonical*, then, in respect to the Old Testament books in the apostolic age, in the sense of including only the books publicly or privately permitted by the Jews to be read. And if we should resort to the Christian fathers for information, in regard to the extent of the Hebrew canon, we should find so much variety in the use of the word *canon*, and such different usages in regard to the religious books to be publicly read, that we could receive no assistance from this quarter.

It becomes a matter of necessity, then, that we should fix upon a sense of the word *canon* which is definite and intelligible; and this being done, we must uniformly adhere to it. I mean, then, by *the Canon of Jewish Scripture in the apostolic age, that class of books which the Jews as a people regarded and treated as sacred, i. e. of Divine origin and*

---

* This account of the origin of making sections from the prophetical books, which was first proposed by Elias Levita, is now justly exploded. If Antiochus, as is asserted, commanded all the copies of the Moses' Law to be burned, it is very unlikely that he should have allowed the public reading of the prophets. D.

SECT. III.   COMMENCEMENT OF THE CANON.   29

authority. This agrees with the present general usage of the churches, as to the words in question, and therefore will occasion no embarrassment and no mistake in regard to phraseology.

The word *canon*, I would remark at the close, seems not to have been in use, in its technical sense as applied to the Scriptures, until the time of Origen. No trace of it can be found in the second century. In his Prol. ad Cant. Cantic., sub fine, Origen employs it; also in Schol. ad Matt. xxvii. 9; in a sense like to that which I have given to it.*

SECT. III. *Commencement of the Canon.*

THAT books of this character existed among the Jews, from the time of Moses down to a period of some extent after the return from the Babylonish captivity, few have denied; and none have been able to show the contrary. It is well known, however, among critics at least, that the *Mosaic* origin of the Pentateuch has, since the days of Semler, been called in question by a considerable number of German critics. At the time when Wolf had assailed the antiquity and genuineness of the Iliad and Odyssey, and spread far and wide his scepticism on this subject, the antiquity and genuineness of the Pentateuch began to be attacked on the like grounds, and about the time of Eichhorn's death, it was considered by the dominant neological party in Germany, as established beyond reasonable contradiction, that the Pentateuch was composed at a period near the captivity, or perhaps even after the return from it. By slow degrees the thousand years over which the Pentateuch was made to leap, in order to find an appropriate birth-day, began to be diminished. By and by it was felt by some to be necessary to assign a date for it which was antecedent to the time

---

* The substance of this section seems to be drawn from Suicer's Thesaurus. It is not very accurate, profound, or satisfactory. The reader who is acquainted with German should consult the minute investigation of the word *canon*, by Credner, in his work Zur Geshichte des Kanons, 8vo, Halle, 1847, p. 1—68.   D.

when a copy of the Law was found by Hilkiah the priest, in the reign of Josiah, B. C. 624. Of late, the date of the Pentateuch, at least of a large portion of it, has receded still more, even back to the times of Solomon or David, B. C. 1000—1040. Lately it seems, in part, to have made another retreat, viz. to the time of the Judges, or possibly even of Joshua. Such I take to be the view of Ewald and Tuch, and also of some other distinguished German critics. The next step may possibly be to a period of time which puts the whole matter *in statu quo*. But be this as it may, I must take for granted the fact now more generally acknowledged, that at least some parts of the Pentateuch were committed to writing in the time of Moses. I cannot indeed even conceive how the most important laws of the Mosaic institution, how the Levitical ritual in all its minutiæ, how the sketch of the tabernacle to be built with all its apparatus, and the account of it as built and provided with such apparatus, should have failed to be committed to writing. The ten commandments, from their importance, would naturally be engraved on some permanent material. The other two classes of composition just mentioned, are of such a nature that no memory could be trusted with them. No later age, in case these minute particulars concerning the tabernacle had not been early designated, yea even by Moses, could have ever dreamed of making, and palming upon the Jews as *Mosaic*, such representations as these. No subsequent age could have admitted a ritual like that of the Jews, provided it was introduced long after the death of Moses and Aaron, and was attributed to them. It is not possible to suppose, that any one age or generation after Moses' time, could be made to believe that things which they had never before heard of in connexion with their two leaders, and things which they had never been taught to practise, originated from them, and had always been obligatory on the Jews.

After the protracted and vehement contest about the origin and antiquity of *alphabetical* writing, which grew out of the Homeric *Wolfian* controversy, and extended itself to sacred as well as profane books, we have at length come to a result, and that result seems to be, that no reasonable doubt can be entertained, that the origin of alphabetical writing among the Egyptians, Phenicians, and Greeks, dates far back before the time of Homer. The *Homeric* controversy was occasioned by the position of Wolf in his Prolegomena, which was that the Iliad and the Odyssey are full of interpolations and probable abscissions, and that they owe their present form and order and unity to the later writers of Greece, near or during the time of Pisistratus. To make this probable, it was necessary to show that the poems of Homer were, for several centuries, not reduced to writing, but only sung by chanters and rhapsodists, ἀοιδοὶ καὶ ῥαψῳδοί. Of course, it became in a manner necessary to show that the art of writing, at least among the Greeks, was not as old as the time of Homer, i. e. did not extend back to about 1000 years before the Christian era. Every nerve has been strained for this purpose; while, on the other side, have recently been enlisted writers of the highest reputation. Among the combatants are Wolf, Heyne, Herder, Voss, Kreuser, W. Mueller, Hermann, Nitzsch, D. C. W. Crusius, and others. Nitzsch, in his *Historia Homeri*, seems to have made an end of the question, whether alphabetical writing is as old as the time of Homer. This is now, so far as I know, generally conceded. But whether alphabetical writing was so common at the time of Homer, that we can reasonably suppose him to have been acquainted with it, and to have availed himself of it—that is a question, in regard to which no inconsiderable number of critics have stood and still stand arrayed in mutual opposition.

It would be incongruous for me to turn aside for the purpose of discussing at length this question. Nevertheless, it has no unimportant bearing on the question which is now before us, viz. *At what period shall we date the commencement of the Jewish canon?* If the art of writing was not in use among the Greeks until the sixth century before the Christian era, then can it be probable, that the Hebrews, less literary than the Greeks, practised it before that period?

It is not essential, indeed, to my main design, to show *when* the Pentateuch was written, nor even *by whom*. It may be a book worthy of all credit, if written by some other hand than that of Moses, or at some later period. If Christ and his apostles have sanctioned it as a *sacred* book, the main question is settled for us. It should be sacred to us, as well as to them.

But to resume the subject of alphabetic writing among the Greeks, for a moment. It is said by the advocates of the *Wolfian* theory, that there is no Greek *prose writer* upon record before the Milesian Cadmus and Pherecydes of Scyros, who flourished about 544, B. C.; and that there is no writer of this class who is of any note, until the time of Hecatæus of Miletus and Pherecydes of Athens, i. e. about 50 years later. About the same time, that is, some 350 or more years later than the time of Homer, the laws of Draco were reduced to writing, and these are said to have been the first *written* laws among the Greeks. Is it probable then, it is asked, that the *poetry* of Homer was reduced to writing at a period some 350 or 400 years earlier?

But on the other hand, we may well ask, Could two poems, one of about 16,000, and the other of more than 12,000 lines or verses, be brought down through so many centuries by mere oral and traditionary communictiaon? Admitting even that there are a few interpolations in the Iliad and Odyssey, yet the unity and order of these poems demonstrate an origin from the same author; as do also their dialect and circle of words and imagery. How could so much be orderly composed by any man, without some means of consulting what had already been composed, as he advanced in his work? In fact, does not the Iliad itself, (Z. 168—9,) by its σήματα λυγρὰ γράψας ἐν πίνακι, advert to a *letter* addressed to Proteus? At any rate, this gives a more probable sense to the passage. See Trollope's Note in loc. Euripides (Hec. 856, seq.) makes Hecuba say, "Alas, no mortal is free! For he is either the slave of money, or of fortune; or else the mass of the city or *written* laws (νόμων γραφαί) coerce him." In Hippol. 856, seq., (ed. Barnes,) the same Euripides represents Theseus as speaking of an *epistle* or *tablet* (δέλτος) written by Phædra to him: "What then is the meaning of this appended epistle (δέλτος) from her dear hand? What news does it communicate?" In the sequel he calls this δέλτος an *epistle* (ἐπιστολάς = literas); and still further on he names it δέλτος again. The time when Euripides represents Theseus as saying what has been quoted, was some 80 years before the Trojan war. In his Iphigenia in Aulis, (l. 35, seq.,) he makes the aged messenger of Agamemnon, about to be sent with a letter to Clytemnestra, thus address this king : " Thou writest (γράφεις) this letter, which thou holdest in thy hands, and again thou dost erase these letters, (γράμματα,) and dost seal them, and then unseal them, and cast the tablet on the ground, pouring forth large tears." The erasing (συγχεῖς, *dost intermingle*) of the letters seems plainly to point to the corrections made on a waxed tablet, which was done by smearing over or mingling (συγχέω) the wax. Here then are all the phenomena of writing, with sealing and unsealing of the letter. And most graphic is the description; for Agamemnon is writing to his wife respecting their daughter Iphigenia, who was to be sacrificed to Diana, in accordance with the direction of the prophet Calchas. He had already sent her one letter, requiring Iphigenia to be given up. Now (l. 108, seq.) he says to the aged messenger, " I now *re-write* in this letter (δέλτον) what is proper to be done, which you, old man, saw me by night sealing and unsealing. But go now, taking this letter [τὰς ἐπιστολάς, like the Latin plur. *literæ*] to Argos. Whatever this letter hides in its folds—I will tell thee by word of mouth all which is written in it." Several times, in the sequel, is the same letter adverted to ; and so as to leave no possible doubt, that Euripides describes a veritable letter, (like the epistles of his own time,) folded and sealed in the same way.*

* In like manner, Orestes, the son of Agamemnon, is represented by Euripides as saying to Hermione: " I came hither, τὰς σὰς οὐ μένων ἐπιστολάς, not waiting for a letter from you ; " Andром. l. 965. This, of course, is just at the close of the Trojan war. In Iphig. in Aul. l. 307, the aged servant says to Menelaus, " Thou must not open the *letter* (δέλτον) which I bear." The servant complains to his master Agamemnon, that Menelaus " had by violence snatched out of his hands the epistle " (ἐπιστολάς) of Agamemnon. In the sequel Menelaus refers to it, and calls it δέλτον. In Iphigen. in Taur., Iphigenia speaks of transmitting " a *letter*, (δέλτον,) which a captive who pitied her had written to her friends." In the sequel she says, that " she had no one by whom she could send her *epistle* " (ἐπιστολάς). And again she speaks of " no mean reward for transmitting her *light letters*" (κούφων γραμμάτων). Orestes afterwards tells her to deliver the *letter* (δέλτον) to a particular person; and she in the sequel says, " I will go, and carry a *letter* (δέλτον) from the temple of the goddess ; " and again, (l. 640,) " I will send to Argos, particularly to my friends, a *letter* (δέλτον) which will tell them," &c. The same *epistle* (δέλτος, ἐπιστολαί) is again mentioned in l. 727, 732,

The simple question now is, whether this distinguished poet would have made out such a description as this, and introduced Agamemnon in such a manner, if the persuasion had not been general, and even universal, at his time, that the art of writing was familiar to the Grecian chiefs at the siege of Troy. One cannot well bring himself to attribute a gross *anachronism* and incongruity to such a writer.

In the like manner Sophocles (Trach. 157) makes Dejaneira speak of a δέλτον γεγραμμένην or *written will* of Hercules, in favour of her, when he left her house. This was some time before the Trojan war. In Sophocles' Antigone, he makes her speak of the ἄγραπτα Θεῶν νόμιμα, in contrast with the Κηρύγματα of Creon. Does not the nature of the contrast here presented allude plainly to the art of writing? And would these two consummate poets, distinguished as much for their knowledge as their skill and taste, commit such an *anachronism* as the Wolfian theory would make them guilty of? Suppose a poet of Boston should write a tragedy founded on the overthrow and death of one of the native Indian kings in this country some five centuries ago, and should introduce him as *writing letters* to his wife? Would a Boston audience endure this without hissing the play down?

I know it has been remarked, in the way of answer to the argument seemingly deducible from this in favour of the early discovery of alphabetic writing, that the poets have liberty to feign what they please, in making out the fable of

and in 734 she calls it γραφάς. A new epistle of joyous tidings to Orestes is written by Iphigenia, after she is delivered from death by Diana, which speaks of her ἐπιστολαί as containing the news, "even the things written ἐν δέλτοισιν." Again, (l. 1446,) she requests Orestes to inform himself what that is which is in her letter (ἐπιστολάς). In the Bacchæ, the servant of Theseus says to the captured Bacchus, "I lead thee captive, ἐπιστολαῖς, by the [written] mandate, of Pentheus." Pentheus, it will be recollected, was the grandson of Cadmus, who lived, it is supposed, nearly 1500 years B. C. The same word, (ἐπιστολάς,) in the like sense, occurs in Hel. l. 1665. As to δέλτος, besides the instances already adduced, see in Hippol. l. 877, 1057. In Iphig. in Aul., (including some instances produced above,) we find δέλτον in l. 35, 109, 155, 307, 322, 891, 894. In Iphig. in Taur. 584, 760, 603, 615, 635, 640, 667, 733, 756, 791. Besides these, several instances occur in the Fragments of Euripides.

In all these cases, let it be called to mind that the writer is speaking of persons and occurrences at or before the siege of Troy. It is impossible, therefore, to resist the impression, that he regarded *epistolary* correspondence as a thing then well known and commonly practised, certainly among persons of the higher rank.

their tragedies. But I am persuaded that this remark must be limited to bounds which forbid absolute and palpable incongruities. Very extravagantly and unaccountably the actors of a fabulous age may be represented as demeaning themselves, and all is well; because extraordinary actions are expected, and extraordinary powers of performing them are presupposed. But this is something exceedingly diverse from evident and monstrous incongruities in circumstantial matters, which belong not to persons, but to *things*. There would not be a man or woman in a Boston audience, present at the exhibition of such a play as has just been mentioned, who would not in an instant perceive the gross incongruity of putting the wild Indian chief to the writing of letters; and who would not feel that the author of the play was stupidly ignorant, or else destitute of all taste, or silly enough to believe that his audience would all be stupidly ignorant. I aver, then, that the familiar and often repeated usage of Euripides, of Sophocles, (and even of Æschylus,) in introducing epistolary communication among the ancients at and before the siege of Troy, implies, of course, a like belief on the part of the Athenian public, who were so sensitive as to even the minutest things in a player, that they would spontaneously correct a false accent or a wrong quantity. But if alphabetic writing began in Greece only about the middle of the sixth century B. C., then this public could not possibly have been brought to the general or rather universal belief, that it was four or five centuries older, to say the least; for in a place like Athens, there must have been some well-grounded knowledge in respect to such a matter. The common usage of the great tragic poets, in the introduction of epistolary communication among remote ancients, shows with certainty what the public sentiment at Athens was, in respect to this matter. And how can any one account for such a public sentiment, on the ground that writing began among the Grecians only in the sixth century? This would be far more difficult than to believe that the sentiment was grounded upon matter of fact.

But we have something perhaps more definite and certain, than these allusions in the great poets. Plutarch, (in Lycurg.,) Ælian, (Var. Hist. XIII. 4,) Dio Chrysostom, (Orat. II. p. 87,) Heraclides of Synope, (Gronov. Thesaurus Ant.

Græc. VI. p. 2823,) all testify that Lycurgus, the great lawgiver of Sparta, brought the poems of Homer from Crete, where he met with them among the posterity of Creophylus; which latter person was (as tradition says) a son-in-law, or teacher, or guest of Homer. Plutarch and Ælian both aver, that in the land of European Greece, previous to this period, only an obscure tradition about Homer's poems existed, and one and another possessed some extracts from them. Lycurgus employed chanters and rhapsodists to recite them to his people, in order to inspire them with a martial spirit. Now Lycurgus lived almost nine centuries before the Christian era; and if he found the complete poems of Homer in *writing*, and copied them, (as is most explicitly affirmed by the historians just mentioned,) this would seem to settle the question as to the antiquity of the *written* works of Homer. Wolf, Mueller, and others, examine this testimony *adunco naso*. No wonder; for it prostrates the fanciful edifice which they have reared. But Crusius (Præf. to his edit. of Mueller) has given the subject a fair investigation.

The appeal to the so-called *Homeridæ, chanters,* and *rhapsodists,* (ἀοιδοί, ῥαψῳδοί,) as evidence that Homer's poems must have been diffused and preserved for a long time independently of writing, is not at all conclusive. The Homeridæ were nothing more than an ancient and higher class of *rhapsodists*. The chanters and rhapsodists differed only in name, and perhaps in some peculiarities in the modes of recitation or *recitativo*. All were the *viva-voce reciters* of Homer; and, in the earlier times, they recited without the immediate aid of manuscripts in the act of recitation. They wandered from place to place, reciting wherever they could find encouragement and remuneration. But to argue from this, as many critics have done, that Homer's poetry could not at the same time have existed in *writing*, betrays but an indifferent knowledge of the customs of antiquity, and especially of the East. The mass of Greeks, in Europe and Asia, could not read in those times. The price of *manuscripts* ample enough to comprise the Iliad and Odyssey, was beyond the reach of any but the rich. Yet the Grecian people were of a romantic and poetic turn of mind. The poems of Homer greatly delighted them. Hence the profitable employment of the rhapsodists. The brief and popular songs of times more ancient than the age of Homer, probably were not committed to writing, but were diffused and preserved merely by oral tradition. They were sung or chanted of course, without the aid, and without the need, of any *written* copy. When Homer came to be sung in like manner, and to be the popular poet of the Greeks, he was *recited* without book. This gave an opportunity for the rhapsodists to do, what their successors in office still do in Egypt and Persia, and other countries of the East, that is, it gave opportunity to *act*, as well as recite, the works of Homer. This was a great advantage to the rhapsodists, since they could impart a much more lively interest to their readers, by adopting such a method of exhibition.

To my own mind, the fact that there were chanters and rhapsodists of Homer's works, soon after they were composed, and for some centuries onward, is far enough from proving that these works were not reduced to writing. Let us look at experience and matters of fact. The Thousand and One Nights of the Arabians has always, from the time of its composition, been in writing, as all agree; for it is a production some centuries later than the era of Mohammed. Yet in Persia and Egypt, even in recent times, very few copies of this most entertaining and truly oriental work exist, since neither of these nations have availed themselves of the art of printing; at least not until these some ten years past, and now only to a small extent. Sir John Malcolm, in his Notes on Persia, tells us, that on festal occasions and at levees, at the court of Persia, the chanters or rhapsodists are a regular part of the entertainment. He speaks of them as ready to recite, at an almost indefinite length, the Thousand and One, the poems of Hafiz, and the works of other distinguished Persian writers, and as being employed by the nobles and the rich for this purpose. He describes them as not simply *reciting*, but *acting*. He tells us that no actor on the stages of London or Paris, ever played his part more significantly and satisfactorily. One of Sir John's attendants, who did not understand Persian, was about to withdraw, on one of the festal occasions, when the rhapsodist rose to commence his exhibition. The latter, seeing him in the attitude of withdrawing, inquired the reason. He was told, that it was because he did not understand the Persian language. The actor replied, that this was of little consequence; for he would make himself quite intelligible to him, notwithstanding this. The English gentleman remained, and the actor most amply redeemed his pledge.

This gives us an instructive view of the interest which the rhapsodists of Homer might, and probably did, impart to their recitations; and shows that they might find full employ, notwithstanding the existence of MSS.

The case is the same in Egypt. Mr. Lane, in his admirable work on the Modern Egyptians, has given us a full account of their rhapsodists. The most numerous class of them is the *Shó'ara*, i. e. reciters of poetry, of which there are about fifty in Cairo. These confine themselves to the romance of Abu Zeyd, which is full of poetic passages. The prose they recite with measured tone; the poetry with accompanying instrumental music. The next class (about thirty of them in Cairo) are called *Mohadditeen*, i. e. Story-tellers; who recite nothing but the Life of Zahir, a romance founded on the story of an Egyptian prince who bore that name. It is very voluminous and expensive; and consequently, a knowledge of the work, such as it is, is mainly kept up by the *viva-voce* reciters. There is, besides these, a small class of reciters of Cairo, who are called *Antereéyah*, in consequence of reciting the romance of Antar, which has been recently translated into English. Occasionally this class of persons extend their recitations to other works.

Such then are the oriental modes of entertainment in the way of reading or recitation. Where the great mass of the population are unable to read; where printing is not introduced, and the price of MSS. is exceedingly dear; where the indolent habits of the Turks, Arabians, and Persians, forbid, or at least dissuade from the effort necessary to read a book; especially where a book needs comment and explanation; rhapsodists come in and find ample and profitable employment. So it doubtless was in Greece; so, in western Asia Minor.

But Mr. Lane states one fact in regard to these rhapsodists, which strikes me as of serious import, in respect to the matter before us. He says, that a few years previous to his sojourn in Egypt, the romance of *Seyf Zul-l-Yezen*, abounding in tales of wonder, and the *Thousand and One Nights*, were the subject of frequent recitation. But as these works became very scarce and very dear, the rhapsodists could not afford to purchase them in order to prepare for recitation, and so *they discontinued the practice*. These last-named works are far superior to the others which are now recited, and would be preferred by the people, if they might have them presented. But this cannot be done for the reasons just stated.

This throws light on the recitations of the Homeric rhapsodists. Had they not been able to resort to some MS. copy of Homer, to refresh their memory, or to store it, they could never, or at least they would never, have brought down two poems of nearly 30,000 lines, through so many centuries. I allow that the force of memory is great, even surprising, where a man of talent gives himself wholly to the cultivation of it. Xenophon expressly asserts, (Sympos. III. 6,) that there were several persons at Athens, in his time, who could repeat *memoriter* the whole of the Iliad and Odyssey. So among the Persians and Arabians there has been many a rhapsodist who could repeat the whole of the Thousand and One Nights, or other works of equal length. But after all, such a gift is occasional, and somewhat rare. On a succession of such persons, so as accurately to transmit the Iliad and Odyssey down through three or four centuries, one can place no safe dependence. The thing is incredible. The Egyptian and Persian rhapsodists every where intermingle, with what they recite, so much of their own compositions, both in poetry and in prose, as may serve to expand, embellish, or explain their author. Often, men of talents among their rhapsodists become so excited by the applause of their audience, that they *improvise*, in a manner that exceeds the originals. So it cannot have fared with Homer; for the present state of his works—so little being in them which is incongruous or superfluous—demonstrates that *improvisation* has not wrought sensibly upon them by additions or diminutions, and of course that they can never have been long subjected to its sole influence.

We may get along quite well as to *oral* tradition, when it is said to have preserved *short* songs, narrations, allegories, or fables, independently of written records. But to think of an *Iliad* and an *Odyssey* being preserved for centuries substantially inviolate, in this manner, requires much more credulity, than it does to believe that alphabetical writing existed a considerable time before the era of Moses. At least, I cannot bring my own mind to a state of doubt or hesitation in regard to this whole matter.

I am fully aware of the testimony of Josephus, in relation to the subject of *ancient* alphabetic writing in Greece. In his *Contra Apion*. I. 2, he draws the contrast between the *antiquity* of Greek and Hebrew letters, and, as might naturally be expected from a Jew, greatly to the advantage of the latter. He says that even the Greeks themselves make their boast of learning their letters from Cadmus; that they have no monumental inscriptions older than the siege of Troy; and no book older than the poetry of Homer. In respect to this, also, and whether the Grecians at the siege of Troy were acquainted with the use of letters, he says questions have arisen, and that the better opinion is, that the Greeks who destroyed Ilium were ignorant of letters. As to Homer, he says: "φασὶν οὐδὲ τοῦτον ἐν γράμμασι τὴν αὑτοῦ ποίησιν καταλιπεῖν, ἀλλὰ διαμνημονευομένην ἐκ τῶν ἀσμάτων ὕστερον συντεθῆναι, καὶ διὰ τοῦτο πολλὰς ἐν αὐτῇ σχεῖν τάς διαφωνίας· i. e. they say that this one [Homer] did not leave his poem in letters, [writing,] but that being kept in remembrance by chanting, it was subsequently adjusted, (composed or put together,) and that it was because of this that so many incongruities were found in it." Such was the impression which Josephus received from Greeks with whom he was conversant, and he was very ready to receive it, because it made directly for the support of his opinion in favour of the greater antiquity of the Hebrew literature. But we learn from him, that it was then a *contested* question, whether the Greeks who besieged Troy were acquainted with letters; so that on the face of his testimony it appears that the point was regarded as a doubtful one. We have seen, however, that Euripides and Sophocles make appeals to Athenian audiences in relation to this subject, about four centuries before the Christian era, which leave no reasonable doubt as to what the general opinion at Athens then was.

Josephus, by using συντεθῆναι in respect to the arrangement of Homer's poems, doubtless has reference to the story so often repeated, and from a period somewhat before the Christian era, (Cic. de Orat. III. 34. Pausan. III. 26. Ælian. Var. Hist. XIII. 14,) viz. that Solon, and especially Pisistratus and his sons the Pisistratidæ, put together the disjointed and Sibylline fragments of the Iliad and Odyssey, and first reduced them to writing, as well as to unity, regularity, and order. All the rhapsodists, as the story goes, far and near, were collected by Pisistratus, and from them he obtained all the scattered fragments of the epic bard, and put them together as well as he could, summoning to his aid all the literary corps of Athens. So much of all this is doubtless true, namely, that Solon made an arrangement of the parts of Homer, which were to be chanted at the Παναθήναια, i. e. the feast of Minerva, which was held once in five years. *All* could not be then sung, and Solon decided how much should be sung, and in what order. Pisistratus, and his son, Hipparchus, pushed criticism much further. They obtained all accessible evidence of what belonged to Homer, and of what quality it was, and arranged the result in the best manner they could. To the famous Aristarchus of Samothrace, (fl. B. C. 200,) is generally attributed the division of the Iliad and Odyssey into twenty-four books each.

Such is the sum of tradition, in regard to this subject. But that *letters* were not known in Greece earlier than the time of Solon and Pisistratus, (about 550 B. C.,) no one will now credit, since the publication of Nitzsch's *Historia Homeri*. But how much the *Diaskeuastai* just mentioned, or others after them, changed the text or the order of Homer, it is in vain now to surmise. The internal evidence of Homer's works is most unequivocally against any considerable interpolation. The unity of his poems, their dialect, the spirit of all the parts, (with slight exceptions,) show a unity of authorship, and a unity of purpose, combined with a plan and a regularity which could not arise from diverse minds. A man might as well say, that the different parts of a watch were, in the first instance, manufactured by different persons without any concert; and that being accidentally brought together, they all perfectly fitted each other, and made a true time-keeper, which all succeeding watch-makers have only imitated. Who would believe such an account of the origin of watches? And yet it is even more credible, than the fabled composition of Homer by poets of different ages and different countries. All agree that Homer's is the greatest poem of antiquity; most say that it is the greatest of any or all ages. How was such a rare union of Homer and Co. brought about? We can find only now and then a solitary example of poetry like his among nations, during the whole period of their existence; a Virgil in Rome, a Shakspeare and a Milton in England, a Dante in Italy. How could Greece, in its barbarian ages, between 600 and 1000 B. C., produce a whole host of geniuses like to Homer, and never one afterwards?

But I am digressing. The interest of the subject has led me away from my more direct purpose. I must simply state the result; which is, that the use of letters was known in Greece some time before the age of Homer; that it was not very common, however, until the sixth century B. C.; that the existence of chanters and rhapsodists of Homer at a preceding period, is no proof at all against the existence of his poems in a written form during that period; that the unity, and diction, and dialect of his works demonstrate unity of authorship, and a good state of preservation in respect to his poems; and that the thing in itself is all but absolutely incredible, that poems of nearly 30,000 lines could have been so preserved for more than three centuries, without having been reduced to writing.

Appeal then to the case of the Greeks, and confident appeal such as has been made in respect to the works of Homer, to prove the *later* origin of letters among the Hebrews, and, consequently, the impossibility of Moses' having *written* the Pentateuch, can no longer be heard with approbation or assent. It is too late to bring forward such allegations among us. In Germany, at the time when, through the example of Wolf and Heyne, the recent *destructive* criticism (as some of our German cousins now name it) was in the ascendant, one was famous "according to the number of axes and hammers which he lifted up" against the ancient temple of the Muses, whether sacred or profane. *Commenta opinionum delet dies.* It is too late to palm upon the literary public any longer the scheme of the *Destructives.*

We return to the HEBREWS. Whether Greece possessed letters very early, or did not, would in reality affect but little the case before us.* Moses and the Hebrews came out of Egypt, after a long residence there. Moses was brought up at the Egyptian court, and was skilled in all the learning of the Egyptians; and Gesenius has come, after all his palæographical researches, and notwithstanding his former opinion that the Pentateuch was composed near the close of the Hebrew monarchy, fully to the conclusion, that alphabetical writing was known in Egypt at least 2000 years before the Christian era, and among the Phenicians at a period but little later. Nor does he stand alone, even among the Neologists. Ewald and von Lengerke, among the most liberal of the Liberals, and both now engaged in publishing a critico-religious history of the Hebrews, have avowed their opinions in regard to the antiquity of writing among the people of Western Asia, in a manner not to be misunderstood. Ewald, in his Geschichte des Volkes Israel, (Israelitish History, 1843,) says, (p. 64,) "In respect to the time of Moses, suggestions from the most diverse sources, even those of the earliest times, agree in this, viz. *that writing was already in use.*" Again (p. 66) he says, "That writing was practised at the time of Moses, the two tables of the Law prove beyond contradiction; and since the art of writing was then actually in existence, the beginnings of *historical* composition must speedily appear, for the importance of the Mosaic period was a sufficient excitement to engage in it." In p. 69, speaking of the nations of Western Asia, he says, "Writing among these nations always appears to be more ancient than any history is able to disclose." Again, on the same page, "So much is beyond mistake, viz. that it [the art of writing] was a privilege enjoyed by the Shemitish nations a long time before Moses made his appearance in history." Once more, on p. 71, he says, "So then the position remains firm, that, since the time of Moses, historical writing in Hebrew might be practised, and was practised." He means to say, that at least it must have begun as early as the time of Moses.

* This is not quite consistent with what is stated in page 31, "It (i. e. the use of alphabetic writing among the Greeks) has no unimportant bearing on the question which is now before us." The statement here is correct, and the digression commencing at page 31 might have been omitted without detriment. D.

Von Lengerke in his *Canaan*, or national and religious History of the Jews, after referring to the ancient name of Debir, viz. Qirjath Sepher, (קרית ספר, i. e. *book-town*,) says, "At all events, it seems historically to follow, from this ancient name, that the use of writing among the inhabitants of the land [Palestine] took its rise in very ancient times, before the *exodus* of the Israelites from Egypt;" p. xxxii. Again (p. xxxiii.) he says, "Among whatever original people of Shemitish origin the invention of writing is to be sought, or to whatever early period it must be assigned, still the invention must be supposed to precede Moses by a long period of time, so far as it respects the Egyptians." Again (p. xxxv.) he says, "Undoubtedly at Moses' time, a commencement of historical writing among the Hebrews had been made."

No one who knows the sentiments of these two distinguished Hebrew scholars and critics, will think of accusing them of any leaning towards *orthodoxy*. They have been forced, by pure historical considerations, upon the acknowledgment of these facts; and so must Mr. Norton have been, had he paid but a moderate attention to the critical history of the art of writing. Even De Wette, the coryphæus of doubters, says, "With Moses, the author and lawgiver of the Hebrew state, the introduction of the art of writing among them may well be assumed as commencing;" Einl. ins. Alt. Test. § 12.* Our own countryman then, Mr. Norton, who so often speaks with not a little severity of the scepticism of the Germans, plainly outdoes the very leaders of dubitation among them, in the case before us.

We may then, in sketching the early history of the Hebrew Canon, assume it as a thing altogether probable, if not quite certain, that in Moses' time the Pentateuch, or at least the leading parts of it, were *committed to writing*. If writing was in use, the fundamental laws and regulations, civil, social, ritual, or religious, must needs have been recorded.

---

* This is scarcely a correct representation of De Wette's statement, at least as it appears in the last edition of his Introduction. Those too who are aware of the aberrations of the Tübingen school, and have read De Wette's late book on *Faith*, will by no means assent to the truth of the assertion, that he is the *coryphæus* of doubters. His words literally translated are these, "The tradition of the Hebrews themselves assigns the first use of the art of writing among them to Moses, the founder and law-giver of the Hebrew state. We cannot ascribe to him the foundation of a Hebrew literature, but merely a feeble beginning of it, perhaps the penning of some laws;" § 12. D.

Such parts of the Pentateuch as the last part of Exodus, which have respect to the sketching of a plan for the tabernacle, and the corresponding detail of the completion of it in accordance with this plan, it could never have entered into the mind of an impostor in after ages to draw out in writing, at least in such a way. That there are a few paragraphs and some occasional glosses of an ancient word, added by a later hand to the Pentateuch, one may very readily concede; e. g. the later succession of the dukes of Edom in Gen. xxxvi.; the account of Moses' death and burial, Deut. xxxiv.; and here and there the more recent names of several towns appended to the ancient appellations. But the very fact that these stand out so prominently from the rest of the composition, is a good argument in favour of the antiquity and genuineness of the book at large.

It does not comport with my design to examine, with any minuteness and in particular, the arguments against the early composition of the Pentateuch, which are alleged to be drawn from the internal state of its various books, and especially from those parts of the several books which wear the appearance of distinct composition, if not the marks of a foreign hand. Nor can I here produce the many arguments drawn from the internal state and character of the Pentateuch, in order to establish its Mosaic origin. In my own private judgment, I must regard the latter as far outweighing the former. But all the detail of these matters belongs only to a *critico-exegetical* Introduction to the Old Testament, on an extended plan, like that of Hengstenberg, of Hävernick, and others. Enough for my purpose, that the Pentateuch is recognised as the work of Moses, by all the historians and prophets of the Old Testament; by the Apocryphal writers, by Philo, Josephus, and all the New Testament writers, and expressly and repeatedly by Christ himself; as will be seen when we come to produce the evidence collected from all these various sources. Enough that this matter rests on the universal tradition and belief of the Jews in all ages; in the same manner as the authorship of the Iliad, or the Odyssey, or of the Eneid, or of the Commentarii de Bello Gallico, or the work de Bello Peloponnesiaco, and the like, rests on the traditionary and universal belief of the nations to whom these works respectively belong. What is concerned with the general critical history of the Pentateuch has already been touched upon. It is clear that *it might have been written* (some small portions of it and some later explanations of ancient names excepted) by the great Hebrew legislator. If we may put any faith in united and constant and invariable ancient testimony, IT WAS WRITTEN BY HIM. At all events, it was in the Jewish Canon before our Saviour's time, and was spoken of frequently by him, and by his apostles, as the work of Moses. This is enough for my main purpose, as I am now more concerned with its *authority* and its *right to a place in the Canon*, than I am with the detail that is connected with a critical dissection of the work, and a discussion of its parts collectively and individually.

I must not, however, dismiss it here, without adverting for a few moments to the fiery trials through which this portion of the Hebrew Scriptures has had to pass.

Soon after the era introduced by Semler, doubts began to be raised concerning the *early* composition of the Pentateuch. Almost every marked period from Joshua down to the return from the Babylonish exile, has been fixed upon by different writers, as a period appropriate to the production of this work. To Ezra some have assigned the task of producing it; in which, if we may hearken to them, he engaged in order that he might confirm and perpetuate the *ritual* introduced by him. To Hilkiah the priest, with the connivance of Josiah, Mr. N. and others have felt inclined to attribute it, at the period when a copy of the Law is said to have been discovered in the temple. Some where near this period, Gesenius and De Wette once placed it; but both of them, in later times, have been rather inclined to recede from this, and to look to an earlier period. The subject has been through almost boundless discussion, and a great variety of opinions have been broached respecting the matter, until recently it has taken a turn somewhat new. The *haut ton* of criticism in Germany now compounds between the old opinions and the new theories. Ewald and Lengerke, in the works cited above, both admit a *ground-work* of the Pentateuch (including Joshua). But as to the *extent* of this they differ, each one deciding according to his subjective feelings. The leading laws and ordinances of the Penta-

SECT. III.   COMMENCEMENT OF THE CANON.   47

teuch are admitted to belong to the time of Moses. Ewald supposes that they were written down at that period. Then we have, secondly, *historical portions* of the Pentateuch, written, as Ewald judges, not by prophets, but before this order of men appeared among the Hebrews—compositions "not earlier than the second half of the Judges' period, and certainly not later than this;" Ewald Volkes Geschich., p. 79. Then come next, according to him, a *prophetic* order of historical writers, about the time of Solomon, or not long after his reign. Next comes a Narrator, distinguished for his talents and his religious zeal, who is to be placed some where near the period of Elijah and Joel (about 900 B. C.). His compositions are of a marked character and style, and easily distinguished from the rest of the Pentateuch. Then comes a fourth Narrator, different from all the others, whose compositions exhibit references to events so late, that we cannot place him earlier than about the middle of the eighth century B. C., not far from the time of Isaiah and Micah. He was followed by the *Deuteronomist*, i. e. the writer of Deuteronomy, who, as Ewald thinks, lived some time during the latter half of Manasseh's reign, and in *Egypt ;* p. 160. Besides all these original authors, and collectors, and redactors, and supplementarists, there are many pieces of composition in the book of Genesis, and several in other books of the Pentateuch, which belong to writers not specified in this statement, and which were selected from all quarters, domestic and foreign. Thus, just before the Babylonish exile, the great *Collectaneum,* or *Corpus Auctorum Omnium,* was brought to a close.

Lengerke, whose work is later, (1844,) admits a *groundwork ;* but, with the exception of some laws, &c., it was not composed until the time of Solomon ; p. xci. Next comes a *Supplementarist,* who must have lived some time in the eighth century ; p. cii. Then comes the *Deuteronomist,* as in Ewald; but he is assigned by Lengerke to the time of Josiah, about 624, B. C. The book of Joshua has only a ground-work and a Supplementarist.

Each of these writers is so confident in his critical power of discrimination, that he proceeds boldly to point out all the respective portions of the Pentateuch assignable to each author or supplementarist ; not doubting in the least, that the internal *indicia* exhibited by the style and matter are plain and decisive in regard to their respective theories. But here arises a difficulty. Let us admit, (as we must,) that both of these critics are fine Hebrew scholars, and very well read in all matters pertaining to the history or philology of the Hebrews; still the question comes up, How can these writers, each being sure that he sees every thing so clearly, differ so widely from each other? Ewald finds internal evidence of a Ground-work, four Narrators, a Deuteronomist, and of many miscellaneous compositions of others that have been introduced by them into the Pentateuch. Lengerke supposes a Ground-work, a Supplementarist, and a Deuteronomist. The respective periods of each (some laws, &c. excepted) are different. And yet each judges from *internal* evidence and *subjective* feeling. Each is sure that he can appreciate all the niceties and slight diversities of style and diction, and therefore cannot be mistaken. Each knows (in his own view with certainty) how many authors of the Pentateuch there are; while still one reckons *six* and the other *three*. And all this—*ex cathedra*, like a simple αὐτὸς ἔφη, or *dixit Magister*.

I will not ask now, "Who shall decide, when Doctors disagree?" But I may, with all becoming deference, be permitted to say, that two representations so widely different cannot be both true. This needs no proof. I do most sincerely believe, that neither of them is true. In some things, however, they both agree; e. g. that writing was known and practised in the time of Moses; and that some of the laws and the ground-work of the system must have come from him (although these critics differ as to the *extent* of this ground-work). They also agree that the Pentateuch is made up by a nameless multiplicity of compositions; "here a little and there a little;" "line upon line," after long intervals of time; and that it was not completed until the latter part of the Jewish monarchy. This *Collectaneum* (I had almost said *Ollapodrida*) is every where dismembered, dissected, separated, and descriptively distinguished, in a measure by the niceties of style and diction. But here is another great principle which is summoned to the aid of the critical analyzers, which is common to both, and heartily sanctioned by both, viz. that *prophecy* or *prediction*, in the strict sense of these words, is an *impossibility*, and therefore is out of the question. All the references, then, in the so-called prophetic parts of the Pentateuch, whether to nations, or events, or characteristics of either, must have been written *post eventum*, i. e. *after* the nations arose, and after the events took place, &c. This is at least very simple; it is also very effectual for the purposes of neological criticism. It makes the assignment of *dates* to the ancient scriptural writings comparatively quite easy and obvious.

It is out of question for me here separately to canvass the particular allegations of these critics. I can only make a few remarks of a general nature, and must then pass on.

That the five books of the Pentateuch were not written in one continuous succession, like an epic poem, or a continuous piece of history, or an argumentative discussion, is sufficiently obvious to any one who reads with discrimination. To me the Pentateuch from the commencement of Moses' active public life onwards through the whole, wears the air of a (historic) *journal*, as well as a record of legislation which was engaged in as often as circumstances called for it. Every thing is more or less minutely recorded, according to its relative importance at the time when it was written down. It looks exactly like the journal of a man, who was often interrupted in writing by the pressure of his other engagements. If Moses was actually the responsible leader of two and a half millions of people for forty years, through the Arabian desert, he most assuredly must have been a very busy man, and have had but little time for writing. His laws were made, from time to time, as circumstances required, and as the people could bear them. Some of them were modified or changed during the journey. All this appears in his journal. It bears the marks of being a series of brief compositions, written in a manner independently of each other; for they were doubtless written at very different times and places, and some of them quite remotely from each other. Deuteronomy, which is set so low by some of the critics, and attributed to a foreign hand by most of the Neologists, appears to my mind, as it did to that of Eichhorn and Herder, as the earnest outpourings and admonitions of a heart, which felt the deepest interest in the welfare of the Jewish nation, and which realized that it must soon bid farewell to them. The repetition of laws is to mould them more into a popular shape, so as to be more easily comprehended and remembered. Instead of bearing upon its face, as is alleged by some, evidences of another authorship than that of Moses, I must regard this book as being so deeply fraught with holy and patriotic feeling, as to convince any unprejudiced reader, who is competent to judge of its style, that it cannot, with any tolerable degree of probability, be attributed to any *pretender* to legislation, or to any mere *imitator* of the great legislator. Such a glow as runs through all this book, it is in vain to seek for in any artificial or supposititious composition.

As to the book of Genesis, it of course must have been matter of immediate revelation to Moses, or else of tradition either oral or written. Now as Luke tells us, that when he was preparing to write his Gospel, he investigated all the things which it contains even up to their original sources, so it may have been, and probably was, with Moses. It was for him to judge, as the traditions were examined by him, what among them was true, and what was false. If we suppose him to have been under Divine influence, (as I do suppose,) then the difficulty as to his judging would surely not be very great. The accounts of former times, then, he has brought together. I have no hesitation in believing that he has combined different ones; and occasionally, where the subject was one of deep interest, he extracted from two or more sources at the same time; e. g. in his history of the flood; of the creation of man and woman; and so of other particulars. For nearly fifty years, all Germany has resounded with reports concerning this matter, which have been greatly diversified. The most general theory is, that *two* different writers are the main sources of the book, viz. the *Elohist*, i. e. the one who uses *Elohim* to designate the Godhead, in his narrations, and the *Jehovist*, (proh pudor! to form such a sacrilegious appellation,) i. e. the one who employs *Jehovah* for the same purpose. Germany is full of books proclaiming the certainty and the importance of this discovery. After all, metes and bounds can be drawn with no certainty between these two sources; and evidently there are compositions in Genesis which belong to neither, and which are of a mixed character. It matters not to us *who* wrote these pieces or *when* they were written. They have passed, as I believe, through Moses' hands, and are authenticated by him. Nothing, moreover, can be more natural than the composition of such a book as Genesis, in order to constitute a kind of introduction to the remaining four books of the Pentateuch.

The account of the creation cannot, indeed, be considered in the light of a historical composition of the ordinary cast; for no man was a witness of the events which it records. It must, therefore, be regarded in the light of a composition that depended on Divine teaching or illumination entirely. At least I look on it in that light. To call it a *creation-song*, with recent critics; or to regard it as a mere poetic philosophem, or philosophical speculation on the origin of things in a poetic way; I cannot. The sublime and awful matter and manner of the composition forbid me to attribute it to mere fanciful conceptions of the mind.

In some such way would I explain the various phenomena of the compositions which make up the Pentateuch. That a book of such claims as it puts forth, viz. as being a work of Moses the great lawgiver, should be composed at six different periods, as Ewald supposes, or at three or four, as Lengerke maintains, and yet admitted each time, by the whole Jewish nation, by prophets, priests, and kings, *as a genuine work of Moses*, requires much more credulity than the commonly received scheme of belief. Scepticism and credulity are, after all, more nearly allied than most persons are ready to suppose. That king of Prussia, who had Voltaire at his elbow to aid and abet him in his attacks upon Christianity, and to foster his scorn of it, was the victim of superstitious deliraments such as are rarely found in the inmates of a hamlet or a cottage.

Still, the critics now before us are entirely free, as one who reads them must suppose, from any doubts as to their power to discriminate between all the various portions of the Pentateuch, and to separate them one from another. Each moves on, as though no impediment or obstacle could be thrown in his way. Lengerke has perhaps even outstripped his compeer, in his march through the province of the *destructives*. He tells us that the promise to Abraham and Jacob, that kings should arise from their posterity, could have been written only after kings arose in Israel; p. xci. Among other things he says, that there is no satisfactory evidence that David composed one single Psalm, in the book which bears his name; p. lxiv. And (which I think to be a rare discovery indeed) he has found out, that the 45th Psalm is an *epithalamium on the marriage of Ahab and Jezebel!* p. lxvii. The tyrant and apostate son of Omri and the Sidonian idolatrous heathen devotee, Jezebel, hardly claimed for themselves, as I wot, such an honour as this.

Each of our critics, as I have said, appears confident that he is in the right; although one makes out *six* redactions for the Pentateuch, and the other *three*. But if we inquire of some other critics, even of the Liberal School, about the matter of style and tone in the Pentateuch, on which all the discerptive process depends, they give us a very different account of the matter. Eichhorn, no mean judge by the way in matters of taste or æsthetics, finds, as he avers, (Einleit.,) most palpably one and the same tone and tenor of diction, from the time when Moses came upon the stage until he quits it. Deuteronomy he regards as the outpourings of a heart ready to burst with interest and solicitude for the Hebrew nation—such outpourings as could come from none but Moses. Herder is of the same opinion; and his taste and discrimination in oriental matters have not often been surpassed. Rosenmueller has avowed the same convictions, after writing a commentary on the whole Pentateuch. Others might be named, to say nothing of the English and other European critics. What are we to say, then, to assumptions such as those of Ewald and Lengerke? Are we, as a matter of course, to give them our assent? And by what process shall we prove their judgment to be so much superior to that of Eichhorn and Herder, in such a matter?

If it were worth our while, it would be easy to show that men, even the best scholars, are liable to mistake in judgments of this nature, which depend on the style and tone of writings. Two or three notable instances, that are recent, may serve to illustrate and to defend this position.

Of Sir Walter Scott's talents and discrimination nothing needs to be said. Especially was he *au fait* in all matters pertaining to Scotch Ballads and Border Stories. Mr. J. H.

Dixon, a literary antiquarian, has recently published some remains of Mr. R. Surtees, a poet of no mean rank; and among the rest a morsel of five pages, entitled *the Raid of Featherstonehaugh*, a mere *jeu d' esprit* of the poet, in which he aimed to imitate the older ballad-makers. Sir Walter not only believed in the antiquity of the Raid, but quoted a whole verse from it in his Marmion, (Cant. I. v. 13, seq.,) and gave the poem at length in his Notes to this work, with a grave comment upon this work, pointing out its distinctive *antiquarian* traits. Surtees, of course, was convulsed with laughter, and thought it good pay for what Sir Walter had so often done to the public, by imposing on them in the way of pretending to quote old Ballads, and particularly that famous author *Mr. Anonymous*.

A more recent affair of a like nature has just come before the public. Dr. Reinhold of Germany, being revolted by such claims as Strauss, Ewald, Bauer, Lengerke, and other Liberals make, to the power of discrimination in all cases between what is ancient and modern, or earlier and later, in writing, in order to put these pretensions and boasts to the test, composed and published the story of the *Amber Witch*, as a "tale of olden time." It was of course furnished with the due apparatus, in the introduction, for carrying on the hoax with success. No sooner had the book been published, than the prevailing opinion appeared to pronounce it to be a genuine production of antiquity, and not a few criticised, and explained, and praised, all in the due and usual order. In particular, the Tübingen Reviewers—the compeers and friends of Strauss, pronounced their infallible sentence, grounded on their unerring skill in discriminating the character of any composition, in favour of the book as a *genuine ancient* chronicle. When the matter had gone so far that there was no retreat, Dr. Reinhold comes out with an avowal, that the whole thing was a mere fiction, got up and carried through solely by himself. Angry and lacerated critics pretended not to believe him. The evidences of its antiquity, they averred, were sooner to be believed than his declarations. Recent report states, that Reinhold has actually been obliged to resort to the testimony of his neighbours and townsmen, who were cognizant of his undertaking in the time of it, in order to confront the assurance of the infallible critics of the New School. So much for this. What shall we say, then, in respect to the power of making out all the different authorships of a book more than 3000 years old, and written in an oriental tongue?

I have a graver matter still to relate. About 1824, a *fac-simile* of an inscription on a stone was sent from Malta to the French Academy, with a *bilingual* writing purporting to be Greek and Phenician, accompanied by some emblematic pictures or outlines of them, at the commencement and the close. The learned Raoul Rochette was then keeper of the Cabinet of Antiquities, and professor of Archæology at Paris. He sent copies to different literati in Europe, and asked assistance to decipher the inscriptions. These were dated in the 85th Olympiad, i. e. some 436 years B. C. Raoul Rochette believed in their antiquity. Creutzer doubted; Boeckh at Berlin also doubted. But Gesenius of Halle and Hamaker of Leyden, two of the best orientalists and antiquarians in all Europe, not only sided with the French professor, but published comments on the inscriptions, which were submitted to the European public. In respect to the *Greek* part of the inscription, it was written βουστροφηδόν, in order to imitate the most ancient Greek; still, there was no difficulty for an antiquarian in reading it. But the so-called *Phenician* part was a matter of serious difficulty. Each antiquarian made out his own scheme of interpretation. Finally, however, Raoul Rochette induced the celebrated Kopp, the author of the *Bilder und Schriften der Vorzeit*, to undertake the deciphering of these inscriptions. This he did with the most complete and triumphant success, and exposed the folly of the claims made for them to all Europe, even to their entire satisfaction. His letter is in vol. vi. of the *Studien und Kritiken;* and it has lulled the Maltese inscriptions of the 86th Olympiad into a sleep, from which they will never more wake. Not even the powerful voice of a Gesenius or of a Hamaker could summon them back from the regions of Morpheus, or (whither perhaps they may have emigrated) from the banks of the Lethe in a darker domain.

So much for *infallibity* in these *antique* matters. How can Ewald and Lengerke expect from us implicit faith in their claims, while facts like these are before us?

SECT. III. COMMENCEMENT OF THE CANON. 55

To sum up my critical creed respecting the Pentateuch in a few words; I believe that the last four books of the Pentateuch contain a record or journal kept by Moses, during the period of forty years spent in the Arabian waste; that this journal is a mixed composition of laws and ordinances and history, written at periods and under circumstances so diverse, that parts of it not unfrequently wear the air of a different authorship; and finally, that the book of Genesis is composed, in a good measure, of different traditions respecting preceding times, either oral or written, all of which passed under the revising eye and hand of Moses. The account of the creation may have been derived from some of the patriarchs, such as Enoch, Noah, or Abraham, whose minds were enlightened in regard to this matter; or it may have come from Moses himself, enlightened in the same manner. Enough that all is now authentic. Why should I be called upon, then, to believe in the discretive and discriminating power of an Ewald or a Lengerke, when these powers are exercised, as they have plainly been, in separating what God and Moses and the Saviour of the world have joined together?

Such was the commencement of the Hebrew Canon. The foundation of the ancient Dispensation was laid by it. How the Pentateuch was diffused and preserved among the Jews remains to be shown. When and in what manner the other parts of the Hebrew Scriptures took their rise, still remains for consideration. In order to place this whole subject in an adequate and appropriate light, it will be necessary to take a survey of the state and means of literature, and particularly of religious writing and instruction, from the time of Moses down to the period when the Canon was closed. When all this is before us, it will be easy to appreciate what is said, respecting the composition and preservation of the sacred books; and without some adequate and proper knowledge of these matters, no just and solid judgment can be formed in relation to the critical history of the Hebrew Scriptures.

SECT. IV. *State of Literature and means of Instruction among the Hebrews.*

In order to present any thing satisfactory in relation to these topics, it will be necessary to take a distinct view of several matters, which stand intimately connected with them.

I. It hardly needs to be said, that the art of printing was unknown at this period, not only among the Jews, but in all hither Asia and Europe. The Chinese, indeed, boast of knowing something of it for a considerable period before the Christian era. But this, as well as many other Chinese boasts, remains to be further examined.

The diffusion of books, even sacred ones, among any people who can employ nothing but *manuscripts* all written out by hand, must every where and at all times be very limited. The expense of material on which writing could be performed, was somewhat considerable; yet this would not compare at all with the expense of hiring a *copyist*. It does not appear certain, what the WRITING-MATERIAL was, in the earlier times of the Hebrew commonwealth. The large *tablet* (גליון) on which Isaiah (ch. viii.) is required to write, not improbably was a tablet of light wood smeared with wax. But in the time of Jeremiah, we find that the *roll* on which Baruch had written his communications, was cut in pieces with a knife, and burned in the fire by Jehoiakim, Jer. xxxvi. 23. Possibly this was a linen roll, or it might more probably be leather or parchment? At a very early period the Egyptians began to write on linen and cotton cloth, smeared over, after the writing, with some diaphanous substance so as to preserve it. They also wrote on what we may name *paper*, i. e. stuff manufactured from the bark of the papyrus. The skins of animals, tanned and made smooth, and adapted to the purpose of receiving impressions from ink of different kinds, were early employed among nations where writing was practised. One cannot well suppose the Jews to be ignorant of any of these materials, who had lived so long in Egypt; and when once known, the use of them can hardly be supposed to be discontinued at any subsequent period. The best kind of parchment was, to be sure, only a late invention, i. e. in the

SECT. IV.   LITERATURE OF THE HEBREWS.   57

time of Attalus the king of Pergamus. But tolerably good writing material may be made from prepared cloth, or soft and smooth skins of animals that have a thin and delicate cuticle. The *roll* which Ezekiel saw, (iii. 9, 10,) and the flying roll of Zechariah, disclose to us that either linen cloth or skins prepared must have constituted the then usual material of writing. Psalm xl. 7, speaks of a מגלת ספר, *a roll of the book*, in which something was written that had respect to the Messiah; see Heb. x. 5, seq. The title of this Psalm ascribes it to David. In his time, then, books were written in such a manner, i. e. on such material, that they were *rolled up*. Cloth or prepared leather they must have been, unless indeed the product of the Egyptian papyrus may be supposed to have been transported to Palestine. To make this *roll of a book* only a decree in the Divine mind, because every thing stands as it were recorded in that mind, (so Mr. Norton has explained it,) is an application of the by-gone doctrine of *accommodation*, about as extravagant as any thing among the German critics with whom he finds fault.

A moment's consideration of the nature of the climate in Palestine, will serve to show how perishable the material of books must have been, unless guarded with extraordinary care. The severe heat during one part of the year, and the extreme moisture during another part, must have both been unfavourable to the cloth and skin material on which books were written. It is easy to see, how the original autograph copies would soon disappear, in such circumstances, and especially such volumes as were exposed to constant use and to the open atmosphere. The original Pentateuch might reach, perhaps, the time of Samuel, or of David; but we can scarcely suppose it to have been extant in the time of Ezra.

II. We can make no thorough comparison of the present state of the Christian world with that of the ancient Hebrews, in respect to education and knowledge, without at once perceiving the almost unappreciable difference that exists between them. Brought up as we are, in a land where from our very infancy the knowledge of letters is impressed upon us, and where it is a rare thing to find an individual who cannot read and write, and rare even to find any one who is not habitually a reader of some kind of book or periodical, or at least of some weekly or daily journal, it is very difficult for us fully to realize the condition of a people, among whom books never circulated, or could circulate, to any great extent, and of whom only a few priests and prophets, or some of the noblemen or of the rich, could even read a book. Yet such was the state of the ancient Hebrews.

If there be any one thing which strikes us with astonishment in regard to the Mosaic legislation, it is, that no provision is made by the great Jewish law-giver for the thorough education and enlightening of the Hebrew nation at large. When viewed in contrast with the present legislation of most Christian countries in respect to the subject of *education*, the Mosaic dispensation would indeed seem to be one of types and shadows, in comparison with that of the gospel. It was only *once in seven years*, viz. when the whole population of the country were required to assemble in Jerusalem, at the feast of tabernacles, that the Law was to be read in the hearing of them all, Deut. xxxi. 10, 11. The usual period of this feast was seven days; and diligent must readers and hearers have been, if all the Law was read during that period. This is all the direct provision made by Moses, for the instruction of the people. Three times in a year, it is true, all the males were to appear before God in Jerusalem, viz. at the feast of unleavened bread or the passover, at the feast of weeks, and at the feast of tabernacles, Deut. xvi. 16; Ex. xxiii. 14, 17; xxxiv. 23.* Doubtless there were some selections from the Pentateuch read on these occasions; but this is not expressly ordered by Moses; nor could the reading have been very extensive, because of other duties to be performed.

* I cannot refrain from noticing here an important circumstance, added in the way of encouragement or assurance, in order to show the Hebrews the practicability of complying with the injunction to assemble thrice each year at Jerusalem. What I refer to, follows immediately the injunction in Ex. xxxiv. 23. to "appear thrice in the year before the Lord," and it runs thus: "For I will cast out the nations before thee, and enlarge thy borders, neither shall any man desire thy land, when thou shalt go up to appear before the Lord thrice in the year." Mr. Norton and others, who speak with undissembled horror of the command to extirpate idolaters from the land of Palestine, probably may not have turned their thoughts to this necessary precaution for the safety of the Jewish people, when celebrating their national feasts during so many days of the year. The withdrawing of the great mass of the male population from their homes, must of course have left the country defenceless.

LITERATURE OF THE HEBREWS.

Besides these means of instruction, *judges* and *officers* of the tribe of Levi were to be appointed in all the Hebrew cities; whose business it was to judge in cases of dispute between man and man, to solve cases of conscience, and instruct those who consulted them as to the mode of performing ritual and ceremonial observances, Deut. xvi. 18; comp. 1 Chron. xxiii. 3, 4. Of this more will be said in the sequel, when we come to inquire what part the *priests* took in the instruction of the people.

The very statute of Moses, which orders all the population of the land to assemble once in seven years in order to hear the Law read, does in itself imply, that this was the only means provided generally for such a purpose. If each family possessed a copy of the Law, and could read it, of what possible consequence would be all the trouble and expense and risk of assembling at Jerusalem in order to hear it merely? The defenceless state of the country, and the heavy expenses of travelling with one's whole family on these occasions, even from the remotest borders of the country, shows that other more facile and more economical means of enlightening the people, and of giving them full views of their religious and civil obligations, were no part of the Mosaic institution. Had they been employed, the general assembling of the whole mass, so onerous and expensive, must have been superseded.

We know indeed that in the times of Samuel, and of Elijah and Elisha, that there were something like *schools of the prophets*, in which young men were trained up for prophetic service. But the number of them could not have been very great. Omitting these, we hear or know nothing of *schools* for the education of the mass of the people. They seem never to have existed. Hence the mass could neither read nor write. Hence too the revolting fickleness and mutability of the Jews, in regard to the worship of the true God. A well-informed population must have viewed with disgust the abominations of the heathen worship. But ignorance is always prone to superstition, and is ready to believe any thing and every thing which superstition will inculcate. The morals of the heathen were of course low; those of the Mosaic system were sound and stern, and as to some features perhaps even rigid. Heathen rites, we may suppose, were naturally revolting to most Jews, so far as bloody human sacrifices were demanded. Yet even Moloch was, at times, worshipped by many of the Hebrews with zeal. But what attracted the ignorant and unthinking was, the loose rein that was held over the passions. Impurity was even a part of the heathen religious rites. In the journey of the Hebrews toward Palestine, while under the guidance of Moses himself, the people joined themselves to Baal-peor, the god of the Moabites; and all this because they were allured to "commit whoredom with the daughters of Moab;" Num. xxv. 1, seq. So down through the whole time of the Judges, and, with few exceptions, down to the Babylonish exile itself, the Jews were continually prone to turn aside from their more rigid and pure and elevated worship, to the rites and ordinances of the heathen. Nothing but the gross ignorance in which they lived, can adequately account for such a phenomenon.

It is indeed true, that Moses commands Jewish parents to "teach his statutes diligently to their children, and to talk of them when they sit in the house, and when they walk by the way, and when they lie down, and when they rise up," Deut. vi. 6, 7. But the instruction is all *oral*. No reference is made to letters or books. What the parents could retain in memory from hearing the Law read once in seven years, they were to inculcate upon their children. But how much the mass of the people, ignorant of letters, would retain and teach, was but too manifest in the subsequent ignorance and proneness to idolatry in all ages of the Jewish commonwealth, down to the time of the return from the Babylonish exile.

Such is the remarkable difference between the effects of the Gospel dispensation, and that of the ancient Law. The votaries of Romish superstition would fain bring the mass of Christians back to the condition of the ancient Hebrews. With them it is at least a practical maxim, that *ignorance is the mother of devotion;* but above all, that ignorance of the Scriptures is the mother of devotion. Hence the Bible itself is not to be put into the hands of the common people. *Religion*, therefore, with them must practically mean, a readiness to submit to all which the pope and the priesthood prescribe. But here even the times of Moses were far in advance. All the people were required to hear the *whole*

Law once in seven years; and parents were also strictly enjoined to urge upon their children all the precepts which they could retain in memory. Moses, of course, did not leave the whole population to be managed only by the priests.

I have only to subjoin under this head, that we must not judge of the policy or skill of Moses, in legislating for the Hebrews, by a comparison of the ancient Jews with our own population of the present day. The Hebrews as a nation were illiterate; and they long continued to be so. A command to set up schools among them, in the then state of things, and to furnish all their children with books, would at least have been deemed by them to be a practical impossibility. We, who purchase elementary books enough at the price of from two pence up to fifty, can scarcely feel what a burden the general provision of books for all the children, and for grown-up readers, would have been in the Mosaic age. It is one of the things that the great legislator felt himself obliged to leave untouched, on account of the circumstances of the Hebrews, and of the times in which he lived. Book-making or reading, and the possession of books, could at that time belong only to a few.

III. Let us now look at this subject in another point of light. I refer to the subject of *religious instruction*.

We who have enjoyed the privileges of the Christian sabbath and of the sanctuary, are but ill prepared for the due estimation of the ancient laws of Moses, in respect to these matters. The Jewish people were forbidden, on the penalty of excision, to kindle a fire in their dwellings on the sabbath, Ex. xxxv. 3. They were even prohibited from leaving their habitations on that day (Ex. xvi. 29); although the spirit of this precept would not seem to extend to leaving their dwellings for the purpose of religious worship. But all idea of religious *social* instruction on the sabbath is entirely lacking here, and is to be excluded. We shall soon see that there was no provision for social worship among the Hebrews on the sabbath, and no order of men whose business it was regularly to superintend their habitual religious instruction. *Parents* are the only persons required by Moses to perform this office; and how well it would be performed by those who could neither read nor write, and had no books, it is not difficult to perceive.

Nothing is plainer, than that the very arrangement of the tabernacle, its ritual, its priesthood, (and so in respect to the temple,) presupposes and takes for granted that there is only *one* lawfully constituted place of public ritual worship. Three times in each year are all the males among the Hebrews to repair to the tabernacle or temple, and spend, on two of these occasions, a week each time, (at the passover and also at the feast of tabernacles,) and at least one day as sacred time at the feast of weeks or Pentecost. The reason why no more time was demanded on this last occasion, which occurred just seven weeks after the feast of the passover, is obvious. It was the beginning of *harvest time*, and the absence for even a few days of the great mass of the population from their homes, would occasion the loss of their main sustenance.

The sacrifices appropriate to these occasions could be offered "only in the place which the Lord Jehovah had chosen." Specially was this true of the *passover lamb*. It must be killed and dressed in the outer court of the tabernacle or temple, while its blood was carried within, and sprinkled upon the altar. Of course there could have been no other lawful places of worship, i. e. of ritual worship, which would have rivalled the tabernacle or temple.

But still, may there not have been houses built in at least the larger towns for public, social, *devotional* worship ? May not the Hebrews from Joshua down to the Babylonish exile have had their *synagogues*, i. e. places of social religious meeting, in order to read and expound the Scriptures, to sing hymns, to communicate instruction, and to give utterance to exhortations ? Nothing is easier, I answer, than for us, brought up as we have been, to suppose this. Indeed it is even difficult for us to suppose the contrary.

We can scarcely credit it, that Moses should have overlooked or failed to make an arrangement so obviously important and useful. But still, when we make the most strict and thorough scrutiny of the Hebrew Scriptures, both in the history which they contain and in the prophecies, we cannot find a trace of any such thing as public social worship, either on the sabbath or on any other day of the week, from the time of Moses down to that of Ezra. *There is not a word in all the Pentateuch of command to the Hebrews to keep the sabbath, by attendance on public worship.* There is no intimation of even voluntary associations of individuals in any part of Palestine, to hold any stated public and social worship, or to procure religious instruction for such occasions.

In the book of Judges, (the brief history of a period of about 300 years,) there is little else but a record of Jewish propensities to idolatry, and of the chastisement which ensued, upon the indulgence of these propensities. There is, however, one notable woman, Deborah, who is called a *prophetess*, whose history is given; but apparently more on account of her political than her religious achievements, Judg. iv., seq. She, as it would seem, was the civil head of the Hebrew nation, during a period of some length. Her triumphal song on account of the victory achieved over Sisera and his army, is on record, Judg. v.; but we hear nothing of any religious instruction that she gave. After this period, when the Midianites invaded Palestine, overran it, and greatly oppressed the Hebrews for seven years, we are told of a *prophet*, whose name is not given, (Judg. vii. 8—10,) who was sent to administer reproof to his countrymen. This is all respecting religious instruction which the history of 300 years presents. Can we suppose synagogues to have been extant, and regular worship to have been carried on during all this time? Nothing is more unlikely, or more foreign to the demeanour of the Jewish nation, at that period. Scarcely did they rise up and free themselves from one neighbouring heathen nation, who had been commissioned to chastise them for their idolatry, before they relapsed again into the commission of the same crime, and again were obliged to undergo the like punishment. Nothing can, to all appearance, be more true than the last verse of the book of Judges, in reference to those times: " In those days there was no king in Israel; every man did that which was right in his own eyes."

This verse, moreover, seems to show that the book of Judges must itself have been written after kings arose in Israel. Whether, as the Talmudists suppose, it was written by Samuel, or whether more probably by some other and later personage, we cannot now stop to inquire. But if the whole book, as it now is, was always the same from its origin, it might seem to have been written at quite a late period of the Jewish kings; for chap. xviii. 30, mentions "the captivity of the land," i. e. seemingly of the ten tribes, which was at the commencement of Hezekiah's reign. But I do not, with De Wette, regard this as decisive of the age of the whole book, any more than I look upon the late protracted account of the dukes of Edom, (Gen. xxxvi.,) or the account of the death of Moses, (Deut. xxxiv.,) as decisive of the age of the Pentateuch in general. Some of the documents, (for several are plainly combined in the book of Judges,) beyond reasonable doubt, are of the more ancient stamp, and might have been written soon after the events which they describe had taken place.

In respect to the book of Joshua, which also is made up of several ancient documents, this could not well have been completed until the reign of David, inasmuch as we have repeated references to *Jerusalem* in it, (Josh. x. 1; xv. 63; xviii. 28,) which was, before the time of David, called *Jebus*, (Judg. xix. 11,) and was subdued by David and made his capital, 2 Sam. v. 1—9. But the registers of the division of the country among the twelve tribes of Israel, and some other matters in the book, it is quite probable are of a date contemporaneous with that of the conquest by Joshua.

Thus it seems to be plain, that for a period of about three centuries after the death of Moses, (B. C. 1451,) there could have been no other Scriptures extant among the Jews, than the Pentateuch, probably some parts of the book of Joshua, and some portion, it may be, of the book of Judges. These Scriptures, instead of being in the hands of the great mass of the people, or of being read every sabbath, could have been possessed by very few, even among the priests and rulers. Indeed it is difficult to find any recognition at all of *priests*, during the period covered by the book of Judges. Mention is made, Judges xx. 28, of Phinehas, the son of Eleazar and grandson of Aaron, at the time when the Benjamites were nearly destroyed by the other tribes. But after this we hear no more of priests or prophets, (with the exceptions above noted as to the latter,) until the time of Eli and Samuel. It does not follow, indeed, that there were no persons of these respective orders among the Hebrews. But that they performed no conspicuous part, that they

SECT. IV. LITERATURE OF THE HEBREWS. 65

were not numerous or active enough to have much influence on the nation at large, seems to be nearly certain from the manner and tenor of the history in the two books before us.

In such a state of things, how was the Pentateuch preserved? By whom was it watched over and guarded, and how much was it diffused among the Hebrews? These questions very naturally arise; but we cannot stop to answer them now, without interrupting the history of religious instruction among the Hebrews. We shall revert to these inquiries as soon as the course of our discussion will permit.

Let us pursue the inquiry respecting social synagogue worship from the era of Samuel down to the Babylonish exile.

Not one word in regard to this subject can I find in the histories comprised in the books of Samuel, Kings, and Chronicles, or in the Psalms, Proverbs, or works of the prophets who lived during this period. When Jeremiah pours forth his pathetic Lamentations over the fallen city and country of the Hebrews, he describes the ruins of the temple, the metropolis, the strongholds, and the villages; he weeps over the multitudes of the slain, the famishing, and the exiled; but not a word respecting the destruction of any *synagogues* of the land, or places of public social worship. The comminations of the prophets in regard to judgments about to be inflicted, all have respect to the objects first mentioned, and not to synagogues. It is affirmed of no invading enemy, whether Babylonian or other foe, that he assaulted or destroyed any such buildings or places of worship.

The great public fasts, on extraordinary occasions of distress and danger, are always proclaimed and spoken of as celebrated in *Jerusalem*. Thus Joel, in a time of famine threatened by the incursion of locusts, proclaims a fast in *Zion*, and the summoning of the solemn assembly there; Joel ii. 15, seq. When several enemies had combined, and were on their march to invade Judea, the pious Jehoshaphat proclaimed and celebrated a fast of the whole nation at *Jerusalem;* 2 Chron. xx. 3, seq. When Jehoiakim, stricken with terror at the approach of Nebuchadnezzar's army, proclaimed a fast to all the realm, this fast was to be held at *Jerusalem;*

F

Jer. xxxvi. 9. Now as the Law of Moses had made no prescriptions in regard to any temple-ritual for such fasts on extraordinary occasions, what necessity could there be of assembling at Jerusalem for services merely devotional, in case there were *synagogues* dispersed through all the land? The nature of the arrangement, on the very face of it, imports that there were no such places of public and social worship, where the people were accustomed to perform their devotions. And this is plainly confirmed by the fact, that when Jehoshaphat sent princes and Levites through all Judea, in order to give the people religious instruction, *they carried a copy of the Law with them*, which they obtained at Jerusalem, in order to aid and confirm their instructions; 2 Chron. xvii. 7, seq. This was surely a needless precaution in case there were synagogues in all parts of the land, and of course copies of the Law in them.

I am aware that it has been alleged by some advocates of the early existence of synagogues, that there is a plain reference to them in Ps. lxxiv. 8, which contains a lamentation over the wasting of Judea—probably its desolation by the Babylonish army. Of the enemy the Psalmist says, "They have burned up all the *synagogues* of God in the land." So runs our English version. The original Hebrew runs thus, כל־מועדי־אל בארץ. The word מועד, here rendered *tabernacles*, means, first of all, a *fixed appointed time* or *season;* then, very naturally, the assembling or convention of men at such appointed seasons; then, thirdly, (like our word *church*, which means *assembly*, and then the *place of assembling*,) it stands for *temple* or *place of assembling*. So Lam. ii. 6, "[The Lord] hath destroyed מערו, *his temple*." But in Ps. lxxiv. 8, the plural number of this word is employed, מועדי־אל. On this account Gesenius says, in his lexicon, "It is difficult to say what this means;" and on the whole he thinks it may refer to the high places at Rama, Bethel, Gilgal, &c. Rosenmueller cuts the knot, which he cannot untie. He says, that the Psalm was doubtless composed in the time of the Maccabees, and refers to the destruction of synagogues by Antiochus. More recent criticism seems to have laid aside the idea of Maccabæan psalms, and we are thrown again upon the difficulty which the case appears to present. But it seems to me much less formidable than it did to

Vitringa, or to the critics just named. Let us compare the synonymous word מִשְׁכָּן, *dwelling-place, temple*, (synonymous with מוֹעֵד when this means *temple*,) and see what the usage of the Hebrew is. In Ps. xlvi. 5; cxxxii. 5, the word (מִשְׁכָּן) is in the *plural* number, with the sense of the singular; in Ps. lxxiv. 7; Ex. xxv. 9; Ezek. xxxvii. 27, the same word with the same meaning is employed in the *singular* number. What difficulty then in interpreting מוֹעֲדֵי־אֵל after the analogy of מִשְׁכָּן, in cases where both words have the same sense? The simple truth of the matter seems to be, that the use of the singular or plural, as to a considerable circle of words, was a matter left to the choice of the writer. Thus he might say אֵל, or אֱלוֹהַ, or אֱלֹהִים; אֲדֹנָי or אֲדֹנִי; and so in the New Testament σάββατον and σάββατα, οὐρανός and οὐρανοί, ἀνατολή and ἀνατολαί, and the like in many other cases. Substantially there is no difference of meaning between the singular and plural forms, where such a usage prevails. The plural may indeed, almost at any time, be used instead of the singular, whenever a writer conceives of an object as *composite*, i. e. as consisting of various parts, and he has reference to this circumstance in the language which he employs; or, when he means to designate *intensity*. When simple unity is designated, the singular number only is of course employed. Finally, inasmuch as the temple, with all its courts, was a large mass of buildings, the plural of מוֹעֵד might very appropriately be employed to designate it, as thus conceived of. How much more easy and simple this philological explanation is, than those of the critics just named, every one may easily perceive. If it be said that כֹּל stands in the way of this and requires the real plural, my reply would be, that the plural form of the noun may well admit כֹּל, while the sense of the whole is not substantially affected by it.*

---

* We regard this interpretation of the Hebrew word in question as wholly unsatisfactory. The כֹּל *all does* stand in the way of it, and still more the succeeding word בָּאָרֶץ, *in the land*. It is very improbable that the plural should be used in this case for the singular. Professor Leo, in his Hebrew Lexicon, assigns to it without scruple the signification of *synagogue*, but there are grave reasons for doubting the accuracy of such a meaning. Perhaps it means *places of meeting*, i. e. places in different parts of the land where the people of the neighbourhood met occasionally for prayer. In this manner we have the first notice of *proseuchæ*, in the Old Testament. D.

If there be any passage besides this in the Old Testament which has even a seeming reference to *synagogues* properly so called, it has escaped my notice. I am aware, indeed, that some have supposed that certain other passages might refer to them; but the probability that they do so refer, is so small, that I do not deem it proper to occupy my own or the reader's time with the consideration of them.

In whatever way, then, the Law of Moses, or any other ancient books of the Jewish Canon were preserved, before the Babylonish exile, it could not have been by the aid of *synagogues*. When these arose; and what was done in them with reference to the Jewish Scriptures; are questions that must be touched upon in the sequel.

One other circumstance of a seemingly extraordinary nature in regard to the Law of Moses, deserves some special attention. In the eighteenth year of the reign of Josiah (about 624 B. C.) the high priest Hilkiah, on occasion of making a thorough repair and expurgation of the temple, "found the book of the Law of the Lord by Moses;" 2 Chron. xxxiv. 14, seq.; 2 Kings xxii. 8, seq. This he announced immediately to the king's scribe, who took the book and read it before the king. The surprise and agitation which this occurrence occasioned in all quarters, are represented as being very great. Josiah immediately convoked the whole realm, and in person read the book of the Law to them, and exacted from them a promise to obey it. What is to be deduced from a circumstance so peculiar and extraordinary as this?

We know what Mr. Norton has deduced from this narration. On p. 430, he says, "The story of its being accidentally found in the Temple, may be thought to have been what was considered a justifiable artifice, to account for the appearance of a book hitherto unknown." Not a few of the German critics have, in like manner, traced the origin of the Pentateuch to the transaction in question. If the Pentateuch was before in existence, it was impossible, they allege, that Josiah and the high priest Hilkiah should have been ignorant of it or destitute of it.

First of all, then, as to the *probability* of such a forgery on this occasion. What kind of persons were concerned in it? Josiah was the most pious king that ever sat upon the throne of Judah, from the time of David down to the captivity. He entered upon his office at the age of only eight years, and before he had arrived at his eighteenth year, he had cut off and destroyed all the idols of the land, with their temples, groves and monuments of every kind, and in the way of disgrace he had burned the bones of idolatrous priests upon the altars where they had ministered. Not only so in Judea, but he went beyond his own specific boundaries, and destroyed all the insignia of idolatry to be found in the land of Israel; 2 Chron. xxiv. 3—7. Having accomplished this work, he immediately set about repairing the ruins of the temple, which had been occasioned by the fifty-seven years of idolatry under his predecessors. Most zealously did he engage in this work; in which he was seconded by the pious and distinguished high priest Hilkiah, who was probably the father of the prophet Jeremiah. In the prosecution of these repairs, the copy of the Law in question was found. That there was no concert between the high priest and the pious Josiah, to introduce a new system of law among the Jews, is quite clear. When the scribe or secretary of state, Shaphan, read the Law to that king, the latter rent his clothes in token of grief and distress; unquestionably because of the heavy denunciations in that Law against idolatry and such sins as were common among his people. Immediately he sent to inquire of a prophetess, what was to be done to propitiate the anger of the Lord, which had been kindled because of the breaches of his Law that had so long taken place. The answer returned was, that 'God would visit upon Jerusalem all the evil that had been done there, but would be propitious to him, on account of his humility and penitence.' Immediately Josiah assembled all Judah; read to them in person all the words of the Law; solemnly engaged to obey its precepts with all his heart; and obliged all the people to enter into the same covenant; 2 Chron. xxxiv. 20—32. He extended the reformation to Israel also; and all his days he departed not from following the Lord, the God of his fathers; 2 Chron. xxxiv. 33. This, moreover, was the king who renewed the passover-rites which had fallen into desuetude, and kept such a passover "as had not been kept from the days of Samuel the prophet, nor by any of the kings of Israel;"

2 Chron. xxxv. 18. And as to Hilkiah, the record of his life and actions is brief, but full of significance. To him were committed all monies for repairing the house of the Lord, even without being required to account for them. The work of repairing was carried on with great zeal and complete success, under the same high priest.

Were these men, now, and others their associates who were evidently of the like character, persons who would undertake to commit a forgery in the name of Moses, and to palm it off as the genuine production of that great law-giver upon the whole Jewish people? Then, moreover, were the people so stupid and tame, as to receive such a book as coming from the hand of Moses, and to swear fealty to all its statutes and ordinances accordingly? Did they not know whether such a book had been received or known by their ancestors, not to speak of themselves aforetime? In short, whatever may be the position in which such a forgery may be placed or argued for, it is a manifest and utter improbability. It scarcely deserves a serious notice. Indeed, such a thing was all but impossible.

But then all difficulties are not removed, by removing this obstacle from our path. How could the pious Josiah, and above all the high priest Hilkiah, have lived and acted so long, (some eighteen years,) without possessing any copy of the Law of Moses?

That all the ordinary routine of temple-rites was well known and familiar to the priests who ministered at the altar, must be quite certain. To suppose these to have been regularly performed by virtue of traditional knowledge, is doing no violence to probability. It is only what has happened in all ages and in many countries; I mean not the performance of the same identical rites, but of others of the like nature, as it respected the religion of the heathen. It is true, that nearly the time of two generations preceding the reign of Josiah had passed away, while idolatry in its grossest forms had pervaded the land under Manasseh and Amon, whose reigns lasted fifty-seven years. Manasseh not only " walked in the ways of Ahab," but he built altars and set up carved images for his idols in the very temple of the true God; he offered up his own children to Moloch, and " did even more wickedly than the Amorites themselves had done." Besides this, "he shed much innocent blood in Jerusalem from one end to the other." To him, Jewish tradition (with much probability) attributes the massacre of Isaiah. He was succeeded by Amon, who trod in his steps, and withal was so tyrannical, that his own courtiers formed a conspiracy against him, and put him to death when he had reigned only two years.

In this history, now, as it seems plain to me, lies the solution of the problem, arising from the fact that a copy of the Law of Moses was found, after so long a time, by Hilkiah. Nearly sixty years of undisguised and most thoroughgoing idolatry, carried out even to the most bitter and bloody persecution of the true worshippers of God, had obliterated nearly every trace or monument of proper religious worship. The number of copies of the Pentateuch had probably never been great, at any one time, among the Hebrews. Those, moreover, which had been in existence, were written upon perishable materials. Such devoted idolatry as that of Manasseh, it is probable, would not permit any copy of the Pentateuch to remain safe, which could be destroyed. Antiochus Epiphanes, when he wished to extirpate the Jewish worship and introduce the rites of the heathen into Judea, ordered all the copies of the Law to be burned. It was an obvious measure for Manasseh, in order to carry through his designs. The story of finding the copy of the Law in the temple, which created so great a sensation in the court and among the people, is a good voucher for the fact, that Manasseh aimed at building heathenism upon the ruins of Mosaism and all its monuments, so far as it lay within his power. In some secret recess of the temple, it is altogether probable, had some pious priest hidden the copy of the Law found by Hilkiah, in order to prevent its destruction by Manasseh. That priest had probably died, or been martyred, during Manasseh's impious reign, and the secret died with him, as to the place where the Law was deposited. In making extensive repairs of the temple, the secreted volume was discovered, to the astonishment and great joy of the king, the high priest, and the mass of the Jewish people, who seem to have been thoroughly disgusted with the reigns of Manasseh and Amon.

If any one should regard it as quite improbable, that the

copies of the Law could be reduced to a single one at this period, let him read the religious history of France during the reign of terror and of atheism. In less than an eighth part of the time in which idolatry prevailed under Manasseh and Amon, France had succeeded so entirely in obliterating all traces of the Scriptures, in and about Paris, numerous as Bibles were in that city at a period preceding the reign of terror, that for many weeks the Committee of the Bible Society could not find a single copy from which they might print a new edition. How much easier to produce a like effect in the time of Manasseh, when the copies of the Scriptures were so very few, and when almost every individual who possessed them must be publicly known as the possessor!

It is true, indeed, that, according to the book of Chronicles, (chap. xxxiii.,) Manasseh was taken captive and carried to Babylon in chains, and after a while, being released, he returned to his kingdom penitent and humbled, and endeavoured to repair the mischief he had done to the true religion, by building up the altars of the Lord, and removing and destroying the images of false gods. Of all this, it is true, the book of Kings says nothing; but still, the history is not the less credible on this account. Even the book of Chronicles, however, does not give us any data by which we can estimate with certainty at what time in the reign of Manasseh his exile took place. But the probability seems to be, that it was in the *latter* part of his very long reign, (55 years,) and that he had not then either the time or the means necessary to repair the mischief he had done. He could not restore the copies of the Law which had been destroyed, if it was a matter of fact that he had destroyed them; and it is altogether probable that he knew nothing of the fact or circumstance, that the Pentateuch roll had been secreted in some part of the temple. Then his son, Amon, walked in the wandering steps of his father, and matters remained as they were until Josiah came to occupy the throne. Mere child as the latter was, he appears to have been deeply imbued with the spirit of piety, and to have commenced the work of reformation as soon as his government was fairly established. The sequel of his history has already been presented to view.

On the whole, strange as the finding of a copy of the Law of Moses after an eighteen years' reign of Josiah appears at first view to be, and much as has been made of it by interested critics against the antiquity of the Pentateuch, it turns out, upon more careful examination, to be nothing incredible, nor even very strange. But thus much at least may be gathered from it which is appropriate to our present purpose, viz. that there were at that time *no synagogues* in the land which were depositories of the Law of Moses, and that few persons indeed, in a time of general idolatry and heathenism, possessed copies of the Pentateuch. We cannot conclude, for certainty, that no copy was extant in Judea at that time, except the hidden one in the temple. There were pious men, beyond all reasonable doubt, among the idolatrous mass of the people; and some of these might have a copy of the Law. When Elijah, in the time of Ahab and Jezebel, complained to God, that he alone of all his true worshippers was left in the land of Israel, he was told by him who is the searcher of hearts, that 7000 were yet left, who had not bowed the knee to Baal. And so it might be, at least in some measure, under the reign of Manasseh and Amon. But still, the fact that Josiah reigned eighteen years before the book of the Law was found, seems to import, that no other copy of this book was then procurable in his dominions.

The fact, then, that before the Babylonish exile there were no synagogues, and no public, social, devotional worship, lies upon the very face of the whole Jewish history. An extraordinary fact, I am ready to confess, it seems to us to be, so different is it from a state in which a Christian education and weekly devotional worship are general, and are regarded as indispensable. On what ground the great Jewish legislator omitted to make provision for the general education of the Jewish people, and above all for their religious education and for their social devotional worship, we do not know. But at all events, such a matter goes fully to illustrate the truth of what the apostle says, when he declares that "the Law was the shadow of good things to come, and not the very image of those things," Heb. x. 1. It seems also to illustrate the declarations, that "the Law made nothing perfect," (Heb. vii. 19,) and that "the first covenant was not faultless" (Heb. viii. 7, 8); yea, in view of these matters, one may even venture to say, with Paul, that the Jews, who had only a public ritual with all its external pomp and show, instead of a religious education and stated, social, devotional worship and instruction, "were under bondage to the elements of the world," Gal. iv. 3. Or one may express the feelings which spontaneously arise in his bosom, after such a survey of the religious state of the ancient Hebrews, by saying, with Paul, " Even that which was made glorious, had no glory in this respect, by reason of the glory [of the gospel] which excelleth," 2 Cor. iii. 10.

That the Jews had no regular places of public and social worship, and no religious services appropriate to these, while in a state of exile and servitude in Babylonia, need not be shown. " How could they sing the Lord's song in a foreign land?" No; "by the rivers of Babylon they sat down and wept; they hanged their harps upon the willows," Ps. cxxxvii.

One might naturally expect an altered state of things, after the Hebrews had returned from a seventy years' exile. The better portion of the people would naturally be the portion who went back to their native land. Some time (about seventy years) after permission to return and rebuild the temple, Ezra and Nehemiah appeared as religious and political reformers among the Jews living in and around their metropolis. The services of these distinguished men were great and important. Indeed, I think we can hardly look upon Ezra in any other light, than as a kind of *second Moses* among his countrymen.

Yet in all the accounts of what these two reformers did, there is nothing which expressly recognises the institution of *synagogues*. Still, the public reading and exposition of the Law, so circumstantially related in Neh. viii. 1, seq., might very naturally lead the people and their governors to see and feel the importance of providing the means for employing the like method of instruction—means that would insure its being often and statedly given. But of this, express mention is not made in the books of Ezra and Nehemiah; and after these, we have no Jewish historical writings on which we can rely, until near the time of the Maccabees, about 170—160, B. C. Nor does even the first book of the

SECT. IV.   LITERATURE OF THE HEBREWS.   75

Maccabees (one of the oldest and most credible of all the apocryphal books) say a word of *synagogues*. But it says of Antiochus Epiphanes, that he burned up τὰ βιβλία τοῦ νόμου, and also intimates that copies of the Law, in the hands of individuals, were not unfrequent; 1 Macc. i. 56, 57. This imports a very different state of things from that which existed, as we have seen, in the time of Josiah.

The Jews themselves have nothing more than mere floating traditions, about the origin and introduction of synagogues. In 1 Macc. iii. 45, 46, mention is made of the Jews, after the sanctuary was laid waste, as assembling for prayer at Massepha, (Mizpeh,) because it was formerly a τόπος προσευχῆς, i. e. a place for prayer. But this merely refers to the occasional worship at Mizpeh, in the time of Samuel, and afterwards, 1 Sam. vii. 5, seq. In the eighth chapter of Nehemiah, we have a history of the reading and explanation of the Law, which might well serve as a model for synagogue worship; but still nothing is said of the institution of synagogues. It is only the Jews of a late period, who refer to Ezra the institution and modelling of synagogue worship. So does Maimonides fully and without scruple'; but yet he supports himself merely by appealing to tradition; see in Vitr. De Vet. Synag. p. 414, seq. Josephus speaks repeatedly of synagogues, in the time of Claudius; e. g. in Antiq. Jud. XIX. c. 5. c. 6. Bell. Jud. VII. c. 21, edit. Colon.   Philo speaks of synagogues beyond the Tiber, at Alexandria, and in other large cities; De Legat. ad Caium.   Of the fact that these were common and numerous, there is no doubt; for the New Testament is full of references to synagogues, both in and out of Palestine.   But all this does not give us any thing to depend on, as to the *first origin* of synagogues.   This is lost in antiquity.   No Jewish author has given us any express and credible history respecting this point.

The Rabbinic tradition about the *Parashoth*, or sabbatical lections of the Law, viz. about ceasing to read these in the time of persecution by Antiochus Epiphanes, and putting the *Haphtaroth* or prophetical lections in their stead, seems not improbable, at first view; and if this was matter of fact, then synagogues would seem to have been in existence in the time of Antiochus; for the Parashoth and Haphtaroth are adapted to synagogue worship, and not to the ritual of the temple.

We are left, then, to conjecture as to what time after the return from the Babylonish exile, the public and social worship of the synagogues commenced. That it began soon after the time of Ezra and Nehemiah, if not in their day, would seem to be indicated by the declaration of the apostle James, (Acts xv. 21,) that "Moses of *old time* (ἐκ γενεῶν ἀρχαίων) hath in every city (κατὰ πόλιν) them that preach him, being read in the synagogues every sabbath day;" comp. Acts xiii. 15, 27. I will not say that such a phrase as ἐκ γενεῶν ἀρχαίων might not be employed in reference to a custom which originated even after the time of Antiochus Epiphanes, i. e. B. C. 170. But such is not the natural import of the phrase in question, in the mouth of a Jew. One can hardly satisfy himself with a period much short, to say the least, of that in which Ezra, Nehemiah, or Malachi lived. The nature of the case appears very much to favour this more extended latitude of meaning. From the time of Joshua down to that of the Babylonish exile, the Jews had been ever prone to fall into idolatry, and to practise all the rites of the neighbouring nations. What could be plainer, than that the want of an adequate religious education was one of the principal causes of their defections? Men of such learning and skill as Ezra, could not help discerning this. What more rational and probable, than to suppose that he and Nehemiah concerted and carried into execution some plan for the general instruction of the Jewish people, especially as to the nature of their religious duties?

I am aware that we should examine with caution the Rabbinic stories respecting Ezra and his colleagues, who are said to be the members of what is called the *Great Synagogue*. But while I would lend no willing ear to the הגיות or romantic conceits of the Jewish doctors, I cannot persuade myself, as many of the recent Liberalists in criticism have done, that there is no proper historical basis on which we may repose confidence, in respect to the existence or achievements of the Great Synagogue. All Rabbinic antiquity takes for granted, that in the time of Ezra and Nehemiah there was a select body of men in Judea, who were named the *Great Synagogue*, and who had much to do with arranging the Jewish Scriptures, making provision for their circulation, furnishing the best text to be had, and, in a word, performing the part which was afterwards performed by the well-known Jewish Sanhedrim. Rau, (De Synagoga Magna,) and Aurivillius of Upsala, (Diss. Sac., edit. J. D. Michaelis, p. 139, seq.,) have endeavoured to undermine the whole of this tradition, and to show that it is unworthy of credit. But after all, nothing but the conceits which the Rabbins have connected with the tradition, seem to demand rejection. If these were a good reason for rejecting the tradition itself, then many, or rather most of the narrations in the Old Testament Scriptures must be rejected in the like manner; for what is there to which the Rabbins have not attached some fantasies not unfrequently bordering upon the ridiculous?

On the other hand; nothing can be more probable, than that two such patriots and men of ardent piety, and sound understanding, and great zeal, as Ezra and Nehemiah, would call into council and active coöperation some of the wisest and best and most influential men among their Hebrew contemporaries and countrymen? The Jews have ever and always believed this, so far as we know. I do not aver, that Josephus has expressly said any thing of the Great Synagogue; and the plain reason seems to be, that he has merely followed the sacred records in his account of those times. Philo had no occasion to speak of the formation of the Hebrew Canon, in those of his writings now extant; and the Son of Sirach, in his catalogue of Jewish worthies, (Sir. xlv.—xlix.,) has even omitted Ezra himself, probably because of his lack of political eminence. No certain conclusion can be drawn from such omission on the part of these writers, against the fact that there was a Great Synagogue. The Mishna (Pirqe Aboth, c. 1) expressly appeals to it; and so do the train of Rabbinical writings in after times.

One striking fact, of a historical nature, will serve to render probable the supposition, that synagogue instruction and worship must have been somewhat early instituted after the return of the Jews from their long exile. We have no knowledge, that the mass of that nation have, at any period since that, become the devotees of heathen and idol worship. Antiochus Epiphanes did his best to corrupt them, both by persuasion and force. He even bestowed the office of high priest on such persons as seconded his views. But all in vain, as to the mass of the people. Only the refuse of the Jewish community hearkened to him. Judas Maccabæus and his companions made opposition, roused the Hebrew nation, and finally expelled all traces of heathen worship from their borders.

What now was it which kept the Jews, for more than five centuries before the Christian era, from becoming idolaters, as they had so constantly been (short intervals excepted) during almost a thousand years before the Babylonish exile? Something must not only have operated, but operated powerfully. Their temptations to embrace idol worship were not stronger or more frequent before this exile, than after it; especially under the Syrian kings, the Seleucidæ. Yet they remained firm and unwavering, with the small exception mentioned that took place during the reign of Antiochus Epiphanes. I cannot imagine any cause adequate to produce such an effect, excepting that of *religious instruction*. Nor can I see any way in which this could be accomplished, excepting in that of reading and preaching in synagogues. The Mosaic institute, that the Law should be read once in seven years to the assembled mass of the Hebrew nation, had been tried for almost a thousand years, and had been found quite inefficacious, particularly as this reading was often neglected. What more probable, than that the enlightened and patriotic and pious Ezra and Nehemiah devised and established the social worship of the synagogues, as a preservative from all inclination to future apostacy and idolatry?

Since we have no express and certain history in regard to this point; since, moreover, we know that synagogues were in being a long time ($ἀπ'$ $ἀρχαίων$ $γενεῶν$) before the Christian era; since the Jews were actually preserved from idolatry and heathen rites, and no means but efficient religious instruction which is general are adequate to produce such an effect; I see no good reason why we may not regard it as altogether probable, that synagogue worship was devised and commenced under the superintendence of Ezra, Nehemiah, and the men of the כנסת גדולה or Great Synagogue.

But there is another branch of this topic respecting *religious instruction*, to which I have hitherto but merely ad-

SECT. IV.   LITERATURE OF THE HEBREWS.   79

verted, but which, standing intimately connected as it does with the topic just discussed, should here be brought more distinctly into view. I refer to the *priests* and *Levites* of the Mosaic dispensation.

Whoever borrows his views of the offices of these from the functions of a Christian pastor, and regards them as having a similar employment among the ancient Hebrews, will find, on examination, that he is radically mistaken. The fact that there were no synagogues before the Babylonish exile, i. e. no places for public reading of the Scriptures and for preaching, of itself shows, that there could have been no regular order of men among the Jews, who performed a public part in social and devotional worship. Had Moses made provision for such an order of men, he would have made provision for the means of performing their proper duties.

A glance at the Mosaic institutes serves to show at once, that the sum of duties attached to the *priestly* office, was the performance of those services which were appropriate to the *ritual* worship of the tabernacle and temple. These duties required so much bodily vigour and activity, that they were limited to those who were between the age of thirty and fifty, Num. iv. 3, 23, 30, 35, 39, 43, 47. To the office of PRIEST, *only Aaron and his posterity were consecrated;* Ex. xxviii. 1; xxx. 30; xxix. 5, seq. All the rest of the Levites were given to Aaron and his sons, as mere subsidiaries in the performance of their duties; Num. iii. 9; viii. 19; comp. Num. iv. viii. throughout. In the time of David, the *priests* had become so numerous, that they were divided by him into twenty-four courses or divisions, each of which in turn served a definite period of time in the temple; 1 Chron. xxiii. 3, 6; xxiv. 3, seq.; comp. Luke i. 5. As to the *Levites*, it appears that there were, at one and the same time, 38,000 males, who were of the age of thirty and upwards. To these were assigned by that pious king, duties appropriate to their condition in accordance with the institutions of Moses; 1 Chron. xxiii. 3, 4; comp. xxvi. 29. The greater part, at that time, were employed in aiding to build the temple to be erected by Solomon. But still, 6000 were appointed to be שטרים ושופטים, *magistrates and judges.* Inasmuch as the verb שטר signifies *to write* or *inscribe*, it would seem quite probable that the *Shoterim* were magistrates who kept *records* for their own use and for the public weal. In a literal sense, שוטר would seem to be equivalent to γραμματεύς; but it is evidently of wider usage in the Hebrew Scriptures, and designates *magistrates*, probably those whose business was connected with *records*. In Deut. xvi. 18, the very same officers are named, and Moses gives commandment that they shall be appointed in all the gates of the Hebrews. Moses does not say that these respective offices shall be limited to the Levites only; but it is quite evident, that since they were the most enlightened part of the Jewish community, on this account they would most naturally receive such appointments.

The manner in which the Levites were disposed of by Moses and Joshua, shows that they were not, and were not designed to be, teachers among the people in the capacity of schoolmasters. God gave commandment to Aaron, that neither he nor his posterity, the *priests*, should have any inheritance in the land of Palestine or any part among their brethren; Num. xviii. 20. At the same time, provision was made for the maintenance and accommodation of priests and Levites. Unto Moses it was said, that he should command the children of Israel to assign unto the Levites cities to dwell in, and the suburbs around them; Num. xxxv. 2. Accordingly, after the conquest of Canaan we find Joshua assigning to them forty-eight cities with their suburbs, scattered over all the country. As they were restrained from the ownership and cultivation of lands for agriculture, (the suburbs of their cities being assigned to them merely for *gardens*,) their fellow citizens were bound to provide for them by tithes, first-fruit offerings, and parts of beasts sacrificed; Deut. xviii. 3—5; comp. xxvi. 12. Special liberality and charity to the Levites are strongly enjoined by Moses; Deut. xii. 19; xiv. 27—29. In return for all these contributions, the Levites were to be the judges and magistrates of the land, in both an ecclesiastical and civil respect. Indeed the one was inseparably connected with the other. It was predicted by the dying Jacob, that the posterity of Levi should be *scattered in Israel;* Gen. xlvii. 7. This was necessary, indeed, according to the arrangement made by Moses. The Levites and priests were the appropriate *juris-*

consults of the nation. They did not go round, and preach and teach in a public capacity; but it was their business to settle and adjudicate all controversies between man and man; to declare the law in all cases of trespass or injury; to decide all dubious cases of conscience about rites and ceremonies; to give counsel, whenever asked, about any thing which pertained to duty; and, in a word, to perform the office of judges and of religious and civil monitors. In this light Ezekiel places the matter, xliv. 23, seq. So Malachi, ii. 7. Thus did Jehoshaphat regard their office, especially the priestly office; 2 Chron. xix. 8, seq. In the same light Moses has placed the whole matter; Deut. xvii. 8—10; xxiv. 9; Lev. x. 10, 11. Ordinarily, to say the least, and at any rate according to strict rule, the Levites were to abide in the cities assigned to them, and not go elsewhere to reside. And if this be so, how could they be religious teachers in synagogues (if such there had been) in all the villages of Palestine?

In Judg. xvii. 7, seq. is an account of a wandering Levite, who, at the invitation of Micah at Mount Ephraim, took up his abode with him, and became his priest. But Micah was an idolater (Judg. xvii. 4, 5); and the Levite of course must have apostatized from the worship of Jehovah, in order to become a priest of Micah. This therefore is no example in point, to prove that the Levites ordinarily wandered through the land, taking up their residence wherever it might suit their convenience. We have also an account of Jehoshaphat's sending a special deputation of princes and Levites "to teach in the cities of Judah," (2 Chron. xvii. 7, seq.,) who carried with them a copy of the Law. But this was an extraordinary, not an ordinary, measure. Indeed, there is nothing in the Old Testament which shows that the priests or Levites were travelling preachers or teachers; nothing which shows that they were teachers in their own limited circle, in the ordinary sense of that word. As judges and jurisconsults, and expounders of the Law in doubtful cases, and helpers in matters of religious doubts or scruples, they were indeed teachers. But this duty they performed only when required to do it. They were passive in the business of teaching, not active and aggressive. It was their business to give an opinion when asked, but not to persuade others to assemble and learn their duty from them.

We must, in justice to the case before us, proceed one step further still. I know of no passage in the Old Testament which enjoins upon priests or Levites, as their ordinary duty, to *pray* with and for the people, and to give them religious instruction by sermons or by reading the Scriptures. If there is any passage in the Old Testament which even hints at *prayer for the people* being a duty of the priests in the temple itself, yea, of even the high priest, it has escaped my repeated and attentive search. I doubt not that all pious priests did pray in the temple. I cannot doubt that every pious high priest especially would intercede for the people, on the great day of atonement, and on other like occasions. But where is this *enjoined?* What part of the Mosaic institutes made it their *duty?*

In Luke i. 10, seq. we have an account of Zacharias in the act of his official duty. And what did he? He burned incense in the temple, while all *the multitude of the people were praying* in the outer court. If it be said that the angel who appears to him, promises the birth of a child in answer to his prayers, (Luke i. 13,) yet we cannot suppose these prayers to have been then and there uttered. They would have been unseemly, unbecoming. And besides this, it appears from ver. 18, that Zacharias had for a long time utterly despaired of offspring, and therefore we cannot suppose him to have been then and there praying for what he plainly deemed impossible. Of course his prayer, to which the angel refers, must have been on some former occasion, and probably in a place more appropriate to such a request, than that of the temple of God, where he had an important public part to act.

Let the intelligent and considerate reader, now, put all these things together, and ask himself, whether there were any regular and stated means of instruction or active instructors for the Jewish nation, before their exile. He cannot find them. But he can find, on extraordinary occasions, fasting, prayers, reading of the Scriptures, a renewal of the covenant, and other religious transactions. But all this is nothing to the purpose of establishing the position, that before the Babylonish exile there were synagogues and regular and stated religious teachers of the people.

One remark here forces itself upon me. To argue from a

Levitical priesthood to a *Christian ministry*, and to prove the validity of the latter institution by an appeal to the former, and especially to compare the official duties of the two respective classes with an assumption that they are parallel—is out of all question. The ancient ritual is abolished. The whole of the sacrifices and offerings, and of course the whole of the rites and forms belonging to them, is *for ever* done away by the death of Christ, if any credit is to be given to Paul, particularly in his Epistle to the Hebrews. And as to the main official duty of a Christian minister, viz. *the communication of religious instruction*, it stands as it were even in direct contrast with that of the priest and Levite, so far as all its active aggressive functions are concerned. If Christian ministers are to find any parallel under the Mosaic dispensation, it must be in its PROPHETS, not in its *priests*.

To complete the course which we have pursued, in making inquiry respecting the state of literature and education and religious instruction among the Hebrews, it is necessary that we should take a brief view of the PROPHETIC ORDER belonging to that nation; and particularly ought we to do this, because of the relation which the prophets sustained to the Holy Scriptures, whose critical history we are endeavouring to pursue.

The word *prophet* has had a variety of meanings attached to it by various critics. The biblical idea, as it seems to me, is fully unfolded and designated in the definition which Knobel has given: "A prophet is a person gifted with superior intelligence, and filled with religious inspiration, who stands in an intimate relation to God, and as the servant of God is active in the promotion of religious purposes, especially those which concern the Divine authority and government;" Knobel, Prophetismus, I. p. 113. The most usual name of *prophet* in the Old Testament Scriptures is נביא.*

---

* The verb נבא, employed only in Niphal and Hithpael, Knobel regards, (and rightly in my apprehension,) as related to the Hebrew verbs נבע, נבח, נבך, נוב, all of which mean *to pour forth, to pour out, to cry out*, i. e. to pour forth words or sounds, *to shoot* or *stream forth*, &c.; and kindred to these are the Chaldee נבע, נבב, נבח; the Syriac ܢܒܥ, ܢܒܣ; the Arabic نَبَغَ, نَبَجَ, نَبَعَ; all kindred in meaning to the Hebrew verbs named above. Hence נבא seems to mean, *to pour forth*, or *pour out*, i. e. *to utter one's internal excitement* or *inspiration*. It is not diffi-

Other not unfrequent names of prophets are חזה *a seer*, and ראה *a beholder*. Of course the meaning is one *par excellence*, denoting a person who sees or beholds what others do not, such as secret things, future events, and the like. In a number of cases prophets are called צפים, i. e. *those who espy, explore*, &c. This refers to the appropriate duty of prophets as the moral guardians and observers of the people. In the same way is the designation שמר, *watchman*, employed, and for the like reason. In reference also to spiritual care for the people and for their proper religious nurture, the prophets are occasionally named רעים, *shepherds*. In regard to the proper work which a prophet has to perform, he is also occasionally named *man of God, servant of Jehovah*, and now and then *angel* or *messenger of Jehovah*. Among these appellations, *man of God* and *seer* are the more ancient (see 1 Sam. ix. 9); נביא, *an inspired man*, is more general after the time of Samuel; and *spy, watchman*, and *servant of Jehovah*, appear more frequently in the later Hebrew writers.

If the reader will cast his eye, for a moment, over the various appellations of the prophets now placed before him, he will gather at once, with a good degree of certainty, what the proper office and duty of a Hebrew prophet was. Instead of being a mere μάντις, i. e. a superintendent of ritual observances, a soothsayer, an oracle-monger, or the like, he

cult, perhaps, to assign a good philological reason, why the verb הִתְנַבֵּא, נִבָּא, is used only in the *reflexive* conjugations; for the generic meaning of these verbs thus employed seems to be, *to exhibit one's self as excited or inspired.* Hence the manifold application of the words in question; for they apply not only to uttering predictions, but to commination, reproof, condemnation, warning, exhorting, consoling, exciting, promising, and the like. In a word, to *prophesy* embraces every thing which a religious and moral teacher may say or utter by the aid of inspiration. Of course it applies to sacred music, i. e. to psalms or hymns sung either with or without instrumental music; see 1 Sam. x. 5; 1 Chron. xxv. 1, 2; 1 Sam. xix. 20: comp. 1 Kings xviii. 28, 29, where the verb is applied to the *shouting* and *cantillation* of the priests of Baal, who attempted an imitation of the true prophets. The Jews, as every reader of the Hebrew Bible knows, have designated the books of Joshua, Judges, Samuel, and Kings as *prophetical* books, probably from the persuasion that they were composed by prophets. According to the broad meaning given to נבא above, any book composed by an inspired writer might be named *prophecy*. And in a similar latitude are the words προφητεία and προφητεύω employed in the New Testament. In the language of the Bible, the uttering of *predictions*, in the appropriate sense of this word, is only a species under the genus *prophesying*.

was the *moral teacher* and *preacher* of his nation. His duty was not like to that of the priests; although occasionally some of the prophets superintended sacrifices and other parts of the ritual, e. g. Samuel, Elijah, and some others. All that was ritual, however, if resorted to on any occasion by a prophet, was merely subordinate and subsidiary, and not his main or appropriate business.

The Old Testament is full of the history, doings, and sayings of the prophets. Nearly one half of it consists of their peculiar discourses or prophetic compositions; of which only a small part is *prediction* in the proper sense of that word. Prophets were the principal instruments in keeping alive the Mosaic religion at all times, whether one looks to the spirit or to the ritual of it. Inasmuch as the Jewish commonwealth was ecclesiastico-political, prophets were politicians as well as preachers. Nothing is more common, than the history of their interposition in matters that concern the political weal of the Jewish state. To give counsel to magistrates, on occasion of exigency, was regarded as one of their appropriate duties.

It is singular that, after Moses and Miriam, no prophet or prophetess is mentioned until the time of Deborah, which was more than a century after the conquest of Canaan. And even she seems rather to be called a prophetess on account of her song of triumph (Judges v.) than on account of her mode of life. It is clear that she was a remarkable woman; for she was at the head of the nation, a שפטה, when she led on the Hebrew army to battle against Sisera; Judges iv. 4. An anonymous prophet is presented to view in Judges vi. 8, seq., who administers severe rebuke. Besides these, we meet with no prophetic personages until we come down to the time of Samuel, which, counting from the death of Moses, makes a period of more than 300 years. If there were no more prophets than appear on the face of the sacred records during this long period, it is no wonder that the Jews, who had been partially idolaters in Egypt, relapsed very often, as the book of Judges tells us they did, into the idolatry of the heathen. This had its attractions. It put no restraint on the passions. It might be, (although it does not seem probable,) that priests and Levites urged the ritual of the Law, and exacted all its ceremonial observances; but if they did, these would have had but little efficacy in preserving the nation from corruption, so long as prophets, the preachers of righteousness, were wanting.

With Samuel opens a new and splendid era, both as to the civil and religious concerns of the Jews. This distinguished servant of God acted not only as prophet, but was also a judge (שפט); and not unfrequently did he act as a priest; see 1 Samuel vii. 9, seq.; ix. 22, seq.; x. 8; xi. 15; xvi. 1, seq. He commenced his duties about 1100 B. C., and the prophetic order, founded (if one may use the expression) by him, continued, with little interruption, down to the time of Malachi, i. e. about 400 B. C. Thus, for some 700 years, was the Jewish nation provided with religious teachers, by special Divine interposition, and therefore they had much less apology for departure during this time from the institutions of Moses, than they had in former days, during the administration of the judges.

Samuel began his career very young, and nobly did he maintain it during a period of some forty years. It was during his life, that *prophetic institutions* or *schools of the prophets* first made their appearance. Doubtless this illustrious reformer saw and felt the necessity of more efficient and more widely diffused religious instruction, than had previously been given. The young men educated at those schools seem plainly to have been designed for the prophetic office. Hence they are frequently named *prophets*, (e. g. 1 Sam. x. 5, 10—12; xix. 20, 24; 1 Kings xviii. 4, 13; xix. 14; xxii. 6, seq.,) in relation to the office for which they were being qualified. At other times, their discipleship or relation to their prophetic masters is pointed out by the appellation *sons of the prophets*; e. g. 1 Kings xx. 35; 2 Kings ii. 3, 5, 7, 15; iv. 1, 38; v. 22; vi. 1; ix. 1, 4. The Hebrews often called a teacher *father* (אב); and of course the pupil or learner was a *son*. So in the New Testament, υἱός, τέκνον, and τεκνίον, are employed to designate disciples or learners.

The notices of these schools, in sacred history, are confined to the time of Samuel, and to that of Elijah and Elisha. We find nothing concerning them at other periods. If such schools existed after the last-named period, it would seem at least that they could not have had any considerable notoriety.

In Samuel's time there were large companies of prophetic pupils in several places; 1 Sam. x. 5, 10; xix. 20. Ahab could, in his day, muster 400 prophets of Baal at a time; 1 Kings xxii. 6. Obadiah, one of his pious officers, concealed 100 of the prophets of Jehovah, from Jezebel's bloody persecution; 1 Kings xviii. 4, 13. Fifty of the prophets at Bethel attended on Elijah and Elisha; 2 Kings ii. 3, 7. Those at Jericho, at the same time, appear to have been still more numerous, 2 Kings ii. 16, seq. In Elisha's time, we find 100 of the prophets at Gilgal; 2 Kings iv. 38—43. Various places also are named as the abode of the *sons of the prophets*, viz. Rama, Bethel, Gibeah, Jericho, Gilgal, and mount Ephraim. They appear, moreover, to have lived together in the manner of Cœnobites, and to have been superintended and instructed by some aged prophet. But sacred history gives us no minute particulars as to the manner of their education. Yet doubtless, as there were to be moral and religious teachers, the Law of Moses must have been the subject of their special study. Even Knobel, who maintains the later composition of the Pentateuch, asserts that they must have been orally instructed in the theocratical Law (as he names it) that was traditionally current at that period; Proph. II. p. 46. That *sacred music*, with the voice and with instruments, was in part an object of special attention, is clear from 1 Sam. x. 5; xix. 20. Saul, who meets with a company of these prophetic musicians, is said, by the sacred historian, to have *prophesied* along with them, because he united in their music; 1 Sam. x. 6, 10—12.* It does not follow, however, that all who attended the schools of the prophets, did actually assume the prophetic office after quitting the schools; but it is altogether probable, that most of the religious teachers among the Jews, from the time of Samuel down to the death of Elisha, (a period of about 200 years,) were first learners in the schools of the prophets.

That the notable age of sacred *lyric poetry* among the Hebrews, during which David, Asaph, Heman, Ethan, the

---

* It is clear that Saul united in their *music*, but that this is all that is meant when it is said, *he prophesied*, is not correct. The Spirit of God came upon him, and he gave utterance to religious sentiments. *He was under a peculiar divine afflatus.* D.

sons of Korah, Solomon, and others, were so conspicuous as poets, connects itself with the instructions given in the schools of the prophets, one cannot well doubt. During the period, moreover, between Samuel and Elisha, we find a considerable number of distinguished prophets as well as poets; e. g. Gad, (2 Sam. xxiv. 11—13,) Nathan, (2 Sam. xii. 15,) Ahijah, (1 Kings xi. 29, seq.,) Shemaiah, (1 Kings xii. 22,) several prophets whose names are not given, (1 Kings xiii. 1—3, 11,) Iddo, (2 Chron. ix. 29,) Oded, (2 Chron. xv. 1,) Hanani, (2 Chron. xvi. 7,) Jehu, (2 Chron. xix. 2,) Jahaziel, (2 Chron. xx. 14,) Eliezer, (2 Chron. xx. 37,) Elijah, (2 Chron. xxi. 12,) and Elisha (1 Kings xix. 16). During the lives of these two last-named prophets, we find repeated mention of hundreds more of prophets, many or most of whom had probably been connected as pupils with the schools which they taught.

As to all the prophets now in view, however, although some of them were most highly distinguished by talents, activity, and usefulness, we have no remains of works written by them, but only a brief account by others of their sayings or doings on particular occasions, which is contained in the historical books of our present Scriptures. It is an assertion of the Talmudic Rabbins, (Baba Bathra fol. 14. c. 4. comp. fol. 15. c. 1,) that "Samuel wrote the books which bear his name, and also the books of Judges and Ruth." The two latter, i. e. the substance of them, it is possible that he wrote. But as to the two books of Samuel, they are out of the question. The death of Samuel is related in 1 Sam. xxv. Consequently he could not have written the remainder. Nor is it probable that he wrote what precedes chap. xxv. The great era of *prophetic* composition commences with Joel, Amos, Hosea, and Isaiah, about 800—730 B. C.

From the more circumstantial history of Samuel, Elijah, and Elisha, it appears that they continued in their office down to the time of their decease. In other words, the prophetic office, as then held and exercised, seems to have been a business of life. Was this so with all the prophets who have been named or adverted to above? Or did they assume the office merely for a temporary exigency, and lay it aside when that exigency had passed by?

With entire certainty we cannot answer these questions.

As to most of the prophets, it seems to me more probable that they held their office permanently; for the moral necessities of the people, which called the office into being, seem to have been such as to render the continuance of it highly important and useful. We meet with aged prophets; and the tenor of the narrations respecting this order of men, favours the idea that the office was one which was regular and long continued, so far as it respected the duty of moral and religious teaching. It is unnecessary to assume that all prophets were endowed with miraculous powers. Such was not the case even with Christian prophets, if we may credit the declarations of Paul in his account of their gifts, in his First Epistle to the Corinthians; and I know of no testimony more authentic than his. But the fact that *the prophets* (נביאים) were *inspired persons*, would seem of course to indicate, that they addressed the people under the special aid and guidance of the Spirit of God. It need not, and should not, be supposed, that at all times, and on all occasions, these prophets spoke and acted under such a special guidance. So much was not true of even the apostles of Christ. Enough that at due times, and in appropriate circumstances, they were specially guided and aided by the Spirit of God.

Their sermons or addresses to the people they did not, as it would seem, commit to *writing* at the period in question. We have therefore, at the present time, only some fragments of what they uttered, which were collected and recorded by others. It is natural to conclude from this, that they regarded themselves as ministers of God and servants of the theocracy, only for their own day and generation. The *permanent* monuments of the prophetic class are of a later date, and commence with Joel, Hosea, and Isaiah.

A glance at facts such as these, especially if we view them as they stand connected with and related to each other, would seem to admonish us quite plainly, that in the prophetic order, if we except Moses the distinguished founder of the Jewish commonwealth, a gradual advance to higher degrees of culture and usefulness is perceptible. Who, except Moses, can compete with those prophets, whose immortal works are still so conspicuous in the Jewish Scriptures? We do truly revere and honour such men as Samuel,

Elijah, and others of the like spirit; but we do more than homage or honour to such men as Isaiah, Joel, Nahum, and their compeers.

To the canon of Scripture some considerable accession was made as early as the time of David and Solomon. There might have been a part of the books of Joshua and Judges extant at that period; and if so, these, with the Law of Moses, constituted the then Jewish Canon. David and his contemporary sacred poets made very valuable accessions to the Jewish Scriptures; especially to the *devotional* part of them. Down to the present hour, the compositions of these men are regarded as excelling those of any or all others, in respect to their adaptedness to be the medium of praise and of devout meditation. I will not say, that these compositions introduced a new element into the Jewish religion and worship; but I may safely affirm, that at least they made a new development of the Mosaic religion, and gave to all ages then to come some of the most exquisite models of expressing devout, grateful, humble, and pious feeling. They will go down to the end of the world with unabated, yea, with increasing honour. The greater part of the book of Psalms was composed by David and his contemporaries; and the few Psalms that have been since added, show that sacred lyrics among the Hebrews had its golden age, and also its silver one, and that the golden age commenced, and attained its highest elevation, under David and his contemporaries. Only now and then did some peculiar occasion afterwards call into exercise talents of a lyric nature, in the composition of devotional psalms and hymns.

The book of Proverbs, moreover, must have been a substantial aid to the prophetic teachers of morals. It would seem, however, that from the 25th chapter onward, the composition lay in an uncopied MS. until the time of Hezekiah; Prov. xxv. 1. But be this as it may, the preceding portion of the book is exceedingly weighty, particularly on the score of morals and circumspect and prudential behaviour. Prophets who lived after the writing of this, certainly had a somewhat ample store of choice texts, for discourses on the subject of morality and sober demeanour.

I have distinguished David and his colleagues, the devotional poets, from the prophets, who were the subject of our preceding consideration. But in so doing, I have rather followed our own common *usus loquendi* than that which is appropriate to the Scriptures. Whatever is written or uttered by the aid of inspiration, the scriptural writers name *prophecy*. The ground of employing the word in this extensive sense, has already been presented in the preceding pages.

Let us now pass to the next and most splendid period of the Hebrew prophetic development. It begins with Joel, in the reign of Uzziah, about 800 B. C., and continues down to the end of the Assyrian dominion, not far from 700 B. C. It has been named the ASSYRIAN PERIOD by Knobel, because most of the prophets during this period have reference more or less, in their discourses, to the Assyrian invasions of Palestine, or to those of the neighbouring countries of the heathen who were under the dominion of Assyria, or were associated with it.

It would not be consistent with my main design, to discuss such questions respecting each prophetic book, as belong only to the specialities of an ample and scientific introduction to the Old Testament. I shall not therefore enter into any minute discussions, the particular object of which would be to vindicate the genuineness of *those prophetical books which bear the names of their authors.* Nor will the plan of my work permit me to canvass at length the question, whether particular parts of Isaiah, for example, or of Zechariah, or of Daniel, are superstitious; which two last works, however, belong to a later period than the one with which I am now concerned, unless indeed (with Knobel and some others) we attribute Zech. ix.—xi. to the Zechariah the son of Berechiah mentioned in Isa. viii. 2. Enough for my purpose, that the Old Testament books which bear the names of their authors, were extant, and were acknowledged by the Jewish nation as genuine works, before and at the period in which Malachi, the last of the Hebrew prophets, lived; that they were regarded as inspired and authoritative; and that Christ and his apostles have sanctioned them as such. On the general subject of the genuineness of the Hebrew Scriptures, I shall produce, in the sequel, a striking passage from Eichhorn. Their authority or sanction does not depend on the fact, whether this prophet or that one wrote a particular book, or parts of it, but on the fact that *a prophet* wrote them. Of course, this is my main point. And since I am not now writing a critico-exegetical introduction to the Hebrew Scriptures, I may dispense in general with all questions which belong merely to minute and special criticism. My object leads me to bring to view the Jewish sacred books as regarded in a general way; and I may be permitted to treat them, when they are not anonymous, as proceeding from the persons whose names they bear.

When I mention then, as belonging to the period in question, the works of Joel, Hosea, Isaiah, Amos, Micah, and Nahum, (and perhaps Jonah,) I need say nothing more to characterize this golden age of the prophets in the capacity of writers. Isaiah is surely without a parallel; and as for Joel and Nahum, all effort to commend them to readers of taste would be useless. In the other prophets just named, there are passages of great splendour; and in all of them there is such a lofty tone of piety, and zeal for God and his honour, with such inflexible morality, as almost transports the reader into New Testament times. Indeed one may well compare the spiritual and elevated views of these writers, with the leading principles of the gospel dispensation as developed by our Saviour in his conversation with the woman of Samaria; John iv. 19, seq. Let us listen for a moment to Isaiah:

"What is the multitude of your sacrifices to me, saith Jehovah?
I am satiated with the offerings of rams and of fatted beasts;
The blood of bullocks and of lambs and of he-goats I do not desire.
When ye come to exhibit yourselves before me,
Who hath required this at your hands—the treading of my courts?
Bring no more worthless offerings;
Incense!—it is an abomination to me.
As to your new moons and sabbaths and summoning of assemblies,
I cannot endure iniquity and solemn meeting.
Your monthly festivals and appointed feasts my soul hateth;
They are a burden to me, I cannot bear with them.
And when ye spread out your hands, I will hide mine eyes from you,
Yea, when ye multiply prayer, I will not hear.
Your hands are full of blood.
Wash ye; make ye clean;
Put away your evil deeds from before mine eyes;
Cease to do evil; learn to do well;
Seek after justice; console the afflicted;
Vindicate the orphan; plead the cause of the widow."

Who cannot easily imagine himself to be listening to the Great Teacher, the Light of the world, when he hears such a passage as this? And many such, i. e. of the like tenor with this, are there in the works of the prophets now before us. In respect to the so-called Pseudo-Isaiah and Jonah, placed by recent critics among the works of the second or *Chaldee* period of prophecy, I shall notice them in my remarks on that period.

The last king of Assyria, of whom any mention is made in the sacred records, was Esar-haddon, who sent colonists from his dominions into the land of the ten tribes, about 678 B. C.; Ez. iv. 2. He was the last of the Assyrian kings, who appears to have possessed any great degree of energy and activity. At all events, we hear no more of incursions into Judea, after his reign; and it was but some fifty years afterwards, that Nabopolassar, a tributary king of the Babylonian province, threw off the yoke of Assyria, and made Babylon an independent kingdom. His son Nebuchadnezzar enlarged its borders, and became master of the greater part of Asia west of the Euphrates. To Babylon then are we to look, from the latter part of the reign of Josiah onward, for most of the annoyances which the Hebrew commonwealth experienced during its last period before the exile; and most of the prophets who lived from the time of Josiah onward to the end of the captivity, in their writings still extant, refer principally to Babylon, or the land of the Chaldees, (which is the same,) or to some of its tributaries or allies, as the enemies whom the Hebrews have most reason to dread. Hence, in classifying the prophets with reference to a predominating element in their discourses, we may name this latter period, in which the prophetic order were somewhat conspicuous, the CHALDEAN PERIOD.

It is remarkable, that from the year 710 B. C. down to 640 B. C., i. e. for seventy years, scarcely a vestige of any Hebrew prophet is to be found in the Jewish history. No wonder at this. The fifty-seven years of unrelenting persecution of the true worshippers of God, and the rank and zealous idolatry even of the grossest kind which made up the reigns of Manasseh and of Amon, must needs have cast off or driven away all the true prophets of God. At first there seem to have been some who warned Manasseh, (2

Chron. xxxiii. 10,) but he would not hearken to them. And so entirely does the Holy Land appear to have been destitute of prophets, in consequence of persecution and idolatry, that they did not make their appearance again, so far as we know, until some time during the reign of Josiah; 2 Chron. xxxiv. 8, 22. Under him we find Zephaniah predicting the destruction of Assyria and its capital, Nineveh, ii. 13—15, which took place about that time. Moreover Huldah, a prophetess, is consulted by Josiah and Hilkiah, on the occasion of finding a copy of the Law in the temple; 2 Chron. xxxiv. 22. Jeremiah began his prophetic duties in the thirteenth year of Josiah, i. e. 629 B. C. If Zech. xii.—xiv. belongs to an older prophet than the Zechariah who lived after the return from exile, it should probably be assigned to the period about 607—604 B. C. (See Knobel, Proph. II. p. 280, seq.) At the same period the prophecy of Habakkuk may most probably be placed. Ezekiel, who was carried into exile about 600 B. C., began his prophetic work about 595 B. C., and continued it until 573. The greater part of his prophecies relate to his countrymen who still remained in Palestine, after the deportation to Mesopotamia in the reign of Jehoiachin. But some of them relate to his fellow countrymen in exile with himself. The brief work of Obadiah seems, by the historical circumstances to which it refers, plainly to belong to the period of the exile. His prophecy is directed against the Edomites; and one may compare with it Jer. xlix. 7—22; Ezek. xxv. 12—14; xxxv. 1—15. Those who maintain the late composition of Isa. xl.—lxvi., also compare Isa. lxiii. 1—6 with the prophecy of Obadiah; and it seems to tally well with this and with the other prophecies just named.

The turn which recent criticism has taken, among a large class of commentators and writers on subjects of sacred literature in Germany, with respect to various and extensive portions of the book of Isaiah, must be well known to all who are acquainted with the recent history of sacred literature. As I have already said, it comports not with my present object minutely to discuss the questions in regard to this matter, which have recently sprung up. But I must at least touch upon this topic, although as summarily as may be.

No allegations are made at present with more confidence by many, than that Isa. xl.—lxvi. belongs to a writer near the close of the exile, to whom Cyrus was known by name, and whose intentions he well understood. To the same period, but (as most of these critics suppose) to a different author, is to be assigned Isa. xiii., xiv. In their opinion, to the author of the latter, perhaps, belongs Isa. xxi. 1—10 ; at any rate, it must be assigned, as they aver, to the close of the exile. Isa. xxiv.—xxvii. belongs, as some of the latest critics say, (e. g. Knobel,) to a prophet who lived near the beginning of the exile. Isa. xxxiv., xxxv. is to be assigned to the middle of the exile. Thus we have, if we may believe these critics, no less than five or six works of so many different prophets, in our present book of Isaiah.

A few hints I may be permitted to suggest, in relation to this critical theory. It seems to me to be pressed with some serious difficulties, from which no adequate relief has yet been found.

(1.) All *ancient Jewish and Christian tradition* is against it. So far back as Sirachides, we have express testimony of the Jewish views. He calls Isaiah "the *great prophet*, and faithful (or, worthy of credit, πιστός) in his vision." He speaks of him as *comforting* Zion, and showing "the things that would happen ἕως τοῦ αἰῶνος, for ever, and hidden things before they take place;" xlviii. 22—25. Does not this specially refer to the latter part of Isaiah? So Philo, Josephus, and the New Testament in very many places from the so-called Pseudo-Isaiah, (indeed altogether most frequently is this part of the book referred to in the New Testament,) which are ascribed to Isaiah ; and so the Christian Fathers and the Talmud. The discovery of diverse authors is one that is acknowledged to have been made but a few years since.

(2.) The *discrepancy of diction*, which is even confidently alleged to be a satisfactory proof of different authorship in the various parts of the book, in my apprehension has no solid basis adequate to support this allegation. The several parts of the book which are conceded to Isaiah, between chap. xiii. and xxxix., are in general more discrepant from the first twelve chapters, (acknowledged to be genuine,) than some of those genuine chapters are from the alleged interpolated portions of the book. In other words; Isaiah differs more from himself than he does from others. These portions, moreover, which are said to be interpolated, are so widely distant from the idiom of Jeremiah, Ezekiel, and other Hebrew prophets during and after the exile; they have so little of the later so-called degenerate Hebrew idiom in them; that to my mind they present a very serious difficulty in the way of believing that they could have been written near the close of the exile, or even at the middle, or the beginning of it. So very different from the work before us are the productions of this period, in regard to diction and style, that even the Liberalists feel compelled to confess, that the Pseudo-Isaiah was a writer of rare talents at imitation of the ancients, and they even allege, that he has *copied* from the true Isaiah. I cannot here exemplify and confirm the position, that the resemblance between the confessedly genuine parts of Isaiah and the suspected parts of his book, are so many and so striking, that even De Wette confesses that "they must arise from *imitation* or *sonstwie*, i. e. in some other way!" Einl. p. 288. To the *some other way* in which these resemblances arose, we may assent; but not to the assertion that the writer in question was an *imitator*. I can only refer the reader, for an ample statement, to Kleinert's *Aechtheit des Esaias*, p. 220—279, and to Hävernick's *Spezielle Einleit. Esai.* p. 192, seq. Every discriminating reader well versed in the Hebrew must feel, as I think, that there is indeed, in some respects, a notable difference between the last twenty-seven chapters of Isaiah and the first part of his work. It seems to me that candour will not—need not deny this. But, as I have intimated above, this difference is not so great, in my apprehension, as the difference between the first twelve chapters of Isaiah and other acknowledged parts of his work between chap. xiii. and xxxix. Let any one compare the circle of imagery, the sources of metaphor and comparison, the historical examples of ancient times appealed to in both parts of the book, the *absence* of particular visions and symbolical actions in both, the insertion of triumphant lyrical songs, and the like, and he cannot refuse to recognise most striking similarities; see Hävernick ut sup. p. 191. 'They that be for the *antiquity* of the alleged adscititious portions of the book, are more than they that be against it.' I am persuaded, that the Neologists have evidently the worst of the argument on this ground; and this is a ground which they are prone to consider as one of their choice positions for defence.

(3.) What example is there, among all the prophets, of a book so patched up by putting together six different authors, five of them without any names? *Who* did this? *Where, when*, was it done? If parts of the book are so late as is alleged, why have we no hint about its compilation, no certain internal evidence of it? How can we account for it that all the minor prophets, even Obadiah with his one chapter, should be kept *separate* and distinct, and this even down to the end of the prophetic period, and yet Isaiah be made up by undistinguished fragments and amalgamations? These surely are serious difficulties; and they have not yet been satisfactorily met.

(4.) In numerous places of chap. xli.—xlviii., the prophet appeals to his own predictions concerning Babylon's fall, as uttered *long before* the time of fulfilment. Even Rosenmueller confesses, (iii. p. 5, 6,) that 'the writer, who lived near the close of the Babylonish exile, has assumed the personage of some ancient prophet.' This same prophet adverts to *localities* and *nations*, to which it would be very strange for a Jew in exile to advert to. E. g. xli. 9, where he speaks of Israel as being "taken from the ends of the earth," i. e. Ur of the Chaldees; which would do well in case he was in *Palestine*, but be quite incongruous if he were in Chaldæa. As to *nations;* Egypt, the land of Sinim, (xlix. 12,) i. e. probably the Pelusiotes, the appeal to offerings of swine, (lxv. 4,) which were made in *Egypt*, but not in Babylon, the frequent appeals and addresses to Jerusalem and the towns of Palestine, all seem to betoken the presence of the writer in the Holy Land, and his familiarity with objects there and in the neighbourhood. Then the *historical relations* are to be added to these. Egypt and Æthiopia are joined, and also the Sabæans; xlv. 14. In xli. 11, 12, the active and *assailing* enemies of those addressed are mentioned; but who were they, during the exile? In lii. 4, the writer adverts to the past captivities of the Jews, and mentions only those of Egypt and Assyria. How could he omit that of Babylon, if it had taken place? In Isa. lxvi. 19, the Jewish exiles are represented as being gathered only from countries connected with Egyptian or Assyrian sway. These things have not been satisfactorily explained by the recent liberal critics. I am not aware how they can be.

(5.) In chap. xl.—xlvii., are very many passages which are addressed to a people under the influence of idols, and who practise heathen rites ; and they are reproved for not presenting the offerings due to God. How could this be, while the Jews were in exile ? They served no idols then and there ; and how could they be reproved for not presenting offerings there, which could lawfully be presented no where but at the temple in Jerusalem ? Besides, the people addressed are represented as seeking *foreign alliances.* Could the Jews in exile do this ? Chap. lxvi. 3, 4, describes the Jews as presenting hypocritical oblations and sacrifices. *How, where, when,*—in the land of Chaldæa ? Even Ewald feels obliged to concede (in Es. II. p. 409, seq.) that he finds no marks of the author's being in Babylonia, but the contrary.

(6.) It seems to be evident, that the latter part of Isaiah is quoted or imitated by prophets who lived before the exile ; comp. Nah. i. 15 and Isa. lii. 1, 7. See also Nah. iii. 7 and Isa. li. 19 ; Nah. iii. 4, 5 and Isa. xlvii. 5, 9. So Habakkuk in ii. 18, 19, comp. with Isa. xliv. 9—20. In Zephaniah are several passages of the same tenor. Jeremiah has strowed passages through his whole book, which lean upon the latter part of Isaiah ; particularly in chap. l., li., which, one might almost say, are made up of extracts from this prophet ; see Hävern. Einl. p. 180. Finally, 2 Chron. xxxii. 32, not merely refers for authority, as to the history of Hezekiah, to the *Vision of Isaiah,* (chap. xxxvi.—xxxix.,) but also to an old book, the *Book of the Kings of Judah and Israel,* which had drawn from the same source ; see Häv. II. 1. p. 198, seq. At all events, when the author of Chronicles wrote, the book of Isaiah was a definite and well-known book.

It were easy to add to these evidences of earlier composition—and of composition in the Holy Land. But my limits forbid. I would merely repeat, in the way of comment, what I said at the outset, viz. that the recent opinions respecting adscititious parts of Isaiah, are embarrassed by very serious difficulties, which have not yet been satisfactorily met.

SECT. IV.   LITERATURE OF THE HEBREWS.   99

As to all the objections made to the early composition of the alleged Pseudo-Isaiah, on the ground that *prediction*, so long beforehand as the time of Isaiah the son of Amoz, is an *impossibility*, I have only to say, that this is assumption and not argument—it is simply *petitio principii*. Even if, with most of the neological critics, we put off the composition of that portion of the book to a period little before the exile, it is still *prediction;* for how could any one foresee what Cyrus would do, either as to the destruction of Babylon, or the liberation of the Jews? But when the composition of these parts of Isaiah is brought down very near to the time of the events described, our sharp-sighted critics say, that a shrewd political observer might easily *conjecture* what would take place; as Burke foretold what would follow in the train of the French Revolution. It happened, as they suggest, that he had made a *lucky guess*. But what if it had turned out, that the Babylonians had been victors, in the contest with Cyrus? 'Why then (as they intimate) the Pseudo-Isaiah would have stood in no repute, and his work would never have come down to us.'

In respect to this, and all that is like it, I have only to say, that it is not critical argument, but a mere result of the *a priori* assumption, that prediction is an impossibility.

An impartial view of the subject before us, however, obliges us to say, that the recent critics who contend for a *Pseudo-Isaiah*, are not wholly destitute of reasons, some of which, to say the least, are quite specious. They allege, (1.) That the later writer does not so much describe an exile which is *to be*, as one which *is*. In this state, he thinks, and feels, and speaks. He describes desolations in Judea and in Edom, which had already taken place; e. g. in chap. lxiii., lxiv., and elsewhere. He dwells on these things; repeats them; goes into minute particulars which savour of the *historical* rather than of the prophetical. All this is contrary to the genius of any prophecy, which for a long time precedes the events described.

(2.) The mention by name of *Cyrus* (xliv. 28 ; xlv. 1) is without parallel. The fact of such a mention shows, that Cyrus was already on the throne.

(3.) Predictions so long beforehand as the time of Isaiah, when Babylon was a mere provincial and tributary kingdom belonging to the Assyrian domain, could be of no interest to the then living generation. Neither Isaiah nor they knew or cared any thing about Babylon. It looks like mere *soothsaying* or *fortune-telling*, to utter such predictions at such a period. And above all, how could Isaiah himself say so much about *deliverance* from exile, and dwell so long and minutely upon it, when he has said nothing of the Jews being carried away into captivity, nor uttered any threats of this nature?

(4.) The whole strain is *hortatory*, and addressed (in this shape) to those then living in exile. The writer addresses them as having present duties to do; prays for them as already in distress and danger; and in fact adjusts his whole discourse as if it were an epistle to the exiles.

(5.) The writer, in chap. xl.—xlvii., appeals to *ancient* prophecy respecting the Babylonish exile. In Isaiah's time, who was there that had already written such predictions?

(6.) Why does not Jeremiah, when he predicts the return from exile, (xxix., xxx., al.,) appeal to the predictions of Isaiah, in the way of confirmation, in case they already existed?

These are the main arguments on which they rely, with the exception of those drawn from the impossibility of miracles, and from the style and manner of the alleged adscititious parts. A few remarks only can be made here respecting them.

As to No. 2, which respects the mention of Cyrus by name, the passage in 1 Kings xiii. 2 is a parallel case. *Agag*, in Num. xxiv. 7, seems to be another. Besides, the name *Cyrus* is, in all probability, like that of *Pharaoh*, a mere *nomen dignitatis*, applicable to more than one king. The proper name of Cyrus appears to have been *Agradates*. In case the matter is so understood, nothing more particular than a reference to *a Persian king* is contained in the prediction. In respect to No. 3, it cannot be said with truth, that Isaiah and his contemporaries knew nothing of Babylon, and felt no interest to know any thing about it, after one reads Isa. xxxix., which contains an explicit prediction, that the descendants of Hezekiah should be carried to Babylon and be eunuchs in the palace there. In Micah iv. 9, 10, is a prediction of the same tenor. Of course this involves the destiny of the nation, (Micah expressly applies it to the nation,) as well as of its king. Is not this " saying something" about being carried into exile? And does not the deliverance which follows come in its proper place?

The *hortatory* strain, objected to the early composition in No. 4, would be convincing, if we could show that the spirit of prophecy could not anticipate future circumstances. Most of the exhortations are of such a nature as to constitute *preaching* applicable to any or all periods, in those ancient times. The appeal to ancient prophecy (No. 5) does not necessarily involve any thing more ancient than what Isaiah himself had uttered, or at any rate Micah. In Micah iv. 9, 10, the Babylonish captivity is very plainly and expressly predicted; and Micah was a contemporary of Isaiah. In respect to No. 6, Jeremiah no more appeals to Micah than he does to Isaiah. The *argumentum ex silentio* has little force indeed, in a case of this nature.

Finally, I deem it proper to add, that the whole dispute in respect to the Pseudo-Isaiah, is after all a matter of less importance, in a *theological* point of view, than many have deemed it to be. If real *prophets* are allowed to have written the alleged adscititious parts of the book, then the *authority* of the book is not impinged, at any rate is not impugned. But most of the recent critics refuse to admit the existence of such men, i. e. to admit them as being properly *inspired* men. But such as do admit of the real prophetic origin of the adscititious part (so called) may ask, If other prophetic works are of Divine authority, why are not these also? It is not pretended, even by the better class of neological critics, that these parts of Isaiah were written *post eventum*. If written before, they are *predictions*. Merely as a *theologian*, then, I should have little to object to the *compound* nature of the book before us. It is in fact of little or no theological or doctrinal importance which way this question is decided. But as a critic, I have serious doubts whether recent criticism has yet made its way clear. There are obstacles in its path, which it seems rather to leap over than to remove.

In the mean time, it must be confessed that there are some obstacles in the way of other and the older critics. The graphic description of desolations in Edom and Judea, which is contained in chap. lxiii., lxiv., seems to plead strongly in favour of the idea, that those desolations had actually taken place. Above all, the difficulty of supposing a deep and present interest, which the Isaiah of Hezekiah's reign had, or could well have, in the *return* from the Babylonish exile, when he has not any where dwelt at length upon the occurrence of being *carried into exile;* and the unparalleled length and particularity of the descriptions or predictions respecting this return; do constitute difficulties, it must be confessed, in the way of the older exegesis, which are entitled to serious consideration. Such, it must be conceded also, is not the manner of most prophets, in regard to mere *civil* or *political* events. Things of *present* interest and of *impending* danger, are for the most part before them, and are the subjects of prophecy. And if Isa. xl.—lxvi. can be viewed as coming from the pen of a prophet in exile, not long before the return from it, its graphic descriptions and its many developments of deep feeling seem to be more naturally and easily accounted for. Is it not possible that another prophet, who also bore the name of *Isaiah*, lived and wrote at this period? I must confess that I have sometimes suspected this to be the case. Most knots which we must now cut, would easily be untied by such a solution. The principal objection to it is, that history has not said any thing of such a man; and it is difficult even to suppose that the name of such a writer, at so late a period, could be covered with entire darkness. Did we know that such a person lived and wrote, we might call him *Deutero-Isaiah*, but surely not (as recent critics do) *Pseudo-Isaiah*. The mistake of redactors in later ages, (in case there were two prophets who both bore the name of *Isaiah*,) in arranging and combining their works together, and placing them under one category, might be very easily accounted for, in such a case. I should feel some inclination to admit this theory, as the most easy and ready solution of the difficulties, if it could only be rendered probable, that such a person as the *Deutero-Isaiah* could have lived, and written such a piece of composition as Isa. xl.—lxvi., and yet not have been conspicuous in Jewish history. The lack of any notice of such a writer, is certainly one of the unaccountable things.

One general remark, which in my own view is of great

importance in regard to the whole matter before us, I must make before I quit the subject. It is only when chaps. xl.—lxvi. are viewed in the light of a great *Messianic* development—a series of predictions respecting the person, the work, and the kingdom of Christ—that the earnestness, the protracted length, the fulness, the deep feeling, the holy enthusiasm, the glowing metaphors and similes, and the rich and varied exhibitions of peace and prosperity, can well be accounted for. The writer, in taking such a stand-point, uses the exile and the return from it as the basis of his comparisons and analogies. It was a rich and deeply interesting source, from which he might draw them. Any other solution of the whole phenomena is, to my mind at least, meagre and unsatisfactory. On no other ground can I account for it, that Isaiah so long beforehand should have dwelt on an exile and a return from it, which were more than a century distant from him and his contemporaries.

In regard to the book of JONAH, it purports to be the work of Jonah the son of Amittai (Jonah i. 1); and in 2 Kings xiv. 25, we have an account of Jonah the prophet, of Gath-Hepher, a town in the district of Zebulun (comp. Josh. xix. 13). Of this latter personage it appears, that he lived and prophesied during the reign of Jeroboam II., king of Israel (825—784, B. C.); of course, at the time when the Assyrian power was just beginning to show its strength in western Asia, and might be dreaded by the Israelites. To him is attributed, by Hitzig and others, the prophecy against Moab in Isa. xv., xvi. And inasmuch as Isaiah himself appears to assign this portion of his book to some other and older prophet than himself, (Isa. xvi. 14,) no very urgent objections against this view of the subject seem to press upon us; although I do not deem it necessary.

As to the prophecy contained in the book entitled JONAH, (but little indeed of the book is *prediction*,) there has been an endless diversity of opinion among modern and recent commentators in regard to the matter and manner of this work. It is clear from Tobit xiv. 8; 3 Macc. vi. 8, and from Josephus' Antiq. IX. 10. 2, that the ancient Jews regarded the whole book as a *narrative of facts*. It seems, moreover, very much as if the Saviour had given his sanction to it as such; Matt. xii. 40, seq.; xvi. 4; Luke xi. 30.

Most of the Christian Fathers have done the same; and the great body of the older modern commentators have inclined to follow in the same path. But not so with all. In recent times, the Liberals, almost to a man, reject the simple historical exposition of the book at large; and not a few, even of those who are more strict in sentiment, have felt compelled to regard it as an *allegory* or *parable*.

The difficulties alleged to be connected with the book are very numerous. First, the mission itself to a very distant barbarian city, the mistress of the eastern world, buried in luxury and idolatry, and looking contemptuously on all foreigners—a mission totally destitute of any thing analogous among all the Hebrew prophets—is thought to be a serious obstacle to the historical exposition. Then comes a host of other difficulties. The sudden and unexpected penitence of the Ninevites, it is said, is incredible. More credible would the story have been, if it had represented them as taking Jonah for a raving maniac. The book of Kings, (2 Kings xiv. 25, seq.,) which gives us some notices of Jonah, takes no notice of such an event. Jonah, a *prophet* too, is represented as expecting to fly from the presence of the Lord, by going in a ship to Tarshish! When the lot falls upon Jonah, as the cause of the tempest which threatened the safety of all embarked, with the same indifference which before had made him sleep quietly in the hold of the ship amidst the agitations of the storm, he proposes to be cast overboard. He is swallowed by a whale; and after being three days in his belly, he is vomited up upon the dry land. The second admonition to go to Nineveh is obeyed. The consequences of this mission have already been adverted to. Then comes the repining indignation of the prophet, because Nineveh was not actually destroyed. A gourd comes up in a single night, and grows to such a size as to shelter Jonah from the burning heat, to which he was exposed in his watch-station. But the next day a worm eats it at the root, and it immediately withers. Jonah then wishes to die, rather than to see his prophecy unfulfilled. These circumstances, it is averred with the greatest confidence, are all of them either very improbable or actually impossible.

So they must have been regarded, it would seem, by many interpreters of the book; for all manner of devices have been resorted to, in order to make out some meaning for it that would comport with facts which the interpreter deemed probable or possible.

The principal difficulty is with the matter of being swallowed up by the fish or whale. A whale, it is said, has not a gullet large enough to receive a man. Then, it is asked, how could Jonah live in his interior? How could such a monster approach the land near enough to throw him upon it? These and the like questions have been discussed, until it would seem that not much more remains to be said, or even invented.

Of the Rabbinical conceits about Jonah, I need say no more than to mention, that one of them is, that the whale swam round the whole continent of Africa in the three days during which Jonah was within him; that he came back by the way of the Red Sea; and that he went through the subterranean passage from that sea to the Mediterranean, and thus brought Jonah safe to his home again. According to some of the Rabbies, Jonah had a not uncomfortable berth for such a long and rapid voyage; and, looking through the whale's eyes, he saw a great many wonders of the deep. Besides this, he performed many devotional exercises. Even Josephus (Antiq. IX. 10. 2) makes the whale to throw up the prophet upon the shores of the *Euxine*. Others have invented a more facile solution of the whole difficulty. The whale (דג, lit. *fish*) is turned into *a boat with a whale painted on its stern or bow;* or it may be a boat of the whalers, as we speak of a *whale boat.* Even Godfrey Less has broached such an exegesis; Verm. Schrift. p. 161. So Jonah, after three days' tossing, is represented as being driven to the land, and thrown upon it by the waves. But the difficulty here is, that the account of Jonah (i. 17) states, that the Lord had prepared דג גדול, *a great fish*, to swallow up the prophet; where the epithet *great* has of course a very appropriate meaning. But how is it with a *great boat?* Then again, the *vomiting* (ויקא) upon the land—appropriate enough to the great fish, but how the *boat vomited* out Jonah, looks rather problematical. Others, therefore, not liking these explanations of the narration, say, that Jonah, when thrown overboard, found a dead fish, on which he got a station, and was thrown, at last, upon the land unharmed. But still, the *swallowing up* of Jonah, and the *vomiting of him out*, are lost sight of even in this exegesis. To remedy this, ingenuity has contrived to make Jonah cut a hole in the fish, so that he could lodge in his interior; and from this he came out, when cast upon the land. But even here, Jonah seems rather to manage the fish, than to be managed by him. The view attributed to the famous Von der Hardt, who wrote several volumes upon Jonah, viz. that Jonah put up a tavern which had the *sign of a whale*, is closely allied to this.

Futile, not to say ridiculous, attempts are all these and the like, to do away the force of a narration, which plainly savours of the *miraculous*. Not but that the whole matter, in respect to the *fish*, might be shown to be a natural possibility. The *Canis Carcharias*, common in the Mediterranean, can surely swallow a man, for it has done so; and so can some other fishes. That a man should preserve life for a while in the stomach of a fish, under certain circumstances, is no impossibility. Living reptiles often spend years in the human stomach; some of them, moreover, are such as need air for respiration, (as indeed what living and breathing creature does not?) As to throwing up Jonah upon the land, there are places enough of deep water up to the very edge of the sea-shore, where this might be done by a large fish. The objection that the stomach of the fish must have *dissolved* and *digested* Jonah, is of no weight; for every one acquainted with physiology knows, that *living* flesh does not digest in the least in the stomach. The gastric juice has no power over it. And last, but not least—the God who meant to punish, but not to destroy, Jonah, could arrange all these circumstances, and also preserve his life, in such a way as is stated in the narration. The same God could cause the fish to throw him out of his stomach; the Bible affirms that he did; Jon. ii. 10.

So would I say, moreover, of the gourd, and its withering, although the latter circumstance is pressed by no special difficulty. Its growth, however, must be supernatural. The panic, the fast, and the penitence of the Ninevites, are doubtless all circumstances extraordinary and without a parallel in sacred history. Yet surely they cannot be deemed *impossibilities*. The mission of Jonah to a distant *heathen* country, in his day scarcely known among the Jews, and not yet having made any incursion upon Palestine, is undoubtedly one of the most serious difficulties that the book presents. The mission of a man who had such a temper as Jonah, to execute a commission so grave, stands next to this. And then—what was the object? What was achieved? What had the *Jews* to do, at that time, with the Ninevites? It is easy to ask many questions of this kind; but it is not so easy to answer them satisfactorily. The book itself presents us with no key to unlock these mysteries.

I cannot much wonder, therefore, that *allegory* or *parable* has been resorted to by so many interpreters, (and of different sentiments too in theology,) in order to explain the book. Jonah, they say, designed to teach the Hebrew nation to feel more liberally towards the heathen; to show them that even the latter were more susceptible of moral impression than hardened Jews; and to impress them with the idea that God was the common Father of all men—of the Gentiles as well as of the Jews. He wrote this allegory, as they aver, in order to accomplish this end; just as the Saviour uttered the parable of the good Samaritan, and of the rich man and Lazarus, or of the sower, in order to illustrate and confirm certain moral truths. In itself this exhibits nothing impossible, or even improbable. Yet the want of all intimations of this nature in the book itself, is somewhat of an objection against this mode of exegesis; although it has been adopted, for substance, by such men as J. D. Michaelis, Herder, Eichhorn, Staüdlin, Meyer, Mueller, Niemeyer, and others. In the Gospels, and generally in the prophets, the *context* gives us a key to the allegory or the parable. I am constrained also to ask: Can what the Saviour says about Jonah and the Ninevites, be reconciled with the idea that the book is only an *allegory*? The first spontaneous prompting of the mind seems to be an answer in the negative. Yet it is asked, Do we not every day refer to the Good Samaritan, and to the Prodigal Son, in the same way as if they were real historical personages? And in fact one cannot deny this; but still there is this difference between the two cases, viz. that in the Gospels the nature of the allegory is palpable. However, at all events, this method of interpretation is much preferable to one lately come in vogue, through Goldhorn, Gesenius, De Wette, and Knobel, viz. that the book has only a few facts at the basis, simple and credible; while all the rest is a mythic romance—a narrative made out of floating popular stories. Jonah, they say, was a prophet. He uttered oracular threats against Nineveh. He made a voyage to sea; was shipwrecked; narrowly escaped the sharks; returned to his prophetic duty; but was indignant that his first predictions had not been fulfilled, and therefore wished for death, through fear of disgrace. So much they allow to be fact. Then as to the *mythic part*, it comes, as they think, from the story among the Greeks, that Hercules, at Sigeum, rescued Hesione, the daughter of Laomedon king of Troy, from the jaws of the sea-monster to which she was devoted. In order to do this, he sprang himself into the monster's jaws, was swallowed down, and there he fought three days and nights in his belly, destroyed him, and came out alive with only the loss of his hair, which had been burned up by the heat within; Diod. Sic. VI. 42. Ovid Met. XI. 211, seq. Tzetzes ad Lycoph. Cassand. 33. This myth, as some of the recent critics suppose, was combined with another, the scene of which is at the shore of Joppa. There Perseus rescued from a sea-monster Andromeda, the daughter of king Cepheus; and Pliny (Hist. Nat. V. 14) and Jerome (Comm. in Jon. i. 3) tell us, that the people of that place were accustomed to show to strangers the rock where Andromeda was chained, and the huge bones of the sea-monster [whales' bones no doubt]. Both of these fables are united, and forthwith out comes the *myth of Jonah*. So even Rosenmueller. To this I have only to say:

> "Humano capiti cervicem pictor equinam
> Jungere si velit, et varias inducere plumas
> Undique collatis membris; ut turpiter atrum
> Desinat in piscem mulier formosa superne;
> Spectatum admissi, risum teneatis amici?" *

What others may do, who have more power over their *risibles* than I, is not for me to say. But for myself, I cannot do otherwise than Horace supposes his friends would

---

* In English thus: "If a painter should undertake to join a horse's neck to a human head, and to cover with variegated feathers the limbs collected from all quarters; so that a woman beautiful in the upper part should disgustingly end in a black fish; if admitted to such a sight, my friends, could you keep yourselves from laughing?"—Ars Poet. 1—5.

SECT. IV.   LITERATURE OF THE HEBREWS.   109

do, when looking at the strange production of the painter whom he describes. Winer (not restrained most surely by any *orthodox* notions from admitting neological exegesis) says, in respect to this *mythical* explanation, "It always must appear very improbable, that a *Hebrew* writer would have found any occasion of working over the materials of a *Philistine* Myth;" Bib. Lex. art. Jonas. It is even worse than Horace's supposed picture; and so we may emphatically ask, *Risum teneatis, amici?* How it is possible thus to overlook the very genius of the Hebrews, and the nature and design of the sacred books, and to suppose that the book of Jonah was written with such views, and admitted to a place in the sacred canon—I leave for those to explain, who have done the deed of making up the monstrous compound. I wash my hands of such high treason against the fundamental laws of sacred criticism.

Doubtless the question will be put by the reader: And what then, after such remarks on the exegesis of others—what do you yourself regard as the object of the book of Jonah? What estimate do you put on the narration? So far as I am able, I am willing to give an answer; but it must be brief, after dwelling so long upon this book.

When the scribes and Pharisees said to Christ, "Master, we would see a sign from thee," he told them that "the men of Nineveh should rise in judgment with that generation, and condemn it, because they repented at the preaching of Jonah," and then immediately added that a "greater than Jonah" was before them; Matt. xii. 41; Luke xi. 32. Did he not mean now to compare one *historical* person and transaction with another? If the Ninevites had been known and regarded only as an imaginary people—the offspring of allegory or romance—there would be no difficulty in the case. The comparison might then be placed on the same ground, on which we now place the conduct and person of any one actually living, when we compare him and his demeanour with the prodigal son, or with the rich man and Lazarus. But the Ninevites are surely historical and veritable personages; as much so as the *queen of the South*, who is joined with them in Matt. xii. 42; and the force of the Saviour's appeal is greatly strengthened by the supposition that they are real personages. Not a word from Jesus to make us suspect that he regarded the matter of the Ninevites in any other light than that of a real historical fact. Again, when Jesus says to the Pharisees and Sadducees, who were seeking a *sign* from heaven and tempting him, that "no sign should be given them but the sign of the prophet Jonah," (Matt. xii. 39, 40; xvi. 4,) does he not compare the abode of Jonah for three days in the belly of the fish, with his own abode in the grave during the same period? Matt. xii. 40. In other words, Does he not compare one *historical* fact with another? It seems so. I know not how to throw off the impression which these passages make upon my mind. When Paul tells us, in Gal. iv. 24, that the narrative in Genesis concerning the son of Hagar and also of Sarah is *allegorized*, we know where we are and what to expect. But is there any thing in the passages just cited in respect to Jonah, which is adapted to make an impression that the story of Jonah and of the Ninevites is an *allegory?* If there be, it has escaped my notice.

The authority of Christ, then, seems to bind me to admit the *facts* as they are stated in the narrative of Jonah. They are indeed strange facts apparently; but not therefore untrue. They plainly are not *impossibilities;* although I acknowledge, very readily, that they are improbabilities, when compared with the common course of things. But are not all *miracles* of this character? Or, putting aside (as I would) *absolute* miracles in regard to the things recognised by Christ with respect to Jonah, do they not border upon the marvellous? Certainly they do; but is all that the Old and New Testament contains, which is of the like character, to be therefore rejected? Neologists say, Yes. But the believer in Divine revelation has no need to join in this answer. He may rank the occurrences in the book of Jonah with other occurrences related in the Scriptures, which are of a similar, i. e. of a miraculous character.

So much for *facts*. Now for the *object* of the book. This is indeed a problem of difficult solution. What can it be, unless it is to inculcate on the narrow-minded and bigoted Jews, (there were many such,) the great truth, that God regards the humble and penitent every where with favour; and that even the haughty, cruel, idolatrous, and domineering heathen, in case they repent and humble themselves, become

SECT. IV.   LITERATURE OF THE HEBREWS.   111

the subjects of his compassion and clemency, and are more acceptable than the haughty Jew, claiming descent from Abraham, but still the devoted slave of ritual observances and of his own evil passions?

So much lies on the face of the book. There is no strange *doctrine* in it, therefore, but a plain and simple truth is illustrated and impressively taught by it. No difficulty, indeed, of a *doctrinal* nature attends the work. Whatever difficulty there is, it lies in the tenor of the narration.

The only question over which darkness seems to a believer in miracles to hover, is, how Jonah alone, of all the Hebrew prophets, should be a missionary to the *heathen?* And, (as connected with this,) why was he sent, in the reign of Jeroboam II., to perform such a service? My *ignorance* as to those things which would make out a satisfactory answer to these questions, can prove nothing against the facts themselves. The time when he was sent, is indeed of no great importance.—These facts, moreover, are in themselves so far from being impossibilities, that, if admitted, they actually help to commend the *prophetic* dispensation to our feelings. We are heartily glad, to see in what manner the Divine Being recognises the relation of all parts of our race to himself, and how willing he is to pardon the penitent. The *unusual* occurrence of such an event as the mission of Jonah, and the apparent *strangeness* of the whole matter, are about the only things, in the end, that afford any serious doubts or difficulties to the believing mind. But I do not think these to be satisfactory or valid reasons for rejecting the book, or for turning it into an allegory or an ethnico-Judaic Myth.

But I must not pursue any further the examination of these particular works. I return to our *Chaldean* period of prophecy, which extends down to the end of the exile; I have only to add here, in regard to the prophetic order, that we have no history of any other than those prophets before mentioned. If there were men capable of writing such compositions as the so-called *Pseudo-Isaiah*, then why, as has already been suggested, is no mention made of them, no hint given respecting them? Could men capable of writing in that manner, have lived in entire obscurity, while Zephaniah, Obadiah, Haggai, and Malachi, not far from the same period, are all distinctly recognised and well known? At least this is something, which those, who feel so free on all occasions to doubt, may allow us the privilege of doubting, until the matter is better cleared up.

In addition to the anonymous prophets already adverted to, (who are brought into being by recent criticism,) another prophet, it seems, must be reckoned. Jer. l., li. is thought by some critics of name, to have been composed about the middle of the exile, and therefore not by Jeremiah the well-known prophet, who most probably must have been dead before that time. But the arguments drawn from the *diction*, in this case, surely make against this, if the whole of the resemblances to Jeremiah are set over against the alleged discrepancies; and there is no historical or critical necessity of supposing the chapters in question to be an interpolation.

If we turn now from this brief survey of the prophets who lived and acted during the *Chaldean* period, to a moment's consideration of their characteristics of style, we shall be struck with the greatly altered tone of their compositions. The brevity, simplicity, majesty, and beauty of the golden age have in a large measure passed by. The dialect, though still *Hebrew* in all its substantial elements, differs much from that of Isaiah, Joel, and Nahum. Allegory, figure, symbol, and parable, are frequent almost every where; and in fact they make up almost the whole of Ezekiel. Jeremiah has a great deal of historic matter, and is less inclined than his contemporary to allegory and symbol; but still the tenor of his style differs so exceedingly from that of the previous writers already named, that one can hardly persuade himself, that more time than is usually allowed did not elapse between the Assyrian and the Chaldean periods of prophetic composition. As to pathos, tenderness, deep-felt grief on account of the desolations of Judea, and still more on account of its wickedness, there is nothing in the writers of any age which exceeds some parts of Jeremiah.

Another circumstance should be noted. Instead of employing *poetry* as the vehicle of instruction, which for the most part the prophets of the golden age did, the compositions during the period in question were generally in *prose;* but not unfrequently in a kind of measured prose. Habakkuk is indeed an exception to this, as well as to the style in general of his times. How now shall we class Isa. xl.—lxvi. with the poetry of this Chaldean period, when the former consists of some of the most symmetrical poetry to be found in all the Hebrew Scriptures? If the so-called Pseudo-Isaiah be indeed of later composition, it stands out as a singular phenomenon amidst the other prophetic remains of that age. A writer of that day, on a theme so interesting as that which is presented in Isa. xl.—lxvi., who could with such wonderful success transport himself into the midst of the golden age and adopt its general manner, imagery, and diction, one would be prone to think must have had some memorial left of him.

Knobel alleges, that the prophets of the Chaldean period exhibit more attachment to the *ritual* Law, than those of the preceding era. What little foundation there is for this remark, seems to me to rest merely on the fact, that Jeremiah and Ezekiel were both *priests* as well as prophets. How natural then that they should look somewhat more to the violated ritual, as well as to the moral law!

We have no history of the Jews during their exile, excepting the hints in Jeremiah and Ezekiel respecting them. But these do not disclose to us any particulars respecting any true prophets of the Lord, if such there were among them. In Jer. xxix. we have an account of several *false* prophets among the exiles, by the name of Ahab, Zedekiah, and Shemaiah. The two former were roasted by the king of Babylon in the fire, (Jer. xxix. 22,) probably because they excited their countrymen to uneasiness in their exile, by false promises made to them. Jeremiah strongly denounces these false prophets; and in a similar manner does Ezekiel denounce men of the same class, who were flattering the exiles with deceitful promises; Ezek. xiii. 1—16. In like manner the false *shepherds* of Israel, (probably false prophets, see on p. 84, above,) are severely rebuked in Ezek. xxxiv. May we not, then, in the absence of direct testimony, assume as altogether probable the continued existence of *true* prophets among the Hebrews in their exile? False coin does not usually make its appearance where there is no true coin. The analogy of former and of subsequent periods would seem to plead in favour of the position, that among the exiles in Babylon were more or less of true prophetical teachers. The people were humbled by this exile. They grew better under their chastisements. Many of them sighed for a return to Palestine, and a renewal of their religious state and privileges. And when they did return from exile, in consequence of the proclamation by Cyrus who gave them liberty, they had such men for leaders as Zerubbabel and Jeshua the high priest; also the prophets Zechariah and Haggai; Ezra v. 1. These, and in the sequel Malachi, contributed important aid in re-establishing the Jewish commonwealth and worship. We can hardly suppose, therefore, that the Jews were at any time during their exile entirely destitute of true prophets, although we have no explicit account of such persons among them.

In 536 B. C. Cyrus attained to the sole regency of the Medo-Persian empire, and during the same year he published his edict, permitting and even exhorting the Jews to go up to Jerusalem and rebuild the temple. About 70,000 persons returned to Palestine, (Ez. ii. 66; Neh. vii. 66, seq.,) the same year, in consequence of this edict, having Zerubbabel, a descendant of David, as their civil head, and Jeshua as their high priest. Great trouble and hinderance were soon given to the Jews, by their heathen and envious neighbours; so that the rebuilding of the temple and city was often interrupted and long delayed. For the following seventy-five years we have no particular account of their religious state, and only a few notices of their civil condition. Who were their prophets, if prophets they had, excepting Haggai and Zechariah, (Ezra v. 1,) we know not. After Darius Hystaspes had come to the throne of Persia, (521 B. C.,) i. e. some fifteen or more years after the edict of Cyrus, those prophets contributed much in stirring up the Jews to go on with their temple-building. In the sixth year of Darius (516 B. C.) was this great undertaking finished. From that time down to the seventh year of the reign of Artaxerxes Longimanus, (457 B. C.—or as some maintain, 460,) we have no historic notices in the Jewish Scriptures of the state of the nation. In the year just named, Ezra, "a ready scribe in the Law of Moses, which the Lord God had given," came up to Jerusalem from Babylon, by leave of the Persian king, and brought with him between two and three thousand of the exiles; Ezra vii., viii. Here Ezra employed himself for several years in the accomplishment of a reformation both in worship and in morals; for both of these had greatly degenerated after the death of Zerubbabel and Jeshua. In about ten years, Nehemiah, the cup-bearer of Artaxerxes, by leave of this king, paid a visit to Palestine, and found the walls of Jerusalem in a ruinous state. These he repaired, and being made governor (Tirshatha) of the place, he resided there some twelve years, (Neh. vi. 14,) and not only did he fortify the city, but contributed greatly to bring every thing both civil and religious into a state of order and regularity. In this he was much assisted by Ezra, (Neh. viii.,) who took the lead in all religious matters. After twelve years he returned to Persia, according to agreement, but within a few days he obtained leave to go back to Palestine; Neh. xiii. 6. There he spent the rest of his life. But of his further actions, excepting for a short period after his return, we have no account, and the history of the Jews after the Babylonish exile ends with the doings of Nehemiah, i. e. about 434 B. C.

It is said of Nehemiah, (Neh. vi. 7,) that he had appointed *prophets* to preach in Jerusalem. Who these were is not said, in the passage to which reference has been made. But that Malachi was among them, scarcely admits of a doubt. That he was later than Haggai and Zechariah, and lived after the building of the temple was completed, is quite manifest to any one who will take pains to consult and compare the following passages; viz. as to completion of the temple, Mal. i. 10; iii. 1, 10; as to duties neglected by priests and Levites, comp. Mal. i. 6; ii. 1, 8, 9, with Neh. xiii. 10, 11, 28—30; as to the people's withholding gifts for the temple, comp. Mal. iii. 8—10 with Neh. xiii. 10, 12, 41; as to marriage with foreigners, comp. Mal. ii. 10—16 with Neh. xiii. 23, seq.; as to oppression of the poor, comp. Mal. iii. 5 with Neh. v. It would seem, then, that Malachi flourished about 440 B. C. When he died, we know not; but it is conceded on all hands, that he *closed* the series of that very extraordinary class of men, the Hebrew prophets.

We have, then, after the return from exile, only three prophets whose names and works are known to us. These are Zechariah, Haggai, and Malachi. But we find kindred spirits in Zerubbabel, Jeshua, Ezra, and Nehemiah; and especially does it seem to me that Ezra had much to do with the republication, arrangement, and completion of the Jewish Canon. But of this, more in the sequel.

I have as yet made no mention of *Daniel,* because he was not a prophet among the people of Palestine, although born in that land. He was very young at the time when Nebuchadnezzar came up against Jerusalem, (606 B. C.,) and was carried away to Babylon as a hostage, by the king; Dan. i. 1—6. Most probably he was the son of a nobleman, or perhaps of the royal family. We have an account of him in the third year of Cyrus, (534 B. C.,) so that he must have lived to the age of eighty or ninety years; Dan. x. 1. He might be placed among the prophets of the third or Chaldean period; for some of his visions were before the close of the Babylonish monarchy; yet some of them, also, were after the edict of liberation to the Jews was issued by Cyrus. Recent criticism has ascribed his book to some writer in the time of the Maccabees; and some have even denied that any such distinguished person as Daniel lived at the Babylonish court and held an office there. The writer of the book, it is averred, has merely feigned such a character, in order that he might compose a work suited to console the Jews who were suffering under the persecution of Antiochus Epiphanes, as the more ancient Jews had done under their Babylonish oppressors. Of course, the book of Daniel is ranked, by critics of this class, as last of all in the prophetic Scriptures.

It would be inconsistent with my present object, to turn aside here, in order to vindicate the genuineness of the book of Daniel. It has found an able advocate in the work of Hengstenberg on its authenticity, *Authentie des Daniel,* 1831; and also in Hävernick's recent *Einleit. ins Alt. Testament.* Nearly all the arguments employed to disprove its genuineness, have their basis more or less directly in the assumption, that miraculous events are impossibilities. Of course, all the extraordinary occurrences related in the book of Daniel, and all the graphic predictions of events, are, under the guidance of this assumption, stricken from the list of probabilities, and even of possibilities. All that is

SECT. IV.   LITERATURE OF THE HEBREWS.   117

said of Antiochus Epiphanes and other Syrian and Grecian kings, is *prophetia post eventum*, i. e. real narration of events past, rather than prediction of events to come. Beyond the objections which are founded entirely on these assumptions, there is little, as it seems to me, to convince an enlightened and well-balanced critical reader, that the book is supposititious. After examining the subject with much attention, I must confess myself to be far from believing that the objections to the authenticity of the book can maintain their stand, before the bar of enlightened and truly liberal criticism.

But be this as it may, it matters but little to the main object of my present work. All agree, that the book of Daniel was written a considerable time before the Christian era; and none can well deny that our Saviour has expressly recognised it, in Mark xiii. 14; Matt. xxiv. 15, as a book of prophecy. Josephus bestows upon it more commendations than upon any book of the Old Testament; Antiq. lib. x. I am aware how much has been said, on account of the Jewish classification of the book in question among the Hagiography or כתובים. This indicates, it is averred, that the book was composed very late, i. e. a very considerable time after the other prophetic books, and that the Jews did not deem it worthy of a place among their prophetic books in general. The questions to which these allegations give rise, are of importance; and some of them will be resumed and examined in the sequel. But nothing more can be said respecting them at present, inasmuch as we are bound now to pursue the interesting theme that has so long occupied our attention. We must not take our leave of the Hebrew prophets without subjoining *a few remarks in respect to the character of these extraordinary men.*

The mental endowments of many of them are sufficiently disclosed by the works which they have left behind them. There is indeed among them, as among the writers of the New Testament, a great diversity of style, and evidently also of taste and capacity. The Spirit of God, when he speaks by men, does not create new mental and psychological powers, but employs those already existing, and acts by enlightening and sanctifying and guiding them, still leaving each individual to develop his own peculiar characteristics of taste and mental endowments. But if there be any compositions which in their kind exceed many of the Psalms, much of Isaiah, Joel, Habakkuk, Nahum, and not a few portions of Jeremiah ; if there ever have been any of any age or nation down to the present hour, which exceed them, I have no knowledge of such compositions, and do not expect to attain to such a knowledge. The prophets need only to be read with intelligence, with candour, and with some good measure of oriental taste, (I believe this to be indispensable,) to take, in one's estimation, an exalted, I would say the most exalted, place among the literary productions of any or of all ages.

Other works of the Old Testament, indeed, besides those which we of the present day usually name *prophecy*, most probably came from the pen of the prophets. But of these, as they are *anonymous*, I do not speak at present. I shall come to the consideration of them, when we have dismissed our present theme. Let us now, at the close of this view of the Hebrew writers, teachers, and means of instruction, bring distinctly before us the question :

What was the moral and religious character of the Hebrew prophets? My answer must be brief; but I cannot forego it, as their character stands in so intimate a connexion with the rise of the Old Test. Scriptures. I must say, then, from both a general and particular survey of their history, that as a body they stand on a lofty preëminence above all their contemporaries, whether judges, kings, priests, Levites, or the common people of the Hebrews. I speak, of course, of *true* prophets, not of pretenders, soothsayers, and fortune-tellers. Not a few of these, from time to time, arose and had a baleful influence. But the Mosaic Law condemns them, and the true prophets of God denounce them in unmeasured terms.

From the first appearance of Hebrew prophets on the stage of action, down to Malachi the last of the series, prominent traits of character mark them as a distinct class of men. One sees in them, at all times and places, an animated zeal for the worship of the only living and true God, and a correspondent, inextinguishable, irreconcilable, stedfast hatred and contempt of all idols and false gods, of their worship, their worshippers, their rites and ceremonies. Conscious of the integrity and uprightness of their own designs, the prophets never shrink from urging their views upon all around them. Do threats of violence, persecution, or even martyrdom, ensue, they never shrink back from their undertaking. It matters not with them whom they are addressing, be they kings, princes, nobles, priests, Levites, or common people. They have but one and the same message for all, and that is the necessity of sincere and hearty obedience to the laws of God. Their courage and resolution never fail, or even seem to abate. Whether Nathan appears before David to accuse him of adultery and murder; or Elijah before Ahab to remonstrate against his oppression and idolatry; or Jeremiah before Jehoiakim or Zedekiah to admonish them and their corrupt courtiers; or Urijah before Jehoiakim, who persecuted even unto death; it matters not as to the fidelity, boldness, zeal, and constancy of the prophet. They do not appear even to have asked themselves whether they might not avoid persecution, or danger, or death, by withholding their message. Enough that they felt commissioned to say, *Thus saith Jehovah*. With them it seems to have made no practical difference, whether the message connected with their commission was to be addressed to the king on the throne, or to the beggar on the dunghill.

On the side of right, justice, humanity, uprightness, sincerity, true kindness, we are always sure to find them. The widow, the orphan, and the oppressed they are ever ready to succour. They spare none who violate the sacred principles of the moral virtues; surely not those who hanker after idols. On the side of law, order, decorum, peaceful demeanour, we never fail to meet with them. Their zeal for the only living and true God, his honour, his worship, his ordinances, never cools, and never permits them to temporize or hesitate, when any of these are in jeopardy. We always find them, moreover, to possess rational and spiritual views of religion. Rites and ceremonies they regard as only subordinate means to an ultimate and higher end. Bigotry and superstition form no ingredients of their character. The Mosaic rites with them are but *rites*, and nothing more. That these were only *the shadow of good things to come*, is the sum of all they ever said, or would say, respecting them.

With all this, they were unflinching, undeviating *patriots*, having the prosperity of their country most deeply at heart. When kings and counsellors erred, and formed dangerous alliances, they always remonstrated boldly. They did not even wait to be sent for and consulted, on such occasions. Urged on by the fear of God and the love of country, they spake with entire freedom on subjects pertaining to the weal of the commonwealth, to the king on his throne even when his menacing executioners were around him, or to the raging multitude who were ready to tear them in pieces.

With all this boldness, yea, indomitable courage, they do not appear to have been rash, or impetuous, or foolishly prodigal of life by exposing themselves unnecessarily to danger which they might anticipate. Elijah, after delivering his prophetic message, fled from the face of Ahab and Jezebel, who meant to take his life; 1 Kings xvii. 1—6. The good Obadiah concealed a hundred prophets in caves, and supplied them with nutriment, when Jezebel persecuted them with relentless fury; 1 Kings xviii. 4. Elisha bars his door against the approach of an assassin; 2 Kings vi. 31, 32. Jeremiah hid himself from the rage of his persecutors; Jer. xxxvi. 26. The like was done in other cases; and so was it afterwards done by the Saviour, and by his apostles. Yet when duty called, suffering and death were met with equanimity and unshrinking boldness by these faithful ministers of virtue and piety. In all this, they differed widely from the raving fanatics, who now and then, in every age, make their appearance, and rush on death with a foolhardiness which makes no distinction between the claims of conscience and duty and those of mere enthusiasm and momentary excitement.

To have maintained such a character, and this through, it may be, a long life, required an unshaken confidence in God. This the prophets did doubtless possess. They were conscious of something within, to which the world were strangers, and which, therefore, the world did not well appreciate. Look at the demeanour of Isaiah, after having severely reproved Ahaz for his league with the Assyrian king, and predicted the overrunning of the kingdom by the Assyrian forces; he seals up the prophecy, and suspending his reputation and not improbably his life on the issue, he waits quietly the fulfilment of what he had predicted; Isa. viii. 16—18. A most vivid picture is drawn in Jer. xv. 10— 21; xx. 7—18, of the agonies which this prophet endured

SECT. IV.   LITERATURE OF THE HEBREWS.   121

in the execution of his office, and also of the fidelity and
confidence which he still exhibited. It would be easy to
enlarge this portion of our sketch, by adding many instances
of the like nature ; but our present limits forbid.

It has been brought as a matter of accusation against the
prophets, that they were rigid and severe, not only against
the heathen in general, but against their own fellow countrymen whenever they betrayed any symptoms of idolatrous inclinations. This charge I do not feel much interested to repel. If the Mosaic law can stand before the tribunal of
criticism in respect to matters of this nature, sure I am that
the prophets may maintain their position. Their prophecies against the heathen are to be regarded in a two-fold
light, viz. in that of *religion* and in that of *politics*. The
heathen were all idolaters. They were of course naturally
enemies to the Jews, who despised their idol-gods. The
heathen aimed to destroy both the religion and the national
independence of the Hebrews. With the prophets, it was
a question whether religion and the people of God should
become extinct or not, when they contemplated the invasion
of Judea by the heathen. How could they speak on such
occasions, either as patriots or as worshippers of the true
God, without strong feeling and much excitement ? And
with respect to the vicious and idolatrous among their own
people, were not such far more guilty than the foreign heathen ? I know well, indeed, after all this, that the times in
which the prophets lived stand chargeable with no small portion of the alleged severity of this order of men. The all
but universal persuasion was, that strenuousness in urging
the claims of justice, and in humbling enemies, was by no
means a trait in the rulers of a nation which could be dis-
approved of or condemned. The oriental world retain that
characteristic down to the present hour. In Persia they
are even now wont to say, that such a Shah as Mohammed
Aga Khan was the kind of king that Persia needed. In
their view he was the model of a great prince. Yet this
same Mohammed Aga fairly outdid Nero in atrocities. I
do not say this in order to justify undue severity, at any
time or in any age. But it is ever to be remembered, that
Judaism is not *Christianity*. LAW and JUSTICE were inscribed on the standards of the Mosaic institutions. We

find there "the mount that burned with fire, and blackness, and darkness, and tempest;" we hear the trumpet proclaiming the law with a sound that shakes the earth, fills the people with awful terror, and makes even Moses himself to tremble; Heb. xii. 18—21. On the other hand, the first proclamation of Christianity is the greeting of the joyful angels: "Peace on earth; good will to men." How can it be, that the principal ministers of the Old Testament dispensation, i. e. the prophets, should not conform to the tenor of the dispensation itself?

And now, let the intelligent and honest reader compare the order of prophets among the Hebrews with any other class of men, not of that nation only, but among all the nations of the ancient world. With the priests and Levites among the Jews one may most naturally compare them. The offices of both orders were important to the purposes of the Mosaic dispensation. But after all, the priests were the ministers of *form* and *ritual*, the prophets of *substantial morality* and *piety*. How little do we hear of the priests in the Old Testament records, excepting now and then in the way of reproof by the prophets for their malversation. Now and then a high priest, a man of superior intellect, piety, and patriotism, meets our view. Yet these instances are few and far between. How could the Jewish people take the same interest in them as they did in their substantial and active religious instructers and advisers? Occasionally, yet quite seldom, a *priest* is also a *prophet;* and then, of course, we may expect from him a prominent part. But otherwise we find that all the Jewish kings go to the *prophets* for advice in their exigencies; and that no affairs of state are regarded by considerate men as promising good, which have not the concurrence and co-operation of the prophets. Certainly it was on these that all sober and pious people among the Hebrews relied, far more than they did upon kings and princes with their counsellors, or upon the priests and Levites.

I would, moreover, solicit a comparison of the prophets, with the men of an alleged similar office among the heathen. What are the μάντεις, the προφῆται, θεσπισταί, χρησμολόγοι, ὀνειρομάντεις, ὀνειροπόλοι, ὀνειροσκόποι, and the ἱεροσκόποι, of the Greeks, and those of corresponding names among the

Romans, in comparison with the Hebrew prophets? The heathen prophets (if we may so name them) made an *art* of soothsaying. They played all manner of tricks, and resorted to all manner of devices, in order to support the reputation of themselves and their pretended oracles. Cicero tells us, that two *diviners* could never look each other in the face without laughing; evidently because both were conscious of the frauds which they practised, and the success of their impositions. And where, in all antiquity, are they presented to us as the zealous defenders of real piety and good morals? Where are their *missions* to guide and instruct the people in matters of morality and real religion? Superstitious they were, indeed, to great excess. The persecution and death of all who were opposed to their views, not unfrequently followed any active opposition. But neither their office, their lives, their favourite objects, or even their influence, at least their influence for *good*, will bear any comparison with those of the Hebrew prophets.

To this extraordinary class of men, now, we owe most, if not all, of the Old Test. Scriptures. What one among them all, if Ezra and perhaps Nehemiah be excepted, came with any certainty from the hands of a priest, who was not also a prophet? Hence in tracing the history of the rise and progress of the Hebrew Canon, it was necessary to bring before the mind a somewhat full picture of the class of men who were active in its composition. They stand on a lofty eminence above all their contemporaries. They bear a character which the tongue even of slander cannot assail with any success. *Perfect* men we need not and do not suppose them to have been. But it would be difficult perhaps to find, under the Christian dispensation itself and among its ministers, men of more unblemished and exalted character. From the prevailing vices of their times they plainly stood aloof. It would seem that in some respects they even went beyond the letter (yet not beyond the true spirit) of the Mosaic Law. I cannot call to mind a single instance of *polygamy* or *concubinage* among them; although the Law of Moses allowed at least the former, or at any rate did not forbid it. The alleged case of the polygamy of Isaiah (chap. vii., viii.) turns out to be wholly without proof or foundation, when the meaning of the prophet is strictly examined. The *virgin* who was to conceive and bear a son, in case we insist on her marriage antecedent to his birth, is not spoken of still as the wife of the prophet, or as about to become his wife. I cannot doubt that the great law of monogamy, which the God of nature has impressed upon our race by dividing it into *halves* between the sexes, was practically recognised and complied with by the prophets as a body.

Such are the men, then, from whom come the books of the Old Testament. God has put an honour upon them far above that which belonged to priests and Levites. How could this have taken place, if the *ritual* was, in his eyes, entitled to the most conspicuous place under the Jewish dispensation?

It would be a most interesting topic of discussion, were we to pursue inquiries respecting the times, places, and manner of prophesying or preaching among the Hebrews. The characteristics of prophetic discourse, its tropical language, its symbol, its allegory, the manner of delivering it and of preserving it, the impression which it made, the topics which were the most usual themes of it—all these and other matters in relation to the subject it would be delightful to discuss. But these belong to an appropriate treatise on the Hebrew prophets, and must, for the sake of brevity and unity of design, be excluded from our present consideration.

SECT. V. *Continued history of the Canon; books supposed to bear the names of their authors.*

It is time to inquire in what position we now stand in respect to the Canon of the Old Test. Scriptures. Beginning, as we have done, with Moses, the greatest prophet of all in ancient days, and following the books down *whose authors are known*, we have, according to the representations made above, the Pentateuch, Isaiah, Jeremiah, Ezekiel, Daniel, (for I cannot regard this work as supposititious,) and the twelve Minor Prophets. If there be any exceptions to these, they must be some parts of Isaiah and of Zechariah, which, as we have already seen, are thought, by most of the recent critics in Germany, to belong to *anonymous* writers;

and possibly the book of Jonah may have been written by a person different from the prophet himself. Whether this be so or not, is a question which belongs to the *special* criticism of the Old Testament, and does not affect at all the nature and design of my present undertaking; for it is conceded on all hands, that even the anonymous compositions among these, (if such there are,) must have sprung from so-called *prophets;* and, with scarcely any exceptions, if any at all, from prophets before the termination of the Babylonish exile. With us the question at present is not, what specific individual wrote this or that book of Scripture, or this or that part of any book, but whether it was written by such men as gave to the composition a right to be placed among the *sacred books* of the Hebrews.

In our historical sketch of the prophets, we have passed in brief review the works which bear their names, and in respect to which we do not think there is any reasonable ground of doubt as to their genuineness. We now come to a second class of books, which, without bearing the name of their authors, seem to ascribe their composition to particular individuals, in the inscriptions affixed to them. In consequence of this, I forbear to put them among the books which all confess to be *anonymous*. Of the books now before us, some appear to be properly assigned, as to most of their contents, to particular individuals; while the inscriptions prefixed to others are of a doubtful character.

We begin with the first class of these. And to this class belongs the book of PSALMS. That this was principally composed by David, has been generally acknowledged. (I have found no one but Lengerke who seems to doubt or deny this.) But there were several coadjutors, some contemporary and others not, in this work. Thirty-four Psalms only are without any inscription; but the inscription does not always give the name of the *author*, for sometimes it merely refers to then existing outward circumstances, sometimes to the music to be employed, and then to some special use of the Psalm. A part of the inscriptions is probably from the hand of redactors, and is not always trust-worthy. About one hundred Psalms are usually assigned to David; some of which perhaps are of doubtful authorship, and some most probably did not come from his pen. To Moses is assigned Ps. xc.; to Solomon, Ps. lxxii., cxxvii.; to Asaph, Ps. l., lxxiv.—lxxxiii., making eleven; to Heman, Ps. lxxxviii.; to Ethan, Ps. lxxxix. De Wette himself concedes, that a number of the anonymous Psalms may not improbably be assigned to David and his contemporaries. Ten Psalms, i. e. Ps. xlii.—xlvii., lxxxiv., lxxxv., lxxxvii., lxxxviii., are usually supposed to be assigned, by the titles, *to the sons of Korah*, i. e. to Korahites, who were priests and sons of Levi. The usual title is, *To the chief musician, for the sons of Korah;* but לבני קרח may also designate the *authorship* of the Psalms, inasmuch as ל often, and even usually, stands before an author's name, as indicating the source whence the composition sprang. What inclines one to doubt that sense of the expression here, is the *plurality* or *partnership* which it would make in the authorship; a thing literally impossible in compositions so brief, and of such a marked character. Moreover, one might almost say of the Psalms in question, A greater than David is here. From one pen and one heart they must have come; and that the *authorship* should be assigned in such an indefinite way as the expression *sons of Korah* would indicate, that a *partnership* in the composition of such pieces should be deemed feasible, are serious difficulties in the way of supposing that *authorship* is indicated by the title.

For our present purpose, indeed, it matters not who was the particular author of this or that Psalm. The authors named, almost without exception, lived at or near the time of David. A few Psalms are unquestionably of later origin; some of them were composed at the period of the captivity, and even after the exile; e. g. Ps. lxxxv., cvi., probably cvii., cxxvi., cxxix., cxxxvii., cxlvii. De Wette himself confesses it to be doubtful, whether any of the Psalms (e. g. xliv., lx., lxxiv., lxxvi., lxxix., lxxxiii., cxix., reckoned by some as of Maccabæan times) are to be assigned to the period of the Maccabees; Einleit. § 270, 3rd ed. That question I take to be now generally regarded as settled by Hassler, in his *Comm. Crit. de Psalmis Maccab.* 1827. Eichhorn and Gesenius, moreover, doubt so late an origin. Rosenmueller unequivocally abandons such a position, in the preface to his compendious Comm. in Psalmos, 1833; while, in explaining Ps. lxxiv. 8, he again adopts it. The fact, that the book of Psalms was long in the process of formation, (if we begin with David, about 1050 B. C., and go down to 536—457, the time at and after the return from the captivity in which some scriptural books were written, we must make more than 500 years for the period of formation,) occasioned it to be compiled in five various books. Thus we have in the first book, Ps. i.—xli.; in the second book, Ps. xlii.—lxxii.; in the third, Ps. lxxiii.—lxxxix.; in the fourth, Ps. xc.—cvi.; in the fifth, Ps. cvii.—cl. At what particular time these various portions or books were collected and published, we do not know for certainty. But it is quite manifest, that in general the older Psalms, i. e. those of David's time, were first collected; and so in succession, as Psalms worthy of introduction were composed. Now and then some more ancient compositions make their appearance in the later books of the Psalms, viz. in the fourth and fifth, which had been overlooked in the former compilations. If any Psalms were added in the time of the Maccabees, it would seem then to be nearly or quite certain, that they would be found in the fifth and last book. But as the alleged Maccabæan Psalms mostly belong to the earlier rather than the later portions of the book, the improbability of their late composition becomes too great to support a critical belief. The early establishment of such musical choirs as belonged to the temple-service, both old and new, would cause all psalms and hymns fitted for that service to be early and earnestly sought for. We may therefore, without any danger of erring, place the completion of the book of Psalms at a period antecedent to the death of Malachi, for it will not be seriously contended that any thing in them obliges us to assume that they are later. On the question, whether the anonymous Psalms were properly included among the contents of the sacred books, we are not competent to pass a judgment which is grounded on historical and minute information, since we have not such information, and cannot obtain it. But it is enough for our present purpose, if we can show that the book of Psalms, as it now is, comes down from a period near the death of Malachi. The contrary of this we may challenge any criticism to establish.

The book of PROVERBS may well be referred to Solomon as its principal author. The Hebrew is of the golden age, and speaks most decidedly against a late composition. The titles which we find in Prov. i. 1; x. 1, ascribe the work to Solomon. Possibly xxii. 17—xxiv. 34, may have originated from another hand, and been incorporated by Solomon. Chap. xxv. 1 gives an entirely new and singular title: "These are the Proverbs of Solomon, which the men of Hezekiah, king of Judah, *transcribed*," or *copied out*, העתיקו. I understand this of transcription from some MS. of Solomon, which had not before (so to speak) been published. The verb העתיק cannot possibly be understood of original *composition*, for כתבו would be the word to designate that. De Wette understands Prov. xxv. 1, as asserting, that the men of Hezekiah *reduced to writing* proverbs that were orally circulated before, and ascribed to Solomon. But this too would require כתבו. Be this matter however as it may, it makes nothing to our present purpose. That the composition is not late, is agreed on all hands. Prov. xxx. is ascribed to Agur; Prov. xxxi. to king Lemuel, as taught by his mother. The time of their composition we know not. But De Wette himself (always inclined to make the origin of books as late as possible) fully concedes that they could not have been written after the Babylonish exile; Einl. § 281.

ECCLESIASTES was regarded by all the ancients as a production of Solomon. But doubts respecting such an origin have recently been brought forward, and seem to be of such a nature as cannot easily be solved. The title (Ecc. i. 1) seems to appropriate the work to Solomon. Yet the like language might be employed by a later writer, whose plan was to repeat the sayings and detail the experience of Solomon. Peculiarly impressive does the book become, in respect to the subject of the emptiness and vanity of all earthly objects and pursuits, when presented as derived from the experience and reflections of such a king, who was at the very summit of human greatness. That this, however, belongs rather to the plan of the book than to the category of realities, seems to be made probable by arguments drawn from the *matter* and *manner* of the book. The complaints, in many parts of the book, of crushing oppression (Ecc. iv. 1); of the exactions of provincial rulers (v. 7); of the exaltation of low men to high offices (x. 5—7); of the present as inferior to the past (vii. 10); of the frequent changes of regents and their unsuitable behaviour—all seem to betoken a book written at a very different time from that of Solomon. How singular it sounds, moreover, when we hear Solomon say, "I *was* king over Israel at Jerusalem" (i. 12); singular, I mean, on the supposition that Solomon was the actual author. Did any one need to be told this? How singular for Solomon himself to say, that 'he was wiser and richer than *all* the kings in Jerusalem before him,' (i. 16; ii. 7, 9,) when David his father was the only king who had reigned there. The *diction*, moreover, of this book differs so widely from that of Solomon in the book of Proverbs, that it is difficult to believe that both came from the same pen. Chaucer does not differ more from Pope, than Ecclesiastes from Proverbs. It seems to me, when I read Coheleth, that it presents one of those cases which leave no room for doubt, so striking and prominent is the discrepancy. In our English translation this is in some good measure lost, by running both books in the same English mould. There is only a single trait of resemblance, which any one would consider as marked or noticeable; and this is, the *sententious* or *apothegmatic* turn of the book. In this respect one is often led to direct his thoughts toward the book of Proverbs, which abounds in, and almost wholly consists of, sayings of such a sententious nature. Yet how very different is the *diction* and *style* of each book, in the original Hebrew! And then the general circle of thought is still more discrepant. The philosophic doubts and puzzles of Ecclesiastes, and the manner of discussing them, have no parallel either in Proverbs, or in any other part of the Hebrew Scriptures. They remind one of many things discussed by Socrates, in the Dialogues of Plato. I cannot help thinking that the writer must have been a Hebrew who had resided abroad, where he had formed some acquaintance with the philosophic discussions of the Greeks. So *unique* is the tenor of his book, and so widely different from the usual circle of Hebrew thinking, that no very probable account can be given of these matters, without such a supposition.

As to the *age* of Ecclesiastes, critics have widely disagreed, ranging from Solomon down to the time of the Maccabees. But the appeal usually made to the *language* or *diction* of the book, in proof of a very late age, will hardly stand the test. Knobel, in his recent and much praised commentary on the book of Ecclesiastes, asserts, and has endeavoured to show, that the book is deeply tinctured with Chaldaisms, and words of the later Hebrew. He even thinks that it savours strongly of the diction of the Rabbins and Talmudists. But the scores of his *Chaldaisms* have been reduced by a later writer, better acquainted with this idiom, (Herzfeld, a German Jew, in his notable work, *Coheleth translated and explained*, 1838,) to some eight or ten ; and his *later Hebrew*, words (some scores more,) to some eleven to fifteen. The investigation of Herzfeld is so thorough, that appeal from it seems to be nearly out of question. And besides the fact, that the quantity of later Hebrew diction and Chaldaism is so small, we must take into view the additional consideration, that the Phenician language, unquestionably of the same character as the Hebrew in its basis, resembles more what is called the *younger* Hebrew, than it does the ancient. The young Hebrew, therefore, may in fact be *very old.* So Gesenius, after all his investigations of the Phenician ; Hall. Lit. Zeit. 1837. No. 81.

There is nothing, either in the matter or diction of the book, absolutely and exactly to settle its age. But the course of thought seems to indicate an acquaintance with philosophical disputes ; and the complaints of oppression, of frequent change of rulers, of the exactions of provincial satraps, and of the toils and dangers of life—all seem to indicate some period of its composition under the Persian government. If the opinion of Josephus is to be relied upon, (Contra Apion. I. § 8, which will be hereafter adduced and examined,) Ecclesiastes must have been composed at some period before the death of Artaxerxes Longimanus, i. e. antecedent to 424 B. C. De Wette and Knobel think, that the end of the Persian period, or the beginning of the Macedonian one, was the time. But there are many and weighty objections against such a supposition, as we shall see in due time.

The CANTICLES present a difficulty somewhat like to that which we have just been considering. The title purports that the book came from Solomon ; at least if לשלמה is to be regarded as indicative of authorship ; which is usually the fact. That it may be regarded in this light, so far as the language is concerned, there is no doubt. But if the idiom of the book, which differs not a little from that of the book of Proverbs, is to be taken into consideration; if, moreover, such passages as Cant. i. 4, 5, 12; iii. 6—11; vii. 5; viii. 11, 12, be attentively examined, the difficulty regarding Solomon as the proper author of the book will not be inconsiderable. That Solomon is the *subject* of the book, there can be no doubt. That some writer contemporary with him may have composed it is quite possible, notwithstanding its idiom. The freshness of all its scenery seems to betoken much in favour of such a view. The diction is neither Chaldaic nor Aramæan in such a degree as to render this either impossible or improbable. Herder and Döpke strenuously maintain the *early* date of the book. De Wette thinks the composition of the poem may have been early, and that it may have been only *orally* preserved for a long time; which, moreover, he supposes may account for the want of regular order and unity in the present arrangement of the book. But I cannot deem this probable, considering that the book obtained a place in the sacred Canon. It is enough for my present purpose, however, that the book was, beyond any reasonable critical doubt, included in the Canon whenever the same was completed. Josephus, at any rate, appears most plainly to include it; for without it we cannot make out the number of sacred books which he specifies.

The *theological* scruples which have raised, or at any rate sought for, objections against the Canticles, stand on the basis of its contents. How, it is asked, can an *amatory* poem be a part of Scripture? This question brings into view the main objection which is felt against the book. On this question I hope to say something in the sequel; but in order to avoid repetition, I must omit remarks pertaining to this part of the subject for the present. One thing seems to be quite clear, viz. that whoever they were that inserted this book in the Canon of Scripture, they must have regarded the work as of a *religious* cast. There is no other example in all the Old Testament of any work of a different tenor. If Ruth or Esther should be appealed to as exceptions to this remark, it would be easy to show, that both of these books have an important bearing on points of consequence in the politico-ecclesiastical history of the Jewish nation.

SECT. VI. *Continued History of the Canon; Books which are Anonymous.*

Thus far of books supposed to be inscribed with the names of their author, with the exception of a few Psalms. We come now to those which are *anonymous*.

Among these the book of JOB stands the most conspicuous, whether we have respect to the splendid poetry which it exhibits, or to the nature of the discussion with which it is occupied. *Who wrote it? When was it written? When annexed to the Canon?* These are questions about which there has been and still is endless dispute. The main difficulty is, first, the want of any proper historical evidence respecting its authorship; then, secondly, the want of internal evidence of a definite and decisive character, as to the age in which it was written. It abounds in references to natural scenery, and to Idumæan and Egyptian localities and objects; but this does not help to decide whether it was written earlier or later. Its idiom, which abounds in Aramæan diction, and often approaches the Arabic, seems to betoken an author who lived out of Palestine, or at least in a border country. But its Aramæan idioms are not sufficient to settle the question in favour of a later age for the book. Very much in this book closely resembles the diction of most of the Psalms and of Proverbs. And besides this, it is an acknowledged fact, that nearly all the poetry of the Old Testament verges towards the dialect in question. The Aramæan hue is to Hebrew *poetry*, something like what the Doric one is to the choruses of Greek tragedy. Nothing decisive, therefore, can be made out from this quarter, as to the age of the book.

It is beyond a question, that the author of this book was acquainted with many of the Hebrew notions of things, with their opinions, their formulas of speech, and the like. With events in general before and after the flood, the book manifests an acquaintance. But all this does not decide any thing for certainty, as to the *time* in which it was written. Carpzov, Eichhorn, Jahn, Stuhlmann, Berthholdt, and the great mass of English critics, give to the book a date anterior to the time of Moses. A number of writers have referred it to Solomon, or to some person of his time. More recently, Gesenius, Bernstein, De Wette, (first two editions of his Introduction,) Umbreit, and others have set the work down to the Chaldee period, i. e. to some period after 610 B. C. De Wette now dates it earlier, (as well he may,) because of Ezekiel's express recognition of Job, in chap. xiv. 14, 16, 20.* Rosenmueller (Proleg. p. 20) places it before the time of Hezekiah. Thus the whole matter is in a floating state; but still, the only question really important to us at present is, whether it was composed either before, or during, the time of the Babylonish exile. If so, it then was undoubtedly a part of the Jewish Canon at the close of that exile.

It is singular to see with what warm zeal the question about the *age* of this poem has been and still is discussed. Not a few writers set about the work of discussion, as if the matter were one *stantis vel cadentis ecclesiæ*. How can it be so to us? Of what consequence is it whether the book is older or younger, if it belong to the Canon, and did belong to it before it was formally closed? Not a few, moreover, appeal to the speeches of Job, Eliphaz, Bildad, Zophar, and Elihu, in support of *doctrinal* propositions; just as if these angry disputants, who contradict each other, and most of whom God himself has declared to be in the wrong, (Job xlii. 7—9,) were inspired when they disputed! The man who wrote the book, and gave an account of this dispute, might be (I believe he was) inspired; he had a great moral purpose in view; but how Job is to be appealed to for a sample of doctrine, who curses the day of his birth, and says many things under great excitement, I am not able to understand. Are we indeed to follow him in the sentiment of chap. xiv. 7, 10, 12? "There is hope of a tree," says he, "if it be cut down, that it will sprout again, and that the

---

* Another reason assigned by De Wette for placing it earlier than the Chaldean period is, that Jeremiah had probably read the book. Comp. Jeremiah xx. 14—18, with Job iii. 3—10; x. 18; xvii. 1, with Job xix. 24; xxxi. 29, &c., with Job xxi. 19. See Einleit. § 291. D.

tender branch thereof will not cease.... But man dieth, and wasteth away; yea, man giveth up the ghost, and where is he?... Man lieth down, and riseth not; till the heavens be no more, they shall not awake, nor be raised out of their sleep." And are we to appeal to his angry friends, who are in the wrong as to the main point in question, for confirmation of a doctrinal sentiment of the gospel? The practical amount of the matter is, that those who refer in such a way to this book, merely select what they like, and leave the rest. They complain, however, in other cases, of doings like to this. They accuse the Unitarians and the Rationalists of very unfair and unscriptural practices, in so doing with other parts of the Bible. After all, it seems to be quite plain, that one might as well appeal to what is said by all manner of persons who are brought to view in the Gospels, as authoritative in matters of doctrine, because what they said stands in an inspired book, as appeal to the speeches of Job and his friends for a like purpose. When will it be understood, that the disputants themselves were not inspired? Did they, moreover, all speak in *poetry*, and all in the same cast of poetry, exhibiting such a unity of style? A rare faculty of *improvisation* those five men must have had, if we assume such a ground as this.

But I am indulging in digression. I return to our immediate object. To my own mind, the strongest objection against the great age of the book of Job is, that it is no where referred to in all the Hebrew Scriptures, except in the case of Ezekiel; and it appears to have produced no influence upon the manner and tenor of the Hebrew sacred writings. I am not able to conceive how such a book should have existed so long, and have produced no more effect; for there is not even a single quotation of it or a reference to it in the other Old Test. Scriptures. Not so with the Pentateuch. I must therefore believe, on the whole, that the book of Job was composed during the troublous times of the Jews, in the later periods of their kingly government. Yet the fact, that there is not in all the book a distinct and certain reference to any thing belonging and peculiar to the Mosaic institutions, rites, sacrifices, and feasts, or to Hebrew personages, or history, is almost astounding, and seems to stand in our way when we assign to the book a later origin.

Especially is this so, when we consider that it was a *Hebrew* who wrote this book; which beyond all reasonable question must have been the case. Yet it is quite possible, that the writer's *plan* definitely precluded references of the nature in question. It was a part of his deliberate plan to compose a book independent of Jewish peculiarities, and based upon the more general views of the patriarchal religion. It is certainly easier to believe this than to suppose the book to be very ancient, and yet not be able to find a trace of its existence or influence, until the time of Ezekiel. To allege, as some have done, that the reference in Ezekiel (xiv. 14, 16, 20) is only to an *allegorical* personage, and therefore proves nothing—is not alleging what seems to be very probable. Were Noah and Daniel, who are joined with Job, mere fictitious personages in Ezekiel's view? If not, it hardly seems probable that this prophet has united real and allegorical personages, and placed them both in the same predicament. Besides this, the Job to whom Ezekiel refers, seems plainly to be such a personage as the book of Job presents to our view.*

If, as has been alleged by some critics, the book of Job was composed by a foreigner, an Aramæan or an Arabian, how came he by such a knowledge of Hebrew diction and rhythm? It would be next to an impossibility. Above all, how came the Jews to admit the book of a *foreigner* into their sacred Canon?

Who composed the book, whether Job himself or some of his friends, we have no means of determining. Exactly *when* it was composed, we cannot decide for want of data. I suppose, however, that no one well acquainted with the book, will doubt its claims to a place in the Jewish Canon, although, before Ezekiel's time, we can find no certain traces of it.

It makes nothing against this, that the genuineness of the

---

* The time to which the composition of the book is here assigned is that given by De Wette, who places it in the declining state of the kingdom of Judah. I have no doubt of its being posterior to the Pentateuch and Joshua; and the period assigned to it is perhaps as nearly correct as we are able to make out at the present time. Hirzel, one of the ablest commentators on Job, thinks that the author was a Hebrew who was carried away by Pharaoh Necho into Egypt. This serves to explain the references and allusions to Egypt which Stickel in vain denies. See Hirzel's Hiob. p. 12. —D.

prologue and epilogue to the book, and also of the speech of Elihu, has of late been often called in question. The criticism of the *Destructives*, as I am inclined to believe, reached its highest point of culmination some time since. Its sun is now descending. Whenever it sets, I hope and trust it will set to rise no more. The same spirit which makes up the Iliad and Odyssey of fragments from a multitude of singing beggars brought accidentally together, has made up the book of Job in the same way, and with reasons equally good. The most recent criticism, however, seems verging back again toward the opinion of all ages and nations, which knew any thing of the book in question, viz. the opinion that the whole of this book belongs to one author, and is one, and but one work. The *numerosity* of the book, i. e. the divisions throughout into groups of *three*, strongly favours the genuineness of the *whole* book. Moreover, the poem, without the prologue and epilogue, if not absolutely unintelligible, would at least lie in every reader's mind in a dark, confused, and unsatisfactory state. De Wette, as usual, not only doubts the genuineness of Elihu's speech, (ch. xxxii.—xxxviii.,) but also of xxvii. 11—xxviii. 28. *Doubting* seems to be an essential element of this critic's literary life; and he appears to derive more pleasure from it, than he does from believing.

Upon the whole, I am disposed to think that few persons who are familiar with the course of the human mind in ancient times, as to doubts and reasonings on difficult problems of morals or of the Divine government of the world, will yield their assent to the probability of the very early origin of the book of Job. The main question of the book, whether the Divine Being constantly and adequately rewards virtue and piety, and punishes sin in the present world, is one that seems to spring from an investigation and a spirit of philosophizing, which is rarely to be met with among the most ancient Hebrews. Ecclesiastes is full of a similar spirit; but as this book is manifestly among the later ones, I am inclined to place the book of Job in the same age, i. e. in the Chaldean period of the prophets, or not long before. The diction decides nothing certain for any particular age. The almost unequalled sublimity of the composition, the rhythmical perfection of its parallelisms, salem. Nothing can be more natural than to suppose that a record would be made of the conquest and the division of Palestine, soon after those events. How could the division and apportionment of it be rendered authoritative and permanent, unless by some *record* of the same ? That it was written *after* the death of Joshua and of his contemporary elders, seems to be certain from Josh. xxiv. 31, where Israel is spoken of as serving the Lord until after the death of these persons. So the death of Eleazar, the son of Aaron, is recorded, (Josh. xxiv. 33,) but not of his successor Phinehas. But if the book be so *fragmentary* as is alleged, then such declarations would only go to show the age of the fragment in which they are contained.

Mr. Parker (in his additions to De Wette, II. p. 188, seq.) has exhibited a graphic specimen of the usual neological reasoning. "The book of Joshua," he suggests, "makes frequent appeals to the Law of Moses; but this *Law* could not have been written until after the time of Josiah; *ergo*, the book of Joshua could not have been written until after the same time." The main proposition is plainly a mere *petitio principii*. But no matter: *Delenda est Carthago*.

The *Samaritans*, along with the Pentateuch, have also a book of Joshua, containing much of what is in the Hebrew book of the same name, with additional fabulous matter of their own. Was there not, then, a book of Joshua, when the ten tribes separated from the two, in the reign of Rehoboam ? Appearances seem to favour this supposition. Those tribes retained the Scriptures then extant, but never added any more. I would not deny the probability, that documents of several kinds are contained in the book of Joshua; but that they passed through the hands and under the revisal of some one compiler, whose office or name gave authority to the book, I cannot well doubt. Many of the alleged contradictions and discrepancies are easily removed, on such a ground; but it comports not with my present object to enter into the discussion of these matters.

The book of JUDGES is also anonymous. The main historical elements of the book end with the biography of Samson, Judg. xvi. 31. Chap. xvii.—xxi. contain an appendix, showing how anarchy and licentiousness were introduced, after the death of Joshua, among the men of the following generation. There is nothing in the diction or style of the book, which would serve at all to prove a late origin. But such passages as those in Judg. xvii. 6; xviii. 1; xix. 1; xxi. 25, which attribute certain evils to the times, because *there was no king* in the land, seem strongly to savour of being written after there was some example of an efficient and orderly monarchical government.

The book is strongly marked with several peculiarities. Except reference in the song of Deborah (v. 4, 5) to the appearance of Jehovah on Mount Sinai, there is nothing in the book of Judges that refers to the Law of Moses, to the priesthood, to the Levitical rites, nor to any prophets, excepting in one case, (vii. 8,) and the instance of Deborah, iv. The truth plainly is, that the writer did not design to give any thing like a regular and connected series of history, during the 300 years which are covered by the book of Judges. (De Wette makes them above 400.) The peculiar sins of the people, their exemplary sufferings in consequence of them, and the signal deliverances which they experienced under this heroic leader and that, occupy the whole book, with the exception of the appendix before mentioned; and this stands in connexion with the general subject. As to the *chronology* of the book itself, I question if any regular and certain series can be satisfactorily made out from it.

The most natural origin of such a book would be, during the prevalence of idolatry in Judah or in Israel. A true prophet would seize such an occasion in order to hold up to view past experiences, as a warning to the idolatrous people of the danger which they were encountering. That he possessed notices, probably *written* ones, of the past, seems highly probable. Even oral tradition would preserve a knowledge of many things related in the book of Judges, which were of an extraordinary and wonderful nature. The tone of piety and zeal for the honour of God as manifest in the book, is elevated and pure. *Ritual* services are plainly quite secondary in the writer's view. But idolatry, and oppression, and other vices he censures with unsparing severity. A spirit kindred to that of David and Samuel must have animated his bosom.

The so-called *myths* ($\mu\tilde{v}\vartheta o\iota$) of the book are numerous.

In other words, (not to speak with the neological critics,) the extraordinary and even miraculous occurrences related in it are not a few. The stories of Gideon and Samson, in particular, elicit a tempest of objections from recent criticism. Among all, however, who accuse the book of anile attachment to fables and myths, I find none who goes so far as Dr. Palfrey, late Professor of Sacred Literature in the Theol. Seminary at Cambridge, in the tone and manner of criticism. In his Academical Lectures, (II. p. 194, seq.,) speaking of Samson, he says, "The character of Samson is but a wild compound of the buffoon, the profligate, and the bravo. With a sort of childish cunning, and such physical faculties as a fantastic invention has ascribed to the *ogre*, he is without a common measure of capacity to provide for his own protection," &c. Dr. Palfrey, if I am rightly informed, has a great and unconquerable aversion to such freethinkers as Mr. Parker, the translator of De Wette on the Old Testament. Yet I recollect nothing in what I have read of Mr. Parker, nothing in Strauss, nothing in any of the neological critics of Germany which I have consulted, (and they are not a few,) which compares with this scornful caricature. Bruno Bauer, (whom I have not read,) if the reviewers fairly represent him, may, under the maddening influence of the potions which he is reported to love too well, have said some things more indecorous than this.* I would hope, however, that such is not the case. How Dr. Palfrey can be so displeased with Mr. Parker and his associates for thorough rejection of the Divine authority of the Scriptures, after writing such a passage as this, is more than I am able to explain. The writer of the Epistle to the Hebrews, who classes Samson with such worthies as Barak, and Jephtha, and David, and Samuel, (Heb. xi. 32,) must have viewed the character of Samson, taken as a whole, in a very different light from that in which the Cambridge Professor has placed him. Samson was not without great faults ; can it be proved that he had not some conspicuous

---

* This sentence should not have been penned. No cause can be served by vague references to the private habits of an individual, especially if such references be founded on *reports*. We should deal with what a man *writes*, and nothing else, in a work like the present. D.

virtues? His zeal against heathenism and idolatry, at least, will not be called in question.

The book of Judges, however, depends not, for its credit, on the judgment of Dr. Palfrey respecting the character of Samson. It was, beyond all doubt, among those books which Christ and the apostles spoke of as being holy Scriptures.

The First and Second Books of SAMUEL are but one work, severed into two parts. The ancient Hebrews always reckoned them but as *one* book ; and so of Kings and Chronicles. They contain the history of Samuel's administration, who was the last of the *Judges*, 1 Sam. i.—xxv.; the partly contemporaneous history of Saul, an account of whose death terminates the so-called First Book of Samuel; while the Second exhibits the history of David's government.

It is generally conceded, that there is nothing in the idiom of these books which indicates with any certainty a late origin. In 1 Chron. xxix. 29, it is said, that "the acts of David, first and last, are written in the book of Samuel the seer, and in the book of Nathan the prophet, and in the book of Gad the seer." From this passage, many in ancient and in modern times have drawn the conclusion, that the so-called books of Samuel were the work of these three different individuals, 1 Sam. i.—xxiv. being from the hand of Samuel, and the rest, (containing history after his death,) by the other prophets just named. The fact that David's *death* is not mentioned at the close of 2 Samuel, would seem to import that these books were written before that event. But I can hardly bring myself to believe, that the authorship of these books belongs to three different persons. Much more probable does it seem to me, that the author made use of the three works in question, in compiling his book; while the conception of the plan of the books, and the selection and association of the parts, are the work of one and the same mind.

De Wette ventures to bestow some faint praise upon these books, on the ground that they have so little of the *mythical* in them, and little or nothing of the ritual and Levitical spirit; Einl. § 178, seq. The story of the witch of Endor, however, he thinks is an instance of "ideal pragmatism," i. e. a representation in which the author labours to account for certain phenomena, the real history of which remains doubtful. The apparent *predictions* in the book, he says, were written *post eventum*. Withal, too, he says there is much disturbance and confusion in these books; but still, that there is much of genuine history in them, and that the narrations are lively and true to nature, § 178. The chronology, moreover, he pronounces to be imperfect and legendary; and he avers, also, that there are some contradictions. But Mr. Parker, his translator and commentator, goes still further in his critical remarks. 'Some passages savour of anthropomorphitic and mean conceptions of God; unworthy actions are attributed to him; there is a sacerdotal spirit in the books; and a few miraculous legends are mingled in the story;' Add. to § 178.

That different sources from which the writer drew, have occasioned some appearances of discrepancy, the attentive critical reader will not perhaps deny. Let him compare 1 Sam. xvi. 14—23; xvii. 31—40, with xvii. 55—xviii. 5, and he will perceive what I mean. The passage in xviii. 54 wears every appearance of a late and very unskilful interpolation. How could David carry the head of Goliath to *Jerusalem*, which came not into possession of the Hebrews for many years after this period? See 2 Sam. v. 6, seq. A fair investigation and candid judgment of the books in question, as it seems to me, will however remove most of the alleged objections against them. I except, of course, those objections which lie against all accounts of miraculous events. But it is not a man's *critical* judgment or skill, which leads him to make objections of this nature; it is his *a priori* reasonings and his *theology* which move him to object on such a ground.

At all events, no doubt can remain that these books were written long before the Babylonish exile. And this is enough for our present purpose.

The 1 and 2 KINGS (one book in two parts) contain the history of the Jewish kings from the reign of Solomon down to the exile; and with this is incorporated the history of the ten tribes, from the time of their separation down to that of their deportation by the king of Assyria.

De Wette allows to these books a *prophetic* origin. He says that "the chief object aimed at, is to set forth the efficacy of the prophets." It is admitted, that there is a uniformity of style and a general unity of design. But the neological critics, of course, are full of objections against the *myths* of these compositions. Some think the accounts are from mere oral and traditional sources; others, that written documents were employed by the redactor as the basis of his work. This latter opinion is rendered more probable by the fact, that the book of Kings refers by name to several other books, as containing a more ample account of particular things, than that which the author of the books in question has given; e. g. the Book of the Acts of Solomon, 1 Kings xi. 41; the Book of the Kings of Israel, 1 Kings xiv. 19; xvi. 5, 20, 27; xxii. 39; and the Book of the Chronicles of the Kings of Judah, 1 Kings xv. 7. From the manner in which the writer refers to these, it would seem plain that he considered them of the same credibility and authenticity as his own book.

As to the *time* in which the books before us were written —the close, at any rate, must have been written late down in the exile; for 2 Kings xxv. 27—30 brings the history down to the thirty-seventh year of the captivity of Jehoiachin. In addition to this, the remark in 2 Kings xxiii. 25 respecting Josiah, viz. that "there was no king before him like to him . . . neither after him arose any like him," shows, that when the books were written several kings after Josiah had arisen. On the whole, there can be no good reason to doubt, that the compilation, as it now is, must have been made near the close of the exile. The arguments mainly employed by De Wette, however, to prove this, amount to nothing in the view of any one who believes in the reality of prophetic foresight. He says, that the return from exile is mentioned in 1 Kings viii. 47; the destruction of the temple, in ix. 7, 8; the dispersion of the people, in xiv. 15; and the Babylonish exile, in 2 Kings xx. 17. All these passages, however, I must regard as merely *prophetic* anticipations of the events in question. But as he rejects every thing of this nature, so he interprets the passages just adverted to as being written *post eventum.*

Who the author was, is not known. The Talmud attributes the authorship to *Jeremiah.* But Jeremiah cannot well be supposed to have lived and been active in the prophetic office in the thirty-seventh year of Jehoiachin's exile, although Hävernick adopts this view; for he must then be at least some 110 years old. Movers supposes, that Jeremiah wrote an older book of Kings, from which most of the present one was taken; *De utriusque Vet. Jer. Indole*, &c. There can be little doubt that, whoever was the author, his work was completed before the return from the Babylonish exile.

The books of CHRONICLES, as we might naturally expect, have been more vigorously assailed than any other historical book of the Old Testament. De Wette made his *debut* upon the stage of historic criticism by an attack upon them, in his *Kritik der Israel. Geschichte*. He has bestowed particular labour upon them in his *Introduction*, occupying some ten pages; which his translator and commentator, Mr. Parker, has, with a special purpose, spread out into sixty-four pages.

The contents of the Chronicles are genealogies and Jewish history, from David downward to the exile. The history of David (1 Chron. x.—xxix.) is of course a repetition, in the main, of that in the books of Samuel, but diversified particularly by minute accounts of Levitical arrangements. The history of Solomon occupies 2 Chron. i.—ix., which stands related in the like manner to that in 1 Kings. The remainder is the theocratic history of the kings of Judah, rarely glancing at that of the ten tribes. It is evidently the writer's design to make an appropriate history of only the legitimate kings of Judah, and of them in particular as they stood related to matters of religion and the priesthood. He brings it down to the period of liberation from exile by the proclamation of Cyrus; 2 Chron. xxxvi. 21, seq. In 1 Chron. iii. 19—24, is a passage of genealogy, which brings us down to the grandchildren of Zerubbabel, who was the leader of the returning exiles. If this passage be genuine, it will bring the book down to a period near that in which Nehemiah and Malachi lived. The orthography (*scriptio plena*) and the idiom of these books also contribute to render probable their very late origin. De Wette (§ 189) reckons the union of the Chronicles with the *Hagiography* an evidence of late origin. But are the Psalms shown to be all of late origin, by the circumstance that they are classed with the Hagiography?

The gravest objections which are brought against these

books, are founded in their departures from Samuel and Kings, in matters of a historical nature. E. g. when Joab numbered the people, i. e. the military force of Israel, at the command of David, it is said in 2 Sam. xxiv. 9, that there were 800,000 soldiers in Israel, and 500,000 in Judah; while 1 Chron. xxi. 5 says that the number in Israel was 1,100,000, and in Judah 470,000. In 1 Kings xxiv. 24, David is said to have bought of Araunah a threshing-floor and a pair of oxen for sacrifice, at the price of fifty shekels of silver; in 1 Chron. xxi. 25, David is said to have given 600 shekels of gold for the same. In 2 Kings viii. 26, Ahaziah the son of Jehoram begins to reign at the age of twenty-two; according to 2 Chron. xxii. 2, he begins at the age of forty-two, this book thus making him two years older than his father, who died at the age of forty, 2 Chron. xxi. 20. In 1 Kings v. 16, the overseers of temple-work are said to be 3300; in 2 Chron. ii. 2, they are estimated at 3600. In 1 Kings xv. 32, it is said that "there was war between Asa and Baasha king of Israel *all their days;*" in 2 Chron. xiv. 1, it is said that under the same king Asa "the land had rest ten years;" and after the invasion by Zerah the Ethiopian, that "there was no more war unto the thirty-fifth year of his [Asa's] reign." In 2 Chron. xiv. 2, 3, it is said of Asa, that "he did that which was good and right in the eyes of the Lord; for he took away the altars of the strange gods, and the high places, and brake down the images, and cut down the groves" (comp. 6. 5); in 2 Chron. xv. 17, it is said, that "the high places were not taken away out of Israel." Possibly the latter may mean 'out of the land of the ten tribes;' but I cannot think this is probable, for Asa had no control over that land. In 1 Kings vii. 15, the two pillars of brass for the temple are said to be eighteen cubits in height; in 2 Chron. iii. 15, they are represented as thirty-five cubits high; and the like in some other cases.*

Besides these and similar discrepancies, the statement of *numbers* occasionally wears the air of something very extraordinary. E. g. in 2 Chron. xxviii. 5, seq., which gives an ac-

---

* See Davidson's Sacred Hermeneutics, p. 544, et seq., and the article on Chronicles in Kitto's Cyclopædia of Biblical Literature, where some of these contradictions, and others not mentioned, are reconciled. D.

count of the invasion of Judah by Pekah king of Israel, and Rezin king of Syria, it is stated that " Pekah slew 120,000 men of Judah in one day, all valiant men." In this connexion we may also note, that Ahaz was twenty years old when he began to reign (2 Chron. xxviii. 1); that in the next year of his reign the invasion of Pekah took place, in which (as is said in 2 Chron. xxviii. 7) a "mighty man of Ephraim [one of Pekah's captains] slew Maaseiah the *king's son*." How could Ahaz, then twenty-one years of age, have a son old enough to bear arms? The implication seems to be such; and yet the meaning may simply be, that Pekah's captain destroyed one of the royal progeny (not in arms); and this is quite possible, as marriages often take place in the East when the husband is only some fifteen or sixteen years old. In 2 Chron. xiii. 17, it is stated, that Abijah, king of Judah, smote of the children of Israel who were led on by Jeroboam, "500,000 chosen men," in one rencontre. Could the ten tribes have possibly furnished such an army as this, from their population and limits at that time? The army of Asa with which he went out to battle against Zerah the Ethiopian, is said (2 Chron. xiv. 8) to be "300,000 men out of Judah, and 280,000 out of Benjamin, mighty men of valour," i. e. five hundred and eighty thousand soldiers from only the tribes of Judah and Benjamin. This would require the population of these tribes, at that time, to consist of two and a half or three millions at least. Could one half of this number have been supported in the small tract of land— small at any rate as to fertile land—within the borders of Judah and Benjamin? 1 Chron. xxii. 14 represents David as having collected for the use of the temple, 100,000 talents of gold and 1,000,000 talents of silver; which, according to the generally accredited reckoning of Richard, the bishop of Peterborough, are equivalent, the gold to 500,000,000 pounds sterling, and the silver to 353 millions; the whole sum amounts to 853 millions of pounds sterling, i. e. about 4,265,000,000 dollars. The precious metals must have been more plentiful at that time, than they ever have been since, to render it possible for the king of a country some 150 (possibly at that time some 200) miles in length and from 70 to 90 in breadth, to have amassed such an unexampled sum as this. The conquests of David, although somewhat extensive, were still limited to countries not rich in the precious metals.

Such are some of the difficulties that meet us in the books of Chronicles. But even these are not all. There seems, at least at first view, to be a design, on the part of the compiler of these books, to cast into the shade, or to keep out of view, some things which would detract from the character of the persons who are concerned with them. In the account of David's domestic relations, (1 Chron. xiv. 3,) no mention is made of his *concubines;* which last are mentioned in 2 Sam. v. 13. In 2 Sam. viii. 2, David is represented, after conquering Moab, as "measuring with two lines to put to death, and with one full line to keep alive," i. e. as putting to a violent death two thirds of its inhabitants; in 1 Chron. xviii. 3, this circumstance is altogether omitted. The Chronicles make no mention of David's adultery and murder, in the matter of Bathsheba and Uriah, so particularly related in 2 Sam. xi. 2—xii. 26. Little or nothing is said in the Chronicles respecting David's troubles on account of Ammon, Absalom, and the rebellious Ahithophel and others. Nothing is said in the Chronicles of Solomon's 700 wives and 300 concubines, nor of their causing him to apostatize; nothing of his building temples for them around Jerusalem to Chemosh and Moloch; nothing of all the disturbances that ensued, caused by Hadad, Jeroboam, and others; all of which are so fully related in 1 Kings xi. In respect to the impious and tyrannical Manasseh, the book of Kings (2 Kings xxi. 16; xxiv. 4) twice mentions his "shedding very much innocent blood, till he had filled Jerusalem from one end to the other;" all of which the book of Chronicles omits (2 Chron. xxiii.); and moreover, it gives an account of Manasseh's penitence, and of his efforts to restore the worship of the true God, (2 Chron. xxiv. 11—17,) all of which is omitted in the book of Kings. Like to these traits are many other things in the Chronicles; and circumstances such as these serve to show the peculiar texture of these books.

The genealogies in 1 Chron. i.—ix. present a variety of difficulties, being quite incomplete in many cases, and apparently at variance with some other portions of the Scriptures in others. Indeed it is very difficult to discover the specific object of these genealogies, unless indeed it was to show the descent of some leading families who had returned from the exile.

We need not wonder, under these circumstances, that those who speak so freely about other historical books of the Old Testament, here find occasion to utter much of disapprobation, and sometimes even to say what is lacking in decorum. E. g. Mr. Parker, in his edition of De Wette, intimates (II. p. 294) that the historian who could omit so many notable offences of kings, as the author of the Chronicles has done, "must write with some other design than that of telling the whole truth." He even makes himself merry with some of the alleged mistakes of the *Chronicler* (as he calls the author). "An *amusing* mistake occurs," says he, (II. p. 268,) " in 1 Chron. xi. 23, as compared with 2 Sam. xxiii. 21." The cream of the jest is, that in the book of Samuel it is said of Benaiah, that " he slew an Egyptian, a man of remarkable appearance," (אשר מראה,) while the passage in Chronicles says, that " he slew an Egyptian, a man of great stature, five cubits high." Now what part of this it is which Mr. Parker pronounces *amusing*, I do not readily perceive. I can easily see that five cubits = 7½ feet, is an uncommon height for a man; yet this is not without a parallel, or rather it is even surpassed, e. g. by the Kentucky giant, in our own day. That a man of this height might be called *a man of aspect*, (איש מראה, for איש is plainly implied here,) as the writer of the Kings has called him, in a *military* respect, (which is what the passage clearly has in view,) there is no good reason to deny. The Latin *aspectabilis* would give the exact meaning; while Mr. Parker has translated it *respectable man!* That the writer of the Chronicles might choose to state with particularity the height of the Egyptian, rather than to say (as in the book of Kings) that he was a *man of aspect*, conveys to my mind no impression which is specially *amusing*. I cannot even suppose a mistake on the part of the *Chronicler*, as to the import of מראה in Kings. I can only see that one writer meant to characterize the Egyptian as a man of remarkable appearance, while the other gives us the specific quality which made him remarkable. After all, there is something to *amuse* us in respect to this matter; and that is, that Mr. Parker has translated the passage which means *aspectabilis* as if it meant *venerandus*. And this is the criticism, then, which looks at the book of Chronicles with scorn !

To be brief: De Wette and most of the Neologists in criticism who sympathize with him, consider and treat the books of the Chronicles as a mere *farrago* of scraps, made up partly from written records, partly from tradition, partly by a superstitious reverence for the priesthood and the ritual law, and partly by the vain-glorious boastings of a Jew in respect to the royal race of David and the tribes which adhered to the Davidic dynasty. Hence they give little credit indeed to the testimony of these books.

The devout and reverential reader of the Old Testament has, it must be confessed, some difficulties of a serious nature to encounter, in regard to such things in the Chronicles as have been pointed out. The tyro in matters of sacred criticism must certainly feel that he has a somewhat formidable task before him; especially if he adopts the theory of plenary *verbal* inspiration. I will state in a few words what my own impressions are; for I have already dwelt so long on these books, that I must not say much more.

I cannot well doubt, that the Chronicles are the last of all the historical books, possibly with the exception of Ezra, Nehemiah, and Esther. That they were written by some Jew, for the use of the renewed Israelitish commonwealth, and that the author was a priest or Levite, seem to me, all things considered, to be nearly certain.* Let any one peruse the prophecy of Malachi, written about the same period as the Chronicles, and he will find it filled with grievous complaints of the neglect and contempt of the Mosaic ritual, exhibited by the Jews. The prophet complains that they offer the lame, the blind, and the sick, in sacrifice; that they have snuffed at the offerings to the Lord; that they have robbed God in tithes and offerings, besides being guilty of many other sins. It was not unnatural that some pious priest, or Levite, or prophet, should essay to remedy these evils, by giving a particular history of past well-known and renowned kings, as to the

---

* The opinion of the Jews is that they were written by Ezra, and for this many considerations might be adduced. See the article in Kitto's Cyclopædia already referred to. D.

efforts which they made to carry the Mosaic institutions into practice. Hence the enlarged account of all David's arrangements in respect to the ark of God, the sacrifices, the priests and Levites, the singers and porters of the temple, and the like; 1 Chron. xv.—xxvii. The same is true in regard to Solomon, 2 Chron. i.—ix.; in regard to Abijah, 2 Chron. xiii.; Asa, ch. xv.; Jehoshaphat, ch. xvii., seq.; Joash, ch. xxiv.; Uzziah, ch. xxvi.; Hezekiah, ch. xxix., seq.; and Josiah, ch. xxxiv. A prominence is consequently given to things of this nature, which is wanting in the books of Kings, for this was written earlier and in different circumstances. The sacred writers of the Old Testament and the New adapt their works to the wants of the times in which they live. Why should they not?

It lies then upon the face of the books of Chronicles, that they were composed with special reference to the state of the time, as to the Mosaic worship and rites. This will account for a great portion of the differences in the narrations between this and the books of Kings. It is equally plain, that the history of the ten tribes, the *anti-Davidic* government, is purposely omitted. The writer found so little to his purpose in the examples of the kings of Israel, with respect to the Mosaic religion, that he chose wholly to omit them. Moreover, as it respects the kings of Judah, it is plain that the writer did not purpose to give a *full* history. His work is rather what the Sept. Version names it, viz. Παραλειπόμενα, i. e. *Supplement*, or *things that remain*, that is, remain to be recorded. The frame-work of his history is of course the same as that of Judah in the books of Kings; but for a particular purpose he has given to it a different finishing or costume. It is no more true of Kings and Chronicles, that what one of them omits is to be considered as fabulous or unworthy of credit, than it is of the Gospels. Silence proves nothing, unless in peculiar cases. There is even nothing particularly improbable in all the accounts which the Chronicles give us, of the arrangements in respect to religious matters made by many of the kings of Judah.

With these considerations in view, we can easily account for the often varying narrations in the Kings and Chronicles. It ought no more to offend us, than it offends a believer of the Gospels, when he finds such a wonderful variety as there is in the style of John and of Luke. Beyond this, however, we have seen that there are apparent contradictions between the Kings and Chronicles, and some apparent inaccuracies in the latter. We cannot refuse to acknowledge this; for we see with our own eyes. It is simply a question of *fact*, not of theological opinion or theory. *Facts* which are presented to us in a record, cannot be altered by any doctrinal theory which we may devise or maintain.

That the *present* book of Chronicles is in a somewhat imperfect state, I must regard as true. Otherwise, how could Amaziah, the youngest son of Jehoram, be made two years older than his father? 2 Chron. xxi. 5; xxii. 2. I am inclined to believe that some of the excessive *numbers* of men, and of the astonishing amount of treasures, have suffered in transcription, or from marginal *addenda*. Almost all the discrepancies between Kings and Chronicles, and almost all of the seeming excesses in statements, have respect to *proper names* or *numbers*. These are plainly the most liable of all things to error on the part of copyists. If it could be shown that the old Hebrew MSS. designated numbers by alphabetical letters, as the later Hebrew does, it would be very easy to make out the probability of error in transcription, and to account for it. But inasmuch as this, though often assumed, has never been rendered very probable, we must content ourselves with the not improbable supposition, that at least some of the apparent errors in question have arisen from transcription or unskilful redaction. We cannot prove this, indeed, by appeal to direct testimony; and the contrary of this, moreover, is not capable of satisfactory proof. But in such a case as that of the age of Amaziah just mentioned, it would be preposterous to suppose that the error came from the pen of the author, for it would prove him to be destitute of common sense; a position which the rest of the book would not permit us to maintain. The like to this might be said of several other apparent errors of these books.

I regard it as more probable, that the statements in Kings are in general the more accurate of the two, when there is a discrepancy between that work and the book of Chronicles. One good reason is, that the book of Kings rarely developes an *excess* in point of numbers. Internal probability is therefore in its favour.

How far the books of Chronicles, in our Saviour's time, were identical with our present books of the same name, it would be difficult to show. That these books have in some way been tampered with, or in some degree negligently transcribed, since that period, appears to be not improbable, when we look at the history of the Canon. In Josephus' time, the Chronicles were arranged or classed with the other historical books, (as we shall hereafter see,) instead of being where they are now, i. e. at the close of the *Kethubim*, and therefore at the end of the Old Testament. What else was done in re-editing them, besides changing their place of arrangement, we know not. But as they now are, there are certainly, as we have seen above, several passages which disagree with other parts of the Old Testament, and some which disagree with other parts of the Chronicles themselves.

It does not strike me, that the omissions in detailing the sins and weaknesses of David, Solomon, and others, are to be much accounted of in the way of objection to these books. If the design of the writer, or a promise on his part, had been to give the lives of the Jewish kings *complete*, I see not how we could then exempt him from the charge of having performed his task in an unsatisfactory way, at least of having left it very incomplete. But this is evidently not his plan. *The theocratic policy and efforts of the Jewish kings are his main object.* And so far as this is concerned, I am not aware that his narrative is open to any serious and well-grounded objections. The few particulars of incongruity that we have found, amount at the most to nothing which is very important.

As to the rest, I have examined the almost innumerable difficulties and incongruities, suggested by De Wette, and presented in English and augmented by Mr. Parker. Very many of them, I am fully persuaded, will not stand the test of a candid critical scrutiny. Others are more apparent at first view, than real. De Wette has made capital for himself out of every thing, even out of a change or variation in the diction, phraseology, &c. So we cannot, or should not, do with the Gospels; so we must not do with the book of Chronicles, if we mean to preserve the reputation of being truly candid and liberal-minded. I will only add, that after all which Keil has said in his *Versuch über die Bücher der Chronik*, 1833; Dahler, *de Lib. Paralip. Auctoritate*, 1819; and Movers, *Ueber die Chronik*, 1834; in defence of the books in question, there is still need of some other labourer in this field, who will do the work more thoroughly. Hävernick is reported to have performed this task; but it has not yet been in my power to examine what he has written.*

The book of RUTH has plainly for its object, to trace the genealogy of David to a source which is honourable. The probability seems to be, that it was written during the reign of David, or soon after. The variations of the language from the usual Hebrew of that period, are not remarkable enough to afford any ground of argument for the late age of the book. The history which it gives, belongs to the period of the Judges; as is expressly stated in Ruth i. 1. Moreover, "the days when the Judges ruled," is spoken of as a period already passed by. Earlier than the time of David, therefore, it could not have been written; and as the special reason for writing it seems to be, to do honour to David in respect to his descent, he must have been a king before it was written; for this was the particular inducement to do him honour. The character of Boaz and of Ruth is truly noble and ingenuous. It is easy to see, moreover, that the poverty of Ruth was not regarded as a matter of any reproach. Riches, in those days, at least in the author's view, constituted no part of true nobility. The whole picture is a delightful one. The simplicity, integrity, and kind feelings of the principal persons exhibited by this book, are altogether remarkable in any age or country. David had at least some ancestors who were nature's noblemen, if not decked with stars and garters. That Ruth was a foreigner by birth, is no objection to the place assigned her. There can scarcely be a doubt that she became a proselyte to Judaism.

The genealogy, at the close of the book, ends with David. The writer of the Chronicles has made use of it in his genealogy, 1 Chron. ii. 11, 12. This shows that the book was

* This is a strange confession, as the part of Hävernick's Introduction discussing the Books of Chronicles was published in 1839, five years before Mr. Stuart wrote. Hävernick, however, has not done much more than Movers and Keil, on whom he has chiefly relied. See Einleit. Zweyter Theil. Erste Abtheilung. p. 174, et seq. D.

extant in his time, and that is sufficient for our present purpose.

On account of the period to which the book of Ruth relates, it is placed in modern times, and probably in more ancient ones, next to the book of Judges; for we shall see in due time, that in the ancient division of the Scriptures, in and before Josephus' age, this book was appended to that of the Judges. The Talmudic arrangement, which tore it away from this connexion and placed it among the Kethubim, was the result of a later and merely artificial disposition of the sacred books.

The books of EZRA and NEHEMIAH contain the history of the restoration of the Jewish commonwealth, after the exile. In classifying the sacred books, they were usually joined together, in ancient times, as one book in two parts; because they both have a relation to the same subject, viz. the re-establishment of law and order, after the return from the exile. I shall, however, consider them separately here.

The various matters of which the book of EZRA treats, and the Hebrew and Chaldee languages which are employed, have led to a great variety of opinion among critics, as to the *authorship* of the book. Chap. i.—vi. contain the history of the return of the first colony from the exile, and connect closely with the end of 2 Chronicles. The decree of Cyrus, (536 B. C.,) a register of the returning exiles, the hinderances to the building of the temple, and the completion of this work in the sixth year of Darius the king, (515 B. C.,) form the first part of the book of EZRA. The principal Chaldee portion of the work comprises iv. 8—vi. 18. The second part of the book gives an account of the immigration of the new colony under Ezra, in the seventh year of Artaxerxes, 457 B. C.; and of course about 79 years after the first company of exiles returned under Zerubbabel and Jeshua. The decree of Artaxerxes, permitting Ezra's immigration with a colony of Jews, is also written in Chaldee, vii. 12—26. The rest of the book details the efforts and arrangements of Ezra, in reforming the people and the priesthood.

Evidently the first portion of the book is constituted in part by two documents, different from the main narrative of the writer of the book. Chap. ii. is a register of those who first returned from exile; which Nehemiah found in a document by itself, and from which he took his copy; see Neh. vii. 5, and comp. Neh. vii. 6—73 with Ez. ii. The Chaldee (iv. 8—vi. 18) seems to have been from another hand than that of the principal author of the book in general; and not only the letter to Artaxerxes written by the enemies of the Jews, and his answer to the same (iv. 11—22) are in Chaldee, but also the narrative that follows on as far as vi. 18. In the sequel of the book, Ezra speaks sometimes in the *first* person, vii. 27—ix. 15; while chap. vii. 1—26 and x. speak of him in the *third* person.

The last part of the book is occupied with the narration of Ezra's efforts to bring about a reformation in various respects, among the Jews; although its *chronology* is not distinctly marked. For aught that appears, these efforts might all have been made in 457 B. C.; for Ezra came to Jerusalem in the fifth month of that year; Ez. vii. 8. Twelve years after this, when Nehemiah came up to Jerusalem from the Persian court, we find Ezra sedulously engaged in the appropriate duties of his office as priest and scribe; Neh. viii. 1—6, 9, 13. But the history in the book of Ezra seems to comprise only the first portion of these 12 years. Whoever wrote the book, then, he seems to have written it soon after Ezra had taken up his abode in Jerusalem; for otherwise we should expect from the author a further account of Ezra. I think we may set it down as nearly certain, that the book was written not far from 456 B. C.

That Ezra himself wrote vii. 27—ix. 15, is plain from the fact that he constantly employs the *first* person in his narrative. Whether he wrote vii. 1—11 and x. 1—44, where the *third* person is constantly employed, is more doubtful; and especially so from the circumstance, that in xi. 6 it is said of him, that he was "*a ready* or *expert scribe* in the law of Moses." It seems altogether probable to me, that some of Ezra's friends, probably of the prophetic order, compiled the book in question from the various documents named above; and that he did this by prefacing and interweaving remarks and narrations of his own. The book has every appearance of authenticity, and of course of credibility. No reasonable doubt can be critically entertained, of its being joined with the Jewish Canon about the period above named.

SECT. VI.   BOOKS ANONYMOUS.   157

The book of NEHEMIAH purports to be from one and the same person. The inscription presents us with the following title: "The words of Nehemiah, the son of Hachaliah." But the Heb. דברי may mean *matters, affairs,* or *concerns,* as it does in the title to the book of Chronicles. It may be regarded then as somewhat uncertain, so far as the inscription is concerned, whether this book is one of those whose names designate the author. Still, as all the narration, down to chap. vii. 5, employs the *first* person, so far it is plain that all comes from Nehemiah. Then follows the register of the names of those who came up with the first colony to Jerusalem; plainly a repetition for substance of that which we find in Ezra ii. Yet the *discrepancies* between these two registers, as to numbers in particular cases, is striking. Let the reader compare the following names and associated numbers in the two registers, viz. Arah, Pahath-Moab, Zattu, Bani (Binnui, Neh.), Bebai, Azgad, Adonikam, Bigvai, Adin, Hashum, Bezai, Jorah (Hariph), Bethlehem and Netophah, Bethel and Ai, Lod, &c., Senaah, Asaph, Shallum, &c., Delaiah, &c.,—in the whole, nineteen cases in this single register, in which the numbers are discrepant in the two copies of it. Yet in Ezra ii. 64 and Neh. vii. 66, the *sum* of the whole is said to be 42,360—a signal proof that the numbers in one or in both copies have, in this case as in many others, suffered as to accuracy by transcription. The sums of gold and silver given, on the occasion of colonizing, by the chiefs of the fathers, are stated very diversely in Ezra ii. 68, 69 and Nehemiah vii. 70—73. Some other and slighter discrepancies occur, in the insertion of *names* in the one, which are omitted in the other; and some still slighter in the mode of writing and pronouncing the names. The sequel (viii. 1—x. 39) seems plainly to be from another hand, and speaks of Nehemiah in the *third* person as Tirshatha or governor. The register of names, in chap. xi., of those who lived at Jerusalem; and in chap xii., of those priests who came up from the captivity with Zerubbabel; seems to me to be from one and the same hand; at all events, xii. 31, 38, 40, shows that the writer again is Nehemiah himself, who uses the *first* person. It may be, however, that the two registers, in xi. 1—xii. 26, are merely copied by him. Of the same tenor is chap. xiii., which gives an account, in the *first* person, of what Nehemiah did after his return a second time from Persia. His first journey to Jerusalem was in 446 B. C., when he had obtained liberty of absence for twelve years from Artaxerxes, in the twentieth year of his reign ; Neh. v. 14. In the thirty-second year of the same king (434 B. C.) Nehemiah returned to Persia, and in a few days obtained leave again to go to Jerusalem and preside there ; Neh. xiii. 6. During his absence there had been a great falling off among the Jews, as to the observance of the law ; and the book ends with a description of his efforts to produce a general reformation.

There is no difficulty in the way of supposing that all the matter of this book passed under the eye of Nehemiah, or was compiled by him, even if we admit that other compositions than his own are inserted. It amounts therefore to the same thing as his own composition, so far as the *credit* of the book is concerned. The history contained in the book closes with 434 B. C., or about that period, and it was therefore probably written as early as the book of Malachi, if not somewhat before it.

There is indeed one serious difficulty in the genealogy of the high priests, xii. 10, 11, 22, which is that (including Jeshua, who was of Zerubbabel's time, 536 B. C.) there are *six* generations registered. Excluding Jeshua, however, as we should do in this case, the remaining five generations must occupy a period of some 160 to 170 years, extending to some 376 or 366 years B. C., i. e. nearly to the time when Alexander the Great came upon the stage of action. The Jaddua of Neh. xii. 11, 22, is supposed by many to be the same high priest who went out to meet Alexander, on his approach to Jerusalem ; and in fact, the time is so near to that period, that one can hardly believe that it is a different person, inasmuch as it may easily be supposed that he lived at that period. But I could not set down the composition of the book in general to so late a period, any more than I should be disposed to regard the book of Genesis as of late composition, merely because of the late genealogy of the dukes of Edom in Gen. xxxvi. The tenor of the book, and the time down to which it brings the narration ; the fact that Nehemiah's own hand is visible in so much of it, and that there is nothing else besides the genealogy in question which betokens a later origin—all combine to persuade me, that the protracted genealogy of the high priests comes from a subsequent and marginal interpolation, or from something of the like kind, at a later period. Why should a later writer not have continued the history of Nehemiah down to the time of his death? It is against all probability, that he would not have done so.

One book remains, viz. that of ESTHER. Of this book De Wette, in his usual manner, says, "It violates all historical probability, and contains the most striking difficulties, and many errors in regard to Persian manners," § 198. *a*. One of the main difficulties is, that there are no certain *data* in the book, by which we can settle its chronology, or (in other words) that determine which of the Persian kings was called Ahasuerus by the writer. That he could not have lived *before* the time of Darius Hystaspes seems to be evident from the fact, that it was not until his reign that the Persian empire was extended from India to Ethiopia; to which the statement in Esther i. 1 alludes. That Darius himself was not the Persian king, who issued such an edict against the Jews as that described by this book, seems probable from his character as known in history, and from his very favourable regard for the Jews, as developed in Ezra v. 6; vi. 15.

The objections raised against the book are various, and some of them, as the text of it now stands, not easily disposed of. "(1.) Ahasuerus gives to all of his high officers a feast of *half a year*; how could they leave their provinces for so long a time? (2.) His command to Vashti, the queen, to appear unveiled before the whole company, at a drinking bout, is incredible. (3.) That Esther is of Jewish descent seems entirely unknown to Ahasuerus, until after the time when Haman's bloody decree was sanctioned; and still Mordecai is represented as a daily attendant at the court, in order to carry on some correspondence with Esther. (4.) Haman himself is a *foreigner;* and such could not be prime ministers. (5.) Mordecai obstinately refuses all courteous respect for him. (6.) Haman designs to destroy a whole nation of some two millions of people, and this merely because of an affront from Mordecai. (7.) He offers the king

10,000 talents of silver to sign the decree, which is equal to about 17,650,000 dollars; a thing incredible," &c.

I cannot enter into any discussion here of these and the like objections to the book; most of which Eichhorn (§ 509, seq.) has satisfactorily answered. In the sequel this subject will receive more attention. I merely observe here that there are two or three circumstances related by the book, which one finds it difficult to explain in a satisfactory manner. The decree of Haman for the destruction of the Jews was issued on the thirteenth day of the *first* month in the year, (Esth. iii. 12,) and this decree is not to be executed until the thirteenth day of the *twelfth* month; Esth. iii. 13. It would seem that Haman betook himself to the *lot*, in order to fix upon the proper day; Esth. iii. 7. The difficulty in this case is, to account for it that Haman should advertise the whole empire of the massacre, eleven months before it was to be perpetrated. "What could be the use," it is asked, "of putting the Jews on their guard so long beforehand? The Sicilian Vespers and the massacre of St. Bartholomew were not conducted thus; and Haman must have been as weak as he was wicked, to do this." One might suggest in answer to this, that Haman probably indulged the hope, that the Jews, through fear, would exile themselves from the kingdom. Perhaps this may be representing him as more humane than he was; but even a murderous tyrant must be supposed to be apprehensive of trouble, from destroying a whole nation that amounted to several millions of men, and above all, when he had given the intended victims nearly a year's notice of what he was about to do. If the decrees of the Persian monarch had not been irreversible, I should be quite disposed to believe that the whole measure, on the part of Haman, was designed mainly to terrify and vex the Jews. But the true solution seems plainly to be, that Haman having *cast lots* for a lucky day, could not change it when it was once fixed by the lot. Superstition did not permit a change.

The decree which Mordecai obtained from the king, amounted to merely a licence that the Jews should arm themselves on the massacre-day, and make defence against any assailants. It is said in the book before us, that when the day came, the higher officers of the king befriended the Jews (Esth. ix. 3); which is not improbable, considering that Mordecai was prime minister. According to the narration in Esther, the Jews, on that day, destroyed 500 men in the palace itself at Shushan, (Esth. ix. 6,) and 75,000 in the provinces; Esth. ix. 16. On the fourteenth day of Adar, (the twelfth month,) they also slew 300 more in the palace; Esth. ix. 18. Yet in all these rencounters, we have no information that a single Jew lost his life, or was even wounded. Could a massacre of 75,000 Persians take place, without any mutual slaughter? And would it be necessary for the Jews to destroy so many, when the people of the empire at large seem to have been so favourably disposed toward them, as the book represents them to be? It would seem, moreover, that "many of the people of the land became Jews," while Mordecai was prime minister or grand vizier (Esth. viii. 17); a circumstance, moreover, not at all improbable, considering the influence which Mordecai had at court. But that 75,000 Persians were slaughtered in this rencounter, after eleven months' warning and preparation of the parties, and none of the Jews destroyed, (the book does not assert the latter, but some have supposed it to be implied,) is one of those facts which can only with difficulty be admitted, unless some miraculous interposition on the part of heaven should prevent the harming of the Jews. But of this the writer has taken no notice.

Some other difficulties press upon the book. There is not even once the name of God to be found in it, or any special recognition of his holy providence in the whole affair. This is altogether the more singular, inasmuch as it has no parallel in any part of the Old Testament, unless in the book of Canticles. All the other sacred writings of the Jews represent God not only as the theoretical, but as the practical, Sovereign of the universe, dispensing both good and ill, prosperity and adversity. Not so apparently with the book of Esther. Even the days of Purim, set apart in commemoration of the deliverance of the Jews, as related in the book, are to be kept as "days of feasting and joy, and of sending portions one to another, and of gifts to the poor;" Esth. ix. 22. This narration, omitting as it does all reference to an overruling providence, shows how transformed as to his style of thinking and writing the writer had become, by living in a foreign country (for I take the author to be a foreign Jew). The fasting and weeping (ch. iv.) betoken, indeed, a sense of religious dependence; and in iv. 14 there is an evident allusion to the promises of preserving the Jewish nation, let the danger be what it might. But whatever the writer's reasons were for a uniform silence on the subject of religion and of Divine interposition, he has not given them to us. It is certainly with no small difficulty that we can make out reasons satisfactory to our own minds.

On the supposition that *Xerxes* was the Ahasuerus named in the book of Esther, there is still further difficulty. That the same Xerxes, who scourged the sea for carrying away his bridge over the Hellespont; who ordered the heads of the builders of the bridge to be cut off, because their structure could not resist the irresistible tide and storm in the straits there; who slew the eldest son of his friend and generous benefactor, Pythias, before his eyes, because he asked for his release from the army of Xerxes in which he had five sons; who suspended the headless body of Leonidas on a cross, because that with a mere handful of Grecians he had withstood many myriads of Persians; who offered by proclamation a great reward to any one who would invent a new pleasure;—that such a man should sanction such a decree as that of Haman, is to be sure not very strange. But if, with the great mass of modern and recent critics, we admit Ahasuerus to have been Xerxes, what shall we do with Esth. ii. 5—7, which tells us that Mordecai was carried away captive from Judea with Jehoiachin, in 599 B. C., and that Esther was his cousin? Now Xerxes did not begin his reign until 485 B. C., and the third year of that reign, when Vashti the queen was rejected, must bring Mordecai to the age of 117, even if his exile took place in his infancy. His cousin Esther, moreover, must at this time have been nearly a century old; while the book of Esther represents her as a *young* maiden. How then can we admit, with Scaliger, Drusius, Carpzov, Eichhorn, Jahn, Bertholdt, Gesenius, Hävernick, Baumgarten, and others, that *Xerxes* is the Ahasuerus of the book of Esther? If we go back to Cambyses, and even to Cyrus, we shall, after all, still find Mordecai to be some seventy to sixty years old—an age hardly congruous with the part which he acts in the book before us. If we go still further back, we must seek for Ahasuerus among the separate kings of Media or of Persia. But we are forbidden to go back, for then we could find neither the 127 provinces of the empire, (Esth. i. 1,) nor were the Jews under the dominion of any Persian or Median king before the time of Cyrus.

All these difficulties, however, are the result of interpreting the text in Esth. ii. 5—7, in such a way as seems, at first view, to be the most natural and facile. The Hebrew runs thus: "There was a Jew in Shushan the palace, and his name was Mordecai, the son of Jair, the son of Shimei, the son of Kish, a Benjamite, who was carried captive from Jerusalem with the company of captives who were carried into exile with Jechoniah king of Judah, who was carried away captive by Nebuchadnezzar king of Babylon. And he brought up Hadassah, (the same is Esther,) who was the daughter of his uncle," &c. The question which we may naturally raise, is, whether *Mordecai* is asserted by this text to be among the exiles that accompanied Jechoniah, (599 B. C.,) or whether this exile is affirmed of *Kish the Benjamite*. The interpretation which adopts the former meaning, is perhaps the most facile and natural, in case there is no obstacle in the way; but plainly it is not a necessary one. The *who* (אשר) at the beginning of ver. 6, may refer to the noun immediately antecedent, (Kish,) and then we are at liberty to place the period of Mordecai just where the genealogy demands. The time, reckoned from the exile of Jechoniah in 599 B. C. to the seventh year of Xerxes, is about 120 years; and this would correspond right well with the *four* generations mentioned in Esth. ii. 5. Why then are we not at liberty to adopt this exegesis? I would not do so merely in order to avoid a difficulty; for we cannot satisfy our own minds in that way. But the Hebrew is fairly open to either construction; and when the question comes up: Which shall we prefer? what hinders our adopting that which best agrees with the time and circumstances presented in the book? Even if the book of Esther be suppositious, it is still a book belonging to the period that soon followed the return from exile, and its anonymous author can scarcely be supposed to have made Mordecai and Esther contemporary with Jechoniah's exile, and at the same time with the seventh year of Xerxes' reign, or indeed with the reign of any Persian prince from the time that Cyrus began to be sole regent of Middle Asia. The parachronism is too palpable to be attributed to any one, who could write as the author of the book of Esther has done.

Some of the most serious difficulties, then, are removed by the interpretation which I have now suggested. In respect to the *early* publication of Haman's decree, commanding the excision of the Jews, I have already made some suggestions. And as to the *passiveness* of the Persians when the day of slaughter arrives, and the *numbers* said to be slain by the Jews, while they apparently remained unhurt; there may be facts, unknown to us, which would render these matters altogether credible. Clearly there is nothing impossible in the case. But it is better to confess our ignorance, than merely to guess at a ground of explanation, and then proffer it as something substantial.

The reader will perceive that I have dwelt much longer upon the books of Chronicles and that of Esther, than on the other books of the Old Testament. I have done so because I deemed it to be necessary. Few readers investigate difficulties of such a nature as these books bring to view; and when they are brought forward by those who doubt or deny the claims of the Old Testament to authenticity and genuineness, most readers feel astounded by them. In presenting these and the like matters to the reader, I hope to satisfy his mind, that my object is not to carry a point *per fas aut nefas*. Truth needs no pious fraud to support and commend it. If the Bible is indeed *the word of God*, it certainly does not shun investigation, but demands it. The example of the noble Bereans, who searched the Scriptures daily in order to ascertain whether what an apostle had preached was true or not, is one which is commended in the word of God, and worthy to be commended to all who reverence his word. Much as my own mind has been sometimes rendered anxious by critical doubts and difficulties thrust upon it, yet I have never for a moment deemed it best to conceal these difficulties, or to look away from them merely to get rid of the trouble of studying and examining. On the same ground I do not think it expedient merely to glance at difficulties, sufficiently to show that one is not altogether ignorant of them, and then to dispose of them by a general condemnation of every thing which approaches minute or doubting inquiry. It may be dexterous management in a pleader before a court and jury, to conceal the weak parts of his cause, and to keep out of sight whatever can be said against his client's interest; but how long will the same jury continue to confide in such a pleader's declarations, or in his management of causes, if he is wont to do this ? If we, who profess to believe in the Divine authority of the Old Test. Scriptures, decline to examine and consider the difficulties which attend a minute and critical inquiry into their condition and contents, how can we expect to convince those who differ from us and reject them ? I do not indeed think it to be the dictate of prudence and sound judgment to anticipate the time and circumstances in which we live, and publish to the world doubts and difficulties that have not yet come before the minds of the community who surround us. But when they do come, it is not sound policy to aim at winking them out of sight, nor to treat them as altogether unworthy of notice, especially when they are apparently founded upon what the sacred text itself seems to disclose. But doubts and difficulties have already been published to our religious community, by the works of De Wette and of Mr. Norton; and no silence on our part will help this matter. I accede, in my own judgment, to what the celebrated Dr. Bellamy of Connecticut used to say to his theological students, in his parting Lecture, "Gentlemen, on the subject of *polemics* I have one piece of advice to give you; and this is, that you should never raise Satan unless you can lay him." But in the present case, I have not raised him; that has been the work of others. Whether I can lay him, is indeed a serious question, and one which it is not for me to decide.

But to return to our subject; that the book of Esther relates a story which is *substantially true*, there is no good reason to doubt. The feast of Purim, celebrated as a memorial of the deliverance of the Hebrews from massacre, has confessedly been celebrated among the Jews ever since the times of the Persian monarchy. Now this is the same evidence that some signal deliverance took place, as our celebration of the fourth of July is evidence, that our independence as a nation was proclaimed on that day. The great numbers of Jews in Persia, in the time of Xerxes; the hatred which foreigners have nearly always borne towards them, on the ground of their peculiar observances; and the envy and jealousy that would exist among the Persian nobility, when any of them were promoted or treated with special favour—are all circumstances which serve to show the possibility, not to say the probability, of the things related in the book of Esther. There can be no good ground for doubt, that *the book has truth for its basis.* But the number of Persians slain by the Jews, and the amount of money promised to the king by Haman, wears an appearance like to that which sometimes belongs to numbers in the books of Chronicles. Yet so far as the *amount of money* is concerned, it is not very difficult to believe that Haman may have promised so much to the king, on the ground that he had liberty to appropriate all the property of the Jews, when slain, to his own use; Esth. iii. 11. Nor is the *amount* so strange a thing. The prime minister of the late emperor of China is said to have amassed more than £25,000,000 sterling, in jewels, money, and costly furniture and array.

For myself, if I may be allowed to speak in my own behalf on this occasion, I confess that the faith which once has come to admit miraculous events, in earlier and in later times, is not seriously staggered by the extraordinary or even apparently improbable events related in the book of Esther. To any one who has become well acquainted with the history of Persian tyrants, it will be no matter of surprise, that an intoxicated Xerxes should order his queen to appear unveiled before a banqueting company, nor that he should, in a like condition, stimulated by favouritism and the love of gain, have signed the decree of Haman. The surprise which Ahasuerus manifests, when told by Esther of this decree, (Esth. vii. 1—6,) wears very much the air of his having signed it in a state when he was unconscious of what he did. Whoever has read the history of the late Mohammed Aga Khan, Shah of Persia, will readily see, that Persian tyrants who could sign such a decree are no impossibility.

The most serious difficulty to a mind which is religiously disposed, is the omission, throughout the book of Esther, of all mention of God or of his providence. And yet it seems to be plain from iv. 14, that Mordecai is acquainted with and fully believes in the special promises made in the Old Test. Scriptures to the Jewish nation. Nor is there room for reasonable doubt, that the writer of the book means to present the Jews in the light of a people specially favoured and protected by Heaven. But he has confined himself to mere simple narration of facts, and does not undertake to be argumentative or parænetic.

So far as the æsthetics of the book are concerned, it has no small claim to merit. There is no narration so long, in any part of the Old Testament, which preserves a unity so compact and unbroken. There is no bombast, no affected pomp of diction. All must admit, that the writer has told his story with much skill, and made it such as to excite a deep interest in the reader. The impression made by the whole is, that the Jews, even in their exile, were under the guardian care of Heaven, and that in the most adverse and threatening circumstances, they had abundant reason to trust in God. Such an impression, moreover, stood intimately connected with the Jewish religion.

There are, however, some circumstances brought to view in the book, which at first sight appear somewhat revolting to the feelings of those who live under the light of the gospel; e. g. Esther's being brought, consentingly as it would seem, into the royal harem, (ii. 8, seq.,) and her vengeance in hanging Haman's ten dead sons upon the gallows erected for Mordecai (ix. 15). But are not these easily accounted for, by the state of manners and the low degree of civilization in Persia? We indeed, with our feelings and views, cannot praise, nor even approve of, any thing like to either of these transactions; but we can see, if we read the ancient work before us in the spirit of antiquity, that queen Esther did nothing which she believed to be wrong, or judged to be inconsistent with justice or decorum. The book, moreover, does not commend such things as those in question; it simply relates them. In Persia, the king has a sovereign right to any woman in his kingdom; and in theory, even the sacredness of the harem cannot guard it from his entrance.

Of the importance of the book of Esther, and also of some others in the Old Testament, to us at the present time, I intend to say something hereafter. But for the present, we must dismiss the critical history of particular books, in order to turn our attention to other circumstances important to the accomplishment of the main object in view.

Sect. VII. *Lost books of the Hebrews, some of which appear to have been canonical.*

According to the views which have been taken of the composition of the canonical books of the Old Testament, they were all in existence as early as 400 years before the Christian era. But the question *when the Jewish Canon was actually completed*, has become, in recent criticism, a question of great importance, and therefore it must receive a separate and distinct investigation. I must solicit the reader's attention, for the present, however, to some things necessary in order to render more complete our view of the ancient Hebrew literature, whether sacred or common.

The point cannot be decided with certainty as to several of the books alluded to or quoted in the Old Testament, whether they were considered as sacred or not. Some, e. g. the *works of prophets*, it seems to be quite plain, were regarded as sacred and authoritative. Others again, e. g. Solomon's works on botany and zoology, and his one thousand and five songs, (1 Kings iv. 32, 33,) we are not bound to regard as sacred. But there is a third class, the character of which, as we shall soon see, is somewhat doubtful. My design is, briefly to mention the works to which the Old Testament refers, and this in the order in which they occur to the reader of our English Version.

(1.) In Num. xxi. 14, the writer appeals, for confirmation of his narrative, to *the Book of the Wars of the Lord*. The title itself seems to import, that the book was of a religious cast, and it is not unlikely that it was regarded as sacred in the time of Moses. Still, a reference might be made to it in the manner of the Pentateuch, without rendering the point of its sacredness certain. It is clear, that it was regarded as a book of grave authority.

SECT. VII.   LOST BOOKS OF THE HEBREWS.   169

(2.) *The Book of Jasher,* i. e. of the upright, seems to have been a book of poetical eulogies, written respecting distinguished men, actors in distinguished events. The writer of Josh. x. 12, 13, appeals to it as confirming his narration in respect to the standing still of the sun and moon, at the command of Joshua. Again, it is appealed to in 2 Sam. i. 18, as exhibiting evidence respecting David's lamentations over Saul and Jonathan. The credit of the book must of course have been good; for otherwise the sacred writers had no inducement to appeal to it. But whether the book was sacred or canonical at that time, is not decided satisfactorily by these appeals.

(3.) When Samuel had anointed Saul as king, it is said that "he wrote the manner of the kingdom in a book, and laid it up before the Lord," 1 Sam. x. 25. Undoubtedly this was authoritative; but of the book itself we have no further notice or knowledge. It has been called, *The Book of the Constitution of the Kingdom;* but no name is given to it in Scripture.

(4.) Solomon's three thousand Proverbs, his thousand and five songs, and his works on natural history, (2 Kings iv. 32, 33,) may have in part been sacred. E. g. the present book of Proverbs may not improbably contain some of the 3000 which he spoke. Possibly some of the songs may have been *sacred* ones; but if they were, we should naturally suppose that some of them would have been preserved, with his name attached to them. I suppose no one will contend, that Solomon's works on *natural history* belonged to the Canon. If the Canticles could be shown to be a work of Solomon, with any good degree of probability, they might be regarded, perhaps, as a part of his Songs. That no more of his poems (if any) have been preserved, may not improbably be the result of that distinction, which the Jews early made between books of a sacred nature and those on other topics. Yet all-destroying time has taken from us not a few books once undoubtedly regarded as sacred.

(5.) The book of *the Acts of Solomon* appears to have been a copious history of his reign and achievements; to which reference is made by the sacred writer in 1 Kings xi. 41, as a standard and authentic work on this subject.

(6.) *The book of the Chronicles of the Kings of Israel* is

appealed to in 1 Kings xiv. 19 ; xvi. 5, 20, 27 ; xxii. 39, as containing copious accounts of five several Israelitish kings, in distinction from those of Judah.

(7.) *The book of the Chronicles of the Kings of Judah* is indicated, in 1 Kings xv. 7, as a more copious source of the history of Abijam, a king of Judah.

(8.) The acts of David, first and last, are said in 1 Chron. xxix. 29, to be written in *the Book of Samuel the seer*, in the *Book of Nathan the prophet*, and in the *Book of Gad the seer*. Such a king as David would naturally have many biographers. In this case, three contemporary prophets, it seems, wrote an account of this extraordinary ruler. Possibly our present book of Samuel may be one of these, or a combination of more than one.

(9.) A copious life of Solomon was also written by Nathan the prophet, and Ahijah the Shilonite, and Iddo the seer. The two last books are entitled, respectively, *prophecy* and *visions ;* 2 Chron. ix. 29.

(10.) The acts of Rehoboam were also written by Shemaiah the prophet, and by Iddo the seer in a work concerning genealogies ; 2 Chron. xii. 15.

(11.) A copious *Life of Uzziah* was written by Isaiah the son of Amoz ; 2 Chron. xxvi. 22.

(12.) *The Book of the Kings of Israel and Judah*, appealed to in 2 Chron. xxviii. 26 ; xxxv. 27 ; xxxvi. 8, may possibly be our present book of Kings. Yet I do not think this to be certain.

(13.) *The Book of Jehu* the son of Hanani (see 1 Kings xvi. 1, 7) contained the history of Jehoshaphat ; 2 Chron. xx. 34.

(14.) A special *Life of Hezekiah*, written by Isaiah the prophet, is mentioned in 2 Chron. xxxiii. 32 ; which is perhaps that portion of our present Isaiah contained in chap. xxxvi.—xxxix. Also the *Book of the Kings of Israel and Judah* is mentioned ; which may be our present book of Kings.

(15.) The biography of Manasseh, that wicked king of Judah, is said, in 2 Chron. xxxiii. 18, to be written in the *Book of the Kings of Israel*. The דברי הוזי in the same passage may mean, and probably does mean, *the words of Hozai*, (a prophet,) who spake to Manasseh in the name of

SECT. VII.   LOST BOOKS OF THE HEBREWS.   171

the Lord. What he said is also recorded in the same book of Kings. Mr. Parker (I. p. 411) represents these *words of Hozai* as being of themselves a book.

(16.) The *Lamentations of Jeremiah* over Josiah's untimely death, 2 Chron. xxxv. 25, seems plainly to be a different book from that which we now have under the like title, and which says nothing of Josiah.

Besides these, mention is made of a book in Ex. xvii. 14; xxiv. 7; in either case it is probably one of the compositions of Moses, which are now embodied in the Pentateuch, to which reference is made. In Isa. xxxiv. 16, the *Book of the Lord* seems most naturally to mean, the Scriptures then extant, and which reveals the certainty that what God had promised he would perform. As to the passages in Isa. xxix. 11; 1 Chron. iv. 22, no particular book is meant, but a book in a genuine sense. In the last case, perhaps, no book at all is meant, for דברים עתיקים may, and probably does, mean *ancient matters*.

From this brief sketch of ancient Hebrew writings, no longer extant, it appears that many books containing more ample histories of all the leading kings of Judah and Israel, and more ample biographies of their distinguished men, have perished. It is in vain to argue against this; as Hottinger (Thes. Philol. p. 534, seq.) does, and many other strenuous Protestants have done. Hottinger assumes the position, that God in his providence would not permit a *canonical book* to be lost; and that the church, the faithful depositary of the Divine records, cannot possibly have been so deficient in its duty, as to suffer the loss to take place. But what has become of Paul's (really *first*) epistle which he wrote to the Corinthians, and to which he appeals in 1 Cor. v. 9? What has become of John's letter to the church with which Diotrephes was connected? 3 John 9. I know of no *a priori* reasoning, on such a question, that can satisfy us. The loss of a writing is a possible thing; in a long series of exile and misfortune even a probable thing; and at all events the question concerning it is one merely of *fact*. As such, in the present case, it is easily decided. Are the books above named now extant? If they are, nothing is known of them, either among Jews or Christians. It will not do to say, as Hottinger and others have said, that the very fact of the *loss* proves that the books in question were never a part of the Jewish Canon. As to the technical sense of the word *canon*, it was introduced only after the Christian era had advanced a considerable period. But the main thing aimed at by employing this word, can, as it seems to me, be well predicated of many, yea of most, of the lost books in question. What were these books? Prophecies, or prophetico-historical works, the *religious* annals of the Jewish nation, both as to historical and biographical matters. Plainly the writers, as a body, were of the order of the prophets. And were not books written by Nathan the prophet, and Gad the prophet, and Iddo the seer, and Isaiah the prophet, and by others of the same office, counted *sacred* by the Hebrews? We can hardly imagine the contrary. But if any one should hesitate to acknowledge this, on the ground that prophets might write other books than those which were inspired, still the *manner of appeal to the works in question which are now lost, both in Kings and Chronicles, shows beyond all reasonable doubt that they were regarded as authoritative and sacred.* For how could a writer remit his readers for fuller authentic information, to those books which he did not regard as standing on the same basis as his own work, in respect to being worthy of credit? Had we now those fuller narratives which are so frequently appealed to in the present books of Kings and Chronicles, who can well doubt that many a seeming difficulty, in these abridgments of Jewish history, would be solved to our entire satisfaction?

I have called these last-named works *abridgments*. In truth all the historical books of the Hebrews that we possess wear the appearance of abridgments, if we except perhaps the books of Samuel, Ruth, and Esther. It is impossible to read, with a critical eye, the historical books of the Old Testament, without being struck with the palpable difference between them and the leading historical works of the Greeks, Romans, and modern nations of Europe. As to *chronology*, there is no general era to which all events are referred, in order to mark the time when they took place. The *localities* are every where supposed to be within the knowledge of the reader, with the exception that sometimes the older and the more recent names of places are both

SECT. VII.   LOST BOOKS OF THE HEBREWS.   173

given. Then as to general plan, the exhaustive or all-comprehensive method of modern history is a total stranger to the Scriptures. It plainly is not the design of the sacred writers to chronicle civil events because they are civil events, and relate to the civil and social state of the Hebrew nation, but because they are events connected with the theocracy, and are more or less connected with the religious developments of that nation. The book of Chronicles, so much decried of late, has above all others this aspect; which perhaps is one of the reasons why so much critical displeasure has been shown toward it. Were it not that the name would sound as a novel thing, and be considered by some perhaps as a little derogatory to the sacred histories, we might name nearly all of them *Anecdota Sacra*, i. e. brief sketches of historical events, which have a connexion with sacred things. This is their character throughout; with perhaps the few exceptions already named. The tribunal of modern historical criticism would doubtless have many a fault to find with them, in respect to historical æsthetics. But this tribunal is one that has been erected by science, and rhetoric, and the strict method which a logical connexion demands. The Hebrew compositions cannot fairly be tried by this. The Hebrews never had schools of science, of rhetoric, or of philosophy. To the technical demands of these they do not respond. All their compositions have a higher end in view, than that of answering the demands of science or philosophy. The all-pervading element in them is that of religion and morality. To be eloquent, to be attractive, to be graceful or amusing in narration, seem never to have been objects distinctly before the minds of the Hebrew writers. To record what concerned the worship of God, the religious state of his people, their chastisements and their blessings, and not unfrequently what concerned distinguished individuals among them; to say or to sing what would make the people wiser and better—these are the objects always before the minds of these peculiar writers. They have followed no models of writing among other nations. All that they have produced is of spontaneous growth. But is it not a vigorous one? Has it not borne much wholesome fruit? Has science, philosophy, rhetoric, the art of criticism —all scientific means and cultivation united—produced compositions of more power, and of higher perfection in their kind, than those of the Hebrews? I know of none. I know of no narrations that surpass in interest some of the scriptural ones; no epics that make a deeper impression than the book of Job and the Apocalypse; no lyrics that exceed those of David and the sons of Korah; no preaching, no moral painting, more elevated, graphic, sublime, soul-stirring, than that which can be found in the prophets.

In passing such a judgment on these books, I do not and would not summon them before the tribunal of occidental criticism. Asia is one world, Europe and America another. Let an Asiatic be tried before his own tribunal. To pass just sentence upon him we must enter into his feelings, views, methods of reasoning and thinking, and place ourselves in the midst of the circumstances which surrounded him. Then we must summon the books of the Hebrews before us; and if, on a fair trial, they are not found to exceed, in the sterling qualities of good writing, those produced by any other nation, I can only say that my partiality for them has misled me.

In the mean time, this matter proffers to the mind of a reflecting person some considerations of serious moment. How came a people, who never had schools of art, science, rhetoric, or philosophy, to write in such a manner, and to attain to such excellence? This is a problem for the Naturalists or Rationalists, who doubt or deny all inspiration; a problem which they have not hitherto satisfactorily solved; one which we may, without any great degree of presumption, believe they will not be able to solve.

But to resume our present theme; it is not difficult to account for the *abridged* histories of the Hebrews being preserved, while the more copious ones, which have been brought to view above, have perished. During the long exile of the Jews in Babylonia, they must have been in circumstances very unfavourable to the cultivation of letters, or to the preservation of their former literature, either sacred or common. Manuscripts were costly; the men who could copy them, in their state of slavery, must have been few. Under such circumstances, the books already written, being extant in only a few copies, and these written upon perishable material, and especially the more copious and therefore

SECT. VII.   LOST BOOKS OF THE HEBREWS.   175

the more costly books, might easily be lost. More particularly may we suppose this to have been the case, after the abridged works of Kings and Chronicles were compiled. It strikes me that both of these works were mainly compiled during the exile, for the very purpose of preserving, in a brief and compact form, the *memorabilia* of the Jewish history. Such abridgments could be copied, and purchased, at a much easier rate than the original and more ample works to which they continually refer. The very fact that references to ampler sources are so frequent, shows the honest and *bona fide* design of the compilers. They were not satisfied themselves that they composed a faithful narration, but they were willing that others should go to the originals and see for themselves whether such was the case.

If any one is disquieted still with the idea that many of the original and more copious sacred books have been lost, he would perhaps do well to ask the question, "How *large* would the Scriptures now be, if all the sacred books had been preserved? The apostle John, in apologizing as it were for the briefness of his narrative, tells us that he has omitted many things which Jesus said and did, because the world would not contain (χωρῆσαι) the books that must be written, if all should be narrated. I do not understand χωρῆσαι here in the *physical* sense, i. e. *to afford place for, to afford physical room for*, but in the tropical sense, viz. that the times would not bear with such copiousness, and that therefore it would be inexpedient. So of the Jewish historical books. We possess abridgments of them—such as are worthy of credit. We have before us the main points of their history that stand connected with the development of religion and of moral character. We possess that portion of it which is adapted to make religious impressions. Curiosity would relish more; but religious exigency calls for no more. The more copious histories now lost, once had their day of usefulness. They were not written in vain, for the ancient people of God. But to make the Scriptures a volume portable, procurable for all, and one which may be read by all, may have been one design of an overruling providence in permitting so many of the more copious books to perish.

If this be still deemed improbable or impossible by any

one, we may ask him to explain *how* or *why* such errors in the book of Chronicles, and in the book of Ezra and Nehemiah, (e. g. in regard to the *numbers* in the register which they have respectively recorded, Ez. chap. ii., Neh. chap. vii.,) have been permitted to creep in and thus deform the sacred text. Why have heresies been permitted to come into the church? Why has the church general, and almost without exception, been suffered to wander far away from the simple and spiritual truths of the gospel, and to substitute rites and forms for penitence and faith? Would it not be easy to show by *a priori* reasoning, (at least as good as that employed to show that no sacred books can have been lost,) that errors in the sacred text or in the church cannot be deemed probable or even possible? Where, it may be asked, are the promises of God to his children, and to his church? What shall be said of his assurance that he will teach and guide them in the way of his testimonies, and make his church always a pillar and ground of the truth? These and the like questions are very obvious ones, and are much more easily asked than answered. The truth seems to be, that some, perhaps many, expect too much of a revelation made in ancient times. It must be absolutely perfect, in all respects, and, moreover, be immutably preserved. And although they have read in Paul's epistles that "the Law made nothing perfect," yet they seem not to recognise the truth of this in any one particular, save in respect to Levitical rites and ceremonies. It is my belief, that the gospel has a high preëminence above the Law; but also, that the Law was as really from God as the gospel. Why should not the Mosaic institution be viewed as being what it actually was, a mere *introductory* dispensation in respect to the gospel? As such it had its time and place, its means, its regulations, rites, laws, revelations—all adapted to accomplish the subordinate objects to which they had respect. Viewed in this light, the institutions of Moses will bear a thorough examination. The fair question in respect to any thing belonging to it always is, Is that thing adapted to answer the end proposed, in a dispensation which is merely prefatory or introductory to a higher and more perfect dispensation? The lost books of the Hebrews may have been subservient to the purpose for which they were composed;

they doubtless were. But if Heaven had judged them to be essential to the prosperity and well-being of Christianity, we may well suppose they would have been preserved. They were not judged to be necessary; at least, if events may explain the designs of Providence, this would seem to have been the case. There are even some parts of our Old Test. Canon, as it now is, which, if they had been lost, would not have changed the face of a single doctrine or duty of Christianity. Yet, while I readily accede to this view of our subject, I should be far from saying that any of the books which we have are useless. But on this part of the subject I hope to say something in the sequel, when our investigations shall have come to a close.

I do not pretend that there is nothing mysterious in the dispensations of Providence, which have permitted some of the sacred books to perish, and others to have been in some slight respects marred, in the course of transcription. I am well aware that a perpetual miracle in order to preserve the Scriptures has not unfrequently been assumed, and zealously maintained. But *facts* contradict this. It is of no use to close our eyes against these. We shall neither convince ourselves, nor any one else, by such a process. But if I reject the Scriptures as a revelation from God on this account, I must reject the church as a Divine institution on the like account. There is not a church on earth, there never has been one, in which some of its members did not entertain erroneous or imperfect views of some truth with which religion has a more intimate or more remote connexion. Yet after all this is conceded, it remains a truth, that there is, and always has been, a real and spiritual church on earth, a spiritual kingdom of God among men. There is nothing which is dependent on the agency and management of erring man, but what will sooner or later, in one way or another, receive some stain from the hands through which it passes, or be in some respect marred by human management. It has been so with Christianity itself. It has been and is so in respect to the rational and moral powers of man. The Bible, in the long and difficult and in some cases even perilous transition of it from one age to another, has come to bear some traces of having been subjected to a like, i. e. to human, care and management. But shall it be urged as a valid objection against the god-like nature of *reason*, that men abuse and pervert this faculty? Is there no evidence that conscience is heaven-born, because there are perverted consciences and seared consciences? And by virtue of a similar process of reasoning, we may also ask, Does it follow that the Bible, in its origin, is not a Divine book, an authoritative book, because, in transmitting some parts of its records for a period of more than 3000 years, and in transmitting all of it, even the latest books in the New Testament, for a period of some 1800 years, (most of this time, be it remembered, by mere chirography in MSS., before the art of printing was known,) some things of comparatively small moment have been disturbed, or by mistake in transcribers and redactors subjected to error? Not one doctrine is changed by all this; not one duty affected; not even the relation of any one historic event has been so disturbed, that the moral impression which it was designed to make is in any important degree subverted. There is surely nothing short of a perpetual miracle which could have prevented some mistakes. But is there any evidence of such a miracle? I know of no satisfactory evidence, to say the least. I am well aware that the time has been, when leading men in the Protestant church maintained the absolute *inviolability* of the Scriptures. The Buxtorfs, and men of that class, gigantic scholars too in their way, did not scruple to maintain, that not only all the Hebrew letters were the same in all the MSS. the world over, but that even the vowel-points and accents were, and always had been, identically the same from the time of Moses down to the then present hour. Investigation has dissipated this pleasant dream. In the Hebrew MSS. that have been examined, some 800,000 various readings actually occur, as to the Hebrew consonants. How many as to the vowel-points and accents, no man knows. And the like to this is true of the New Testament. But at the same time it is equally true, that all these taken together do not change or materially affect any important point of doctrine, precept, or even history. A great proportion, indeed the mass, of variations in Hebrew MSS., when minutely scanned, amount to nothing more than the difference in spelling a multitude of English words. What matters it as to the meaning, whether one writes *honour* or

SECT. VII. LOST BOOKS OF THE HEBREWS. 179

honor, whether he writes *centre* or *center*? And what matters it in Hebrew, whether one writes קל or קול, קיר or קר, ימלך or ימלוך? Indeed one may travel through the immense desert (so I can hardly help naming it) of Kennicott and De Rossi, and (if I may venture to speak in homely phrase) not find game enough to be worth the hunting. So completely is this chase given up by recent critics on the Hebrew Scriptures, that a reference to either of these famous collators of MSS., who once created a great sensation among philologers through all Europe and America, is rarely to be found. So true, cogent, and applicable to the case in hand is the old maxim of critical jurisprudence, *De minimis non curat lex*.

But still, the ground taken by most of the older Protestant writers, in regard to the *inviolability* of the sacred text, has been shown to be altogether untenable. *Facts* contradict their theory; and there is no arguing against facts.

Why, moreover, should the advocates of this antiquated view of the subject before us, (for there are not a few of them even at the present time, although they are rare among the more enlightened part of the religious community,)—why should they be so strenuous in regard to a thing which is not only disproved by fact, but altogether unnecessary to an enlightened belief in the Divine authority of the Scriptures, or to the well-grounded advocacy of this authority? I am ready to say, that their fears about concession here are vain; their hopes of convincing others, who examine critically into matters of this kind, are vain; and, I would add, the confident expectations of those who disclaim and oppose the Divine authority of the Scriptures, so far as objections of this nature are concerned, are also vain. We freely yield our assent to the allegation, that in our present copies of the Scriptures there are some discrepancies between different portions of them which no learning or ingenuity can reconcile. *Humanum est errare*. The Bible has passed through the hands of erring men for a series of ages; and even the most sacred waters, flowing through a channel that has some impurities in it, must contract some stain, or undergo some depreciation.

But what then? As I have said once and again, not a doctrine is changed, not a duty altered or obscured, not an important historical fact perverted. If so, we have no special interest in labouring with the Buxtorfs and others to establish views of the sacred text, which are contradicted by facts that lie upon the very face of the Scriptures. The honesty of their purpose, and even the warmth of piety which gave birth to it, I readily acknowledge and approve. But zeal without adequate knowledge does not always propose the best ends, nor choose the best means to accomplish those ends. In the case before us, we may confidently take the position, that their theory, or at any rate their mode of maintaining it, is destitute of solid support. On the other hand, when Mr. Norton, De Wette, or his translator, and a large portion of the German critics, assail the Scriptures, particularly the Old Testament, on the ground of discrepancies and contradictions, (and they habitually do this,) we need not say, in reply to them, that absolutely no discrepancies and no contradictions exist in our present scriptural text; but we may say truly, at least such is the view which I feel constrained to take of the subject, that these are so easily accounted for, they amount in the whole to so few, they are in fact of so little importance, that they make nothing of serious import against the claims which the matter, the manner, and the character of the Scriptures prefer as the stable ground of our belief and confidence and obedience. One thing is absolutely certain. There is not in the world—there never has been—any such book as the Bible. There is none which looks to ends so lofty, so worthy of our highest interest and regard. If the Bible be not true, the destiny of man still remains enveloped in more than Egyptian night.

SECT. VIII. *Manner of preserving the sacred Books.*

SINCE the art of printing was discovered in Europe, there has been little or no difficulty as to the preservation of valuable or interesting books. Copies being multiplied by thousands at a time, and this being repeated at intervals of time, such an occurrence as the absolute loss of a valuable book has hardly been possible. It is difficult for us who

SECT. VIII.   THE SACRED BOOKS.   181

live amidst the doings of the printing press, of Bible Societies, and Tract Societies, to make a correct estimate of the state of the ancient Hebrews in regard to the diffusion and preservation of written compositions.

Nothing is clearer, than that the art of writing, and even of reading, in the time of Moses, and indeed for centuries afterwards, was very limited among the Hebrews. The *Shoterim*, (שטרים,) however, a class of officers or magistrates among them, one must naturally suppose, were acquainted with the art of writing, and of course with reading; for the verb שטר, of which the above word is a regular participle, means, both in Hebrew and Arabic, to *write*. The literal translation of שטר is *scriba*, γραμματεύς, *scribe*. We find this class of men among the people in Egypt, Ex. v. 6—19, and in the desert, Num. xi. 16. We trace them down to the latest period of the Jewish commonwealth; see in 1 Chron. xxiii. 4; xxvi. 29; 2 Chron. xix. 11; xxxiv. 13. We are not, however, to understand that this class of men were mere copyists or chirographers, but magistrates, probably of different gradations, who kept written records of the things which they transacted. Besides these, the priests, at least some of them, and probably some of the Levites, were acquainted with reading and writing; for being the *jurisconsults* of the nation, one cannot well divine how intelligent men among them would think of discharging their duties well, without being able to read the Law of Moses.

There must be still less doubt as to the *prophets* among the Hebrews. They were the *preachers* of the Mosaic religion. The office which they performed was, as we have seen in the preceding pages, altogether analogous to that of ministers of the gospel. *Priests* neither preached nor prayed, i. e. as public teachers and in their official capacity; but they gave advice, when consulted, as to matters of law, of duty, and of conscience. Ministers of religion, in the sense of being its *public teachers* and *defenders*, they were not. Above all the men in the Jewish community, it behoved the prophets to be acquainted with the Mosaic Law, and, from time to time, with such other Scriptures as were added to it. The very essence of their official duty as preachers of righteousness, consisted in inculcating the doctrines which their sacred books and their holy men had taught.

Still, plain as all this seems to be, there is no very definite and certain evidence that priests and prophets themselves always, or even in general, were actually possessed of copies of the Mosaic Law ; and so, after the time of David and Solomon, in respect to other portions of Scripture written during their reigns. Had the Mosaic Law been obeyed by all the kings of Judah and Israel, each king must have written out a copy of the Law for himself ; for so Deut. xvii. 18 enjoins. That David, whose delight was "to meditate on the *Law* of the Lord by day and by night," complied with this requisition, there can be no room for rational doubt. Perhaps as little doubt can be entertained respecting Solomon, who, in the former part of his reign, was much devoted to study and to the promotion of the interests of religion. The like was doubtless done by other kings, who were distinguished for their piety and the spirit of obedience to the Law.

It will be recollected that from Moses to Samuel, (about 300 years,) we scarcely find mention of a prophet. Only one makes a momentary appearance in the book of Judges ; Judg. vi. 8, seq. Almost as little, also, seems to be said concerning *priests*, during the same period, as concerning prophets. But from the time of Samuel down to Malachi, there was a succession of *prophets* in all probability unbroken, and *priests* are not unfrequently brought to view. Were the Old Test. Scriptures in their hands ? Were the copies of the Law, and other Scriptures, as they arose, so multiplied that all who wished could have access to them ?

A question not devoid of interest ; but one which can scarcely be decided by any direct testimony within our reach. We can reason quite conclusively in respect to the subject, if we assume that all classes of the Hebrews, the Shoterim, the priests, the Levites, kings and other high officers of state, did their duty in regard to seeking the information requisite to discharge well and faithfully the functions of their office, under the Mosaic constitution. But it lies upon the very face of the Jewish history, that all of these classes of officers did not usually perform the duty of making themselves familiar with the Mosaic institutes, except as they gathered them from common and traditional report. The frequent lapses of the nation into idolatry, which are every where recorded, are satisfactory proof that the Hebrews were not well instructed in the Mosaic laws, and that oftentimes the magistrates who governed them must have been ignorant as well as themselves. It is impossible to suppose with any degree of probability, that the nation would have so often attached themselves to idol-worship, had the light of the then existing Scriptures been generally diffused among them. Moses did not make provision for schools, nor for early and efficient instruction in the Scriptures. Hence, when there were no prophets, (as seems to have been the case in the time of the Judges,) or afterwards when there were but few in comparison with the wants of the people, it is no wonder that the mass of the nation fell into a state of the grossest ignorance. The Mosaic provision for reading the Law only once in seven years to the whole population, (Deut. xxxi. 10—13,) could not possibly be efficient enough to prevent this. Besides, in times of general declension from the spirit of piety, and above all in times of devotedness to the worship of idols, it was a matter of course that this public reading should be neglected. The history of circumcision, of the passover, and of other public feasts, shows that such was the case in regard to these institutions. In times of idolatry, the people would not be duly summoned by the magistracy or the Levites to hear the Law; and if they were, they would not listen to the summons. The very fact that Moses provided for such a public reading and ordered it, shows that *he did not expect his written laws to be circulated in manuscript among the mass of the people.* In times of alienation from the worship of the true God, when the leaders of the people were themselves their misleaders, is it rational to suppose, that they would have subjected themselves to the trouble and very serious expense of procuring for themselves copies of the Pentateuch? Few indeed of the kings either of Judah or Israel (probably none of the latter) ever took pains to copy the Law; at least, the history of them gives us reason to believe that such was the case.

A few occasional notices of arrangements made by some of the pious kings of Judah, serve to show that the statements just made are in all probability correct. The pious Jehoshaphat, in the third year of his reign, sent out, as teaching missionaries among his people, some of the princes, Levites, and priests, and they went round among all the cities of Judah, and *carried the book of the law of the Lord with them;* 2 Chron. xvii. 7—9. Now clearly if these princes, Levites, and priests, had each a copy of the Law, which was their own property, and if this were a common thing among them, it never could have occurred to the historian to make mention of such a circumstance. In giving the history of missionaries now, does any one ever think of specifying the fact, that they carry a *Bible* with them in their journeys? If not, then does it seem altogether probable, that in the case before us, the missionaries were required to take the copy of the Law from the temple where it was deposited, in order that they might appeal to it in all their public instructions? Could other copies of the Law have been accessible among the Jews, at that time, when this copy in the temple was permitted to be taken? It seems, at least, to be very improbable. Who should have such copies, if not princes and Levites and priests who attended on the court, and who were sent on this mission?

In the great reformation under Hezekiah, we find an express recognition of celebrating a famous passover "according to the law of Moses" (2 Chron. xxx. 16); but there is nothing mentioned in this connexion which would cast light on the subject before us, excepting the fact, that many came to the passover unsanctified, and of course unprepared to celebrate it in a legal manner; 2 Chron. xxx. 17—20. Must not this have been in consequence of ignorance respecting the Mosaic law? It seems probable, at least; and the more so, inasmuch as Hezekiah admitted them to the passover, and prayed the Lord to forgive their sin of ignorance, which prayer was granted. A circumstance this, I may add, which is replete with instruction to those who place too much stress upon the rites and forms and externals of religion.

In Josiah's time, it seems nearly certain that the copies of the Law were reduced to *one;* at least that no more could be found or were accessible. The astonishment of the king and his court, yea, of the high priest Hilkiah himself, who found a copy in the temple, is such as to show, that none of these persons possessed a copy of their own; 2 Chron. xxxiv.

14, seq. We have already seen, that the fifty-seven years of idolatry under the reign of Manasseh and Amon had probably occasioned this dearth of copies; and also that the bitter and bloody persecution of that time was probably the cause why the copy had been hid which was found by Josiah. But be this as it may, it is clear enough that the supposition of a general circulation of the Scriptures in MSS. among the Hebrews before the exile, is out of all question. It seems to be almost equally clear, moreover, that kings, princes, priests, and Levites, did not ordinarily take any pains to possess themselves of a copy of the Scriptures. Individuals among all these classes there might be, and more probably still among the prophets, and some also even in private life, who did possess copies of the Law; I mean that such might be, and occasionally was, in all probability the case. But the perishable materials on which these copies were written, and the little interest that would be felt in them in times of deep and general declension from the spirit of true religion, sufficiently account for the speedy loss or destruction of most codices once (as we express it) in circulation.

That the fear of an entire and utter loss of the Pentateuch, after the occurrence already spoken of in the time of Josiah, would probably lead to a considerable multiplication of copies, there can be no good room to doubt. That the brief reigns of Jehoahaz, Jehoiakim, Jehoiachin, and Zedekiah, (only some twenty-two years in the whole,) before the exile, would destroy all, or even most, of these codices, cannot be deemed very probable. These kings did not persecute in such a furious manner as Manasseh had done. When the king of Babylon " burnt the house of God, and all the palaces thereof, and slew the young men with the sword in the house of the sanctuary," (2 Chron. xxxvi. 19, 17,) it is not probable that he destroyed the sacred books in the temple; for as the city of Jerusalem had sustained a siege of about two years' continuance, sufficient warning must have been given to priests and prophets to take care of those books.

The story in 2 Macc. ii. 1, seq., respecting the part which Jeremiah acted, when the temple was burnt, is very curious; and although mixed with a spicing of fable, in all probability has some truth for its basis. The substance of it is, that this prophet took some of the holy fire and the book of the Law, and committed them to the charge of some of the exiles, with strict injunction to keep them safely and never neglect them. At the same time, (which is the fabulous part of the story,) the prophet, moved by a special revelation, commanded the tabernacle and the ark of the covenant to follow him to Mount Sinai, where he hid them, with the altar of incense, in a cave, until the time of restoration and prosperity should return. The writer appeals to ἀπογραφαί and to γραφή as containing this account, verses 1, 4. He relates, moreover, what Nehemiah did in collecting sacred books for the renewed commonwealth of the Jews; but this belongs to a subsequent part of our subject. In respect to this whole matter, it seems altogether probable, that such a man as Jeremiah, himself a priest and having ready access to the temple, would preserve the sacred records deposited there, and secure them against destruction. However this may be, it is at least certain, that Zerubbabel and Jeshua arranged the ritual of Jewish worship according to the *Law of Moses*, when they came up with the first colony of the returning exiles; Ezra iii. 2. Afterwards, when it is related that Ezra came up with a second colony, (Ez. vii. 1, seq.,) he is spoken of as "a ready scribe in the Law of Moses, which the Lord God of Israel had given;" Ez. vii. 6. That the Law, therefore, and probably other scriptural books, were in the hands of the Jews, i. e. of the literary part of them, during the exile, seems quite certain. Private individuals doubtless possessed some copies; and surely such a man as Ezra must have had it in his power to be a diligent student of them, while he was yet in exile.

Let us advert, for a moment, to the account which is given in the Hebrew Scriptures themselves, of the preservation of at least some of the sacred books, as they came from the hands of their authors. In Deut. xvii. 18, Moses speaks of *a copy of this Law in a book*, to be made by each king with his own hand, and then speaks of that book as being *before the priests the Levites*, i. e. under their inspection or guardianship, and of course in the temple. In Deut. xxxi. 9, it is said that "Moses wrote this law, and delivered it unto the priests the sons of Levi," i. e. he committed it to them for safe keeping. In Deut. xxxi. 26, Moses is said to have commanded the priests who bore the ark of the covenant, to "take the book of the Law and put it in the side of the ark of the covenant," there to be kept as a permanent witness against the Israelites, in case they should break the covenant. It is not essential to our present purpose, whether the whole of the Pent., or of Deuteronomy, or only a portion of the latter, is here designated by the phrase ספר התורה הזה; although no one can give a satisfactory reason why one portion of Deuteronomy should be so preserved and not another. But still, the word ספר is employed to designate a writing which is complete in itself, whether longer or shorter, and it can hardly mean merely *extracts* from the Law, or a certain *small portion* of it. That there was a book in Moses' time, a record in which were written important laws, arrangements, and occurrences, and which was deposited by the ark, seems to be nearly certain from the manner in which it is so often adverted to ; e. g. Moses is commanded (Ex. xvii. 14) to write an account of the contest with Amalek בספר, *in the book,* (not in *a* book,) and of course in some noted or well-known book ; in Ex. xxiv. 7 it is said, that "he took *the book of the covenant* and read in the audience of the people," which doubtless means the laws in Ex. xx.—xxiv. ; in Deut. xxviii. 58, Moses speaks of the *words of this Law* written בספר הזה, lit. *in this here book* (which is the most exact translation that we can make of the phrase in English) ; and in Deut. xxviii. 61, he speaks of *the book of this Law ;* and in these two latter cases, what he says was in an address to the people. To be intelligible, he must have referred to a *well-known* book, probably to one which was held up before them while he was addressing them. This same book, called the *book of the Law* in Deut. xxxi. 26, was the one which Moses commanded the Levites, who bore the ark of the covenant, to take and put *by the side,* or *at the side,* or *on the side,* (מצד, מ being often used in Hebrew to denote proximate or dependent localities,) *of the ark of the covenant.* There is nothing inconsistent with the supposition that the book of the Law, i. e. the Pentateuch as a whole, was kept in that place, in the assertion made in 1 Kings viii. 9, and 2 Chron. v. 10, viz. that "there was nothing *in the ark* [when it was transferred to the sanctuary of the newly built temple] save the two tables of stone which Moses put there at Horeb." The Hebrew here is בארון, *in the ark*, which is quite a different phrase from the מצד ארון, *on the side of the ark*, in Deut. xxxi. 26 ; although De Wette in his Introduction has confounded them, and endeavoured to make some capital out of this circumstance for his purpose of *destructive* criticism. The Epistle to the Hebrews (ix. 4) speaks in the same way of only the tables of the covenant, i. e. the stone tablets on which the ten commandments were engraved, as being *in the ark* ; see Ex. xxxi. 18 ; xxxii. 15, 16 ; xxxiv. 1, 28 ; Deut. ix. 10, and particularly x. 1—5. Josephus repeats the same idea, Antiq. VIII. 4. 1, " The ark contained nothing else except the two tablets of stone, which preserved the ten commandments spoken by the Lord to Moses, and written upon them at Mount Sinai."

Traces of the fact that the Law of Moses was deposited in the sanctuary along with the ark of the covenant, for safe keeping, may be found in subsequent parts of the Old Testament. In Josh. xxiv. 26 it is said, that " he wrote *these words* [which most naturally means the two addresses that he made to the people near the close of his life, Josh. xxiii., xxiv.] in the book of the Law of God ; and he took a great stone and set it up there [as witness between him and the people] under an oak that was by the sanctuary of the Lord ;" in other words, he wrote down his solemn addresses and joined them to the Pentateuch or words of Moses kept in the sanctuary.

Again, in 1 Sam. x. 25 it is said, that this prophet " told the people the manner of the kingdom [of Saul], and wrote it בספר, *in the book ;*" which of course must mean a well-known book ; and what other one could this be than " the Law of the Lord," to which Joshua had annexed his admonitions ? The solemnity and importance of the occasion demanded such an authentication as would be made by this circumstance, and perpetuity, moreover, would thus be secured to the written constitution of the kingdom.

Of course we are prepared by occurrences like these, to expect what is related of the Pentateuch in the time of Josiah, viz. that it was found *in the temple ;* although in this case surely not in its usual place by the side of the ark. It had been withdrawn and hidden by some pious hand, to save it from the desolating fury of Manasseh.

Does not, moreover, the passage in Isa. xxxiv. 16 refer to the holy *bibliotheca* in the temple, surnamed *the book of the Lord?* After predicting various evils to Edom, the prophet says, "Seek ye out of *the book* (מעל ספר) *of the Lord*, and read; no one of these shall fail." That this expression does not refer to what the prophet had himself just uttered, Knobel has clearly shown in his Commentary on this book; although Rosenmueller and others have defended this mode of interpretation. Gesenius supposes him to advert to a *collection of sacred books*, with which his own was to be associated. That he refers to some prophecy or predictions in other and sacred books, seems to be quite certain from the tenor of the passage and the nature of the reasoning. But whether these books were a part of our present Canon or not, it would be more difficult to say. Still, the phrase *book of the Lord*, and the certainty of the writer that what was contained therein would take place, show that the book in question was a well-known and definite one, and one also of sacred authority. There was therefore, at the period when this was written, a collection of sacred writings; and the expression, *book of the Lord*, may refer either to the Divine origin of the book, or to the fact that it was kept where God was supposed to dwell, viz. in the inner sanctuary. It is quite possible, moreover, that the prophecy referred to may be virtually contained in the declarations of Isaac respecting Esau in Gen. xxvii. 37, seq., so that the Pentateuch itself is the book of the Lord to which reference is made.

That what was done in ancient times, in respect to the sacred books of the Hebrews, was done at a later period, after the second temple was built, seems to be manifest from various passages in Josephus. Speaking of Moses' bringing water from the rock, (Antiq. III. 1. 7,) he says, "That God had foretold this to Moses, δηλοῖ ἐν τῷ ἱερῷ ἀνακειμένη γραφή, the Scripture laid up in the temple shows." Speaking of the day being prolonged during the battle of Joshua with the five kings, (Antiq. V. 1. 17,) he says, "This is shown by the writings laid up in the temple, διὰ τῶν ἀνακειμένων ἐν τῷ ἱερῷ γραμμάτων." This last quotation shows, that the deposit of books in the temple was not confined to the Pentateuch, for it has reference to the book of Joshua.

Again, Josephus, in describing the triumphal procession of Vespasian and Titus at Rome, when the Jewish war had been completed, says, that the spoils of the temple were made conspicuous above all the other things carried in the procession, and that "last" [and consequently most eminent] "among these spoils was borne the *Law of the Jews*, ὁ τε νόμος ὁ τῶν Ἰουδαίων ἐπὶ τούτοις ἐφέρετο τῶν λαφύρων τελευταῖος," Bell. Jud. VII. 5. 5. Again (§ 7. ib.) he says, that Vespasian erected a temple to *Peace*, and there he deposited the furniture of the temple at Jerusalem, while "he commanded to keep laid up in the palace *their Law*, [viz. the Law of the Jews,] and the purple veil of the temple, τὸν δὲ νόμον αὐτῶν καὶ τὰ πορφυρᾶ τοῦ σηκοῦ καταπετάσματα προσέταξεν ἐν τοῖς βασιλείοις ἀποθεμένους φυλάττειν." I can scarcely doubt that in both of these cases the word νόμος (*law*) comprises, as it sometimes does in the usage of other writers of that period, the whole of the Jewish Scriptures recognised by Josephus as such. The Rabbinical use of תורה = νόμος in such a sense, is well known to all Hebrew scholars; see Buxt. Lex. Talmud. and Hottinger Thes. Philol. p. 94. If there be any doubt of this, it would seem to be dissipated by Josephi Vita, § 75, where he says, that Titus, at his request, "made him a present of the sacred books, βιβλίων ἱερῶν ἔλαβον χαρισαμένου Τίτου." It does not appear with certainty from the context, whether this copy of the Scriptures was one taken from the temple or not; but on the whole this is the impression made upon my mind by reading § 75 throughout. If I am not in an error, there was then, at that time, more than one copy of the sacred books laid up in the temple; for the copy given to Josephus and retained by him, must be different from that which was carried in procession by Vespasian and laid up in the temple of Peace.

It would seem to be a matter of course, that the Jewish high priest and Sanhedrim, who were the supreme judges of the nation in all matters pertaining to religion and morality, should have kept a copy of the sacred books near at hand, i. e. near to the place where they usually held their meetings; which was either in a part of the temple, or in the house of the high priest in its neighbourhood. If so, what place could be so appropriate for those books as the temple?

There is other evidence also, of an indirect nature, in regard to the keeping of the Scriptures, after the return of the Jews from exile. We have already seen (p. 81, seq. above) that *synagogues*, in which the Jewish Scriptures were read, in all probability originated soon after that return. In these it would seem, if we are to credit Jewish tradition, that only the Law of Moses or Pentateuch was at first read, and that this custom continued down to the time of Antiochus Epiphanes. That tyrant, in his persecution of the Jews, compelled them to destroy all the copies of the Law which could be found; in particular he commanded, that the public reading of the Law of Moses in the synagogue, on the sabbath, should be entirely abolished. The reading of the Law in the synagogues being thus prohibited on pain of death, the Jews chose an adequate number of selections or extracts from the *prophetical* books of the Scriptures, as substitutes for them, and thus continued their scriptural readings.

Such is the usual account given of the origin of the *Haphtaroth*, or prophetical lections, which are designated in the margin of all the better Hebrew Bibles. Van der Hooght has given a catalogue of them at the close of his edition of the Hebrew Bible; marked the corresponding *Parashoth* or sabbatical lections of the Pentateuch, for which the prophetical lections, as said above, were substituted; and finally pointed out at the same time the difference in the prophetical selections, in twelve cases, between the Jews of southern and those of middle and northern Europe. The tradition about the origin of these, as stated above, is vouched for and fully stated by Elias Levita, (Thisbi, ad h. vocem,) and admitted by the great mass of biblical critics; among whom are Eichhorn and Bertholdt. The latter makes defence of Elias. Still the story about the origin of the Haphtaroth is doubted by De Wette, (Einl. § 80,) for doubt falls in with his usual style of criticism; but it is also called in question by Vitringa, Vet. Synag. p. 1007, seq., and somewhat doubted by Carpzov, Crit. Sac. p. 148. The ground of doubt as to the origin of the Haphtaroth, is the lack of historical testimony. In 1 Macc. i. 56, 57, the writer, in recounting the persecuting measures of Antiochus Epiphanes, says that "he burned τὰ βιβλία τοῦ νόμου," and that "wherever βιβλίον διαθήκης was found with any one, or any showed pleasure in the Law, the judgment of the king [Antiochus] condemned him to death." Carpzov remarks on this, that the object of the tyrant was not merely to destroy the Pentateuch, or to stop the sabbatical readings in the synagogue, but to heathenize the Jews, and to prohibit all exercises of their religion; and of course he must have laboured to destroy the Prophets as well as the Law. Josephus, in his narration respecting Antiochus, says that "he destroyed all those with whom was found βίβλος ἱερὰ καὶ νόμος" (Antiq. XII. 5. 4); which seems to favour the view of Carpzov and Vitringa.*

But however or whatever the origin or the occasion of reading the Haphtaroth on the sabbath in the synagogue may have been, it matters not as to our present object. In the apostles' time the custom of reading them was usual, or rather, as we may well suppose, universal among the Jews. Thus in Acts xiii. 15, "after the reading of the *Law* and the *Prophets*," (a frequent designation of the Old Test. Scriptures in general,) the rulers of the synagogue asked Paul and his companions to address the assembly." In ver. 27 of the same chapter, it is said of the persecuting people of Jerusalem, that "they knew not the voices of the *Prophets which are read every sabbath day*." This puts the matter beyond a question as to the *prophetical* books being kept in the synagogues for use; and if they were there, they would of course be in the temple. But these passages do not settle the question, *how long* the prophets had been so read. Yet the apostle James, in Acts xv. 21, has decided that the custom of reading the Scriptures in this way, at least of reading the *Law*, was in his time quite an ancient one: "For Moses of old time hath in every city them that preach him, being read in the synagogues every sabbath day." That he names only Moses here, results merely, as I apprehend, from the nature of the appeal which he makes in the passage. The preceding passages which have just been quoted, (Acts xiii. 15, 27,) show the exact state of the

---

* I have already remarked, that this account of the origin of sections from the prophets given by Elias Levita, is now abandoned by the best biblical critics. D.

SECT. VIII.   THE SACRED BOOKS.   193

whole matter at that period. Now how long a period may be comprised under the ἐκ γενεῶν ἀρχαίων of James, it would be difficult to say with exactness. But that a period farther back than that of Antiochus (175—164 B. C.) is meant, seems to me altogether probable. I must therefore, with Vitringa and Carpzov, believe it probable that the religious zeal of the Jews, at or soon after the time of Ezra and Nehemiah, gave birth to the reading of both the Law and the Prophets in the synagogues.

This being conceded, or even so large a period as that which reaches back to the time of Antiochus being conceded, for the reading of the Prophets in all the synagogues, it will be seen at once what effectual provision had been made for the preservation of the Hebrew Scriptures, after the return from Babylon. Such an accident as occurred in regard to the Law of Moses in the time of Josiah, was no longer possible. In confirmation of the fact, that the Prophets were read in the synagogues, (James says, Acts xv. 21, *in every* πόλει=town or village,) we may appeal to Luke iv. 17—19. Jesus being in the synagogue at Nazareth is invited to read the Scriptures, and the volume of Isaiah is given him, which he opens at chap. lxi. and commences reading in it. The suggestion that he did this in an *extraordinary* manner, i. e. merely by virtue of his own peculiar authority, is favoured by nothing in the narration of Luke. On the contrary, he is requested to read; is directed where, i. e. in what book, he shall read; and no one expresses any offence at the manner, but at the *matter* of his discourse. I understand the evangelist as saying, that Jesus had been accustomed to read in the synagogue antecedently to this occasion: "he entered *according to his custom* into the synagogue on the day of the sabbath, and stood up to read;" where κατὰ τὸ εἰωθὸς αὐτῷ may naturally, and I doubt not that it does, qualify both clauses. If the action of reading had been an unusual one, would the volume of Isaiah have been given to him, and all in the synagogue have peaceably and attentively waited for his subsequent discourse?* It is

---

* It is very unlikely that the phrase *according to his custom* refers to more than the first clause, *he entered into the synagogue*. The volume would have been given to him though he had not been accustomed to read in the synagogue; for the reading was not then confined to any one. D.

O

true, indeed, that the portion of Isaiah which he read, (lxi. 1, 2,) is not at present included in the Haphtaroth; for one of them ends with the preceding chapter. But this is not an argument of any weight to show that the reading of the passage in question must be regarded as something singular or extraordinary; for as the Haphtaroth differ (this we have seen above) among the Jews of southern and of northern and middle Europe, so, in ancient times, Isa. lxi. 1, 2 may have been included in them.

It follows from all the preceding considerations, that the Law and the Prophets had been read on the sabbath day, in every town in Judea, for a long period, ἐκ γενεῶν ἀρχαίων; and of course, that there must have been some established Scriptures from which the selection for reading was made. The destruction or even material change of the Scriptures, after such a custom had commenced, was put out of all question. The destruction of one copy would only be the loss of one out of a great number; interpolations or alterations in one copy, would not affect the others which remained unmutilated. Indeed any one who has read the *Tractatus Sopherim* may well believe, that Jewish superstition, if nothing better, would have prevented any considerable change in the text of the Scriptures at this period.

It is unnecessary to dwell here on the inquiry, how much, or what portion, of the Scriptures were called *prophetic*. We have seen above, that the idea of a *prophet*, among the Hebrews, was not confined to those who predicted future events, but was extended to all who preached, wrote, or taught by Divine inspiration. Hence in the division of the Hebrew Scriptures, made we know not how long before the Christian era, the *historical* books, as well as those which we now call prophetic, were assigned to the prophets. Joshua, Judges, 1 and 2 Samuel, and 1 and 2 Kings are called נביאים ראשונים, *the first* or *early prophets*. This is a Talmudic arrangement. We shall see, in the sequel, that Josephus, and probably Philo and Jesus Sirachides, include the other historical books, viz. 1 and 2 Chronicles, Ezra, Nehemiah, Esther, Ruth, and probably Job, among the *prophets;* and these books, with the others now usually named *prophetic* among us, and by the Hebrews called *the later prophets*, were all comprised under the general appellation of *Prophets.* The Haphtaroth or prophetical lections extend, therefore, to the *historical books,* as well as to the books now called *prophetic* by us. And when it is said, (as it has often been of late,) that the Kethubim or Hagiography was a *late* collection, so late that no lections were made from it, the more ancient division of the sacred books is not only overlooked, but the fact that the book of Esther has always been publicly read in the synagogues, since the events which it commemorates took place, at the feast of Purim in the twelfth month, (which book is one of the *Hagiography,* according to the Talmudic division of the Scriptures,) is ignored or very conveniently forgotten. Whatever might have been the reason, on account of which the Talmudic Rabbins classed the last-named historical books with the Kethubim, it was not that they regarded them as uninspired. Nor was the *latest* composition the criterion of what belonged to the Hagiography, as classified by them; for most of the Psalms, the Proverbs, Ruth, Job, Ecclesiastes, and Canticles, (the two last with the Proverbs, according to them, from the pen of Solomon, the book of Ruth from that of Samuel, and most of the Psalms from that of David,) were regarded of course as being older than a number of the books among both the former and latter prophets, e. g. Kings, Haggai, Zechariah, and Malachi, and (I may add) Jeremiah, Lamentations, and Ezekiel.

According to the later Rabbinical division of the Scriptures, then, portions of all the three great divisions of the sacred books were publicly read in the synagogues, long before the Christian era. We can have no doubt, therefore, that each and every part of the Jewish Scriptures was deposited in the synagogues respectively, and of course in the temple.

As to the more ancient *Hagiography,* viz. Psalms, Proverbs, Ecclesiastes, and Canticles, (such we shall see is the classification of Josephus,) I will not undertake to say with certainty what was the reason that no lections for the synagogues were taken from them. But as there is a correspondence, real or supposed, between the lections from the Pentateuch and those from the Prophets, it would seem probable that those who selected these lections did not find a satisfactory correspondence in the books just named, and so they omitted to select from them; at least this may be regarded as probable in respect to Proverbs, Ecclesiastes, and Canticles. In regard to the Psalms, many correspondences as to matter might indeed be easily found; but it should be remembered, that the Psalms were very extensively employed in the public singing at the synagogue, and needed not to be read in the lections.

If tradition has any weight in this matter, it would seem to be quite plain and certain, that all three parts of the Jewish Scriptures were used, as the basis of selection, in the Jewish synagogues, long before the Christian era. This usage, we cannot reasonably doubt, originated not long after the complete arrangement of religious matters at Jerusalem, under Ezra and Nehemiah. The facility of perpetuating the Hebrew code in this way is very obvious. For more than 1800 years now past, it has been perpetuated in the synagogues, in the same way; and, moreover, by private copies. The custom of individuals having these in possession, so far back as the time of Antiochus Epiphanes, is clearly adverted to in 1 Macc. i. 57, "And whenever the book of the covenant was found with any one ($\pi a\rho\acute{a}$ $\tau\iota\nu\iota$) . . . the sentence of the king inflicted death upon him." The deplorable experience of former ages, as to turning away from the true God to the worship of idols, had taught the Jewish nation, that "to be without knowledge was not good for the soul." Ezra and Nehemiah appear to have entertained very enlightened views in regard to this subject. Hence the pains taken to read, circulate among the people, and inculcate the Scriptures, since the second establishment of the Jews in Palestine. Hence the departure from the ancient custom of remaining at home all day upon the sabbath, and the resort of worshippers and learners to the synagogue. And the consequence of all this was, that the Jews never have relapsed again into idolatry; a few renegades only excepted in the time of Antiochus, or when under the yoke of some other foreign tyrant.

To bring our present topic, viz. the preservation of the Scriptures, to a close; I cannot help remarking, that the wisdom of Providence seems to be conspicuous, in directing matters so that the Jewish Scriptures were laid up or deposited in the *temple*. There, constant guardians of them were always found, by day and by night. There, of course, the mutilation or interpolation of them would be a difficult, if not an impossible thing. Well has Abarbanel (on Deut. xxxi. 26) said, "God deposited there [in the sanctuary] the book of the Law, that it might remain as a testimony faithfully preserved, and that no one might vitiate or mar it [the Scriptures]; for no one could act thus basely toward writings which were surrounded by the family of priests." The absolute impossibility of corrupting the sacred books, indeed, need not be assumed, and could not well be maintained; for the priests, the keepers of them, were not all of them at all times good men and true. But the improbability that such a thing was done in a place so public and sacred, may well be maintained.

One other remark is naturally suggested by the topic before us. This is, that the introduction into such a place of books as sacred and as worthy of being kept there, must usually be a thing of more than ordinary deliberation and solemnity. I cannot well conceive, since the *prophets* were wont to be consulted on all the graver matters of church or state, that a book could have been placed there which was not sanctioned by their judgment. It matters not whether the writer of the book were professionally a prophet or not. There might be *occasional* inspiration, in some cases, where the subject of it was not, or at least had not been, a prophet. But if the advice of a prophet was in fact followed, in depositing any book as sacred in the temple, then that book has as much of the *authentic* in it, as the work of the prophet himself would have. That this was so, viz. that the authority of prophets was needed and resorted to, in order to give any book a claim to be considered as *scriptural*, would seem to be almost conclusively shown by the fact, that *when the succession of prophets failed, the reception of any more books into the Canon of the Old Testament ceased*. Indeed, I can hardly imagine a case, while the order of prophets continued, in which I should deem it probable that any effort could be made to add supposititious books, or parts of books, to the holy bibliotheca, without detection and exposure by some of the prophets, whose special duty it was in all things to watch over the interests and preserve the purity of the Mosaic religion.

If I were disposed to bring the usages of other countries, in respect to books that were deemed sacred or specially important, into comparison with that of the Hebrews, I might show the probability of the Hebrew usage from analogy, even if no special reference be had to the fact of their supposed inspiration. It is well known, that among the ancient Egyptians and Babylonians, the priesthood was the literary or learned class; and to them were confided the safe keeping of books regarded as holy or very valuable. Most of these were composed by persons belonging to the priesthood. It was a matter of course that such books, being their own productions, should be laid up in the temple where they ministered, for safe keeping, and also as a testimonial of honour to them. The Greeks called these literary priests of foreign countries, ἱερογραμματεῖς, i. e. *sacred scribes.* Among themselves, moreover, the Greeks had men of the like class, whom they named γραμματεῖς ἱεροί or ἱερομνήμονες; Æl. Hist. An. XI. 10. Aristot. Pol. VI. 8. Demosth. pro Cor. c. 27. Among the Romans, also, the most ancient literature, viz. songs and annals, was the production of priests; Niebuhr Röm. Geschichte, I. p. 247, ed. II. Bähr, Gesch. d. Rom. Lit., pp. 53, seq., 250, seq. It is no matter of surprise, then, that Strabo (Lib. XIV. p. 734, ed. Xyl.) calls temples πινακοθῆκαι, i. e. *tablet* or *book depositories.* In accordance with this is the account given of Sanchoniathon, the Phenician historian, who, about the time of the Trojan war, or perhaps earlier, compiled a work out of *temple-archives*—a work which was translated into Greek by Philo Biblius (c. A. D. 100,) in nine books, and then was quoted largely by Porphyry, and also by Eusebius (Præp. Evang. I. 9). Sanchoniathon himself quotes older writers; all of which, by the way, has a decisive bearing on the question about the antiquity of alphabetical writing. Berosus, in the time of Ptolemy Philadelphus, (c. 280 B. C.,) wrote, in three books, the Antiquities of Chaldea and Babylonia, the materials of which he drew from the archives of the temple of Belus, where he was a priest. The kings of Sparta, who were also *priests*, kept prophetic writings in the temple, which had respect to their country; Herod. VI. 57. At Athens, oracles, and secret compacts important to the welfare of the city, were kept in the Acropolis, in order to

SECT. IX.   GENERAL CONSIDERATIONS.   199

prevent all falsification ; Dinarch. Orat. cont. Demosth. 91. 20. Heraclitus deposited his Work upon Nature in the sanctuary of Diana at Ephesus, in order to withdraw it from the eyes of the profane ; Diog. Laert. IX. 6. So also the Romans kept their Libri Fulgurales in the temple of Apollo (Serv. ad Æn. VI. 72) ; their Libri Lintei, in the temple of Juno Moneta (Liv. IV. 8. IX. 18) ; the Sibyls, priestesses of Apollo, kept their Carmina in the Capitol ; Niebuhr, Röm. Geschichte, I. p. 256, seq.

A practice of this kind could hardly have become so general, without some obvious reasons for it. In all cases of this nature it is quite plain, that the sacredness of the place was relied on as likely to secure the inviolability of the books ; and the permanent structure of the building was also relied on, as affording good assurance of preservation. In the case of the Hebrews, many reasons combined to induce them to institute and keep up such a usage. The priests were the masters of the ritual, which was exceedingly minute and circumstantial ; and they were also the *jurisconsults* and *ecclesiastical judges* of the nation. The necessity of having the code of laws always at hand, would compel them to have *temple-archives*. That they did so admits of no reasonable doubt.

SECT. IX. *General Considerations respecting the Genuineness of the books in the Old Testament Canon.*

I HAVE now gone through with some account of the books comprised in the Canon of the Old Testament, in regard to their origin and authorship, and also in respect to the manner in which they were preserved in the early ages. It may not be improper to introduce, at this juncture, a few considerations of a general nature, in regard to the collection of books which we name the OLD TESTAMENT.

Whoever is acquainted with the works of the late J. G. Eichhorn of Göttingen, knows full well, that for some thirty years he was the sun of the neological firmament. Doubtless his writings, many of them being at the same time both popular and learned, did more than those of any other person of his time to bring forward and consummate the great revolution in theology and criticism, which has taken place in Germany and the bordering countries. Such a man no one will suspect of *orthodox* prejudice. All his feelings and his writings were alien enough from this. Still, on mere subjects of *critique* and of æsthetics, he was usually a candid and fair-minded man. At all events he rarely says any thing that is not worth listening to, and he may put in a just claim at least to a respectful attention.

In his Introduction to the Old Testament, (3rd edit. § 12, seq.,) he has given his views of the GENUINENESS of the sacred books in general; and he has expressed them in such a way, that I have thought it on the whole better to employ his words than my own, in reference to the topic under consideration. If I am suspected of being *juratus in verba magistri*, as doubtless I may be by some who do not know me, he at least is removed far enough from all possible suspicion of this sort. If the *Destructives* will not listen to my suggestions because, as they say, I *must talk orthodoxly*, at least they ought to listen to him, who claims so near a relationship to them.

Having described the general nature, names, and order of the Old Testament books, Eichhorn proceeds as follows:

I. *They do not arise from the forgery of any* ONE *individual*.

Whoever is endowed with adequate knowledge, and investigates with impartiality the question, *whether the writings of the Old Testament are* GENUINE, must surely answer it in the affirmative. No *one* deceiver can have forged them all—this every page of the Old Testament proclaims. What a variety in language and expression! Isaiah does not write like Moses; nor Jeremiah like Ezekiel; and between these and every one of the Minor Prophets a great gulf of style is fixed. The grammatical edifice of language in Moses has much that is peculiar; in the book of Judges occur provincialisms and barbarisms. Isaiah pours forth words already formed in a new shape; Jeremiah and Ezekiel are full of Chaldaisms. In a word, when one proceeds from writers who are to be assigned to early periods of time to those which are later, he finds in the language a gradual decline, until at last it sinks down into mere Chaldaic turns of expression.

Then come next the discrepancies in the circle of ideas and of images. The stringed instruments sound aloud when touched by Moses and Isaiah; soft is the tone when David handles them. Solomon's Muse shines forth in all the splendour of a most luxurious court; but her sister in simple attire wanders, with David, by the brooks and the river banks, in the fields and among the herds. One poet is original, like Isaiah, Joel, Habakkuk; another copies, like Ezekiel. One roams in the untrodden path of genius; another glides along the way which his predecessors have trodden. From one issue rays of learning; whilst his neighbour has not been caught by one spark of literature. In the oldest writers strong Egyptian colours glimmer through and through; in their successors they become fainter and fainter, until at last they entirely disappear.

Finally, there is in manners and customs the finest gradation. At first, all is simple and natural, like to what we see in Homer, and among the Bedouin Arabs even at the present time; but this noble simplicity gradually loses itself in luxury and effeminacy, and vanishes at last in the splendid court of Solomon.

No where is there a sudden leap; every where the progress is gradual. *None but ignorant or thoughtless doubters can suppose the Old Testament to have been forged by* ONE *deceiver.*

The colouring which the painter has here employed is vivid, but the objects are true and real, and are not formed by his fancy. It is impossible to read the Hebrew Scriptures, with the exercise of any discriminating judgment and æsthetical feeling, without acceding in the main to what Eichhorn has stated. Thousands of nice touches and dashes of light and shade, in the original objects, are lost in our English version, where all are mingled together, and melted so as to become one mass in the Anglo-Saxon crucible. But as to the critical reader of the *Hebrew*—if he has one spark of æsthetical fire in him, or if he carries along with him even the feeblest torch of discrimination, he must accede to the truthfulness and the sound judgment of Eichhorn, as to this matter in general. A forgery of all these books by *one* person, would be a greater miracle than any which the books have related. But let us join again the company of the Göttingen Professor :

II. *They are not the forgery of* MANY *deceivers.*

"But perhaps," some one may reply, "perhaps *many* forgers have made common cause, and at the same time, in some later period, have got up the books in question."—But how could they forge in a way so entirely conformed to the progress of the human understanding? And was it possible in later times to create the language of Moses? This surpasses all human powers. Finally, one writer always supposes the existence of another. They could not then all have arisen at the *same* time; they must have existed successively.

"Perhaps then," it may be further said, "such forgers arose at different times, who continued onward, in the introduction of supposititious writings, from the place where their deceitful predecessors had stopped. In this way may all the references to preceding writers be explained; in this way may we explain the striking gradation that exists in all its parts."

But, (1.) How was it possible that no one should have discovered the trick, exposed it, and put a brand upon the deceiver, in order that posterity might be secured against injury? How could a whole nation be often deceived, and at different periods? (2.) What design could such a deceiver have had in view? Did he aim at eulogizing the Hebrew nation? Then are his eulogies the severest satires; for according to the Old Testament, the Hebrew nation have acted a very degrading part. Or, did he mean to degrade them? In this case, how could he force his books upon the very people whom they defamed, and the story of whose being trodden under foot by foreign nations is told in plain blunt words?

These remarks seem to me to be equally just with the preceding ones. A *series* of forgers, in such a succession of ages, all developing an intimate acquaintance with predecessors, and still true to their own particular age in all their characteristic features! And a nation distinguished above all others for activity and shrewdness, tamely receiving and submitting to all these impositions! The thing is unheard of; it is improbable; nay, it is absolutely impossible, in the common course of things. *Impostors* and *forgers* write Isaiah, and Joel, and Habakkuk, and Nahum, and Job, and the Psalms! It is impossible. It is altogether more incredible than any so-called *myth* in all the Old Testament. The story of Jonah and of Samson, which have set in motion the whole circle of obstreperous and vituperative criticism, is a matter quite within the reach of ordinary faith, in comparison with such a figment as this.

I must solicit the attention of the reader to one point in particular, to which Eichhorn has adverted, and which is peculiarly characteristic of the writers of the Old Testament. It is this, viz. that they disclose the *faults* as well as the virtues of men whom they hold up to view, and of the people to whom they belong. What shall we say of Adam, Noah, Abraham, Isaac, Jacob, Moses even, David, Solomon, Asa, and others, in every way so conspicuous as ancestors or as kings of the Jewish nation? Is there one whose faults are not unveiled? One even whose weaknesses are not revealed? And what can we say of the whole history? —the history of God's *chosen people*, distinguished from all the nations of the earth—the posterity of Abraham—the nation "to whom belongs the adoption, and the glory, and the covenants, and the giving of the Law, and the service of God, and the promises?" Is there a history on earth of any people, (unless it be some caricature sketched by the hand of an enemy,) which is half so full of narrations that respect their perverseness, and disobedience, and rebellion, and gross idolatry and immorality ? Where is there such a history ? Who wrote it ? Or if such a one exists, where is there an account of its being received by the very people whom it characterizes, and regarded as a book replete with truths that are Divine ? The challenge to produce it may be fearlessly made. The result is beyond a question.

Will any one explain to me, now, how such a matter as the reception of the Jewish Scriptures as *sacred* was brought about, in the natural course of things ? The historians and the prophets, one and all, charging the nation with ingratitude and rebellion, and threatening them with subjugation and exile, with sword and famine and pestilence—and yet these historians and prophets admitted as counsellors and guides, and their works *canonized!* There is something of the extraordinary in all this, which is no *myth*, to say the least. Naturalists are bound to *untie* the knot ; we cannot permit them to cut it.

But when one adds to all this the consideration of the matter as connected with *forgery* and *imposture*, it becomes quite unendurable. *Forgers* and *impostors* so elevated and honoured for characterizing a people in such a way, as must cause the cheek of every ingenuous Hebrew to blush for his nation ! Is there nothing *mythic* in this ? Men too of such a stamp as forgers and impostors, filled with overflowing zeal on all occasions for the worship and honour and glory of the true God, and for the holiness and benevolence and justice and integrity of the Hebrew nation ? Is this the character of men of such a stamp ? It is a downright contradiction of all that belongs to the history of our race. It is neither more nor less than a moral impossibility. " Quodcunque ostendis mihi sic, incredulus odi."

Romancers have in view the exaltation of their hero. Even the gravest and most tasteful of them scarcely glance at a fault. How has Xenophon presented his Cyrus ; Homer his Achilles ; Virgil his Æneas ? Whatever we, judging by our standards, may find in them which is faulty, it was not the intention of these respective writers to hold up any faults to view. Is it so with the picture of David, in the book of Kings? So with the picture of even "the wisest of men?" And if it be said that the books of Chronicles have kept the faults of these distinguished personages out of view, the reply is easy: The story was already told in the book of Kings, and the chronicler had in view principally what these Jewish monarchs did to accommodate, arrange, and complete the worship of God in the manner prescribed by Moses.

No; the histories of the Jews are unlike those of all other nations. God and his honour and worship and ordinances are the *nucleus* of them all. Men—the whole nation —are but secondary actors in this great drama. A David and a Solomon come before the tribunal of the historian, at his bidding, laying aside their crowns and their heroism and their wisdom, and standing there to be judged for their vices as impartially as the meanest subject in their kingdom. Is this so elsewhere, and in respect to men whose virtues are preëminent? I cannot find it.

How then was all this brought about? Not by *forgers* and *impostors;* not by the ordinary tactics of national historians and the writers of memoirs. There is an honesty, an integrity, a boldness, an independence, a love of truth, and a hatred of sin in every form, which stands out to view so prominently in all the historians and prophets of the Hebrews, that I feel compelled to say, The hand of the Lord is here; his Spirit breathed into these writers the breath of a piety which could not die; it kindled a flame in their breasts, whose light all the surrounding darkness could not extinguish.

But I must desist. Once more then let us listen to the former Coryphæus of Neology. He gives us some diagnostics by which we may judge in respect to the *genuineness* of the books in question, § 13.

The Old Testament bears all the marks of *genuineness* enstamped upon it. (1.) The very same grounds which are available in a contest for Homer, establish the genuineness of all and particular the books of the Old Testament. Why should one deny to these the equity which he extends to heathen writers? If a profane writer plants himself in some particular age and country, and if all the external and internal circumstances of his book accord with this, no impartial inquirer refuses to acknowledge him. Yea, one does not hesitate at all to determine the uncertain age of any writer, by internal arguments drawn from his works. Why should not the critical inquirer respecting the Bible, walk in the same path?

(2.) No one has yet, with any good grounds, been able to overthrow the integrity and credibility of the Old Testament. On the contrary, every discovery in ancient literature has hitherto only served for the confirmation of the Hebrew Scriptures. No one has shown that any writer of the Old Testament has exhibited a style, or knowledge, or introduced circumstantial matters, which are not appropriate to the age assigned to him.

(3.) In brief, all the books of the Old Testament, which bear the names of their authors, are marked with the stamp of integrity on the part of these authors. And with respect to the books that are anonymous, internal grounds demonstrate that we must regard them as genuine. The book of Joshua, for example, whose author is unknown, goes so deep into the detail of the most ancient geography, that a forger must have wrought miracle upon miracle, in order to put himself in a condition so as to compose it.

Let one examine this matter in a discriminating way and without prejudice, and I am certain that he must convince himself of the integrity of the Old Testament.

Eichhorn goes on, in the sequel, to show, that even on the ground that new accessions have been made to some of the books, and that several of them are compounded of various authors, no argument of any force can be drawn from this source to confront the allegation of integrity. Such things have happened to most of the early writers among other nations. Not a few books of the Scriptures are professedly drawn from other sources; and others, not professedly so, exhibit internal marks of the fact. But a book compounded in this way may be as genuine and worthy of credit as any other book.

Thus thought and wrote the great leader of the new array, in the war against the Divine authority and obligation of the Scriptures. With him, when writing here, the question was one merely of critical judgment and feeling. Nobly has he managed the cause of what I believe to be sound criticism, and justly has he decided it. With all his freethinking and independence of mind, he is left, in the race of neological criticism, immeasurably behind De Wette, Ewald, Lengerke, Mr. Norton, and their compeers.

Leaving all *theological* bearings of our matter out of question for the present, I do not see how, as fair-minded critics and exegetes, we can refuse to adopt the sentiments of Eichhorn, as exhibited above. I would not undertake to prove.

that all which this writer has published will harmonize with these views. But I am gratified to have it in my power to express, in language borrowed from him, the views which I entertain in respect to this very important subject.

SECT. X. *Time when the Canon of the Old Testament was completed.*

This has, in recent times, become a much contested question. The criticism that has been moving on in the wake of Wolf, Heyne, and their compeers, (who discovered that Homer's Iliad and Odyssey are nothing but a mere farrago of many songs composed in different ages and countries, and that the art of alphabetic writing was unknown in the time of Homer, and of course in the time of Moses,) has made the like discoveries in regard to almost all the books of the Old Testament. According to recent critics, every book of the Old Testament, with the exception of Ruth, Esther, possibly Canticles, (but here they differ,) Ezekiel, and some of the minor prophets, is a patch-work of cloth and colours of all textures and all varieties. The time in which most of these books were composed, was, according to them, at or after, in some cases long after, the Babylonish exile. In particular, the book of Daniel is placed deep down, even into the time of the Maccabees, i. e. about 160—140 B. C.; as also some of the Psalms, and not improbably various other portions of books the body of which may be older. The question in respect to this matter is one of deep interest to sacred criticism; although it would not be very important to my present main purpose, which is to show what that canon of Old Testament books consisted of, which was sanctioned by Christ and his apostles. Even the most loose of the so-called liberal critics do not pretend that any of the Old Testament books have been added to the Canon since the commencement of the Christian era; so that, come into being when or how they may, if they existed before the Christian era, and were sanctioned as of Divine authority by the author himself of Christianity, and by his apostles, it

SECT. X.   COMPLETION OF THE CANON.   207

would be enough for my special purpose. But, as I said at commencement of this treatise, I have a more general object in view, as well as the particular one just named ; and this is, to give the outlines of the critical history of the Old Testament Canon in general. To do this, it is indispensable to investigate, with some particularity, the point which is brought before us by the heading to the present section.

I begin with the testimony of Josephus in relation to the matter in question, because, although it is not the most ancient, it is still the most definite and particular that can be found in any writer of the more remote antiquity. It is found in his work *Contra Apionem*, against whom he is defending the credibility and authenticity of the Hebrew Scriptures. After appealing to the agreement between profane and Old Testament history as to many important facts related in the Hebrew Scriptures, he then goes on to express himself as follows :

We have not a countless number of books, discordant and arrayed against each other; but only *two and twenty books*, containing the history of every age, which are justly accredited as Divine [old editions of Josephus read merely, " which are justly accredited "—θεῖα comes from Eusebius' transcript of Josephus in Ecc. Hist. III. 10] ; and of these, *five* belong to Moses, which contain both the laws and the history of the generations of men until his death. This period lacks but little of 3000 years. From the death of Moses, moreover, until the reign of Artaxerxes, [Euseb.—'from the death of Moses to that of Artaxerxes' —and so most of the Codices, omitting ἀρχῆς, *reign*,] king of the Persians after Xerxes, the prophets who followed Moses have described the things which were done during the age of each one respectively, in *thirteen* books. The remaining *four* contain hymns to God, and rules of life for men. From the time of Artaxerxes, moreover, until our present period, all occurrences have been written down ; *but they are not regarded as entitled to the like credit with those which precede them, because there was no certain succession of prophets.* Fact has shown what confidence we place in our own writings. For although so many ages have passed away, no one has dared to add to them, nor to take any thing from them, nor to make alterations. In all Jews it is implanted, even from their birth, to regard them as being the instructions of God, and to abide stedfastly by them, and if it be necessary, to die gladly for them." (For the original Greek, see Appendix, No. III.)

Of the historian from whom this passage is taken, it is not necessary to say much. Josephus was perhaps more distinguished and learned than any other man of his time belonging to the Jewish nation. His father was a priest in the regular order of the twenty-four courses ordained by David; and his mother was a lineal descendant of the Maccabæan kings, who also were priests. His father, Matthias, was a man distinguished not only for his noble birth, but for his praiseworthy deeds. To his son Joseph, or Josephus, born about A. D. 37, he gave the best education in his power; and so effectual were the means employed, that at the age of fourteen this boy was consulted by the chief priests and leaders of the city respecting difficult passages of the Law. So Josephus himself has told us; and this seems to render altogether improbable the allegations made here and there not unfrequently, that Josephus had no tolerable acquaintance with the Hebrew. At the age of sixteen he began his inquiries respecting the several Jewish sects, and actually spent three years in solitude with Banus, one of the Essenes, in order to become thoroughly acquainted with the principles of that sect. At the age of nineteen he joined the sect of the Pharisees, which was altogether predominant at that period. At the age of twenty-six he went to Rome as advocate before Nero Cæsar for some falsely accused Jewish priests, and procured their liberation. Not long after this the Jewish war broke out, and Josephus, espousing the part of his countrymen, was put in command, and made a most gallant defence of Jotapata against Vespasian. But there, at length, he was taken prisoner, was subsequently kept by Vespasian and Titus as a medium of communication between them and the Jews, and finally, when the conquest of Judea had been completed, he was taken by Titus to Rome, where Vespasian assigned him a dwelling in a part of the palace, with honorary maintenance. There he wrote his great works, the Antiquities and the History of the Jewish War. Later in life he wrote his Treatise against Apion, in defence of the Jewish religion and their sacred books. Apion was a grammarian of Alexandria, who, under Caligula's reign, wrote a violent attack upon Philo Judæus and upon the Jewish nation. Near the close of the first century, Josephus wrote the Treatise in question; so that it is to be regarded as the fruit of his most mature reflections and studies.

His knowledge of Greek literature is spoken of by Jerome with astonishment. There is abundant evidence of it in his Contra Apionem. His knowledge of the history of his

SECT. X.   COMPLETION OF THE CANON.   209

own nation is sufficiently testified, by his two great works in relation to this subject. It has been thought that he was but moderately skilled in Hebrew, because he usually appeals to the Sept. Version. But for this, two good reasons can be assigned; the one, that he fully believed in the miraculous rise of the Septuagint, as is shown by his account of this matter; the other, that the Romans, for whom he wrote the history, could read the Septuagint but not the Hebrew Scriptures.

That of all the men of his time among the Jews, he was best qualified to give an account of Jewish affairs and Jewish opinions, there can be no reasonable doubt. I can see nothing that could sway him to give a wrong account of what his countrymen and himself believed, in regard to the history of the Jewish Canon. What that belief was, his rank in life, his office as a priest, and, above all, his great learning, must have rendered him able to know. Can any good ground be assigned for the supposition, that he has not given a true account of this matter?

The sect of the Pharisees, among whom he formed his religious opinions, were of all men the most tenacious of traditions and of the customs of former days; and when he assures us of this and that opinion among the Jews of his time, I do not know of any writer among the ancients, the sacred writers excepted, who is more trust-worthy than he.

Thus much that the reader may understandingly appreciate the testimony which we have before us. I return to the consideration of that testimony.

My first remark is, that there is no ground to suppose that Josephus gives us any other than the general and settled opinion of the great mass of the Jewish nation. To the party of the Pharisees this mass assuredly belonged. The Sadducees were powerful only by virtue of wealth, and perhaps learning. They were but a small party. The Essenes lived mostly abroad, in desert or lonely places, and avoided mixing with the world. Josephus then gives us not a *peculiar* opinion of his own merely, but speaks evidently in behalf of the great mass of the Jewish people. Finally, if there were any thing merely sectarian in the views of the Pharisees respecting the Hebrew Canon, Josephus would not have been likely to embrace that in the latter part of his

r

life, inasmuch as he evidently lost, in later life, his early zeal for Pharisaism, as appears from many passages in his Antiquities. On the whole, we can hardly conceive of any one in a better condition to give a clear and impartial account of the light in which the Hebrew Scriptures were viewed by the Jews of that period.

Secondly, we might be in some doubt what king of Persia was meant by the Artaxerxes of Josephus, (inasmuch as this same name is given by some to several Persian kings,) had not the historian been so explicit as to dispel all doubt on this point, by saying, that the Artaxerxes in question was the follower of Xerxes upon the throne of Persia. This Artaxerxes (Longimanus) began his reign in 464 B. C., and died in 424 B. C. Of course he reigned forty years. *Later than 424 B. C., then, no part of the Hebrew Canon can be, if the testimony of Josephus is well grounded.*

Thirdly, Josephus assigns all the historical books of the Canon to *prophets:* "The *prophets*, after Moses, described the events which took place in their respective periods, in *thirteen* books." The word *prophets*, therefore, is plainly used by him, in the sense in which I have defined and employed it in the preceding pages. What books are included in this enumeration of thirteen, is an inquiry that will be made in the sequel.

Fourthly, he states in the most plain and unequivocal manner, that since the reign of Artaxerxes down to the time in which he himself lived, passing events had been fully noted—γέγραπται μὲν ἕκαστα—but "credit was not attached to these histories, in like manner as to the earlier ones, [the canonical books,] *because there was no certain succession of prophets*" during that period. Here then are two facts on which he rests the opinion that he gives; the first, that the sacred books were completed in the reign of Artaxerxes; the second, that other books, continuing the history of the Jews, were composed by those who were not prophets, and therefore could not claim that credit which belonged to the former.

How well this view of Josephus accords with what I have stated in the preceding pages, viz. that books were not admitted to the Jewish Canon unless regarded as of *prophetic* origin, must be obvious to every reader. Had Josephus been an ignorant or unlearned person, who had no knowledge of other books than the Jewish Scriptures, we should attribute less weight to his opinion. Such a man could have examined only one side of the question. But here is a witness who, as we may reasonably say, has read all the books which pertain to Jewish affairs, and who still draws a distinction wide and broad, between those that are sacred and fully credible, and those which can be regarded only as the works of erring men. No reasonable advocate for the claims of inspiration at the present day could ask for stronger or more definite and intelligible expressions, than those of Josephus.

I know not how language can make it more certain than that of Josephus has made it, that he knew well, and made definitely, the distinction between the now called *apocryphal* books and those of the Canon. It is beyond a doubt that he was acquainted with both; for he has drawn from both in his Antiquities.

In order that we may have no doubts left as to the exact meaning of Josephus, we must advert to the order which he has followed in the historical narrations of his Antiquities. In Lib. XI. he presents us with the history of the Jews from the time when the decree of Cyrus for their liberation was issued (536 B. C.) down to the time when Palestine was overrun by Alexander the Great (331 B. C.). In chap. v. of this book he has presented us with an account of events recorded in the book of Ezra, in respect to this distinguished priest and leader of the new colony of Jewish immigrants; and he places all these events under the reign of Xerxes I., taking him to be the king which, in Ezra viii. 1, seq., of our Scriptures, is named Artaxerxes. The journey of Nehemiah and his friends to Jerusalem, he assigns to the twenty-fifth year of the same king's reign, (Antiq. XI. 5, 7,) while the Bible assigns it to the twentieth year of Artaxerxes, Neh. ii. 1, (comp. v. 14,) i. e. about twelve years after the immigration of Ezra. Whether the error lies in the reading of the codices of Josephus, or in his oversight, in this case, it would be difficult to decide, and it is not of any importance to my present object to make a decision. Xerxes' reign lasted but twenty-one years. There are, moreover, other small discrepancies of the like nature between Josephus and the Scriptures; e. g.

as to the time (fifty-two days) in which the walls of Jerusalem were completed under Nehemiah, (see Neh. vi. 15,) while Josephus assigns two years and four months as the period of completion; Antiq. XI. 5, 8. But still, nothing is plainer than that this historian abridges and copies the whole book of Nehemiah, for substance, into his own, and he represents the death of this distinguished leader as taking place under the reign of Xerxes I. In XI. 1, seq. he gives, in like manner, a sketch of the events related in the book of Esther; or rather, we might say, an account more copious even than that which is contained in the Scriptures. All these events he assigns to the reign of Artaxerxes (Longimanus), who reigned more than forty years (464—424 B. C.). The Persian king of the book of Esther is uniformly called *Ahasuerus.** At what time during the reign of this king the deliverance of the Jews, as recorded in Esther, took place, Josephus does not say. I must believe, however, that if one reads carefully the passage from him which is printed on page 207 above, he will perceive on the whole that it makes for the position, that it was at a late period of his reign. If we read the clause, ἀπὸ δὲ τῆς Μωϋσέως τελευτῆς μέχρι τῆς Ἀρταξέρξου τοῦ μετὰ Ξέρξην Περσῶν βασιλέως ἀρχῆς, with an omission of the final word ἀρχῆς, (which is omitted in Eusebius Ecc. Hist. III. 10, and in most of the manuscripts of Josephus,) then it is clear that Josephus intends to fix his limit at the death of Artaxerxes, (424 B. C.,) beyond or since which no book that has been written has any just claim to be considered as a part of the Hebrew Canon. The manner in which he has drawn up his account of these times, proves beyond a doubt that he regarded the book of Esther as the last in the Canon of Scripture, as well as that he considered it a *sacred* book. Beyond this and further on he draws indeed from other histories of the Jews; and so in all the latter part of his Antiquities; but he compiles here much more loosely than before, and evidently proceeds as considering himself more at liberty to depart from his sources, as we may learn by comparing his history, e. g.

* Josephus seems to have considered *Ahasuerus* as the proper name of only one Persian king; whereas it is plainly an appellative, (like Pharaoh, the czar, &c.,) and belongs to Cambyses, Ez. iv. 6, and to Astyages the father of Darius the Mede, Dan. ix. 1. The meaning of the name, as developed by the cuneiform writing recently deciphered, is *lion-king = hero*; see in Ges. Lex.

of Antiochus Epiphanes, with that in 1 Macc. It is to be deeply regretted that he has not given us a particular account of his *sources*, as he had the fairest opportunity for doing it at the close of his Antiquities, XX. 11. 2, where he has made a statement of the object which he had in view in the composition of his work, and of his qualifications to accomplish it. But he goes no further in mentioning his sources than to say that he has given an account of ancient historical events, "ὡς αἱ ἱεραὶ βίβλοι περὶ πάντων ἔχουσι τὴν ἀναγραφήν, i. e. in accordance with the description of them in the sacred books;" ib. 11. 2. Of the estimation in which he held books subsequent to the time of Esther, he has given us an account in his Cont. Apion. § 8, as stated above. After having said that the twenty-two books of the Jews were τὰ δικαίως θεῖα πεπιστευμένα, *deservedly regarded as divine*, he says of the others, written after the time of Artaxerxes, that πίστεως δὲ οὐχ ὁμοίας ἠξίωται τῆς πρὸ αὐτῶν, i. e. that they are not worthy of the like credit with those before them. In respect to his qualifications for writing his *Antiquities*, he says, in a modest way, (XX. 11. 2,) that "he was acknowledged by most of his countrymen as excelling in a knowledge of what belonged to their country, and that he had given himself to Greek literature, until every thing but the niceties of pronunciation was familiar to him." He says, moreover, that the study of Greek literature was disreputable among his countrymen; and for this reason, not more than some two or three besides himself had attained to any eminence in it. Of his knowledge of *Hebrew*, the fact that he was employed as interpreter by Vespasian and Titus, and the fact that he first wrote his *Jewish Wars* in Hebrew, are sufficient evidence. That he was a highly intelligent Jewish priest, would of itself be a sufficient pledge.

We will suppose now that the opinion of Josephus was merely the result of his private judgment in regard to the *order* of the book of Esther. Let it be that Chronicles, Nehemiah, and Malachi are later; all this will not affect the question now before us. Josephus does not specificate any particular time during the long reign of Artaxerxes, when the events related in Esther took place, nor when the book was written. There might be sufficient time, for aught we know to the contrary, for writing those several books after

Esther was written, and yet before the death of Artaxerxes. On the other hand, the book of Esther may have been written *after* them, and therefore the last of all, even in case the events which it commemorates had happened some time before they were written down. The probability as to matter of fact seems to be, that the events commemorated in Esther happened during the reign of Xerxes I., inasmuch as he was a king whose character well fitted him for such actions as are ascribed to the Persian monarch in the book of Esther. In this respect Josephus may have formed an erroneous judgment. Still, there is nothing in the book of Esther, which of itself will determine the date of the work. The events which it commemorates commenced indeed, in the third year of *Ahasuerus*, whoever he was; but how long they were in progress, if we include the whole of them, is not quite certain; and of course we cannot decide exactly as to the age of the book itself. But in respect to Nehemiah, we know that he went a second time from Persia to Palestine, in the *thirty-second* year of Artaxerxes; Neh. xiii. 6. Josephus must have read this book, therefore, without due regard to the notations of time, since he represents the death of Nehemiah as taking place under Xerxes I., Antiq. XI. 5. 8, whose reign lasted only 21 years. But *anachronisms* in Josephus are no strange thing.

But be it that Josephus has erred, as to the reign under which the events recorded in the book of Esther took place, it does not at all affect the statement which he has made, in a manner so explicit and ample, that *the certain succession of prophets ceased with the reign of Artaxerxes*. Much dispute there has been about the meaning of ἀκριβῆ in the phrase μὴ ... ἀκριβῆ διαδοχήν as applied to the prophets. To me it seems, that the simple meaning of Josephus is, that the *succession* of any prophet, after the reign of Artaxerxes, to the series of earlier prophets, who wrote the sacred books, is *uncertain*, i. e. it was a thing which, although some might regard it as true, in his judgment and in that of his countrymen (for he speaks their views) could not be established or rendered certain. Of course, as he regarded those books only as canonical which were composed by prophets, or men of a prophetic spirit, there could be no good ground for admitting any book, after the period

SECT. X.   COMPLETION OF THE CANON.   215

just named, as canonical. Διαδοχήν does not mean *series* or *ordo*, as it has often been translated, but the *succession* of one thing or person after another of the like kind. Ἀκριβής (from ἄκρος, *pointed, sharp*, and this from ἀκή, *point sharpness*,) literally means *pointed, sharp*, but, figuratively, (as in the case before us,) *exact, certain*. This view of the words accords entirely with the explanation given above.

It has been said by those who feel an interest in fixing upon a later period for the closing of the Old Test. Canon, that Josephus cannot mean to assert what is here attributed to him, because he himself attributes to John Hyrcanus (prince and high priest, 135—107 B. C.) the gift of *prophecy*. Josephus, who is loud in the praises of Hyrcanus, does say of him, indeed, that "he *alone* obtained the three most excellent things, viz. the principality of the nation, the high priesthood, καὶ προφητείαν, and *the gift of prophecy*." In order to confirm the last declaration he adds, "For the Divinity (τὸ δαιμόνιον) was conversant with him, so that he was ignorant of nothing which was to come;" Jos. Bell. Jud. I. 2. 8. But let the reader observe, that Josephus says of John Hyrcanus, that he *alone* attained to such a union of gifts as he mentions, and that the stress of this affirmation falls on *prophecy* is plain enough from the fact, that many others united in their persons the office of ruler and high priest, and from the immediate explanation which Josephus himself gives of what he had meant specially to assert. Besides, although Josephus admits of dream-interpreters, (e. g. Simon of the Essenes, Antiq. XVII. 13. 3,) and various prognosticators,* especially during the period near the destruc-

---

* In Antiq. XV. 10. 5, Josephus introduces one Menahem, of the Essenes, as prognosticating the future dominion and fortunes of Herod, and says of him that "πρόγνωσιν ἐκ θεοῦ τῶν μελλόντων ἔχων," i. e. he had from God a foreknowledge of future things. Again (ib.) he says of the Essenes, that "many of them, on account of their good and honest life, were honoured with skill in Divine things." In Bell. Jud. II. 8. 12, he says of the Essenes, "There are among them those who profess to foretell future things;" and in the sequel he subjoins, "Seldom do they err in their prognostications." In Bell. Jud. I. 3. 5, he relates a prediction of Judas, one of the Essenes, "who never lapsed or spoke falsely in his predictions." In Bell. Jud. II. 7. 3, one Simon, of the same sect, is introduced as a prognosticator. All these cases are of the same character. The Essenes, who were of a contemplative and enthusiastic turn of mind, gave their attention to prognostication, and obtained uncommon skill in it. Many cases of the like nature are to be found among most nations.

tion of Jerusalem, yet it is plain enough, that after the reign of Artaxerxes he never introduces any one in the character of an Old Test. prophet. It is plain, too, in respect to the case of Hyrcanus, that the gift of prophecy is ascribed to him rather in a way of *post mortem* eulogy, than of accurate and earnest historical narration. At all events, Josephus makes no allusion to any *written* prophecies of Hyrcanus, so that there is nothing in the case of this individual which can come in competition with the claims of the earlier Hebrew prophets; nothing indeed which contradicts or is opposed to the true spirit and meaning of what he says in Cont. Apion. I. 8. What he there declares is, that there was no proof of the existence of any prophet (after the reign of Artaxerxes) who was the author of a canonical or holy book—that no pretended succession of such a nature to the former prophets was *certain*, ἀκριβῆ. What he says of John Hyrcanus, or of any other individuals as prognosticators or the like, does not contradict this, and is not inconsistent with it.

Thus much for the testimony of Josephus, in regard to the *terminus ad quem* of the Hebrew prophets. But as this is a point of great importance, (at least it strikes me in this light,) we must see what others have said and thought, as well as Josephus, in relation to this matter.

The author of the First Book of the Maccabees, (written not long after the death of Simon, about 135 B. C.,) when describing the calamities that came upon Judea, in consequence of the death of Judas Maccabæus, says, (ix. 27,) that "there was great affliction in Israel, such as was not ἀφ' ἧς ἡμέρας οὐκ ὤφθη προφήτης ἐν αὐτοῖς, *from the time since no prophet made his appearance among them.*" Comp. Jos. Antiq. XIII. 1, where, in describing the same events, he says, "The Jews had not experienced so great calamity μετὰ τὴν Βαβυλῶνος ἐπάνοδον, *since the return from Babylon.*" That the author of Maccabees means as much as to say *for a very long time*, is altogether plain and evident. In his day, then,

and in every age. Josephus, no doubt, was a believer in their occasional extraordinary gift of foresight; but still it is easy to see, that, with all his wonder at their attainments in "second sight," he neither thinks nor speaks of them as being prophets in the sense in which the ancient Hebrew prophets were. [See *Koester's* work, entitled, Die Propheten des Alten und neuen Testaments, u. s. w. Leipzig, 1838. D.]

it was counted a *long time* since any prophet had appeared among the Jews. From the time of this author back to the time of Artaxerxes, is about 300 years.

In 1 Macc. iv. 46, the Jews, who had been removing the stones of the altar in the temple which had been profaned by Antiochus Epiphanes, are represented as laying them aside, " μέχρι τοῦ παραγενηϑῆναι προφήτην τοῦ ἀποκριϑῆναι περὶ αὐτῶν, until the coming of some prophet to decide respecting them," viz. to decide what should be done with them. In 1 Macc. xiv. 41, it is said, that " Simon was constituted leader and high priest for ever, until τοῦ ἀναστῆναι προφήτην πιστόν, *some faithful prophet should arise;*" thus intimating plainly, that they knew of no such one at that time, but expected one in future; i. e. (as I apprehend) the Messiah.

That Malachi, (fl. 430—424,) in the reign of Artaxerxes, was the last of the Hebrew prophets, at all events the last who bore any comparison with the old Hebrew prophets, is a point that has been almost universally conceded by such as had no particular purpose to accomplish by making out a different representation. " With this prophet," says Knobel in his recent Prophetismus, (II. p. 365,) "the Old Testament prophetic office expires."* The author of the famous Rabbinical book Cosri, (Pars III. § 65,) speaking of the series of prophets, says, that "Those which remained of them, after the return to the temple [from Babylon], were Haggai, Zechariah, Ezra, &c. In Seder Olam Zuther, fol. 35, col. 2, the writer says, " In the fifty-second year of the Medes and Persians, died Haggai, Zechariah, and Malachi ; at the same time prophecy ceased from Israel." The Rabbinic author of this book, with most of the earlier Jewish chronologists, supposes the Persian empire to have lasted only fifty-two years, instead of more than 200, which is the real state of the case. The rest of his affirmation is in unison with the general voice. Jerome (Comm. on Isa. xlix. 21) says, in a metaphrase which he puts into the mouth of the Jewish church: "Quis mihi istos genuit ? . . . Post Aggæum, Zachariam, et Malachiam, nullos alios prophetas usque ad Johannem Baptistam videram ;" i. e. "Who hath begotten me these ? . . . Since Haggai, Zechariah, and Ma-

* So also a much abler writer than Knobel, viz. Koester, p. 119. D.

lachi, I have seen no other prophets down to John the Baptist." So Augustine: "During all that period since they [the Jews] returned from Babylon, after Malachi, Haggai, and Zechariah, *non habuerunt Prophetas usque ad Salvatoris adventum*, i. e. they had no prophets until the advent of the Saviour;" De Civ. Dei, XVII. 24. That the agreement of the ancients is all but universal, in respect to this matter, no one acquainted with critical history will pretend to question.

If there be any uncertainty, after all, as to the time when Malachi lived, it may be removed to any one's satisfaction who will take the pains to compare this writer with Ezra and Nehemiah. (*a*) As to breaches of the Law by priests and Levites in taking foreign wives; Mal. iii. 10, comp. Ez. ix. 1; Neh. xiii. 23—29. (*b*) Withholding tithes from Levites; Mal. iii. 10, comp. Neh. xiii. 10—12. (*c*) Neglect of Divine worship; Mal. i. 13; ii. 8, comp. Neh. xiii. 15, seq. (*d*) The application of פחה, *præfect*, to Nehemiah the then present governor of Jerusalem, shows that Malachi could not have lived after Nehemiah; for he was the last ruler there who bore the title in question; [פחה = the modern *Pasha*]. That Malachi lived after the temple was completed, and of course after the time of Haggai and Zechariah, is shown by Mal. i. 10; iii. 1, 10. That he was regarded as the last of the Hebrew prophets, is shown by the place assigned to his book, which closes the series of the prophets.

I cannot refrain here from reminding the reader how very inconsistent this historical development, in regard to the cessation of the prophetic gift during the reign of Artaxerxes Longimanus, is with the favourite theory of De Wette and most of the so-called liberal critics, viz. that the book of *Daniel* was written during the Maccabæan times of trouble, and after the death of Antiochus Epiphanes, whose history it gives.* How could the writer of 1 Macc. say, at the close of these distressing times, that there was no *prophet* in Israel, in case a new prophetical book had then just made

---

* See Von Lengerke on the liberal side, and Hengstenberg on the other. Compare also Hävernick on Daniel, whose Neue kritische Untersuchungen ueber das Buch Daniel, (Hamburg, 1838,) are particularly appropriate and valuable. D.

SECT. X.   COMPLETION OF THE CANON.   219

its appearance, and been received by the Jews as authentic? Or was it, that the Jews, in order to admit the claims of the newly written book, were persuaded by the writer to believe, that the true work of Daniel, which had lain in concealment some three and a half centuries, was now first brought into the light and edited by him? One or the other of these positions must be true, viz. either that there was a prophet at the period, (contrary to the book of Maccabees, inconsistent with the representations of Jesus the son of Sirach, and at variance with the declarations of Josephus and the voice of all antiquity,) whose authority could give authenticity to the book, or else the forgery must have been accomplished with so much dexterity as to mislead the whole of the Jewish people. These considerations are serious drawbacks from the capital of all the Liberals, in regard to the time when the book of Daniel was written.

But to return to our theme; it seems to me, that the dealings of Providence with the Jews, in regard to the matter of religious instruction, are worthy of particular consideration. When the Hebrews had no synagogues, and scarcely any copies of the Scriptures that were current among them, then were commissioned that distinguished order of religious teachers, the נביאים and the רואים. The only copy extant of the Law of Moses might indeed be hidden in the temple, (as in the time of Josiah,) and yet there must have remained adequate or competent teachers of true religion, guided by the Spirit of all wisdom and knowledge. The Jews, after their exile, were so well satisfied of the sin and folly of idolatry, that they used efficient means to guard in future against it; and these were, the multiplication of the copies of the Scriptures, and the erection of synagogues, where the holy books were read every sabbath day. When this custom was fully established, the order of prophets ceased. I cannot doubt that the institution of synagogues was introduced, either in the latter period of the life of Ezra and Nehemiah, or very soon after their death. The Scriptures themselves, which were thus read every sabbath, occupied the place of the earlier prophets. It would seem, since the Law made nothing perfect, and was only a dawning toward the gospel day, that Providence withheld one of the modes of instruction, to which I have adverted, during the time that the other was in full force ; while under the gospel both methods are employed in combination, and with much greater success.

Let me be indulged in one remark more before I dismiss the present topic. How came it about, that the Jewish nation, among whom were prophets from the time of Moses down to that of Malachi, (about a thousand years,) should all at once cease to have them at this latter period ? It is a conceded point, that whatever one or another might say of this or that fortune-teller or prognosticator, at the later period, yet no such persons as Isaiah, Jeremiah, Hosea, Joel, Amos, and the like, appeared among the Hebrews for about four centuries before the Christian era. Had the Jews become so enlightened at this period as no longer to give ear to the pretensions of prophets ? as Neology often and not obscurely intimates. Or was there no true zeal for the Mosaic institutions, and for the customs of the fathers, and no longer any desire to obtain a knowledge of future events ? What had become of the pride and glorying of the Jews in the order of prophets, as showing their superiority over all other nations ? These and the like questions may be urged with the more force, inasmuch as there is no pretence that the Jews, after returning from their exile, ever relapsed into their love of heathen idolatry. Unless it were matter of fact, that the order of prophets ceased with Malachi, I see no way of accounting for the universal impression among the Jews that such was the case. How could they be brought to disclaim a matter of so much precedence and honour to their nation, in any way excepting by the impossibility of establishing any valid claims to an order of prophets beyond the period of Malachi ? I must regard it, therefore, as one of the best established facts in their ancient religious history, that the order of prophets ceased at, or very near, the close of the reign of Artaxerxes Longimanus, i. e. near to 424 B. C.

At all events this cannot be gainsayed, viz. that we have no credible testimony to the contrary. It cannot be controverted, that Josephus, the most enlightened man at that time of the Hebrew nation, as to its antiquities and history, gives it as the established opinion of that nation, that for some four hundred years they had had no prophets who wrote Scriptures, or who could properly have the credit of being sacred writers. All the writers subsequent to the reign of Artaxerxes he explicitly distinguishes, as to the credit due to them, from the prophets who preceded; πίστεως δὲ οὐκ ὁμοίας ἠξίωται τῆς πρὸ αὐτῶν. Nor is this all. He says, in the same connexion, that "although so great a length of time has elapsed, [since the days of the ancient prophets,] no one has dared to add any thing to them, or to take any thing from them, nor to alter any thing." How could this be, if many Psalms, and the book of Daniel, not to mention smaller portions of many other books, have been *added*, as the liberal critics aver, in the time of the Maccabees, or even later? A matter so recent as the events of the Maccabæan times, and especially a matter of so great importance as that of augmenting the Holy Scriptures—how could it have failed to be known to Josephus, so thoroughly versed as he was in the history of his nation? But not a word of this nature from him. And yet he was under strong temptation, in writing his history, to show that the importance and precedence of the Jews had not suffered any degradation or decrease in later periods. Still, in spite of this feeling so natural to the human breast, in spite of all his patriotic ardour, he most amply asserts that the end of Artaxerxes' reign was the close of the prophetic order of his countrymen. The impartiality of the testimony adds much to the regard which is due to it. If the witness be interested, it is that he should say things to the honour of his nation which he does not say. And how should the proud and vain-glorious and boasting Jews of his time believe *en masse*, that no prophets had, for centuries, risen among them? It is very difficult, at least, to answer these questions on any ground, except that which admits the truth of Josephus' asseverations.

We may also ask other questions, in respect to the introduction and reception of *new* books during this period. Of all the nations of whom history has given any account, the Jews have been the most *conservative* and immutable. Subdued and nearly destroyed by Vespasian and Titus, the remnant were, and from that time have continued to be, scattered over the face of the whole earth. Never have they had a dominion or government or country of their own.

But after 1800 years have past, what are they now? The mass is just what they were in the days of the apostles, bigoted fanatics who are zealous in "tithing mint, anise, and cummin," and excessively attached to all the rites and forms that have come down to them by tradition, standing alone amidst all the nations of the earth, unmingled and incapable of being mingled with the people among whom they live. No nation on earth ever exhibited such a uniformity of character, and such a tenacity of traditions. Indeed, their separate and distinct existence, without any approach to amalgamation with other nations, is in itself a standing miracle, an exception to all analogies among the human race. Have they added to, or diminished from, their Scriptures during all this period of 1800 years? Not in the least. Their Rabbies have indeed introduced the Mishna and the Talmud, and commended them to the study of all. But they have never essayed to join these to their Canon of Scripture, or to mingle them therewith. Their BIBLE has remained inviolate.

Is this the people, then, who, a short time before the Christian era, stood on the alert to admit new and unheard of books into their sacred Canon? After enduring all the persecutions of Antiochus on account of their religion, just at the close of such a period would they have admitted a new book among those for which they were ready to die even joyfully—a book purporting to have been written by a man at the head of the court, when the decree of liberation from exile went forth, and which still had never made its appearance before, during nearly four centuries? How any one can be so yielding as to give a ready assent to historical statements so utterly improbable, and yet, on account of a few critical difficulties, become so entirely sceptical and incredulous as to the claims of this book—is a phenomenon that even Neology would find it difficult to account for, although its disciples in general take such a position.

Nor is even this all that may be said about the later admission of books into the Canon of Hebrew Scriptures. When did the rigid, and punctilious, and unchanging sect of the Pharisees take its rise? Was it not between the time of Artaxerxes and the Christian era? On what ground did this sect stand? On the ground of inflexible adherence to the traditions of the fathers. And is it not one of those traditions, as Josephus has stated it, not to add to, diminish from, or alter, the sacred books? In Antiq. XVIII. 1. 2, Josephus says of the three sects among the Jews, viz. Pharisees, Sadducees, and Essenes, that they had existed ἐκ τοῦ πάνυ ἀρχαίου τῶν πατρίων, i. e. from the very ancient times of the fathers. Under Jonathan, a Maccabæan prince, (159 —144 B. C.,) he speaks of this sect as being in full vigour; Antiq. XIII. 5. 9. That their origin lies so much in obscurity, is in itself a circumstance which shows their antiquity. The famous John Hyrcanus, so much extolled by Josephus, being traduced by one of the Pharisees, abandoned this sect to which he had belonged, and went over to the Sadducees; as Josephus relates in Antiq. XIII. 10. 5, 6. On this occasion the historian says of the Pharisees, that "they had so much influence with the people, as to be credited even when they spoke any thing against the king or the high priest." Did this sect, then, admit a new book among their Scriptures? Or if they had done so, would they not have been opposed and exposed by the Sadducees, who were strict *Scripturists*, i. e. strenuous advocates of the sentiment, that we must abide by the Scriptures only, without any of the traditions of men superadded? Plainly it was as much impossible to introduce a new book, (e. g. Daniel,) or new Psalms, at such a period of sectarian jealousy and dispute, as it would now be to introduce an addition to the New Testament, among the contending sects of Christians. Whatever may be said by critics about their difficulties in respect to the earlier composition of the book of Daniel, they can never meet and overcome the insuperable obstacles which the history of the religious state of things in the Maccabæan times throws in their way. And if the sects of Jews described by Josephus, and apparent throughout the New Testament, were, as he avers, ἐκ τοῦ πάνυ ἀρχαίου τῶν πατρίων, then is the probability of new books being introduced into the sacred Canon after the time of Malachi, a matter utterly incapable of being made out.

If indeed we are still urged by critics to admit the later addition of books to the sacred Canon, why, I would ask, was not Jesus Sirachides admitted? In Sirach. l. 27 he says, "I have written the instruction of understanding and knowledge in this book, I Jesus, the son of Sirach, of Jerusalem, who poured forth wisdom from his heart." Nor is this his only claim; for he goes on to say, "Blessed is he who shall occupy himself with these things, and whosoever lays them up in his mind shall become wise. For if he shall do these things, he shall become all-powerful, for his footsteps shall be in the light of the Lord." This is a high claim. Few of the biblical writers have made a higher one. But this is not all. In xxiv. 32—34 he says, "I will radiate forth instruction as the morning light, and disclose those things far away. I will pour forth instruction as *prophecy*, I will leave it to future generations. Behold, I have not laboured for myself only, but for all those who seek for it" [instruction] In xxxiii. 16—18, he represents himself as gleaning after others, (Solomon,) and goes on to say, "Consider that I have not laboured for myself, but for all those who receive instruction. Hear me, ye chieftains of the people, and ye who lead in the assemblies, give ear." Now, as we know from the preface to this work that it was written in Hebrew, and by a Jew of Jerusalem peculiarly devoted to sacred studies, and written *before* the time of the Maccabees, to say the least, what should have prevented the reception of such a book into the Jewish Canon, in case the Hebrews were not adverse to making any additions of this nature? The book exhibits a morality that is pure and elevated; the style has a strong resemblance to parts of Proverbs and Ecclesiastes; and it is evident that great regard was entertained for the work by the Jews in Egypt, where the grandson of Jesus found it and translated it. The Romanists extol it much, and assign good reasons, as they think, for the reception of it into their deutero-canon. To me it seems, that if the Jews were in such a state, in the Maccabæan times, as to admit a forged Daniel and recently composed Psalms into their Canon; and, in a word, if they had no more religious zeal and no more knowledge than all this implies; the Book of the Son of Sirach must have taken the place which the above passages quoted from it seem plainly to claim. No Romanist or Neologist can give a satisfactory reason why the Jews did not admit it. On the other hand, admitting the truth of Josephus' statement, viz. that since the order of prophets had ceased, no book was admitted into the Jewish Canon, then all becomes plain and easy. The Jews could not admit the claims of Jesus the Son of Sirach, because he was no prophet. On the like ground they could not admit the 1 Macc. into their Canon, although a very credible history and gravely written, and composed indeed only a short time after the book of Sirachides. Scarcely any thing in the Hebrew Old Testament history is a matter of more interest to one who seeks after a historical knowledge of the Jewish nation, than the 1 Maccabees. It covers a period of forty of the most eventful years that the Jews ever experienced, and exhibits this nation in the most interesting of all attitudes —contending against a force vastly superior, for their God, their religion, their country, and their homes. Yet 1 Macc. never had any place in the Palestine Jewish Canon, as all agree. I regard it as equally certain, that it had in reality no place in the Canon proper of the Egyptian Jews, at least in the time of Philo and of Christ and the apostles, notwithstanding it was originally written in the Hebrew language. *Practically* the Jews followed out the principle which Josephus states. They included in the Canon those prophetic or inspired writers, whom they knew, or supposed that they knew, to have lived before the close of Artaxerxes' reign. All other writers they left to stand merely upon the footing to which the æsthetical or historic worth of their works entitled them.

Mr. Norton has suggested, that *all* the writings of the Hebrews, which were extant at the time of return from the Babylonish captivity, were collected by the Jews, and combined in their so-called Scriptures. This has often been asserted by Neologists. But the proof of this has not yet been produced. I doubt not that literature among the Jews, during the exile, must have been generally in a low state. But as it will not be contended that the Jews were unacquainted with the art of writing at that time, so I cannot but deem it quite improbable, that nothing was written during the seventy years' captivity, except what appears in the Old Testament. Is it probable that such men as Shadrach, Meshech, and Abednego, brought up at the court of Babylon, and educated in all the Chaldean discipline, never wrote any thing? Is it probable that such men as Ezra, Nehemiah, and Mordecai, at the court of Persia, never wrote any thing, except the books of Ezra, Nehemiah, and Esther, (if these are to be attributed to them,) on any of the subjects which must be of interest to themselves and their nation? And Ezekiel among the exiles on the Chebar—was he the only one of them who could or would employ his pen? I must deem this to be quite improbable. But if these men, and other persons in a similar condition as to information, did engage in the composition of various works—what has become of them, it may be asked? And if it should be, the answer is not very difficult. What has become of the great mass of Greek and Roman writings, at a later period than this? What has become of many, and some very distinguished, works of early Christians? All-devouring time has accomplished their destruction. And should the question be asked still further, how some of the Hebrew books came to survive, while others perished, the answer is not unlike that which might be given in regard to Greek and Roman works, viz. the most important, with few exceptions, have survived. In the case of the Hebrews, such an answer may be given *a fortiori*. They distinguished between books sacred and those which were not so. The relative importance of the former to a people attached to their ancient religion, will not be denied. This consideration is sufficient, without entering upon any comparison of an æsthetical nature, between sacred and other writings. Indeed we cannot do this, for the character in this respect of books that are lost, is of course unknown to us. If it be asked, Who made the selection of books that are preserved? My answer would be—*prophets*, i. e. inspired men. If this be not a well-grounded answer, how comes it about that *the reception of books as sacred ceased when the order of prophets ceased?* So Josephus directly asserts; and the history of the Canon, so far as we can trace it, corresponds with this assertion.

SECT. XI. *Evidence that the Canon of the Old Testament was early completed, arising from the ancient divisions of it which bore specific appellations.*

EVERY reader of Hebrew knows familiarly that the Old Testament Scriptures as presented to us, (and so in the Hebrew MSS. and in the printed editions ever since the art of printing was discovered,) are divided into three parts, viz. *the Law, the Prophets,* and *the Hagiography.* The last is only a *Greek* name which we have borrowed; for the Hebrew name is כתובים, i. e. *writings,* or (which is equally literal) *Scriptures.* That writings *par excellence* or *sacred writings,* are meant by this appellation is clear; and hence the Greek name *Hagiography,* which has this signification. How long has such a division of the Jewish Scriptures been made? A question of no small importance; for these technical appellations of course imply a well-ascertained and *definite* number of books which are comprised under them. Such names could have no tolerable significancy, on the ground that each or either division was left in a floating or uncertain condition. Discrepancies of opinion there might be, in time, about the question, whether this or that book belonged to this class or that; but what books were comprised within this *Corpus,* could hardly have been a question, at a time when the names before us were definitely applied. Civilians have no difficulty in believing that the *Pandects* of Justinian comprise a definite collection of *ancient* Roman laws, nor that the Novellæ of the same comprise the more *modern* laws of that empire; although it is quite possible that the claims of one and another section to stand under the former or latter category might be doubtful.

We begin with the testimony of Jesus Sirachides, because it is the oldest to which we have access. The controversy about the age of the *Wisdom of Sirach* has never been fully settled. The main difficulty lies in the fact, that we cannot ascertain with entire certainty two personages mentioned in the book. In chap. i. Simon the high priest, the son of Onias, is highly extolled; and in the preface to the book by the translator, who was the *grandson* of the author, he says that he performed his work of translation in the reign of [Ptolemy] Euergetes. Now it so happens, that there were two Simons, both high priests, and both sons of Onias; also two Ptolemies with the surname of Euergetes. About a century elapsed between the first high priest and king and the second; so that only the circumstances adverted to in the book can settle the question of its age with probability. The current seems recently to run in favour of the latest date, which would assign the composition of the book to about 170 B. C. Its translation by the grandson of the author, must then be assigned to about 130 B. C. I will admit, for the present, the probability of the later dates; for I cannot now turn aside to discuss the question; and I do not wish, in fixing on the time, to go beyond what critics in general will admit, viz. that the book must have been originally composed before the time of the Maccabees. It is impossible to believe, had it been otherwise, that the Maccabees would have been omitted in the eulogy of Hebrew patriots and prophets, contained in chap. xliv.—l., and more especially since Simon the high priest is there lauded beyond measure.

In respect to the third division of the Jewish Scriptures which has been named כתובים=γραφαί, it is plain that only by the use of the article with such a name, whether in Greek, Hebrew, or English, could it have been made specific. In itself the word is generic, and may be applied to any kind of writings. But when it is employed in connexion with the *Law* and the *Prophets*, and has also the definite article before it, the import of the word cannot well be misunderstood.

Thus much for the name *Kethubim*, since it has been introduced. But this was not very early. We first meet with it in Epiphanius, who translates it literally by γραφεῖα; in Panario, p. 58. A strictly *technical* name the third portion of the Hebrew Scriptures does not appear to have had, before the Christian era, or during the early part of it. We shall see, that while the other two names are very ancient, the ancient designation of the now-named *Kethubim* or *Hagiography* was very various.

In the preface to Sirach, the translator states, that many and signal had been the benefits conferred on the Hebrew nation " by the Law, and the Prophets, and *the other* [books] *which follow in the same spirit,* τῶν ἄλλων τῶν κατ' αὐτοὺς ἠκολουθηκότων." Such is the designation of the triplex parts of the Scriptures. It lacks a proper name for the third division. See the whole of the Preface in Appendix, No. I.

Again, in the same preface, the writer says, that "his grandfather Jesus applied himself ἐπὶ πλεῖον, for a long time, or very much, to the reading of the Law, the Prophets, and *of the other patrical books,* τῶν ἄλλων πατρίων βιβλίων." I have made a new adjective here which rather *transfers* than translates the Greek, because there may be some doubt, perhaps, whether the writer means books *belonging to the fathers,* i. e. books which they received, or books of which *the fathers were the authors.* In either case the meaning indeed is for substance about the same, or nearly so; but at all events and plainly a third division of the Scriptures, not comprehended in the two preceding ones, is here designated, although not by a technical name.

Once more, speaking of a variety as to modes of expression in different languages, he says, that "there is no small difference, also, among the books belonging to the Law, the Prophets, καὶ τὰ λοιπὰ τῶν βιβλίων, *and the rest or remainder of the books.*" Here is still another designation of the third division of the Hebrew Scriptures. THE REST *of the books* must of course be some definite or well-known remainder of them; else the readers of the Preface could have no definite idea of what the writer meant. Indeed τὰ λοιπά is susceptible of no other certain and definite meaning, than such an one as I have just assigned to it. It was not the object of the translator to assert that his grandfather gave himself to the diligent and long-continued reading of all books without distinction, but only to those sacred books which would particularly aid him in the composition of his work. Moreover, if the *Law* in this case designates a definite and well-known portion of the Scriptures, and the *Prophets* another, (as surely they do,) the τὰ λοιπὰ τῶν βιβλίων, in the position and relation in which it stands, must also be equally definite in the view of the writer and reader of that day. Βιβλίων, then, i. e. the plural of βιβλίον, is here used just as we employ the word *Scriptures,* viz. the plural form of the word is used to designate the idea, that the book as a whole is made up of many separate parts. Both Greeks and Latins, at a subsequent period, employed βιβλία and *biblia* to denote the volume of the Scriptures. It is like employing the Latin *literæ*, to designate a single epistle, because it consists of many *literæ* united together. Of course, when the grandson of Jesus Sirachides employs τὰ λοιπὰ τῶν βιβλίων, he uses it just as we should use the phrase *the rest of the Scriptures*, immediately after mentioning the Law and the Prophets. Of necessity this has a definite meaning; and if so, the Bible, at that time, was a well-known and definite book.

I will not affirm, that what the grandson says for the purpose of designating the Hebrew Scriptures, renders it certain that these designations already existed in the time of the grandfather. Yet I am persuaded that his words imply thus much. At all events, so much must be plain, viz. that the grandson means to tell his readers what and how many books his grandfather diligently studied. If the *names* which he employs in order to describe them were not in use in the time of Jesus Sirachides, yet there must have been some circumscription to the limits of the original author's study, and some expressions which would mark it as a well-known and definite circle of reading. Such being the case, in the days of Sirachides the Hebrew Bible must have already attained to a definite whole or *corpus*.

But is there not something in the book itself, as it came from the pen of Sirachides, which speaks to the like purpose? In the proem to his πατέρων ὕμνος, or Eulogy of the Fathers, (chap. xliv. seq.,) he speaks generally of what had been done by the Hebrew worthies. Among other things he says, "They gave counsel by their understanding, they preached—made public declarations, ἀπηγγελκότες—by their *prophecies;*" xliv. 3. Again, of some others among them (ver. 5,) he says, "They sought out the melody of music, they composed poems in writing, διηγούμενοι ἔπη ἐν γραφῇ. This latter clause De Wette translates, *Dichteten Lieder schriftlich* (with the same meaning as above); and in its connexion, this seems to me plainly to be the only true meaning. Here, then, are the two latter divisions of the Bible; for, according to Josephus, (cont. Apion. I. 8,) the third part consisted principally of *poetry*. In chap. xlv., when the writer comes to speak of Moses, he says, that God "gave him commandments by personal intercourse, the Law of life and knowledge, to teach Jacob his covenant, and Israel his judgments." Here, then, according to the view of Sirachides himself, are virtually the same triplex divisions or portions of the Scriptures, which are mentioned by the grandson and translator in his preface to the book. To make this language intelligible, there must have been a known and recognised distinction among the Hebrew sacred books at that time, to which the mind of the reader would of course advert, when these different portions were named.

PHILO JUDÆUS (flor. 40 B. C.) is our next witness, in regard to the point before us. In his book *De Vita contemplativa* (Opp. II. p. 475, ed. Mang.) he is speaking of the Essenes as peculiarly devoted to such a life, and as withdrawing into their secret apartments, from which every thing pertaining to the refreshment of the body was excluded, and there, says he, "they receive only the *laws* and the oracles uttered by the *prophets*, and the *hymns* and *other* [*books*], by which knowledge and piety are augmented and perfected."* In other words, they admit to their meditation-closets nothing but the *Holy Scriptures.* That this is his meaning, is plain from that which he immediately subjoins : " For addressing themselves to the Holy Scriptures, (ἐντυγχάνοντες γὰρ τοῖς ἱεροῖς γράμμασι,) they philosophize after the manner of their country," &c. Immediately after this he says, " They have, moreover, the writings of ancient men, the leaders of their sect, who have left many memorials of their views, in regard to allegorical matters." Here the express separation of their sectarian books from the Scriptures before mentioned, leaves no room to doubt what the meaning of Philo is ; see Append. ut supra. Such, then, in Egypt, as well as in Palestine, was the well-known division of the Hebrew Scriptures before the Christian era. How exactly it coincides with the division in the apostolic age, we shall soon see.

In the NEW TESTAMENT we find the most explicit testimony to the same purpose. Jesus says to his wondering and doubting disciples, after his death and resurrection, in order to calm and satisfy their minds with regard to these

* See Appendix, No. II., for the whole passage.

events, "All things must be fulfilled which are written in the *Law of Moses*, and *the Prophets*, and *the Psalms*, concerning me ;" Luke xxiv. 44. In the 27th verse of the same chapter it is said of Jesus, that "beginning from Moses and from the prophets, he explained to them [to his disciples] in all the Scriptures the things which concerned himself." This passage is virtually the same with that above. Two divisions of Scripture are here alluded to by name, and the third is separated from them by a phraseology which necessarily imports, that there were other portions of Scripture besides the two named, which Jesus interpreted for the disciples, as he first had done in respect to the Law and the Prophets. That the third portion has not a specific appellation, is the same phenomenon that we have already seen in Sirachides and in Philo. Philo, however, adverts to the third division under the general designation of *hymns* (ὕμνοι); and Luke, or rather the Saviour himself, refers to it in the same way, only he calls it ψαλμοί, which is altogether equivalent to the ὕμνοι of Philo. The obvious reason of this designation seems to be, either that the Hagiography began (as now) with the book of Psalms, and then the maxim, *a potiori nomen fit*, guided the choice of a designation ; or else the third class of books was called *Psalms*, because it consisted principally, if not altogether, of *poetry*.* That the Scriptures in a specific form are here meant, there can be no doubt ; for after speaking of the things written in the Law, the Prophets, and the Psalms, concerning Christ, it is said of Jesus, that "he opened the mind [of the disciples] to understand τὰς γραφάς, *the Scriptures*," viz. those Scriptures which he had quoted and explained.

We have already seen, that Josephus, after naming the Law and the Prophets as constituting the first two parts of the Jewish Scriptures, says of the other books, " Αἱ δὲ λοιπαὶ τέσσαρες ὕμνους εἰς τὸν Θεόν, καὶ τοῖς ἀνθρώποις ὑποθήκας τοῦ βίου περιέχουσιν, i. e. the other four books contain hymns to God, and maxims of life for men ;" Cont. Ap. I. 8. See Append. No. III. Here, again, is plainly the same thing which we have found in Philo and in the New Testament, with only this difference, that Josephus, in adding *maxims of*

---
* The latter opinion is the more probable. See Hävernick's Einleit. p. 78. D.

life for men, has definitely alluded to the books of Proverbs and Ecclesiastes, while the other writers have merely comprised them under generic names.

In the later catalogues of the Old Testament books among Christians, viz. that of Melito in the second century, and of Origen in the first part of the third, the *names* of the books are merely given, without mention of the general *triplex* division adverted to by all the preceding writers who have been quoted above. Melito, however, adverts in the context to the Old Test. Scriptures, (see in Euseb. Hist. Ecc. IV. 26,) under the designation of the *Law* and the *Prophets*, in the same manner as is sometimes done in the New Testament. But in Jerome, incomparably the best Hebrew scholar and critic among all the ancient Christian fathers, (indeed we may say, the only really thorough Hebraist among them all,) who spent some twenty years in Palestine, and made himself familiar with every thing pertaining to the Hebrews—in Jerome's *Prologus Galeatus*, the same *triplex* division reappears: "Ita fiunt pariter Veteris Legis libri *viginti duo*, id est, *Mosis* quinque, et *Prophetarum* octo, *Hagiographorum* novem; i. e. thus at the same time are made twenty-two books of the Old Testament, that is, of *Moses* five, of the *Prophets* eight, of the *Hagiography* nine." Down, then, to the time of Jerome this ancient division of the Jewish Scriptures was in full use, although, as we shall hereafter see, the books assigned to the second and third divisions had suffered some change of location respectively since the time of Josephus, who reckons the Prophets as comprising more books than Jerome assigns to them, and the Hagiography of course as comprising fewer.

Lastly, the Talmud, in the fifth or sixth century, put the final seal upon this usage, so far as the Jews and the Hebrew Bible are concerned. This compilation by learned Babylonish Jews of all the traditions among their Rabbies in respect to the Scriptures and to the subject of religious rites and ceremonies, was probably made in the latter part of the fifth and the beginning of the sixth centuries (some portions of it possibly earlier, and some still later). In the Gemara of it, *Tract. Baba Bathra*, fol. 13. c. 2, we find the following declaration: "Our wise men say, that the whole is one, and each part is one by itself; and they have transmitted to us the *Law*, the *Prophets*, and the *Kethubim*, united together as one, "והביאו לפנינו תורה נביאים וכתובים מדובקים כאחד." After this, the passage goes on to recite the order in which the books are arranged, and to specificate those which belong to the three divisions respectively. The *Law* is of course the same in all the arrangements of the ancients; the *Prophets* contains, as usual, Joshua, Judges, 1 and 2 Samuel, 1 and 2 Kings, Jeremiah, Ezekiel, Isaiah, and the twelve Minor Prophets, thus making *eight* books for the second division, as in our common Hebrew Bibles, and as in Jerome quoted above. In the *Kethubim* or *Hagiography*, the Talmudists reckon *eleven* books, while Jerome makes but *nine*. The difference consists merely in the mode of combination. Jerome joins Ruth to Judges as one book, and thus brings the former into the circle of the Prophets; he also joins Lamentations with Jeremiah, and arranges it of course in the same way; while the Talmudists separate these two small books, and throw them both into the *third* division. Jerome's division is more in conformity with the ancient number of the scriptural books. That of the Talmud depends on a new mode of numbering these books; of which more in due time.

What the Talmud thus sanctioned, has come down to the present hour, among the Jews, substantially the same. The only exception is in the *order* of some of the books; which has always been a matter that admitted of change, and has indeed been very various in different countries and in different ages. The Talmudists have one arrangement; the Masorites another; the German MSS. follow the former, while the Spanish MSS. exhibit the order of the latter; and thus with the editions of the Hebrew Bible that are respectively copied after each.

From a remote time, then, even before the Christian era, a *triplex* division of the Jewish Scriptures has been made, which necessarily involved a special relation of each part to the other, and of course rendered it necessary, that the extent of each part should be definitely and well known. If the *Law* was definite, if the *Prophets* was definite, then the *Kethubim* also was definite. For when Sirachides (in his preface) speaks of "the Law itself, and the Prophecies, καὶ τὰ λοιπὰ τῶν βιβλίων," if the two first parts are circumscribed, definite, and intelligible, then the third division must be equally so; for otherwise it would mean simply *all other books*. To suppose this last to be the meaning, would be an absurdity.

This brings us, then, again to the position, that for a long time antecedently to the Christian era, the Old Testament was a definite, well-known, accredited collection of writings, regarded by the Jews as their sacred Code of Laws, and distinguished by them from all other books. But of the estimation in which these books were held, it will become necessary hereafter again to speak.

In order to render this view of the manner in which the Old Test. Scriptures were designated, even in very ancient times, more complete, I must not omit to mention, that as all names of things of which frequent use must be made in common parlance, become, in case they are long, almost without exception abridged for the sake of convenience, so it fared with the triplex and full designation of the Holy Scriptures. Oftentimes the Old Testament was spoken of merely as one book, or one code of religious laws and history, and then a single name of a generic nature was applied—the very same that was technically employed, at a later period, to designate the third division of the Scriptures, viz. γραφαί=כתובים, exactly in the sense of our word *Scriptures*. Examples of this are easily found in the New Testament; e. g. Matt. xxi. 42; xxii. 29; xxvi. 54, 56; Luke xxiv. 32, 45; John v. 39; Acts xvii. 2, 11; xviii. 24, 28; Rom. xv. 4; xvi. 26; 2 Pet. iii. 16. In Rom. i. 2, Paul names the Old Testament γραφαὶ ἅγιαι, in reference to their inspiration by the Holy Spirit, and to the same purpose ἱερὰ γράμματα in 2 Tim. iii. 15. When the speaker wished to appeal to Scripture in a still more *generic* way, (leaving out of view its various component parts,) he employed the singular number of the noun γραφή, especially when he cited a passage from Scripture without stopping to designate the particular place whence he took it; e. g. Mark xii. 10; xv. 28; Luke iv. 21; John vii. 38; x. 35; xiii. 18; xvii. 12; xix. 28, 37; xx. 9; Acts i. 16; viii. 32, 35; Rom. iv. 3; ix. 17; x. 11; xi. 2; Gal. iii. 8; 1 Tim. v. 18; James ii. 8; 1 Pet. ii. 6. In a way a little different from this usage, and in the mere generic sense of Scripture generally, we find γραφή employed

John ii. 22; Gal. iii. 22; 2 Pet. i. 20. In 2 Tim. iii. 16, Paul speaks of πᾶσα γραφή, i. e. every component part or portion of Scripture, (πᾶσα ἡ γραφή would mean *the whole of Scripture* as a totality, Winer, N. Test. Gramm. § 17. 10,) and avers that it, i. e. each part or portion of Scripture, is θεόπνευστος, *divinely inspired*.

The *Law*, as being the leading and preëminent part of the Old Testament, is not unfrequently employed to designate comprehensively the Scriptures in general. Nothing is more common than such a metonymy or synecdoche, where the name of a part stands for the whole, and especially of a preëminent or leading part. The old maxim, *A potiori nomen fit*, also explains this. In such a generic sense does the word seem plainly to be employed in Luke xvi. 17; John x. 34; xii. 34; xv. 25, for the *Law* (to which the speakers in these cases refer) is not any passage in the Pentateuch, but in other parts of Scripture. So is it, also, with 1 Cor. xiv. 21, where a quotation from Isaiah xxviii. 11, 12, is named the *Law*. In John i. 17, however, we have a plain recognition of the word *Law* as employed in the limited and technical sense: "The Law was given by Moses." Rabbinic usage agrees with the custom of the New Test. writers in the employment of the word *law* in a general sense; and so does the usage of our own theological dialect at the present day, e. g. in such cases as 'the Law and the Gospel,' 'the Divine Law has forbidden or sanctioned this or that,' &c. Comp. 2 Macc. ii. 18.

It will be no matter of surprise, after this view of the manner in which appellations are bestowed on the Old Test. Scriptures, to find that the second portion of them, i. e. the *Prophets*, as well as the first and third, sometimes lends its name to designate the whole collection. Examples of such a usage may be found in Mark i. 2; Matt. xxvi. 56; Luke xviii. 31; xxiv. 25; John vi. 45; Acts iii. 21; xiii. 27, 40; xv. 15; xxvi. 27; 2 Pet. iii. 2. This accounts for the use of the plural number, προφῆται, in some cases where merely one single prophet is quoted; e. g. Matt. ii. 23, and many of the passages to which reference is made in the preceding sentence.

The reverse of this, viz. the use of the *singular* number, προφήτης, to designate the whole of Scripture, (like γραφή

SECT. XI. ANCIENT DIVISIONS OF THE CANON. 237

instead of γραφαί,) I believe cannot be found in the New Testament. There is an obvious reason for this. All the writers of the Old Testament, in the language of the Jews, were called *Prophets*; so that all were virtually placed on the same basis or in the same rank. No one of these (the singular number would indicate only a single individual) was so preëminently or exclusively the author of the Scriptures, as to cause them to be named from him. Between γραφή and γραφαί there is no such contrast, because neither of the words are indicative of *persons*. We cannot solve the difficulty then in Mark i. 2, seq., where passages in two prophets are quoted, while they are introduced by the formula, "As it is written *in the prophet*," by saying that the singular number, προφήτης, stands for the whole collection. The solution lies in another quarter. Griesbach, and those who follow him, employ the singular number here, προφήτῃ. But Hahn, the Vulgate text, and the earlier critical editions, read προφήταις; Lachmann himself confessing that the authority of it is equal to that which adopts the singular number. In such a case to prefer the *more difficult reading*, as it is called, to the one which is congruous with the context and with good sense, is what I must name an *abuse* of a good thing—a real perversion of the rational laws of criticism. But we cannot dwell on such matters.

Finally, the *two* leading appellations of the *triplex* division of the Scriptures are not unfrequently joined together, in order to make the name somewhat more complete than one appellation only could make it. Thus *the Law and the Prophets* in Matt. xi. 13; xxii. 40; Luke xvi. 16; John i. 45; Acts xiii. 15; xxiv. 14; Rom. iii. 21. Exactly in the same sense, and for the same purpose, *Moses and the Prophets* is used in various passages; e. g. Luke xvi. 29, 31; xxiv. 27; Acts xxviii. 23.

I would merely remark, at the close of this exposition of Scriptural usage as to *names*, that the New Test. writers could never have employed all these different appellations, and so often interchanged them without superadding any explanations, if the definite import of each and all had not been well understood by themselves and by those whom they addressed. The Old Testament must have been as definite then as it is now, and its limits as well known. Every Jew that could read, must have known what books belonged to it, when copies of the Scriptures had become common.

SECT. XII. *Sameness of the Jewish Canon in early times shown by the Number and Names of the Books.*

WE have seen that Jesus Sirachides adverts only to the triplex division of the Holy Scriptures in his time, but does not give us either the names or the number of the books contained in them. This division is brought to view so frequently in the Wisdom of Sirach, (including the Preface,) that there can be no reasonable doubt of its designating a limited and definite collection of books; and by comparison of the same triplex division brought to view also by subsequent writers in early times, and this in connexion with the *number* and *names* of the books, we learn what estimate we should put upon the designations by Sirachides of the various portions of the Scriptures. We argue from the nature of the case, that his designations must imply a definite and ascertained number or circle of books; but we must go to other writers to learn with exactness the dimensions of this circle.

Josephus has testified (in the passage *cont. Apion.* I. § 8, as fully quoted above, p. 207, see Append. No. III.) in the following manner: "*We have* TWENTY-TWO *books, comprising the history of every age, which are justly credited as Divine.*" *Five* of these he assigns to Moses; *thirteen* to the prophets; and of course *four* to the Hagiography. Would that he had given us the *names* of each, and of those to be classed under each division! But as he has not, we must supply this deficiency in the best manner that we can. I believe it may be done to the entire satisfaction of every reasonable reader.

The earliest writer after Josephus, who has given us an account of the sacred books of the Jews, is Melito, bishop of Sardis (fl. 170 A. D.). He travelled from Sardis to Palestine, mainly, as it would seem by his own statement, for the purpose of ascertaining the exact names, number, and order of the Jewish Scriptures. The result of his visit he communicates to his brother Onesimus, in the following letter, preserved by Eusebius in Hist. Ecc. IV. 26. See the original in App. No. IV.)

"Melito to Onesimus his brother, greeting. Since you have often requested, through the earnest desire that you cherish for the word [of God], that you might have a selection made for you from the Law and the Prophets,* which has respect to our Saviour and the whole of our faith; and since, moreover, you have been desirous to obtain an accurate account of the *ancient books*, both as to their number and their order; I have taken pains to accomplish this, knowing your earnestness in respect to the faith, and your desire for instruction in regard to the word; and most of all, that you, while striving after eternal salvation, through desires after God, give a preference to these things. Making a journey therefore into the east, [Palestine,] and having arrived at the place where these things [i. e. scriptural events] were proclaimed and transacted, I there learned accurately the books of the Old Testament, which I here arrange and transmit to you. The names are as follows: The five books of Moses, Genesis, Exodus, Leviticus, Numbers, Deuteronomy. Then Joshua of Nun, Judges, Ruth, four books of Kings, two of Chronicles. The Psalms of David, the Proverbs of Solomon, (also called Wisdom,) Ecclesiastes, the Song of Songs, Job. Prophets: Isaiah, Jeremiah, the Twelve in one book, Daniel, Ezekiel, Ezra. From these I have made selections, distributing them into six books."

It will not be pretended, I presume, by any considerate man, that the Jews in Palestine had altered their Scriptures between the time of Josephus (born A. D. 37) and that of Melito. The thing was impossible; first on the ground of their own opposing parties, the Pharisees, Sadducees, and Essenes; secondly, on the ground of rivalship between Jews and Christians. I might add a third consideration, peculiarly applicable to those times, and this is the sectarian zeal with which the Pharisees guarded all the traditions and customs of their forefathers.

* These plainly stand for the whole Scriptures, according to New Test. usage pointed out on page 237 above.

(1.) My first remark on this testimony of Melito is, that it comes from a very distinguished and enlightened man. Cave says justly of him, "Vir pietate non minus quam doctrinâ clarus;" and Tertullian (a contemporary) testifies of him, that most Christians called him a *prophet;* in Hieron. de Script. c. 2. 4. His knowledge was acquired, moreover, by a special effort and much caution; for he was not content with what he learned at Sardis, but must needs go to Palestine itself, in order that he might know the ἀκρίβειαν, *the exact truth* of the whole matter respecting the Jewish Scriptures.

(2.) It seems quite probable, if not altogether certain, from the *names* of the books, as given by Melito, and from their *order*, that he learned them by consulting a *Greek* copy or copies of the Scriptures, and not a Hebrew one. Neither the names, in some cases, nor the order, nor the classification, compares altogether with the Hebrew, but rather with the Version of the Seventy; yet in some respects, not even with the Septuagint as we now have it in our printed copies. But in making the four books of Samuel and Kings into one book with one and the same designation, viz. *Kings*, he plainly follows the Septuagint; in placing Chronicles next to them, he does the same, but here it is far from certain that the Hebrew at that time differed in respect to this from the Septuagint. The sequel of his catalogue differs, as to *order*, both from the Jewish and Septuagint lists of the books of the Old Testament which have come down to us; as also from the order of these books as given by Origen, Jerome, and others. But, as I have already remarked, the *order* of classification has always been subject to variation in the second and third classes of the Hebrew books; and that of Melito helps to confirm this view of the subject.

(3.) As the copy or copies of the Greek Scriptures, from which Melito took his list, contained none of the *apocryphal* books, (so called,) so it is plain and quite certain, that near the close of the second century the Greek Scriptures, as circulated and used in Palestine, contained none of the so-called *deutero-canonical* books, i. e. apocryphal books. Whatever may have been the condition of the Old Testament *Greek* Scriptures at Alexandria, at the period in question, the "books written *after* the time of Artaxerxes Longimanus" were *not* included in the Scriptures which Melito consulted. The Romish church will find, therefore, in this almost primitive father, but a very slender support, (indeed none at all, but the contrary,) for their *deutero-canon*. If it be said, (as it has been,) that the clause in Melito, Σαλομῶνος παροιμίαι ἢ καὶ σοφία means *the Proverbs of Solomon and also Wisdom*, (i. e. the Wisdom of Solomon, one of the apocryphal books,) the reply to this suggestion is easy. "Nearly all the ancients," remarks Valesius on this passage, "called the Proverbs of Solomon *Wisdom*, and sometimes σοφίαν παναίρετον." Accordingly Dionysius of Alexandria calls the book of Proverbs ἡ σοφὴ βίβλος; Cap. 28, Catena in Jobum. The author of the Jerusalem Itinerary, speaking of a certain chamber in Jerusalem, says that "Solomon sat there, and there he wrote *Sapientiam*," i. e. the book of Proverbs. Melito means, then, merely to say, that the work of Solomon called παροιμίαι, had also the name of σοφία. The pronoun ἢ also imports this. We cannot alter the accentuation and make it an *article*; for to a title of a book the article does not in such a case belong.

(4.) Counting the books as arranged by Melito, we find them twenty-one in number; which lacks one of the number as given by Josephus. As the list of the bishop now stands, the books of Nehemiah and Esther seem to be omitted. The solution of the difficulty in respect to Nehemiah is easy. Both Jews and Greeks, at that time, reckoned the books of Ezra and Nehemiah as being but one; for so it appears by the lists of the sacred books among the ancients, Origen, Jerome, Concilium Laod., Canones Apost., Hilary, &c. Only one book, then, is lacking in Melito, and this is the book of *Esther*. How the problem which this omission raises is to be solved, critics have not been agreed. Eichhorn supposes Esther to be included by Melito under the denomination Ἐσδρας; but the like to this is not found elsewhere among the ancient modes of reckoning the sacred books. Herbst, in his recent *Einleitung*, supposes Melito to have had access to a Greek Manuscript which contained the apocryphal additions to Esther, and which, as he was told by the Jews that they did not admit the authenticity of the book in that interpolated state, he rejected from his

Canon. I deem it more satisfactory to suppose, with others, an omission here of the name of Esther by Eusebius, in copying the document. Precisely such an one occurs in his copy of Origen's Canon, Ecc. Hist. VI. 25. Origen says, even as copied by Eusebius, that *twenty-two* books belong to the Canon, and he then proceeds to name them. But in doing this, the twelve Minor Prophets (in one book) are omitted by Eusebius, so that, as represented by this historian, Origen makes only *twenty-one* books. Besides this, Ruffinus' translation of Origen gives us the missing book, and restores the Minor Prophets to their proper place. Herbst thinks that Melito himself must have omitted Esther, because, as he avers, Athanasius and Gregory Nazianzen reject it. But Gregory remarks in respect to it, "τούτοις [i. e. to or with the other books of the Old Test.] προσεγκρίνουσι τὴν 'Εσϑὴρ τινές, i. e. with these some reckon Esther;" Carm. XXXIII. Tom. II. It would seem probable that he himself doubted of the book. Athanasius also omits it, probably on a similar ground; but Origen, the Council of Laodicea, (about 360—364,) Can. 59, Canones Apostol. LXXXV., Cyrillus Hieros. Catech. IV. No. 33— 36, Epiphanius de Mens. et Ponder., c. 22, 23, Opp. II., Jerome in Prol. Gal., in their respective lists, all expressly *insert* it. It must be admitted, I think, that either Gregory and Athanasius both had doubts about the canonical authority of Esther; or that in their lists of sacred books, they have merely copied from Eusebius, who, it seems plain, had accidentally omitted it. The whole current of Christian antiquity is evidently in favour of such a view. And as to the *Jews*, the very copious extracts which Josephus has made from the book of Esther, as also the time in which he supposes it to have been written, render it altogether certain that it was in his Canon of the Jewish Scriptures.

Thus much for Melito. A most important witness, moreover, he is, because he is so early, and withal so intelligent and candid. We have then the books which Josephus' number *twenty-two* comprised. We cannot omit Esther at all events, so far as Josephus is concerned; and our next object is to inquire how these books in question came to be reckoned at *twenty-two*.

In whatever way we regard the *number* of the sacred

SECT. XII. SAMENESS OF THE JEWISH CANON. 243

books of the Old Testament, as reckoned by the ancient Jews or Christians, we are obliged to confess that there is something of the arbitrary and the fanciful in it. Still, it is a circumstance in itself so immaterial, that we need not take any alarm at the phantasies which have controlled this matter. Jerome, who spent many years in Palestine in studying the Hebrew language, customs, and opinions, and who, as I have said, was by far the best critic and exegete of all the ancient Fathers, has doubtless given us the true secret of the number *twenty-two*, as applied to the Hebrew Scriptures. Let us hear him, as he speaks in his *Prologus Galeatus:* "Viginti et duas literas esse apud Hebræos, Syrorumque quoque lingua et Chaldæorum testatur quæ Hebrææ magna ex parte confinis est. Nam et ipsi viginti duo elementa habent, eodem sono et diversis characteribus. ... Quomodo igitur *viginti duo elementa* sunt, per quæ scribimus Hebraice omne quod loquimur, et eorum initiis vox humana comprehenditur; ita *viginti duo volumina* supputantur, quibus, quasi literis et exordiis, in Dei doctrinâ tenera adhuc et lactens viri justi eruditur infantia; i. e. that there are *twenty-two* letters among the Hebrews, the Syriac and Chaldee languages testify, which for the most part are kindred with the Hebrew. For they have twenty-two letters, the same [as the Hebrew] in sound, but differing in form... As then there are twenty-two letters by which we write in Hebrew every thing that we utter, and the human voice is comprised within their constituent initial elements: so twenty-two volumes are reckoned, by which the tender and as yet unwearied infancy of the just man is instructed, as by elementary letters, in the doctrine of God."

It is in vain to ask what could have directed the minds of those who arranged the Scriptures to such a fanciful comparison. But to say the least, it is certainly not an unnatural mode of reckoning. 'Letters instruct, and there are twenty-two of them; the Scriptures instruct, and there are twenty-two of them.' Such was the analogical reasoning. I do not know that critics have taxed Aristarchus with folly or weakness, because he divided the Iliad and Odyssey into *twenty-four* books each, according to the number of letters in the Greek alphabet. It was an easy way of designating and distinguishing the different parts of those poems. Why should it be thought strange, that not far from the same time some zealous student of the Jewish Scriptures divided them in a similar manner? Even if you reply, and say that unnatural combinations of different books into one were resorted to, in order to make the number twenty-two; still this has no solid foundation. Aristarchus has combined the poems of Homer, in some cases, in the like manner, where the matter would have pointed to a division different from that which he has made. Yet his division is without any serious inconvenience. So the Jews in several cases combined books together as *one* which seem to be *two*, and are so reckoned in our present Bibles. The ancient lists of the scriptural books show, that at first this combination was made thus: Judges and Ruth were united as one; 1 and 2 Samuel as one; 1 and 2 Kings as one; 1 and 2 Chronicles as one; Ezra and Nehemiah as one; Jeremiah and the Lamentations as one; the twelve prophets as one. The reason of the combination of the first five cases is very plain. The historical matter of the books is continuous and successive. In the sixth case, it is very plain that Jeremiah is reckoned as including the Lamentations, because both are the work of one author, and the latter is an appendix which shows the fulfilment of his prophecy. As to the twelve Minor Prophets, it would seem that they were comprised in one, i. e. in one roll or volume, on account of their brevity. Jerome (ut sup.) speaks of the Hebrews as usually counting five of the books as double, because they have the same number of letters in the alphabet which have two forms, viz. כ, ם, נ, פ, צ; and, corresponding with these, they reckon Samuel, Kings, Chronicles, Ezra, and Jeremiah, as being double, or consisting of two parts.* But this is somewhat more fanciful or arbitrary than the numbering of the books in general according to the letters of the alphabet; inasmuch as it does not reach or account for all the cases of combination. The union of Judges and Ruth, and also of the twelve Minor Prophets, still remains to be accounted for.

With the light which we obtain from Jerome, we may now go back to Josephus, and ask how he must have made out his *triplex* division, viz. the Law, the Prophets, the

* See the passage of Jerome in the Appendix, No. XIV.

Hymns and Maxims of Life, and at the same time have made only *twenty-two* books in the whole.

The matter is easy and obvious. (1.) The *five* books of the Pentateuch, in the order in which they have always stood and still stand. (2.) We must call to mind, that *prophets* is a designation, among the Hebrews, of any writer who is, or is believed to be, *inspired;* and that of course it may, and does, comprehend the *historians* as well as those who uttered predictions. According to Josephus, then, *Prophets* comprises all the books which are historical or predictive. Of course his second division which, as he tells us, is comprised ἐν τρισὶ καὶ δέκα βιβλίοις, i. e. "in *thirteen* books," must include, (1.) Joshua. (2.) Judges and Ruth. (3.) 1 and 2 Samuel. (4.) 1 and 2 Kings. (5.) 1 and 2 Chronicles. (6.) Ezra and Nehemiah. (7.) Esther. (8.) Isaiah. (9.) Jeremiah and Lamentations. (10.) Ezekiel. (11.) Daniel. (12.) The twelve Minor Prophets. (13.) Job. All these are historical or predictive. The book of Job is not an exception ; because Josephus doubtless regarded it in the light of a real history of Job, and as much a history as the book of Ruth, or Esther, although written poetically. That he did so reckon is plain, because the αἱ λοιπαὶ τέσσαρες, i. e. *the other remaining four books*, he describes as consisting of ὕμνοι καὶ ὑποθῆκαι τοῦ βίου, i. e. hymns and maxims of life. I suppose it will not be contended that ὕμνοι does not characterize the Psalms; and the other books must of course be the Proverbs, Ecclesiastes, and Canticles. And although the designation, *hymns* or *maxims of life*, will not strictly apply to Canticles, yet here, as is common in other cases, *a potiori nomen fit*, the name is given to four books from the altogether predominant part of them. Canticles is neither predictive nor historical, and so it would not class with the Prophets or second division of the Scriptures. The conclusion seems to be a necessary one, therefore, that Josephus arranged his twenty-two books in the manner that has now been specified.

This conclusion seems to amount to satisfactory certainty, when we examine all the early lists of the Old Testament books, which other writers have transmitted to us. The list of Melito combines the books of the Old Testament in the same manner as that which we have attributed to Josephus, with the single exception, that Judges is separated from Ruth, and 1 and 2 Samuel and 1 and 2 Kings are combined into one book in four parts, as they were in the Septuagint, and are still, even down to the present time. Origen, who was familiar with the Hebrew MSS. of his day, gives the combination of books in just the same way as that which has been attributed to Josephus. The Council of Laodicea, (360—364,) in Can. 59, follow the same track, making *twenty-two* books, in the same way as Josephus does. The only departure is in the case of Jeremiah, where they join Baruch and the epistles in the same book with that prophet, as well as the Lamentations. It has been supposed, that the apocryphal Baruch was the one here designated, and so that it was anciently included in the book of Jeremiah. But of this I must doubt. Whoever reads Jer. xxxvi., xlv., will be satisfied, especially if he reflects on the disjointed condition in which the writings of this prophet formerly were, that the portions of Jeremiah's words which were written down by Baruch, and on a separate roll, might occasion the mistake here supposed to be made in the enumeration.

In the same manner as Origen, Cyrill of Jerusalem reckons in his Catech. IV., thus making expressly *twenty-two* books. Gregory of Nazianzen (Carm. XXXIII.) follows in the same steps. Athanasius (Epist. fest. Opp. I. 961) has the same reckoning as Cyrill, only that Ruth is separated from Judges, and Esther is omitted, still making the number of books to be *twenty-two*, as usual.

If we go to the Latin church, we find Jerome, the real head of that church and of all the Fathers, as to criticism, making, (in Prolog. Gal.,) as has already been stated, *twenty-two* books, and coupling and combining several of them in the same manner as Origen. It is true, indeed, that he makes a somewhat different division of the books in so far as they belong respectively to the Prophets or to the Kethubim; but this division exhibited by Jerome was a more recent affair among the Hebrews; for so I think we shall, in the sequel, see reason to believe; just as the practice of counting *twenty-four* books (instead of twenty-two) had recently begun in the time of Jerome. This last usage, sanctioned by the Talmud, occasioned of course a separation of some of the books which had been combined together, in order to

SECT. XII. SAMENESS OF THE JEWISH CANON.

make out the number *twenty-two*. Important consequences are connected with the establishment of these suggestions, and on this account they must, in due time, occupy some of our attention.

What is wanting in Josephus, in respect to *specification* of particulars, (and also in Sirachides and Philo,) is fully and adequately supplied by writers who lived shortly afterwards, and by some who had an undoubted acquaintance with the Jewish language and literature, viz. Origen and Jerome. There is, as we have seen, such a uniformity in ancient testimony, as to the books which were combined and thus counted as one, that no reasonable doubt can remain in respect to this point; above all, it would seem that none could remain, when nearly all the ancient writers, who have given us lists of the sacred books of the Old Testament, have, in the same manner as Josephus, made out *twenty-two* books as belonging to it, and told us what several books were combined in order to count respectively as *one*.

One consequence, of no small importance in criticism, may be drawn from the result of this investigation. This is, that the so-called *Hagiography*, or third portion of the Hebrew Scriptures, was not, very anciently, what it is now, or what it was reckoned to be about the time of Jerome, and of the origin of the Babylonish Talmud which was not long after. If this can be established, then the leading argument employed by the Liberalists to show the *lateness* of the composition—a lateness extending even down to the Maccabæan times, of Daniel, Chronicles, many of the Psalms, and perhaps some other scriptural books, or parts of books—is deprived at once of all its force. The argument runs thus, "No reason can be assigned, except the *lateness* of the composition, why Daniel and the Chronicles should be placed among the Kethubim or Hagiography, since the first belongs to the class of the latter prophets, and the second, like Samuel, Kings, &c., to the class of the former prophets. The fact, then, that Daniel and Chronicles are joined with the Kethubim, shows that they were written after the second class of the scriptural books, viz. the Prophets, was fully defined and completed. Now as this class comprises Haggai, Zechariah, and Malachi, so we have conclusive evidence that Daniel and Chronicles must have been composed, or at all events introduced into the Canon, at a period subsequent to that of Nehemiah and Malachi, which was about 430—420 B. C."

This is specious, to say the least, at first view. But then it takes for granted some things which cannot be proved; nay, I will venture to say, the contrary of which can be proved, or at least rendered highly probable. It takes for granted, that the Hieronymean and Talmudic limits of the Prophets and the Hagiography are the ancient and original limits; which is far enough from being capable of proof. It takes for granted, that the main reason for inserting books among the class called the *Hagiography*, was the *recent* origin of the books, which must have been written, as they say, after the *Prophets* had become a definite and completed class. But, not to speak of the doubtful age of the book of Job, what shall be said of the great body of the Psalms, and of the book of Proverbs? David and Solomon surely were not *Maccabæan* writers; not to mention that the Jews, so far back as we know any thing of their opinions, have always held the books of Ecclesiastes and Canticles to be the work of Solomon. Why were these, then, put into the Hagiography? for there they have been ever since the triplex division of the Jewish Scriptures was made. Such an argument, therefore, hits wide of the mark. *Lateness* of composition is *not* essential to a classification with the Hagiography. Moreover, the Neologists take for granted, that the Prophets and the Kethubim have been, since their completion, fixed and uniform as to the number of books in each, and these always the same as they were at first; so that one may even build an argument on this assumption. But the sequel will show how little foundation there is, on which any one can erect such a superstructure.

I am fully aware to what extent the Talmudic apportionment of the Hagiography has been admitted and sanctioned. Even Buxtorf, when he quotes the words of Josephus, descriptive of the third division of the sacred books, viz. "αἱ δὲ λοιποὶ τέσσαρες ὕμνους εἰς τὸν Θεόν, καὶ τοῖς ἀνθρώποις ὑποθήκας τοῦ βίου περιέχουσιν, i. e. the remaining four [books] contain hymns to God, and maxims of life for men," feels compelled to add, "Obscure hoc, nec satis distincte," Comm. Mas. p. 28. He takes it for granted, that the Talmudic arrangement and partition of the books, is the genuine and most ancient one. So have the great mass of writers done; as it would seem, without investigating the subject *de novo*. Josephus, it has been said, makes a classification peculiar to himself, and one which he constituted merely by having respect to the contents or matters discussed in the several books. But when the proof of this is demanded, we are merely referred to Jerome and to the Talmud. To such a reference, however, I must beg leave to take some exceptions.

It is clear at all events from Josephus, since he has affirmed that the Hebrews have only *twenty-two* books, and also that five of these belong to the Pentateuch and *thirteen* to the Prophets, that of course only *four* books can be left for the Hagiography. These he says consist of *hymns* and and *practical maxims*. This limitation of the number and description of the contents obliges us to resort to and fix upon the Psalms, Proverbs, Ecclesiastes, and Canticles, as the constituent elements of the ancient Hagiography. This classification comes from a man, let it be remembered, who had a more intimate knowledge of Hebrew opinions and history, than any other man of his time. He had no temptation, in this case, to represent the matter different from what it was. Nothing in regard to the interests of himself, or of his nation, depended on his mode of representing the Hagiography. He must have been acquainted with the custom of his nation, in regard to the matter of making the appointment or division of the sacred books. There was no inducement that we can conceive of to depart, in his representation, from the usual opinion—usual among the priests—in respect to the whole affair. A competent, an enlightened, an impartial, an honest, a disinterested witness, has always a fair claim to be heard, and to be believed too, so long as what he testifies is neither impossible nor improbable. Josephus was all this as a witness in the present case, and the thing testified looks altogether more probable and more inviting to confidence, than the Talmudic division of the *Prophets* and *Kethubim*. The division of Josephus (the word *Prophets* being understood in the sense which the Hebrews attached to it) is founded on a rational ground, viz. on the ground of the respectively different materials or contents of the several classes of the sacred books. *Hymns* and *Maxims of life* are neither history nor prediction, and so they are classed by themselves, according to Josephus. But the Talmudic division of the sacred books depends on some conceits about the different *gradations* of inspiration, which are not only incapable of any satisfactory proof, but are in themselves quite improbable. The story of the Jewish doctors is, that the books of Moses take the precedence above all others, because God spake with him mouth to mouth; that the Prophets who came after him, were such as, whether sleeping or waking when they received revelations, were deprived of all the use of their senses, and were spoken to by a voice, and saw prophetic visions in ecstasy; that the third and lowest class of the sacred writers were those, who, preserving the use of their senses, spake like other men, and yet in such a way that, although not favoured with dreams or visions in ecstasy, they still perceived a Divine influence resting upon them, at whose suggestion they spoke or wrote what they made public. Of this last class, according to the Rabbins, were the authors of the Kethubim; see Carpzov. Introd. ad Lib. Bib. V. Test. c. II. § 4; Abarbanel, Præf. Comm. in Job.; D. Kimchi, Præf. in Psalm.; Maimon. Moreh Neb. II. c. 45.

Now that Moses, as the founder of the Jewish religion and leader of the nation when achieving its independence, whose laws were to be their statute book in all future generations until the coming of Christ—that such a distinguished personage is entitled, from these considerations, to be placed at the head of all the Jewish teachers and leaders of ancient times, no one will doubt. That extraordinary revelations of God were made to him in a peculiar way, we need not call in question. Certainly, if we take the Pentateuch as our guide in such a matter, this must be conceded. But still, although the *manner* of communication with him was peculiar, it does not follow that what he uttered was more worthy of credit, than that which was uttered by other scriptural writers. Truth is truth, and cannot be any more than this. If the *Hagiographal* writers uttered what was true, (and the Jewish doctors all with one voice affirm that they did,) then the Hagiography stands on the same level with the Pentateuch, in regard to its authenticity, and of course in regard to the credence which we should give to it and the respect that is due to it. I am far enough from as-

SECT. XII.   SAMENESS OF THE JEWISH CANON.   251

serting, that the contents of any and every book in the Old Testament are all of equal interest and importance. This is not and cannot be the case. In a great temple, built by one and the same architect, there are many parts of the edifice that retreat from notice, and are scarcely thought of by the beholder, and yet they are essential to the completeness of the building, and were as really the result of the architect's skill and plan, as the more prominent portions which throw themselves into the notice of all. So is it with God's ancient edifice. The Pentateuch constitutes, if you please, the portico, the pillars, the *façade*, and the main apartment; but there is many and many a subordinate portion of such a building, presenting itself scarcely at all to our notice, which is as really necessary to its full completeness, as the most conspicuous parts of the same.

Even granting, then, that the Hagiography was written by men who, according to the Rabbins, used their senses, and were only occasionally inspired, it would not follow, that any derogation from its authenticity or credibility can be made out from this circumstance. Indeed they do not even pretend to say this. But still it is difficult, after admitting their grounds of classifying the Scriptures, to avoid the idea of a difference in the authority of each class, and in the credence due to each. Yet if the *subject-matter* of the scriptural books is really to be taken into account, and at the same time if it be conceded (as it is by them) that all the books are *inspired*, then we have a right to call on them to show us, how and why the book of Psalms and that of the Proverbs (each included in the Hagiography) are, or are deemed to be, of inferior station or consequence. Nay, so far is the true state of the case from this, that we may safely say, that these two books are of more *practical* avail under the Christian dispensation—more to the purposes of devotional piety and a well-regulated life, than any other portion, I had almost said, more than all the rest of the Old Testament.

Thus much for this renowned Rabbinical division of the Scriptures, as to this point of view. But there are other difficulties with it. "The *prophets*, forsooth, were men who were deprived of all use of their senses, when in an ecstatic state, and report to us only what they saw in visions and heard addressed to them!" And is this so? What, then, is the *seeing* or the *hearing*, in this case? But passing by this, I would ask, Had they no use of their senses when they wrote down the revelations made to them? Besides, Paul taxes the Corinthian prophets with the abuse of their miraculous powers or gifts; how could they *abuse* them, if they were not free agents when possessing them? Paul says, too, that "the spirits of the prophets are subject to the prophets" (1 Cor. xiv. 32); which could not be true of such prophets as the Rabbies imagine. Besides, what evidence is there to show, that such extraordinary and peculiar revelations were made to the writers of Joshua, Judges, Samuel, and Kings, while the Divine influence was altogether of a lower kind, which rested upon the writers of the Psalms, the Chronicles, Ezra, and the other books of the Jewish Kethubim?

In fact, the lowest gradation of inspiration, ascribed by the Rabbies to the authors of the Kethubim, is as high as Christianity demands, or, one may say, even permits us to ascribe to men. No man, not even Moses or Isaiah, was uniformly and always inspired. Of all God's messengers, only one received the gift of the Spirit without measure; and he was the only one who never erred and never sinned. Others were inspired for a particular purpose, and (it may be) remained so, until that purpose was accomplished. Then they returned to their usual state. So it was with even Moses; and so with all the other prophets or priests concerned with the writing of the Old Test. Scriptures. How is the higher inspiration of the authors of Joshua, Judges, Samuel, and Kings, to be proved, when no one can even tell who wrote these books? Or in what respect as to the credence due to them, do these compositions differ from those of Ezra, Nehemiah, Esther, and Chronicles?

In fact, the whole affair is a mere Rabbinical conceit, hatched out during the dark ages of Rabbinism that preceded the composition of the Babylonish Talmud.

Nor is the fact that there is no justifiable ground for the position of the Jewish doctors in respect to the Prophets and the Kethubim, the only thing to be considered. Such a division, I acknowledge, might exist at an earlier period, although founded on phantasy or on caprice; for there is

SECT. XII.   SAMENESS OF THE JEWISH CANON.   253

enough of both these in the Mishna itself to show us, that a talent for the production of such things abounded among the Rabbies of earlier times. The question recurs, after we have seen the division which Josephus made of the sacred books, *Whether others of the more ancient authorities agreed with him?* If they did, then has Josephus given us the *usual* division of the Scriptures at his time.

The grandson of Jesus Sirachides, in describing the third class of Scriptures, or the Hagiography, calls them "the other [books] which follow κατ' αὐτοὺς, in accordance with them [the Prophets] or of a like spirit;" also "the other patrical (πατρίων) books;" and finally, "the rest of the Bible, τὰ λοιπᾶ τῶν βιβλίων;" see p. 229 above. Sirachides himself describes the third division, by saying of the ancient Hebrew worthies, "They sought out the *melody of music*, they composed *poems* in writing;" Sirach. xliv. 5. Philo says of the Essenes, that they read not only the Law and the Prophets, but "*hymns and other [books]*, by which knowledge and piety are augmented and perfected;" see p. 231 above. In the New Testament, Jesus himself speaks of "the Law, the Prophets, and the Psalms;" Luke xxiv. 44, comp. xxiv. 27. The Psalms was in the same manner the leading book in the Hagiography of Josephus.

In Melito, who comes next after Josephus, we find no express designation of the *triplex* portions of the Old Testament; for we find him following in all probability the arrangement of the Greek copy which he consulted, and which may or may not have agreed with some Hebrew copies of that time. Still he makes only *twenty-two* books, even if we include Esther, (which is now omitted in his list as represented in the extract from Eusebius, but) which was in all probability originally included by Melito himself; see p. 239 above. In fact he makes, as we may say, a *quadruplex* division, the *Law*, the *Historical Books*, (including Chronicles, but excluding Ezra,) the *Hagiography*, (which he arranges in one continuous body, Psalms, Proverbs, Ecclesiastes, and Canticles,) and the *Prophets*. But he has evidently gone in the steps of Josephus as to the *number* of the books, and the combinations of them in order to make twenty-two. See App. No. IV.

So is it too with Origen, who expressly declares there

are *twenty-two* books, and who arranges the historical books in like manner as Melito, i. e. after the tenor of the order in the Sept. Notable is it, that he places Job and Esther last of all. *He also brings the Hagiography of Josephus into immediate and local connexion and consecution.* In his list, moreover, which is cited by Eusebius, (as in the case of Melito above,) one link in the chain of twenty-two is omitted, viz. the twelve Minor Prophets; doubtless by mere mistake in transcribing; see p. 242 above. There can be no reasonable doubt that the canon of Josephus is the Canon of Origen, although he has yielded some deference to the Septuagint as to the arrangement of some particular books. See the original in Appendix, No. V.

Exactly in the same way are the books of the Old Testament reckoned in the fifty-ninth Canon of the Council of Laodicea. These books are expressly said to be *twenty-two;* and, moreover, the Chronicles immediately follow the Kings, and are followed themselves by Ezra, just as they are in the list of Origen; i. e. here also the arrangement is partly in conformity with that of the *Septuagint.* In the same manner the Canon of the Council ranges together the books of the Hagiography, in conformity with what is indicated by Josephus. See Appendix, No. VI., for the original.

Cyril of Jerusalem (Cat. IV.) presents another list, in which he says expressly that there are but *twenty-two* books. His arrangement also is Septuagintal, and is the same as that of Origen, save that he assigns an earlier place to the book of Esther, along with the other historical books; see App. No. VII. So is it with Gregory Nazianzen, II. Carm. XXXIII.; see Appendix, No. VIII. The like is true of Athanasius; who (in his Epist. Fest. I. p. 961) makes in general the same number and order of books as Cyril of Jerusalem, i. e. *twenty-two* books arranged generally in the manner of the Septuagint. But there is this difference between them, viz. Athanasius counts Ruth by itself, and omits Esther; which seems to favour the supposition that he meant to omit Esther, inasmuch as he makes twenty-two without it. Indeed in the sequel, he expressly mentions Esther among the books "οὐ κανονιζόμενα μέν ... ἀναγινωσκόμενα δέ, *not canonical, but permitted to be read,*" viz. by the catechumens, and these books, he tells us, were such as the Wisdom of Solomon, the Wisdom of Sirach, Judith, and Tobit. See Appendix, No. IX. In the Synopsis Script. Sac. in Athanas. Opp. II. p. 126, seq., the very same thing is said respecting Esther and the apocryphal books, with the declaration that "they are read only by catechumens," i. e. they are not publicly read with the proper Scriptures. See Appendix, No. X.

Epiphanius (De Mens. et Ponder., c. 22, 23) avers, that the Hebrews numbered only twenty-two books, so as to correspond with their alphabet, making five of the books double, "just as five letters of the alphabet are double," i. e. have two forms. He includes Esther in his list; but he makes a different division of the books from that of any other ancient writer. Job is placed after Joshua, the Psalms after Judges and Ruth, the Chronicles *before* Samuel and Kings, the Twelve Prophets before the others, &c.; evidently an attempt at a kind of chronological arrangement in conformity with the views of the author. See App. No. XI.

The Council of Hippo, (A. D. 393,) in Can. XXXVI., admit indeed several of the apocryphal books into their Canon; but they preserve all the Jewish ones, and put Daniel between Jeremiah and Ezekiel, and Chronicles next after Kings; thus showing that no regard was paid by them to such an order as the Talmudic; see Appendix, No. XII. With this agrees cap. 47 of the *third* Council of Carthage (A. D. 397); Mansi, Concil. Coll. III. 891. See in App. No. XIII.

Jerome, (Prol. Gal.,) as we have seen p. 233 above, makes twenty-two books of the Hebrew Scriptures, and arranges the Law, the Prophets, and Hagiography mostly in like manner with the Talmud; but still he comprises only *nine* books in the Kethubim, while the Talmudists make eleven. He then goes on to say, that "some [so did the Rabbins of that day] enrol Ruth and Lamentations among the Hagiography, [instead of uniting them with Judges and Jeremiah, as he does,] and think that they should be reckoned among their number, and thus the books of the Old Testament would amount to *twenty-four*." Here, then, is the very first notice of this novel method of making out *twenty-four* books; and at the same time it is the first express information which we have of a triplex division of the Scriptures differing, as to the particular books comprised, from that of Josephus. The Rabbins of his day, with whom he studied so long in Palestine, had, as it would seem, already made this innovation upon the ancient arrangement both as to order and as to number, and from them he learned it. See the whole passage in Appendix, No. XIV.

Hilary (Prol. in Psalm.) states the books of the Old Testament to be twenty-two; but he adds, that "to some it seemed good, by adding Tobit and Judith, to make out twenty-four books, according to the number of letters in the Greek alphabet." The *some* here spoken of must of course have been found among Christians; for that the *Jews* admitted the books in question to their Palestine Canon, there is not one spark of evidence. Every thing shows the contrary. See App. No. XV.

Rufinus, (Expos. in Symb. Apost.,) a contemporary of Jerome and Hilary, reckons *twenty-two* books, following in the main the order of the Septuagint. In his Canon all our present scriptural Hebrew books are included; Daniel is placed where we place him, and Psalms, Proverbs, Ecclesiastes, and Canticles, come last; the very copy, in this respect, of Josephus' Canon. See App. No. XVI.

From this somewhat extensive range of investigation, it seems perfectly evident that the *Hagiographal* division of the Scriptures, as taught by Rabbies to Jerome, and afterwards sanctioned by the Talmud, belonged at this period only to some of the Jewish schools, and had no concern with the usual and general classification. I can find nothing in all antiquity that hints at such a classification as theirs, before the notice which Jerome takes of it; although it has so often been talked about, and reasoned from, as if it had long preceded the Christian era.

The question I take to be now finally settled, that the Babylonish Talmud itself was not originated until after or about the time of Jerome, i. e. at the close of the fourth and the beginning of the fifth century, and not completed at least until the sixth century. The traditional authors, who commenced the work, were Rabbi Ashi and Rabbi Jose. The huge *mish-mash* which this work contains, must have been the production of many heads and many hands. But the authority, which it has ever retained among the super-

SECT. XII. SAMENESS OF THE JEWISH CANON. 257

stitious and Pharisaic Jews, is almost without limits. In fact, like the Romish traditions, it has been placed above the Scriptures themselves. The Rabbins are accustomed to say, "The Scripture is water, but the Talmud is wine." Hence it is easy to see why it has had so much influence on the arrangement of the Hebrew Scriptures, for some 1200 years. The passage which has settled this matter for the Jews is in the Tract. Baba Bathra, fol. 14. col. 2, and runs as follows: סדרן של נביאים יהושע ושופטים שמואל ומלכים ירמיה יחזקאל ישעיה ושנים עשר ... סדרן של כתובים רות תהלים ואיוב ומשלי וקהלת שיר השירים וקנית דניאל אסתר ודברי הימים: i.e. "the order of the Prophets is thus: Joshua and Judges, Samuel and Kings, Jeremiah and Ezekiel, Isaiah and the Twelve [minor prophets] ... The order of the Kethubim is thus: Ruth, Psalms and Job, and Proverbs, and Ecclesiastes, the Song of Songs and Lamentations, Daniel, Esther and the Chronicles."

I have omitted the Pentateuch, because the *order* of that is every where and always *one* and the *same*. I would further remark, that as to the *order* of the books in the Prophets and Kethubim, and even the *number* of them respectively, there is no uniformity among the highest Jewish authorities. The Talmudists make twenty-four books, and arrange them as above. But the Masorites, whom I should regard as of higher authority, arrange the leading prophets thus: Isaiah, Jeremiah, Ezekiel, the Twelve; while the Kethubim are thus arranged: Psalms, Job, Proverbs, Ruth, Canticles, Ecclesiastes, Lamentations, Esther, Daniel, Ezra, Chronicles. Both make twenty-four books, but in quite a diverse order. The Spanish MSS., and all the Hebrew Bibles printed from them, follow the Masorites with some slight variations under the Kethubim; the German MSS. and printed editions mostly follow the Talmud, but also with variations of the like kind. In making out *twenty-four* books, Ruth is separated from Judges, and Lamentations from Jeremiah; which, on the contrary, Jerome unites respectively in one book, and so makes *twenty-two* of the whole. Nearly all antiquity counted 1 and 2 Samuel, 1 and 2 Kings, 1 and 2 Chronicles, and Ezra and Nehemiah, respectively, as one book; the Septuagint count the four first of these as four parts of one and the same book, which they name *Kings*.

s

Different from the order both of the Talmud and the Masorites, is that of Origen and Jerome. Both of them make only *twenty-two* books. But Origen places Chronicles and Ezra immediately after Kings; Jerome, near the end of the Kethubim (for with him the closing part of the Canon stands thus: Chronicles, Ezra, Esther). Origen places Psalms, Proverbs, Ecclesiastes, Canticles, Job, next after Ezra (including Nehemiah): Jerome's arrangement after the book of Kings is thus: Isaiah, Jeremiah, Ezekiel, the Twelve. Origen arranges after Job thus: the Twelve, Isaiah, Jeremiah, Ezekiel, Daniel: Jerome puts Daniel among the Hagiography, and next before Chronicles. As the extract from Origen in Eusebius omits the *Twelve*, we should not know how Origen arranged them, had not Rufinus given us a version of him. In this the *Twelve* stands next after Canticles and before Job. Comp. the lists of Origen and Jerome, in App. Nos. V. XIV.

I have now given the reader a fair specimen of the leading arrangements of the Hebrew Scriptures in ancient times, as it respects the Prophets and the Kethubim. No two are alike. Even the Masorites and the Talmudists differ from each other; Jerome differs from both, and Origen from him. And so, if we compare Melito, the Laodicean Council, the Apostolic Canons, Cyrill, Gregory Nazianzen, Athanasius, Hilary, Epiphanius, the Council of Hippo, Jerome, Rufinus, &c., scarcely any two of them are alike throughout. And this is almost the case even with MSS. and editions in later times.

As to the conceit of *twenty-four* books, instead of twenty-two, it must have been a late affair, as has already been suggested. The Talmud made this out by separating Judges and Ruth, Jeremiah and Lamentations. Sixtus Senensis, in his Biblioth. Sanct. I. p. 2, has given us the alleged reasons of the Jews for such an arrangement. These are a fit accompaniment of the arrangement itself. The substance is, that the ancient Jews wrote the unpronounceable name of Jehovah thus ''', i. e. with three Yodhs, (which of course comprise great mysteries,) and so they added two more books to the number 22, in order to correspond with the Yodh thrice repeated in honour of the name of Jehovah. The Greek Versions would naturally and easily adopt the

SECT. XII.   SAMENESS OF THE JEWISH CANON.   259

number twenty-four, because it corresponded with the Greek alphabet. The Christians had another reason, according to Sixtus, for admitting twenty-four books; which was, that John, in the Apocalypse, has introduced twenty-four elders as adoring him who was about to open the sealed book!

Trifling and futile as all this is, yet from the authority and example of the Talmud, *the Twenty-Four* has even become a technical name of the Hebrew Scriptures; and it stands on the first page as a title (עשרים וארבעה) to the majority of MSS. and editions. All antiquity however made, as we have seen, but *twenty-two*; and in this respect the assertion of Josephus, that the Jews have twenty-two sacred books, stands most amply sustained and justified.

Important consequences flow from these investigations and conclusions. I can mention only a few of them, which have respect to views often presented by some recent critics, and which have a slender support indeed in the history of the Canon.

(1.) It has become general to speak of Chronicles as the *last* book in the Hebrew Canon, and to draw important conclusions as to the authenticity of this composition from this source. Eichhorn, (Einl. § 7,) De Wette, (Einl. § 10, and Comm. in Matt. xxiii. 35,) and many others, appeal to Matt. xxiii. 35 as certain evidence, that the book of Chronicles was the *last* in the Old Testament in our Saviour's day. The words in question are, "That on you [the Jews] may come all the righteous blood shed upon the earth, from the blood of the righteous Abel unto the blood of Zacharias, son of Barachias, whom ye slew between the temple and the altar." Here, says Eichhorn and others after him, is an example taken from the first and the last part of the Jewish Scriptures, and the design of Jesus evidently is, to say that on the Jews should come the consummation of punishment for all the martyrdoms related from first to last in their Scriptures. Consequently the book of Chronicles must have stood *last* in their sacred volume.

Notwithstanding the all but universal assent to this method of reasoning, I must still believe that it has not any solid basis. How does it follow, that the book of Chronicles is the *last* in the whole volume, when the Kethubim of Josephus, viz. Psalms, Proverbs, Ecclesiastes, Canticles, yea all the

s 2

books that we commonly name *prophets*, might have stood after the Chronicles, and yet the reasoning have still been the same as most critics now suppose it to be? The reasoning is founded on the *historical* part, and that only, of the Old Testament; and it is enough of course to answer all its demands, that the book of Chronicles was the last in the *historical* series. It is mere gratuitous assumption to suppose any more; for the present arrangement in our English Bibles would support the reasoning in question, just as well as the present Jewish arrangement of the Hebrew Scriptures.

But there are several things, on the other hand, to show that the whole process of the reasoning here, as well as the assumed historical basis of it, is altogether incapable of any adequate defence. (1.) The Zechariah of 2 Chron. xxiv. 19 —22, to which the critics in question appeal, was the son of *Jehoiada*, and not of Barachias, as Christ declares. The conciliation of the two passages, by supposing that Zechariah's father bore both the names of Jehoiada and Barachias, is unsatisfactory in this case; for why should we suppose that the Saviour appealed to any other name of Zechariah's father than that which is mentioned in the Old Testament, in case he really meant to designate the Zechariah of 2 Chron.? But the Neologists have a shorter method, 'The evangelist's recollection was faulty, and he wrote *Barachias* where Jesus had named *Jehoiada*.' I am not prepared, however, to admit this solution. I cannot bring myself to believe, that Jesus would have made such an appeal as is here supposed. Examine for a moment the *chronology* of this martyrdom; for its date must at least be some 840 years before Christ. And are eight centuries and a half to be leaped over, in such a representation, because no martyrdoms, no persecutions by the Jews, could be found in all that period? This is contrary to probability, and contrary to fact. I affirm the latter, because Jeremiah (xxvi. 23) tells us, that Jehoiakim (about 600 B. C.) brought Urijah the prophet out of Egypt, whither he had fled, and slew him with the sword. Here, then, is a martyr-murder 200 years and more after that of Zechariah the son of Jehoiada. What is to be said also of Manasseh's murders, who "filled Jerusalem with innocent blood," more than a century after the murder of Zechariah? And besides all this, did not the partisans of Antiochus Epiphanes, such men as Jason and his compeers, persecute and destroy pious persons living in their days? The denial of all this would be in part a denial of what is certain, and in part of what in all respects is probable. Jews who could sell themselves to Antiochus in order to introduce the heathen rites, must needs persecute those who stood in the way of their nefarious designs. In a word, to *terminate* the history of Jewish persecutions at a period of 800 and more years before the Christian era, in an indignant charge of accumulated guilt upon the nation, is in itself incredible; I must say—to my mind it is preposterous. Yet such is the reasoning of the critics in question.

(2.) It is not at all essential or capable of proof, that the histories which we have of the Jews after their return and down to the Christian era, altogether imperfect and few as they are, should have preserved an account of the murder of Zechariah, as mentioned by the Saviour. A comparatively recent murder of such a man might have taken place, and yet not have been related at all by Josephus; for we well know that his *silence* is not any proof that certain things did not take place, e. g. the massacre by Herod at Bethlehem, the Saviour's appearance, claims, miracles, &c.* That we lack the history of the son of Barachias, is no evidence that there was no such person. A *prophet* he is not said to be in Matt. xxiv. 35; it is only said that his blood was that of the *righteous*. And if in Luke xi. 51 he seems to be called a *prophet*, yet it is plainly in that sense in which distinguished pious men in general are sometimes called *prophets* in the Old Testament; (e. g. in 1 Chron. xvi. 22; Ps. cv. 15;) for here *Abel* is also named as a prophet, in the same sense as Zechariah. No good reason can be given, then, why Jesus should not, or did not, refer to some *recent* event in the way of murderous persecution. The very nature of the case renders this highly probable. Particularly does the mention of the minute circumstance, that "Zacharias was slain between the temple and the altar," savour of an event which was fresh in the recollection of the Jews who

---

* After all the defences that have been made of the passage in Josephus respecting Christ, I feel constrained to say of it, Sapit emendatorem. To me it seems that Josephus must have said more, if he said any thing.

were addressed. And then the charge implied in ἐφονεύσατε, YE *slew*, has all the appearance of imputing *personal* guilt. In fact it must involve it.

(3.) But if any one insists that we must needs have some other historical account of the murder of a later or recent Zacharias, than that apparently contained in the evangelist; why may we not give credit to Origen, who (in Tract XXVI. in Matt.) states that *Zacharias, the father of John the Baptist*, was murdered by the Jews in the temple? He again asserts this in Tom. XI. in Matt. p. 225, ed. Huet. Basil, Gregory of Nyssa, Cyrill of Alexandria, Peter of Alexandria, Theophylact, and others, agree with Origen in this statement; Thilo, Cod. Apoc. N. Test. I. Prol. LXIV. In the Protevangelium Jacobi, the most respectable and perhaps the oldest of all the apocryphal Gospels, (Origen makes mention of it,) the murder of the same Zacharias is circumstantially related, cap. XXIII., seq. It is plain, then, that a very general tradition existed in ancient times, as to the murder of Zacharias the father of John, by the Jews, and probably by Herod's instigation. It is no objection to the truth of this, that the father of Zacharias is not mentioned in Luke i. 5. Barachias was a very common name among the Jews, and might well have been the name of Zacharias' father. The probability that the opinion of Origen and other ancients is correct here, is even strengthened by that exegesis of Luke xi. 51, which would make Zacharias a *prophet* in the usual sense of that word; for Luke i. 67—79 plainly represents him as uttering prophecy.*

Why may we not conclude now, that neither the evangelists have made a mistake about the son of Barachias; nor the Saviour charged on the Jews the commission of a deed done more than eight centuries before? And above all, why may we not say, that the whole of the conclusions about the book of Chronicles and its location, which are built on assuming for it the *last* place in the Hebrew Scriptures, is "such stuff as dreams are made of?" Nay, I venture to say, that the assumption in question is historically and demonstrably

---

* Plausible as this reasoning may appear, and forcibly as it is presented, its correctness may still be doubted. We cannot but think that the Zechariah of 2 Chron. xxiv. 20, 21 is referred to. See Davidson's Introduction to the New Testament, vol. i. pp. 134, 135. D.

false. Josephus so represents the Kethubim, that the Chronicles are excluded, and must have been united with the division of the Prophets; as Philo had done before him, and also the New Testament. The first list of the successive and particular books of the Hebrew Scriptures which we have, is that of Melito, (about 170 A. D.,) which places Chronicles next after Kings; the same does Origen in his list; the same does the Council of Laodicea, the Canones Apostol., Cyrill of Jerusalem, Gregory Nazianzen, Athanasius, the Synopsis Scripturæ in Athanas. Opp., Epiphanius, (who even puts it *before* Kings,) the Council of Hippo, (A. D. 393,) Hilary, and Rufinus. Jerome, who drank in Rabbinical lore for twenty years, is the only Father among all of any name, who puts Chronicles among the Kethubim; and he puts after it Ezra (including Nehemiah) and Esther. Besides all this, the very fact that the Septuagintal arrangement preserves the same order as all the early Fathers, in regard to the book of Chronicles, shows that the Hebrew MSS. from which they translated did not exhibit the Talmudical arrangement, but plainly that of Josephus. Most of the lists of books, to which I have now referred, specifically declare, that *they give the books as they are arranged by the Jews.*

It is out of all critical question, then, to admit that Chronicles was the *last* book of Scripture in our Saviour's time; and out of all question to admit those views in criticism, which are built merely on the assumption of such a fact. The Liberalists must give us some reasons better than such ones, in order to induce us to walk in the paths that they pursue.

In this connexion, let us return once more, for a moment, to the book of Daniel. As I have already stated, the main argument against the genuineness of the book, independently of its account of miraculous or strange events, is that which is drawn from the alleged fact, that the work has been assigned to the division of the Kethubim; and so, as the process of reasoning is, it must have been composed long *after* the time when Daniel is said to have lived, and after the division embracing the Prophets was brought to a close and completed. But what says *fact?* Josephus' arrangement necessarily, as we have seen, includes Daniel among the Prophets. Of course when this is settled, it follows with almost absolute certainty, that the son of Sirach, Philo, and the New Testament writers, do the same, inasmuch as they classify the sacred books in the same manner as he does. We know for certainty this fact in respect to the book of Daniel, as it concerns the later writers; for we have their lists both of the names and the order of all the books. Melito places Daniel among the Prophets and *before* Ezekiel. The same does Origen. The Council of Laodicea place Daniel next after Ezekiel, and of course among the Prophets. The same do the Canones Apostol., Cyrill of Jerusalem, Gregory Nazianzen, Athanasius, Synopsis Scripturæ in Athanas. Opp. (in Epiphanius, de Mens. et Ponder., the book is by some mistake omitted). The Council of Hippo, like Melito and Origen, place it *before* Ezekiel, as also does Hilary; and Rufinus places it next after Ezekiel. Like Josephus, too, this last writer puts at the close of the sacred volume the Hagiographal books, viz. Psalms, Proverbs, Ecclesiastes, Canticles. Jerome alone, in giving an account of the Rabbinical usage in his day, puts Daniel among the Hagiography; and after it he puts Chronicles, Ezra, (with Nehemiah,) and Esther.

The Talmud then stands alone in placing the book of Daniel among the Hagiography, with the exception that Jerome makes the like arrangement, in giving an account of what was customary in his time among the Rabbins who had taught him. But even he does not accord with the Talmud, either as to the number or the order of the books in the Prophets and Kethubim. All this proves, beyond a question, what a variety there was in the arrangement of particular books of the Scriptures, and how little of significance was originally attached to this circumstance. The Septuagint Version, it must surely be admitted, was made from Hebrew MSS.; and how comes it to pass that the arrangement is so different here from that of the Talmud? The proof that Daniel, among the ancients universally, was regarded as one of the *prophets*, is above all exception. The fact that Josephus extracts so copiously from him, and speaks of him as one of the greatest of all the prophets, cannot be disguised. Near the close of Antiq. X. he says, "Daniel was distinguished and illustrious because of the glory of being the friend of God. . . . He was wonderfully fortunate as *one of the greatest prophets;* and during his life-time he had much honour and fame from kings and from the multitude, and now when dead he has an everlasting remembrance." Our Saviour too has said of a certain prediction, that it was "uttered by Daniel the *prophet;*" Matt. xxiv. 15; Mark xiii. 14.

We have now had opportunity to see, how utterly incongruous the Talmudic arrangement of the Scriptures is with all the other ancient testimony respecting this matter—testimony, by the way, which is all of it older than that of the Talmud. Even the Masorites of Tiberias, although they agree with the Talmudists as to the *twenty-four* books of Scripture, and as to the number of books respectively belonging to the Hagiography and to the Prophets, do still refuse to accede to the preposterous arrangement of placing the greater Prophets in the order of the Talmud, viz. Jeremiah, Ezekiel, Isaiah. The Masorites and every ancient authority, one and all, unanimously declare the order to be thus: Isaiah, Jeremiah, Ezekiel. It is worth our while to listen for a moment to the reason of the Talmudists for their peculiar arrangement, in order that we may learn how to appreciate their decision in such matters: כיון דמלכים סיפיה חורבנא וירמיה כוליה חורבנא ויחזקאל רישאה חורבנא וסיפיה נחמתא וישעיה כוליה נחמתא סמכינן חורבנא לחורבנא ונחמתא לנחמתא; i. e. 'since the book of Kings ends in desolation, and all of Jeremiah is desolation; and Ezekiel in the commencement is desolation, and at the close, consolation ; and Isaiah is all consolation, they [the men of the Great Synagogue] joined desolation to desolation, [Jeremiah to the close of the book of Kings,] and consolation to consolation [Isaiah to the last part of Ezekiel].' Yet so incongruous is this, that Abarbanel (Pref. in Comm. in Is.) does not hesitate to say, " Truly our predecessors, the sons of the captivity, did not arrange the books thus, [viz. as the Talmud does,] but they placed Isaiah at the head."

Enough for this topic. Clear as the light is it, that if any regard is to be paid to all the testimony of antiquity which precedes the Talmud, the decisions of the latter as to the *number* or *order* of the books in the Prophets and Hagiography, are entitled to little or no authority. All the reasoning and conclusions about certain books in the Bible, which are built on the Talmudic arrangement of particulars, must of course be without any good foundation. In fact, as already remarked, the Septuagintal arrangement of the Scriptural books, which at all events preceded the Christian era, does of itself demonstrate, that when it was made, the Hebrew originals did not follow the Talmudic order.

If the reader has still any scruples whether he is not to be bound by the decisions of the Talmudic doctors, in relation to critical matters of this kind, it is proper that he should turn his attention for a moment to their decision in regard to the *authorship* of the Old Testament books. It runs thus: "And who wrote them? [the Old Testament books]. Moses wrote his book, and the section of Balaam, and Job. Joshua wrote his book, and eight verses in the Law. Samuel wrote his book, Judges, and Ruth. David wrote the book of Psalms, with the assistance of ten of the elders, by the aid of Adam the first man, of Melchizedek, of Abraham, of Moses, of Heman, of Jeduthun, of Asaph, of the three sons of Korah. Jeremiah wrote his book, and the book of Kings and Lamentations. Hezekiah and his assistants wrote Isaiah, Proverbs, Canticles, and Coheleth [Ecc.]; the symbol of which is ימש"ק. The men of the Great Synagogue wrote Ezekiel and the Twelve, Daniel and the volume of Esther; the symbol of which is קנד"ג. Ezra wrote his book and the genealogy of the book of Chronicles down to himself.* Talm. Bab. Megil. fol. 10. c. 2.

Much comment on this would be unseemly here. The assertion that Moses wrote Job, will hardly stand before the tribunal of criticism. That Samuel wrote his book, (which of course includes 1 and 2 Sam.,) which continues the Jewish history down to more than forty years after his death, it would require strong faith to believe. What Psalms Adam, Melchizedek, and Abraham wrote, the Talmudists might find it somewhat difficult to show. That Jeremiah wrote the book of Kings, which carries the history down to the

---

* ומי כתבן משה כתב ספרו ופרשת בלעם ואיוב: יהושע כתב ספרו ושמונה פסיקין שבתורה: שמואל כתב ספרו ושופטים ורות: דוד כתב ספר, ההלים על ידי עשרה זקנים על ידי אדם הראשון על ידי מלכיצדק ועל ידי אברהם ועל ידי משה ועל ידי הימן ועל ידי ידותון ועל ידי אסף ועל ידי שלושת בני קרח: ירמיה כתב ספרו וספר מלכי וקנות: חזקיה וסיעתו כתבו ימש"ק סימן ישעיה משלי שיר השירים וקהלת: אנשי כנסת הגדולה כתבו קנד"ג: סימן יחזקאל ושנים עשר דניאל ומגילת אסתר: עזרא כתב ספרו ויחס של דברי הימים עד לו:

thirty-seventh year of Jehoiachin's captivity, is very improbable. He must, at any rate, have been more than a century old by that time. That Hezekiah and his helpers wrote Isaiah, Proverbs, Ecclesiastes, and Canticles, is downright folly to assert, in any other sense than that they *made a copy* of these books, or (as we say) *copied them out*. It is singular, that the word כתבו, which the Talmudists have here employed, should have been so much controverted. Bertholdt, and after him Hävernick and others, insist upon its being rendered *introduced*, as if it were the equivalent of הביאו; which seems to me little short of a monstrosity in philology. Others have supposed כתבו to mean, as often elsewhere, *wrote* in the sense of *composing*; which would be attributing more absurdity to the Talmudists than they were probably guilty of. The truth of the matter seems to be very simple. כתב in Hebrew, like the verb *write* in English, may mean either the composition of a book, including the act of writing it down, or it may mean merely the act of an amanuensis or copyist which reduces it to writing. There can be no reasonable doubt, that the Talmudists borrowed the sentiment respecting the doings of Hezekiah and his assistants from Prov. xxv. 1, where it is said, "These are the Proverbs of Solomon, which the men of Hezekiah king of Judah העתיקו, copied out." So our English Version; and it seems to have hit the mark exactly. The verb עתק, in conj. Hiphil, means to *transfer;* hence to transfer from one book into another, i. e. to copy out; see Ges. Lex. The Talmud, instead of saying *the men of Hezekiah*, (as the Bible does,) says *Hezekiah and his assistants* (סיעתו); and instead of העתיקו, they employ כתבו as its equivalent. But as the part of Proverbs thus copied out comprises only five chapters, where they obtained ground for naming the whole book as copied out, and for adding Canticles and Ecclesiastes to this, i. e. adding all the supposed works of Solomon; above all, whence they obtained the information that Isaiah was also copied out by Hezekiah and his assistants; is more than I can conjecture. Not improbably the interest which that good king took in this renowned prophet, and the deference that he paid to him, may have occasioned the guess in question; for more than *guess* it does not seem to be.

The men of the Great Synagogue are said 'to have *copied*

out [for public use?] Ezekiel, the Twelve, Daniel, and the volume of Esther.' Here כתבו is employed in the same way as before, beyond all reasonable doubt. So De Wette, Einl. § 14; and to the same purpose Rashi, i. e. Rabbi Solomon Jarchi, († 1105,) who undertakes to explain and to vindicate this passage of the Talmud in his Comm. in Baba Bathra. His words are worth quoting, in order to display the genius of Rabbinic commentators: " The men of the Great Synagogue wrote out (or copied) Ezekiel, who prophesied in exile. And I know not why Ezekiel did not write it [the book] out himself, except that prophecy is not given for any one to write it in a foreign country. They [the Great Synagogue] wrote it out after they returned to the Holy Land. And so, in respect to the book of Daniel, who lived in exile; and so, in regard to the volume of Esther. And as to the Twelve Prophets, because their prophecies were brief, the prophets did not themselves write them down, each one his own book. But when Haggai, Zechariah, and Malachi came [to the Holy Land], and saw that the Holy Spirit was about to depart, inasmuch as they were the last prophets, then they rose up and wrote down their prophecies, and joined those of the minor prophets with them, and thus made one large book, so that they might not be destroyed (or lost) on account of their smallness." *

It is with great difficulty that one can be brought to believe, that a man of so much intelligence as Jarchi was really serious in giving such an account of this matter. Men, forsooth, according to him, could be inspired as prophets, when in exile, but it was unlawful to write down their compositions while in that state! And then nine prophets of the twelve did not write down their own compositions, because they were *short!* Were the Psalms, then, which are shorter still, not written down by their authors? And could not the nine prophets who composed without writing,

* אנשי כנסת הגדולה־כתבו יחזקאל שנתנבא בגולה ואיני יודע למה לא כתבו
יחזקאל בעצמו אם לא מפני שלא נתנה נבואה ליכתב חוצה לארץ וכתבו אלו לאחר
שבאו לארץ וכן ספר דניאל שהיה בגולה ובן מגילת אסתר ושנים עשר מתוך שהיו
נבואתיהם קטנות לא כתבו הנביאים עצמם איש איש ספרו ובאו חגי זכריה ומלאכי
וראו רוח הקדש מסתלק שהיו הם נביאים אחרונים ועמדו וכתבו נבואתיהם וצירפו
נבואות קטנות עמם ועשאום ספר גדול שלא יאבדו מחמת קטנם:

foresee the danger of their works being lost or perverted, while committed to the keeping of merely oral tradition, as well as the three who provided against such a catastrophe? But it is useless to reason against the putid conceits of Rabbins devoted to the Talmud. And besides all that has been now said, I would merely ask the question, Is it not plain, that, even on Talmudic ground, the real authorship of many of the Old Testament books, and parts of books, remains undisclosed? The information given is neither extensive enough to cover the ground which it professes to cover, nor in any measure satisfactory as to that which it does cover.

Such are the *authorities*, then, for the ancient division of the Hebrew Scriptures into *twenty-four* books; such for arranging Isaiah after Jeremiah and Ezekiel; such for mixing together prophecy, history, and lyric poetry and proverbs, all under one category, the *Kethubim*, when the nature of the case and the voice of antiquity were against it. It is in vain to inquire now what conceits led them in such a direction. No one can fathom the depths of Talmudic criticism. The only possible way to receive it, is to take it upon credit and without examination.

Is there not abundant reason, then, to say, that arguments against the genuineness of Daniel, of Chronicles, or of any other book in the Hagiography, on the ground of its present *arrangement*, are utterly futile; inasmuch as they have no solid basis? Indeed this is one of those cases, in which we may say, that the negative is capable of critical demonstration.

After a minute investigation of this whole matter of the classification and order of the sacred books, one may well be surprised at finding such an intelligent critic as Hengstenberg, in his *Authentie des Daniel*, (p. 23, seq.,) admitting, as it would seem, without any question, the *antiquity* of the Talmudic arrangement, and striving to explain the location of Daniel among the Hagiography, on the ground that the book was not written in Palestine, and was not from the hand of one who was a prophet by office, or who could claim the highest degree of inspiration. Certain it is from all the authorities before Jerome and the Talmud, that Daniel was never classified in this manner by the more ancient Jews

This is the shortest and best answer to all arguments against the genuineness of that book, on the ground of its location. In fact this matter is so plain, that I am strongly tempted to believe, that in the disputes between Christians and the Jews about the Messiah, and the time of his coming, during the first three and a half centuries, the Jews felt themselves to be so pressed by the apparent prediction in Dan. ix. respecting the seventy weeks before his coming, that they sought to give the book a lower place than it had occupied before, and thus to remove it somewhat from an association with the other prophets. It was too late to exclude it from the Canon.

Hävernick, in his recent Introduction to the Old Testament, has made the same admission of the antiquity of the Talmudic arrangement in respect to the Kethubim. And he has not only done this, and in addition to it maintained that the Talmudists made distinctions in the order of the prophets, which were founded on the *degree* of their inspiration and the continuance of it, but he has laboured at length (p. 54, seq.) to show, that even the Scriptures themselves make a distinction—a palpable one—between נביא *a prophet*, and ראה or חזה *a seer*. Labour surely bestowed in vain; and, on account of the fundamental error which it involves, having a tendency only to make his readers distrustful in regard to statements of this nature when made by him. How easy to have prevented such a mistake as he has made, by duly consulting a Hebrew Concordance! Had he done this, he must have seen that נביא and ראה or חזה are undistinguishingly used to designate the very same individuals: e. g. Samuel is נביא in 1 Sam. iii. 20; 2 Chron. xxxv. 18, and ראה in 1 Sam. ix. 11, 18, 19; 1 Chron. ix. 22; xxvi. 28; xxix. 29; Gad is נביא in 1 Sam. xxii. 5; 2 Sam. xxiv. 11, and חזה in 1 Chron. xxix. 29; Iddo is *prophet* in 2 Chron. xiii. 22, and *seer* in ix. 29; Jehu is *prophet* in 1 Kings xvi. 7, 12, and *seer* in 2 Chron. xix. 2. So Amos is called a חזה in Amos vii. 12, and the whole body of the prophets collectively appear to be called *seers* in 2 Kings xvii. 13; 2 Chron. xxxiii. 18; Isa. xxix. 10; xxx. 10; Mic. iii. 7. In 1 Sam. ix. 9 it is expressly stated that נביא and ראה are equivalent by usage, the latter being the more ancient word, and the former being then but recently employed. Both designate the same class of persons, although etymologically considered the words bear diverse shades of meaning. נביא marks one as an *inspired* person uttering the thoughts which his inspiration suggests ; חזה or ראה designate a person as *seeing* things concealed from others, whether by being future, or because they are difficult to find out. Pity that a writer of so much learning and vigour as Hävernick should take such a false position, especially when it was so easy to shun it!

It is true, indeed, that neither Hengstenberg nor Hävernick appears to lay any stress upon the Rabbinic conceit of *different gradations* of inspiration, as being matter of fact. They introduce this view of the Talmudists, in order to account for the arrangement of so many books among the class of Kethubim. Yet even this will hardly be accomplished by it; for how came Lamentations to be put among the Kethubim, and Jeremiah among the Prophets? What sort of inspiration was that which was given to David, in his Messianic views as exhibited by the Psalms? Or what, in respect to devotional feeling and instruction? There is no view that we can take of this subject which does not show its futility. And when the question is once asked, By what diagnostics could the Rabbies discern and decide the gradations of inspiration? all the answer is made to this whole matter that needs to be made, or which it deserves. It is like a thousand thousand other conceits with which the Talmudic writers abound, and which even the later Jewish writers virtually acknowledge, by calling them *Haggadoth*, i. e. *tales* or *stories*, meaning pleasant or entertaining stories.

With good reason, then, do we take the position, that *the son of Sirach, Philo, the New Testament, Josephus, and all the earlier Christian writers, down to the middle of the fourth century, testify in favour of an arrangement of the Hebrew Scriptures, which classes* FOUR BOOKS *together that are of like composition and matter in some important respects, and regards* ONLY THESE *as belonging to the Hagiography.* All that differs from this is later, and is the invention of those who have sought for or made distinctions that are only imaginary, and show more of the ingenuity of romancers than of the sound judgment and discretion of sober critics.

SECT. XIII. *General Results of preceding Investigations.*

THERE are some results, which are so plain, and lie as it were so much on the very surface of what has been exhibited, that they cannot well escape the notice of the reader, even such a reader as may be unskilled in criticism. These are, that the books, which for ages past have belonged to the Hebrew Canon, and which now belong to it, are the very same books which belonged to it in the time of Christ and the apostles, and for several centuries before this period. There are some particulars in the history of them which has now been traced, that place this position beyond all reasonable contradiction. The Son of Sirach refers to them, at least 180 years (perhaps 280) before the Christian era, precisely in the same manner, and by substantially the same names or designations, as does Philo, (fl. 40 B. C.,) the writers of the New Testament, and Josephus. The manner of the reference implies of necessity a defined and well-known collection of books, intelligible to every educated reader, and no more liable to be mistaken than our word *Scripture* or *Bible* now is among us. The Christian Fathers who follow, down to the fifth century, have made the limits of the Jewish Canon entirely definite by specifying, in different countries and by many distinguished persons, the identical books which belong to the Jewish Scriptures. No room is left for mistake on this important point. Such is the state of facts.

In the next place, we argue that such must necessarily have been the case, from the circumstances of the Jews, their views and feelings in relation to religious matters, and the opposing party-divisions which existed, first among themselves, and then between the Jews and Christians. To begin with the Jews; it is certain, from the repeated testimony of Josephus, and indirectly of Philo, that the sect of Pharisees and Sadducees existed long before the birth of Christ. The Saviour and his disciples found these sects in full vigour, and in strong action, at the time of their ministry. When we go further back, we find ourselves unable to trace their history to its origin. Josephus first mentions them in Antiq. XIII. 5. 9, under the high priest Jonathan (159—

144 B. C.); but he mentions them (together with the Essenes) as sects already fully and definitely formed. Winer thinks, and with good reason, that the spirit of Judaism, soon after the return of the Jews from their Babylonish exile, gave rise to a feeling which led to the formation of the Pharisaic party; and that this very naturally called forth an opposition, which embodied itself in the Sadducæan party; art. Pharisäer, in Bib. Lex. In the time of John Hyrcanus, nephew of Judas Maccabæus, Josephus speaks of the Pharisees as having such influence with the common people, that "they would be believed even in case they uttered any thing against the king or high priest." To them were opposed the Sadducees; and the main subject of division between them, was not the denial of angel or spirit, or the Sadducæan rejection of the Pharisaic doctrine of predestination, (as has been often alleged,) but the *cardo rei* was that the *Scriptures are the only rule of faith and practice*. In opposition to the Pharisees, the Sadducees rejected all traditions and ordinances of men, not expressly sanctioned by the Scriptures. So Josephus most explicitly: "Their custom was, to regard nothing except the Laws [i. e. the written Laws=the Bible]; for they reckon it as a virtue to dispute against the doctors in favour of the wisdom (σοφίας) which they follow;" Antiq. XVIII. 1. 4. Again, in Antiq. XIII. 10. 6, he says, "The Pharisees inculcated many rules upon the people, received from the Fathers, which are not written in the Law of Moses; and on this account the sect of the Sadducees reject them, alleging that those things are to be regarded as rules which are written [in the Scriptures]," but that the traditions of the Fathers are not to be observed. In a word; the Sadducees of old were *Scripturists*; and in respect to this point they occupied the same ground in opposition to the Pharisees, which Protestants now occupy in relation to the Roman Catholic traditions. That sect has long been defunct among the Jews; but it has notoriously been succeeded by the so-called *Karaites* (קראין, *Scripturists*); see Triglandius, Syntagma de Sectis Judeorum, &c. The idea that has been broached and defended by some, that the Sadducees admitted the authority of only the Pentateuch, is entirely without foundation. How could they have been, as they often were, members of the Sanhedrim, and high

priests, and no objection of this nature have been brought against them by the Pharisees? That their speculations led them to reject the existence of angels and unembodied spirits, is true indeed; but, as I have already said, the *cardo rei*, in respect to the dispute between them and the Pharisees, was what has just been stated; see Winer, Bib. Lex. art. Sadducäer, who has taken considerable pains in the investigation of these matters.

Back, then, to a time which preceded the Maccabees, at all adventures, we must put the rise of the Pharisees and Sadducees. From the moment that the parties were fully formed, the *extent* of the Jewish Scriptures was of course a matter fully and permanently decided. It is impossible to suppose, that the Sadducees would concede to their antagonists the right or the power to introduce new books into the Canon. This would be giving up the very essence of the matter in dispute. No one but a prophet divinely commissioned, and so endowed as to be acknowledged by both parties, would or could be intrusted with the introduction of a new sacred book. But no such prophet, as is conceded by all, made his appearance at that time. Of course we cannot listen to the affirmations of Neologists, however confident and often repeated, that Daniel, Chronicles, Jonah, many of the Psalms, and what not, first made their appearance at the Maccabæan period. It was impossible to procure admittance for them to the Canon, if such were the case. The very essence of the dispute between the two great parties among the Jews, turning as it did on the specific point of *adherence to the Scriptures only*, must of course have rendered it impossible for either party newly to introduce a sacred book, which would be acknowledged by the other. Yet we have not a whisper in all antiquity, that tells us of any dispute in relation to the rejection of any book now in the Jewish Canon, or of any doubt about its authenticity by either party. Even the Pharisees never attempted to add their traditions to the Scriptures, in the way of incorporating them together. They produced them at first as *oral* law, brought down merely by oral tradition. They formed, at last, their Mishna, and their Talmud, in order to embody them and make them permanent; but in all this they meddled not with the integrity of the Scriptures. In forbidding the young to read Canticles and the first and last part of Ezekiel, they did not pretend to undervalue these books, but merely manifested their opinion that they were not adapted, by reason of their peculiar style and matter, to the capacity, comprehension, and profit of youthful readers.

We may in a moment realize the validity of the argument under consideration, by asking the question, Whether any one of the sects of Christians, at present, could introduce another book into the New Testament, which would be acknowledged by all? Has it yet ever been possible to make Protestants receive Judith and Tobit, and the Apocrypha in general, since the beginning of the Reformation? The Council of Trent did their best to effect this; and in what has it resulted?

We have seen how matters stood before the Christian era; let us now inquire into the state of them since the commencement of that era. Two parties existed among the Jews. Many of the Jews became Christians, and were not only opposed and controverted by the others, but persecuted even to death. The Scriptures were in the hands of both. Which party could add to or diminish from them, and yet persuade the other to accede? Surely neither. When the Alexandrine Christians, (whether Jewish or Gentile Christians we cannot perhaps decide with certainty,) after the lapse of some time, introduced slowly and gradually the Apocryphal books into their churches, did the Jews ever receive or admit them as Scripture? Not in the least. Melito, Origen, and others tell us specifically what the Jewish Canon was, at an early period; Hilary, Epiphanius, Jerome, Rufinus, the Talmud, tell us what it continued to be at a later period. No one will even pretend to say that it has been changed since. Jews and Christians have always been too sharply opposed to admit of any change in the Scriptural documents, since the fifth century. It would be useless to attempt any proof of a matter so obvious, certain, and acknowledged by all. Whatever a part or a party of Christians have done, in the way of foisting in the Apocrypha, has never produced the least influence upon the Jews, nor upon the limits of their Canon. The books which we now have as theirs, and which are appealed to and quoted in the New Testament, still remain as documents which are quoted and referred to by Christians, and by all the Jews the world over. If there ever was a people on the face of the earth, whose superstitions even, to mention nothing better, would have put it out of all question either to add to or take from their sacred books, that people was the Jews. With what unbending obstinacy have they adhered, for more than a thousand years, even to all the conceits and egregious trifling of much that is in the Talmud ! Have they been less superstitious in regard to their Scriptures ?

Whatever may be the difficulties existing in the minds of some, and even of some conscientious persons, about a part of the Old Testament books, they have no bearing on the historico-critical question before us. Our inquiry respects a matter of *fact*, not of doctrine. And this fact stands before us, not in the obscurity of night, nor in the doubtful glimmerings of twilight, but in the full blaze of a noon-day sun.

The question how much AUTHORITY is to be attributed to the Old Testament, or to any part of it, has not yet been distinctly considered. It remains for more particular discussion ; and to this we shall proceed, as soon as one more inquiry has been made. This is :

SECT. XIV. *Did the Egyptian Jews admit the same Canon as the Jews of Palestine?*

IN order rightly to appreciate the importance of this question, it will be necessary to glance at the condition and the number of the Jews in Egypt, at the period of about 320 B. C., and thence downwards to the Christian era.

To Ptolemy Lagus, one of the military officers of Alexander the Great, was assigned, after the death of that king, the government of Egypt. In the contests which followed, among the ethnarchs of Alexander's empire, Ptolemy overran and took possession of Judea, Samaria, Phenicia, and Cœlosyria. Josephus relates that Ptolemy came in person to Jerusalem, and offered sacrifices in the temple there. In order to secure the tranquillity of the newly conquered countries, he took with him a great number of hostages to Egypt, and among these were many thousand Jews. Some of the latter were sent to Cyrene, (then under Ptolemy,) but the body of them settled in the newly built city of Alexandria.

From time to time, after this, great accessions were made to their numbers; for they were treated with special favour by most of the Egyptian kings, in order to secure their fidelity and their aid. Finally, about 153 B. C., Onias, a son of the high priest Onias III., who was massacred at Daphnæ under the reign of Antiochus Epiphanes, fled to Egypt; and not long after this, he so gained the favour of Ptolemy Philometer, then king of that country, that he was made commander-in-chief of the Egyptian army, and governor of the Nome of Heliopolis; while the second in command was Dositheus, another Jew. Onias, on account of the great number of Jews in Egypt and its dependencies, conceived the idea of having a temple built in that country, in order to accommodate Hebrew worshippers, and save the expense and trouble of journeying to Palestine, in order to pay their devotions there. The king consented, and a temple was built at Leontopolis, in the Nome of Heliopolis, in which Onias became high priest, and subordinate priests and Levites were gathered around him. The temple itself was built after the model of that at Jerusalem; and the whole routine of worship in it was simply copied from that at Jerusalem. This state of things continued, until the temple of Leontopolis was destroyed by Vespasian, during his war with the Jews.

Now there is not the least intimation from any quarter, that either any new books or new ritual of worship were ever introduced here. The whole arrangement bespeaks the contrary. Even so late as the time of Philo Judæus, (40 B. C.,) the attachment to the religion of the father-land was not diminished among the Jews of Egypt. They sent Philo to Jerusalem, there to make offerings in the name of the people, i. e. of the Egyptian Jews. Philo himself was descended from a family of the priesthood. He was a Pharisee, and zealous for the religion of his fathers. Yet, in all his voluminous works, he never once refers to any of the apocryphal books as Scripture, nor ever makes them the basis of any of his allegorizing; and all this, when at the same time it is manifest from numerous hints, and occasionally from his diction, that he was familiarly acquainted with the apocryphal writings. Of this indeed there can be no doubt, considering his station and his literary ardour. How is it possible, that neither he, nor Josephus, ever intimates a word of any difference of views about the Jewish Scriptures between the Jews of Palestine and Alexandria, if any such difference really existed? The fact that Philo has quoted most of the Jewish books as authoritative and Divine, is a pledge that he recognised the Jewish Scriptures in their usual extent.* The fact that Josephus never intimates any departure from Jewish views on the part of Egyptian Jews, proves, beyond any fair contradiction, that he was not aware of any such departure. After the minute account he gives of the Pharisees, the Sadducees, and the Essenes, should we not of course expect him, when he describes the building of the temple at Leontopolis and its ritual, to take notice of any peculiarities in the views of his Egyptian brethren in regard to the Scriptures?

It seems probable, indeed, that most of the books which we now name *Apocrypha*, first came into being, or at least into circulation, in Egypt. Alexandria was, for a long period, the great literary workshop of the times. Such of them as were written before the Christian era, (which seems to have been the case with most,) must of course have been written by Jews. But they were nearly all written in *Greek*; and no Jew ever thought of uniting a Greek book with the Hebrew ones. Hence, although some of the apocryphal books made their way to an association with the Septuagint version, yet they were never joined to the He-

---

* This assertion is scarcely correct. Many of the canonical books are not quoted by Philo. Still it is remarkable that he never quotes the apocryphal books as authoritative, although he always used the Septuagint version, with which they were incorporated, and which version too he looked upon as inspired. On the unity of the Alexandrian and Palestinian Canon, see *Movers'* Loci quidam hist. Canon. Vet. Test., (Vratislaviæ, 1842,) who, however, has made several rash statements and hasty inferences. The connexion between the Jews in both countries, and the manner in which those in Egypt looked to Palestine, favour the view that both had the same canonical writings. Nor has any good argument been adduced to prove diversity of opinion between them in this particular. D.

brew Scriptures. Even the production of Jesus the Son of Sirach, who was a Jew of Jerusalem and wrote in *Hebrew*, made no claim, at least none which was admitted, to scriptural authority. Much less could the books written originally in Greek prefer such a claim. Vulgar and uneducated readers, who had no discriminating taste or judgment, and who knew only the Greek Scriptures, might unwittingly unite the apocryphal books with them, because of their religious tone. Yet it would be difficult to prove that this was done before the Christian era. At all events, such men as Philo, although he quotes only the Greek Scriptures, never once thought of doing any such thing.

We may safely come to the conclusion, then, that the Canon of the Hebrew Scriptures was the same among the Jews both of Egypt and Palestine. Our next step is the inquiry:

SECT. XV. *In what estimation were the Hebrew Scriptures held by the Jews, at, before, and soon after the commencement of the Christian era?*

WE begin with the testimony of the Son of Sirach. In the proem to the Greek version of his book, his grandson has told us respecting him, that "he gave himself $\epsilon\pi\grave{\iota}\ \pi\lambda\epsilon\tilde{\iota}o\nu$, for the greater part of the time, or very much, to the study of the Law, the Prophets, and the other patrical books," in order to prepare for writing his own book. At the outset the translator speaks of the "$\pi o\lambda\lambda\tilde{\omega}\nu\ \kappa\alpha\grave{\iota}\ \mu\epsilon\gamma\acute{\alpha}\lambda\omega\nu$, *many and important things* which were imparted to the Jews by the Law, the Prophets, and the other books of like tenor." The estimation put upon the Scriptures, by Sirachides and his grandson, is very plainly disclosed by these declarations. The Bible, for the first, was the highest source of all true wisdom and knowledge; in the view of the second, it was the efficient cause of procuring the distinguished blessings and privileges enjoyed by the Hebrews.

Every where does Sirachides refer to the Scriptures, either by borrowing their phraseology, or by appealing to them, mostly in an indirect way, as the source of all true wisdom, virtue, piety, and happiness. The Law is often the subject of reference, and is regarded as an authority in all matters. In the eulogy of Wisdom, (ch. xxiv.,) there is a manifest and designed imitation cf Prov. viii. In the πατέρων ὕμνος, i. e. *Eulogy of the Fathers*, (xliv.—1.,) there is every where the most plain and manifest recognition of the authority, credibility, and excellence of the scriptural representations. The writer begins with Enoch, and follows the train of biblical history, down to Nehemiah. He quotes the promises to Abraham. Moses was beloved of God, and to him commandment was given in respect to his people. Joshua was a follower of Moses in the *prophetic* office. Most of the kings of Judah sinned by forsaking the Law. Jeremiah was consecrated, while in his mother's womb, to the prophetic office. Ezekiel saw visions of glory, which were shown to him by him who rode upon the cherubim. All the offerings and rites of the Levitical ritual are excellent and deserving of veneration; strong attachment to them, and particularity in the observance of them, is worthy of high commendation. This and the like matter in the book of Sirachides show beyond the possibility of doubt, that with him the sacred books were τὸ πάνυ, the all in all. Philo and Josephus have designated their views much oftener by the use of significant attributives applied to the Scriptures (as we shall soon see); but they have shown no deeper reverence for the authority and excellence of the Scriptures, than the Son of Sirach. "He that runneth may read" this, in every part of his work.

We come next to PHILO. He has been more explicit in stating his view of the matters under consideration. Nothing can be more certain than his belief in *the Divine inspiration and authority of the Scriptures*, in the very highest sense that can be affixed to these words. The edition to which I refer in the view subjoined, is that of Mangey, 2 vol. fol.

1. *Philo's view of the prophetic office and of inspiration.* In Opp. I. p. 222, speaking of Moses as a prophet, he subjoins, "Ἑρμηνεῖς γάρ εἰσιν οἱ προφῆταί Θεοῦ, καταχρωμένοι τοῖς ἐκείνων ὀργάνοις πρὸς δήλωσιν ὧν ἂν ἐθήλησε, i. e. Prophets are the interpreters of God, he employing their organs for the disclosure of whatever he pleases." In his De Legibus Special., II. p. 343, he comes out most fully and ex-

plicitly with his views: "Προφήτης δὲ μὲν γὰρ οὐδὲν ἴδιον ἀποφαίνεται τὸ παράπαν, ἀλλ᾽ ἔστιν ἑρμηνεύς, ὑποβάλλοντος ἑτέρου πανθ᾽ ὅσα προφέρει, καὶ καθ᾽ ὃν χρόνον ἐνθουσίᾳ γεγονὼς ἐν ἀγνοίᾳ, μετανισταμένου μὲν τοῦ λογισμοῦ καὶ παρακεχωρηκότος τὴν τῆς ψυχῆς ἀκρόπολιν· ἐπιπεφοιτηκότος δὲ καὶ ἐνοικηκότος τοῦ θείου πνεύματος, καὶ πᾶσαν τῆς φωνῆς ὀργανοποιίαν κρούοντος, δὲ καὶ ἐνηχοῦντος εἰς ἐναργῆ δήλωσιν ὧν προσθεσπίζει, i. e. a prophet exhibits nothing at all which is his own, but is an interpreter, another suggesting whatever he utters; and so long as he is inspired, he remains unconscious, his reason departing and quitting the citadel of the soul, and the Divine Spirit entering and inhabiting it, and giving impulse to all the organism of the voice, and uttering sounds for the clear discourse of those things which he prophesies. Here, then, is a representation that will satisfy even the warmest stickler for *passivity* in persons inspired. I regret to add, that down to the present hour there have been and are not a few, who have laboured to support the like extreme view of this matter. Even Hengstenberg tells us, that "when the Spirit of God comes in, the spirit of man goes out;" the mere echo of what Philo said more than 1800 years ago. It is not my present business to examine theologically this view of inspiration. How the weight or authority of what is communicated, is augmented by the supposition that the organ of communication ceases to be a rational and conscious being, is what no one has yet shown. At all events Paul did not believe in such a view of this matter, when he declared, (for the purpose of enforcing obedience to his injunctions among the Corinthian prophets, and of showing their obligation and ability to obey,) that "the spirit of the prophets is subject to the prophets." To Philo such a suggestion, it seems, would have appeared little less than blasphemy. My view of it is indeed very different. It appears to me to be simple Christian rationality and truth. But enough of this.

No one will deny, then, that whatever books Philo considered as Scripture, or as revealed, they, in his view, bore the stamp of the highest possible authority and credibility. He often repeats this sentiment. In his Quis Rer. divin. Hæres sit, (Opp. I. 510,) he says, "A prophet utters nothing of his own, but all things are from a foreign source, another giving them utterance." And again in II. p. 417, "A prophet is an interpreter, uttering from within the things that are spoken by God." Whoever then is called a *prophet* by him, is of course regarded as an instrument of Divine and authoritative communication. Whatever books were ranked by him as Scripture, were also of course, in his view, entitled to all the authority and reverence which such a character of their authors could claim. It remains for us to see how he characterizes, in particular, both the sacred writers and their books.

II. *Philo's particular view of sacred authors, and of their books.* The most general designation of the authors is *prophets*, προφῆται. With this word, and for the sake of variety in his diction, he not unfrequently exchanges other names, which, as he employs them, are altogether equivalent. For example, we find frequently in him, προφήτης ἀνήρ, *prophetic man*, ἱεροφάντης, *hierophant*, i. e. exhibitor of sacred things, θεσπέσιος ἀνήρ, *oracular man*, Μωϋσέως ἑταῖρος, *disciple or companion of Moses*, Μωϋσέως θιασώτης, *a follower of Moses*, (lit. a *thiasos, associate,*) τίς τῶν φοιτητῶν Μωσέως, *one of the followers* or *frequenters of Moses*, τοῦ προφητικοῦ θιασώτης χοροῦ, *a companion of the prophetic choir;* all of which names are applied to various sacred writers, and which an artificial eloquence led Philo thus to vary, while his meaning is ever the same. Moses is referred to in some of the cases above, as the perfection of the prophetic character, the *ideal* of an inspired person.

The books written by such men he calls ἱεράς γραφάς, *sacred Scriptures*, ἱεράς βίβλους, *sacred books*, ἱερώτατον γράμμα, *most holy writing*, ἱεροφαντηθέντα, *sacred disclosures*, προφητικὸν λόγον, *prophetic word*, προφητικὰ ῥήματα, *prophetic sayings*, sometimes λόγιον, *oracle*, λόγιον τοῦ Θεοῦ, *oracle of God*, and sometimes χρησμόν, *oracular response*, or τὸ χρησθέν, *what is uttered oracularly*. Like the preceding designations of prophets, all these, as employed by him, are entirely synonymous, and the variety belongs merely to his rhetoric.

Any of these names bestowed on writers, or on their books, indicate, of course, the fullest belief on the part of Philo, that they were divinely inspired, and therefore of paramount authority. Our next object then will be, to inquire in what manner he has bestowed these appellations.

III. *Books and persons designated by Philo as inspired.* Moses he almost every where names προφήτης, *prophet*, or ἱεροφάντης, *hierophant.* His inspiration is of the highest stamp; his books are the *prophetic word* or *sacred books.* Genesis he calls ἱερὰς γραφάς, *sacred Scriptures* (De Mundi Opif. I. p. 18); Exodus is ἱερὰ βίβλος, *sacred book* (De Migrat. Abrah. I. p. 438); Leviticus is ἱερὸς λόγος, *sacred word* (Allegor. III. Tom. I. p. 85); Numbers he calls ἱερώτατον γράμμα, *most sacred writing* (Deus sit immut. I. 273); and Deuteronomy χρησμιόν and ἱερὸν λόγον, *oracle* and *sacred word* (De Migrat. Abraham. I. 454, and De Somn. I. 657).

Joshua he cites as λόγιον τοῦ ἱλέου Θεοῦ, *the oracle of the merciful God* (De Confus. Ling. I. 430).

1 Samuel (which, following the designation of the Septuagint, he calls 1 *Kings*) is cited as ἱερὸς λόγος (De Temulent. I. 379).

Ezra is cited as containing τὰ ἐν βασιλικαῖς βίβλοις ἱεροφαντηϑέντα, *things sacredly revealed in the royal books* (De Confus. Ling. I. 427).

Isaiah he names τὸν πάλαι προφήτην, *the ancient prophet* (De Somn. I. 681). His prophecies are προφητικὰ ῥήματα, *prophetic sayings* (De Mutat. Nom. I. 604).

Jeremiah he calls *prophet, hierophant*, and μύστης, *one initiated in sacred mysteries;* and his work is χρησμός, *oracle* (De Cherub. I. 147, 148). Again he says of this prophet, that he was τοῦ προφητικοῦ ϑιασώτης χοροῦ, ὃς καταπνευσϑεὶς ἐνϑουσιῶν ἀνεφϑέγξατο, i. e. *an associate of the prophetic choir, who being animated by the Spirit spake in ecstasy* (De Confus. Ling. I. 44). In another place he says, "The Father of the universe predicted by the *prophetic mouth of Jeremiah*" (De Prof. I. 575).

In respect to the Minor Prophets, (always *one* book in ancient times,) he refers to two of them, viz. Hosea and Zechariah. A passage in Hos. xiv. 8 he names χρησϑὲν παρά τινι τῶν προφήτων, *spoken oracularly by one of the prophets* (De Plant. Noe, I. 350). Again, he calls Hos. xiv. 24 "a glowing oracle predicted by a prophetic mouth" (De Mutat. Nom. I. 350). Zechariah he calls *the companion of*

Moses, Μωϋσέως ἑταῖρος (De Confus. Ling. I. 414). Of course, in referring to these two prophecies, or to either of them, he recognises the whole book of the *Twelve*, which was always counted as *one* book, so far back as we can trace the history of the Canon.

The Psalms are often quoted by Philo as Scripture; and David, whom he regarded as the principal author of them, is called by him προφήτης, *prophet* (De Agric. I. 308); προφήτης ἀνήρ, *prophetic man* (Quis Rer. div. Hæres, I. 515); θεσπέσιος ἀνήρ, *oracular man* (De Plant. Noe, I. 344; comp. De Mund. Opp. I. 362); Μωϋσέως θιασώτης ὃς οὐχὶ τῶν ἠμελημένων ἦν, *an associate of Moses, who was not of those that are lightly regarded* (De Plant. Noe, p. 219, edit. Francof.); and sometimes ἑταῖρος Μωσέως, *the friend of Moses* (Quod a Deo mitt. Somnia, I. 691).

In like manner he speaks of Solomon, whom the Jews of that day regarded as the author of Proverbs, Ecclesiastes, and Canticles. He says that he is ἐκ τοῦ θείου χοροῦ, *of the Divine choir* (De Ebriet. I. 362); and he names him τινὰ τῶν φοιτητῶν Μωσέως, *one of the disciples of Moses* (De Cong. quær. erud. Grat. I. 544).

The book of Judges, viii. 9, he quotes in De Confus. Ling. I. 424. Job xiv. 4 is quoted in De Mutat. Nom. I. 584. Our First Book of Kings (Philo names it as in the Sept., the *third*) is quoted in De Gigant. I. 274, and in six other places. The book of Psalms, already mentioned as quoted by him, he quotes in all the five parts or divisions of the books, so as to show that it was the same in his day as in ours; see in Eichh. Einl. I. p. 97, edit. III.

Quotations are not found in him from Ruth, Esther, Chronicles, Daniel, Lamentations, Ecclesiastes, and Canticles. But the two latter are doubtless acknowledged by the reference to Solomon as "of the Divine choir." Of the others it is sufficient to say, that he did not find occasion to quote them. It is no argument against their existence and canonical rank, that they are not quoted by him, when he no where undertakes to gives us a list of the Scriptures, but only to refer to such passages in them as are to his purpose. Would any man think of drawing the conclusion in these days, that certain books of the Old Testament were not acknowledged by this theologian and that, because they have not quoted them in their publications? Nothing could be more weak and false in reasoning than this. And equally so is it, when applied to Philo.

After all, in fact the books not quoted by him are almost none, if we reckon the universal manner of the ancients in distributing the books. E. g. Judges and Ruth were by them regarded as *one* book, and he quotes Judges; Jeremiah and Lamentations were one book, and he quotes Jeremiah; the books of Ezra and Nehemiah were one, and he quotes Ezra. There is left then only Chronicles, Daniel, and Esther, which he has not quoted. The wonder is, not that so many remain unquoted, but that so many have been quoted.

Moreover, as the grandson of Sirachides had, long before Philo's time, repeatedly adverted to the triplex division of the Jewish Scriptures, *the Law, the Prophets, and the Other Books;* and as Philo acknowledges the same division, in speaking of the studies of the Essenes (Opp. II. 475); we may conclude that he has virtually referred to every part of Scripture, inasmuch as this triplex division must have consisted of books whose number and order were well defined and well known at that time. Philo was a Pharisee, and of priestly origin. He was zealous, also, in matters pertaining to the Jewish religion. His embassy to Palestine shows this; and his works every where bear ample testimony to it. In fact, it seems impossible rationally to doubt, that the Canon of Philo was the same as that of Josephus and the New Testament writers, considering how near he lived to the times in which they lived, and in what manner he has described the contents of the Scriptures which he regarded as Divine.*

That Philo was, as has already been said, acquainted with the apocryphal books, there can be no doubt. YET HE NEVER QUOTES THEM, NOT EVEN FOR THE PURPOSES OF ALLEGORIZING. No imaginable reason can be given for this, excepting that, like Josephus, he made a distinction wide and broad between *inspired* and other books. This account of Philo's practice in regard to the apocryphal books may be

---

* These two paragraphs respecting Philo approach to the character of special pleading. The argument is sufficiently good without them, and it is matter of regret that they should have been added. D.

relied on, for Hornemann (Observatt. ad illustr. Doctrinæ de Canone Vet. Test. ex Philone) assures us of this; and he read through the whole works of Philo, as he states, in order to ascertain this very point. His competency and his candour as a witness will not be called in question. Eichhorn gives him full credit; Einl. I. § 26. In fact, Philo shows his contempt of the apocryphal books, (for which some in his day doubtless began to entertain a high regard, so as to treat them as a kind of Scripture,) by treating them with more neglect than he has even the heathen productions; for he often quotes Plato, Philolaus, Solon, Hippocrates, Heraclites, and others, while he never does this honour to the Apocrypha.

Such, then, was the state of this matter respecting the Canon in Egypt, the very hot-bed of apocryphal Scriptures, at a period antecedent to the Christian era. The most distinguished philosopher and writer of the Jewish nation, at that time, takes no cognizance of apocryphal Scriptures, when, if he regarded them as other Alexandrians afterwards did, even Christian writers, he must have found very numerous occasions for quoting them, or referring to them. But this is an honour which he utterly withholds.

Next, as to the OPINION OF JOSEPHUS. We have already examined the testimony of Josephus, as to the number and nature of the sacred books, (pp. 207—216 above,) and but little more seems necessary to be here said, under the present category. My particular object now is, to render more prominent the distinction which he makes between the books of Scripture and other works.

The famous passage in Cont. Apion. I. § 8, (see p. 207 above,) presents this distinction to us in a very clear and commanding light. After enumerating the various portions of Scripture and reckoning the number of the sacred books, he says, "From Artaxerxes until the present time, every occurrence is recorded; but these [narrations] are not regarded as worthy of the credit due to those which preceded them, because there was no certain succession of prophets. By our conduct we show what credit we give to the proper Scriptures; for although so long a period of time has passed away, no one has ventured to add any thing to them, or to take any thing from them. It is implanted in every Jew, from his birth, to regard them [the Scriptures] as the statutes of God, to abide by them, and (if necessary) gladly to die for them." See App. No. III. A broader and more palpable distinction no Protestant pen could now sketch.

Elsewhere he testifies the same feelings and views. He calls the Scriptures ἱερὰς βίβλους, *sacred books*; τὰς τῶν ἱερῶν γραφῶν βίβλους, *the books of the sacred Scriptures*; ἱερὰ γράμματα, *sacred writings*; τὰ ἐν τῷ ἱερῷ ἀνακείμενα γράμματα, *the writings laid up in the temple*; and also βίβλους προφητείας. Besides these appellations, he names the Scriptures ἀρχαῖα βιβλία, *ancient books*; βίβλοι Ἑβραίων and βίβλοι Ἑβραϊκαί, *Hebrew books*.

If now there be any suspicion (arising from the fact that the books of Daniel and Esther are *not quoted* by Philo) that those books did not belong to the Jewish Canon at that period, it is entirely dissipated by the course which Josephus pursues. Of no books in the Old Testament has he given more copious extracts, in proportion to their length, than he has from these. In all respects he credits the accounts which they give. And as he unquestionably assigns these writings to a period antecedent to the close of Artaxerxes' reign, so no doubt can remain that they were a part of what he recognises as Scripture. The same is true of the book of *Jonah*, to which so many exceptions have recently been taken. In Antiq. IX. 10. 2, he gives an account of Jonah at length, and says that "he tells the story of this prophet just as he finds it written ἐν Ἑβραϊκαῖς βίβλοις, *in the Hebrew books*;" and at the close he repeats the declaration, that "he has gone through the narration as he found it in writing."

The manner in which Josephus expresses himself in regard to books before and after the close of Artaxerxes' reign, shows that all the Hebrew books which were within the circle of his acquaintance, and were written before the death of Artaxerxes, were included within his Canon. It is indeed doubtful, whether any of the more ancient Hebrew writings, the sacred books excepted, were really extant in the time of Josephus. But be this as it may, it seems evident that none of the more ancient Hebrew books, the Scriptures excepted, were known to him.

The Pentateuch he often speaks of in the highest terms,

and bestows upon it appellations like those employed by Philo; e. g. he calls it ἱερὰς βίβλους, Antiq. I. end of Pref.; III. 5. 2; IV. 8. 48; IX. 2. 2; X. 4. 2. Another appellation is αἱ τῶν ἱερῶν γραφῶν βίβλοι, cont. Ap. II. 4. Comp. with these the various declarations of a similar tenor respecting the sacred nature of the Pentateuch, in Antiq. I. p. 4; XX. 5. 4; III. 6. 5; IV. 8. 44; X. 4. 2; XVI. 6. 2.

Of Isaiah Josephus says, "Cyrus read the book of the *prophecy of Isaiah*, which he composed 210 years before;" Antiq. XI. 1. 2. Elsewhere he calls Isaiah προφήτης, *a prophet*; X. 2. 2. Speaking of Hezekiah he says, that "he learned accurately of the *prophet* [Isaiah] the things that were to come;" XI. 13. 3.

He calls Jeremiah "a *prophet*, who predicted terrible events which were to take place in respect to the city;" X. 5. 1.

Of Ezekiel he says, " Not only did he [Jeremiah] foretell these things to the multitude, but also the *prophet* Ezekiel;" X. 5. 1.

The book of Daniel he classes among the ἱερὰ γράμματα, i. e. *the sacred writings;* X. 10. 4. He speaks of his προφητείαν, *prophecy*, as being "uttered 408 years before;" XII. 7. 6. In X. 11. 7, he says, "All these things he [Daniel] left in writing, God exhibiting them to him; so that those who read, observant of the events, must needs look on Daniel with wonder, on account of the honour done to him by God." Besides, Josephus has made copious extracts from all the historical parts of Daniel, with some comments of his own. He makes this prophet a leading character among the men of the prophetic order; see Antiq. X. 10 and 11.

The twelve Minor Prophets Josephus regards as one book, and places them by the side of Isaiah. In Antiq. X. 2. 2, he says, " Not only this prophet, [Isaiah,] but the other Twelve as to number did the same thing. Every thing, whether good or evil, that has taken place among us, has happened according to their *prediction*, προφητείαν."

Of Jonah we have already spoken above. He places his book among the βίβλους Ἑβραϊκάς, *the Hebrew books*, IX. 10. 1. Nahum is called προφήτης, *a prophet*, and the fulfilment of his predictions is lauded; IX. 11. 3. Haggai and Zechariah are called *two prophets*, δύο προφῆται; XI. 4. 5.

Of Joshua, he says, that it is "among the books laid up in the temple;" V. 1. 17.

The history of Elijah contained in the book of Kings, he couples with the history of Enoch; and says that these histories "are written in the sacred books;" IX. 2. 2.

The Psalms he calls ὕμνους εἰς τὸν Θεόν; Cont. Ap. I. 8. He speaks of them as "the songs of David," because David was the principal author; VII. 12. 3.

In Antiq. X. 5. 1, he speaks of Jeremiah as the author of the Lamentations. And as to all the historical books, Joshua, Judges, 1 and 2 Samuel, 1 and 2 Kings, 1 and 2 Chronicles, Ezra, Nehemiah, and Esther, he every where extracts from them at great length in his Antiquities, following them step by step in their narrations, and only here and there intermingling something of his own, occasionally, but rarely, a wonderful story, and sometimes glosses of the Hebrew narrations. He appeals to them as of the highest and most undoubted authority.

Josephus' historical office did not lead him to quote all of the ancient Hagiography. He has not made excerpts from Proverbs, Ecclesiastes, or Canticles. But he speaks of Solomon as having composed βιβλία ᾠδῶν καὶ μελῶν, *books of songs and chants,* and as having "written 3000 books of parables and similitudes." No doubt can remain, that he regarded him as the author of several of the sacred books.

The book of Job, being foreign to the objects of his history, is not at all mentioned by him. But there can be no doubt that this book was included in his Canon. Ezekiel makes recognition of this book, xiv. 20. Philo quotes from the book of Job; De Mutat. Nom. I. p. 584. It is necessary to include it, in order to make out the *thirteen* books which Josephus includes under the second class, viz. the Prophets. It is recognised in the New Testament; James v. 11. It is reason enough that Josephus does not speak of the book, that the history of Job is that of a *foreigner,* probably an Arabian, who, if a Jew by descent, (as seems not improbable,) has not once in all his work adverted to Jews or Judaism. The silence of Josephus, in such a case, makes nothing against the book. The positive testimony of Ezekiel, Philo, and the New Testament, makes the point altogether clear, that the book was written before Artaxerxes' time, and was therefore regarded as one of the sacred books by Josephus, according to the rule which he lays down in Cont. Apion. I. 8.

SECT. XVI. *Summary of the testimony of Sirachides, Philo, and Josephus.*

It needs but a brief space to exhibit this. The book of Sirach presents to our view a then (at least 180 B. C.) well-known and definite triplex division of the Jewish Scriptures, in which all the books deemed sacred were included. Philo has presented us with the like divisions of the same books, in his notice of books which were studied by the Essenes. Josephus has also presented us with Scriptures which exhibit the same division, viz. *the Law, the Prophets, and the other Books.*

Sirachides has furnished us with no adequate means of ascertaining what, or how many, the sacred books of each division were. Philo has not told us of the *number*; but he has referred to the books themselves as being parts of Scripture, and in such a way, that, if we reckon in the ancient manner of combining, in several cases, two or more books and naming them as one, we make out in him a distinct recognition of all the books excepting Esther, Daniel, and Chronicles. The want of a reference in him to these books, however, proves nothing against their canonical credit. The only case in which it could do this would be, where he should undertake to make out a list which in his view would be complete, and still omit the books in question. But this he has no where undertaken.

Josephus has told us the number of books in the whole collection, viz. *twenty-two*. Of these, *five* belong, according to his statement, to the Law ; *four* to the Hagiography ; and the rest (of course *thirteen*) to the Prophets. His description of the Hagiography of necessity limits it to Psalms, Proverbs, Ecclesiastes, and Canticles, with which agree all the most ancient lists of books among the Christian Fathers, down to Jerome. The same Josephus has revealed to us, in another way, what books he regarded as sacred. The Pentateuch and all the historical books he quotes, and makes excerpts from them at large. The only books which he does not quote, are Proverbs, Ecclesiastes, Canticles, and Job. But what he says of Solomon as an author, in Antiq. VIII. 2. 5, seems plainly to show, that he regarded him as the author of the first three of these books; for so he has been generally regarded by the Jews in all ages since the beginning of the Christian era. Job, then, is the only book left; but this is vouched for by Ezekiel, by Philo, and by the New Testament.

Our Old Test. Canon, then, is complete, if we rest the question respecting it upon *Jewish* testimony. The witnesses before us can neither be impeached for incompetence, partiality, or a proneness to state what is false. What reason is there, that they should not be believed? Their testimony is *disinterested*. They have no party ends to accomplish by it, in this case. They were all Jews; and none could so well understand the matter in question as Jews. Moreover, they were all *priests*, or the descendants of priestly families. At most, only Sirachides can be excepted from this; and I doubt seriously whether we should be justified in excepting him. Intelligent priests, one would naturally suppose, must know what books were deemed sacred.

SECT. XVII. *Nature and importance of the testimony of the New Testament, in respect to the Old Testament.*

WE come now to the consummation of our work—to the great point toward which all else that has been examined converges. Of a considerable number of books in the Old Testament, we do not even know who the author was. Respecting others no explanatory declaration is made by each particular book itself, or by other sacred writers, and we find no special assertion that their origin is Divine. Who tells us expressly, that Joshua, Judges, Ruth, Samuel, Kings, Chronicles, are of Divine authority? Who has told us the secret of the *authorship*? In what light have any of the Old Testament writers placed Esther, Ecclesiastes, or Canticles? Or what do these books say respecting themselves? It seems, indeed, at first view, as if the authorship of Canticles and Ecclesiastes was assigned to Solomon; yet a nicer critical examination shows, that this conclusion is probably not well grounded. The books *have respect to him*—he is the leading personage in them—but this seems to be all that we can necessarily make out from the inscriptions and the tenor of the books themselves. And besides all this, the three books last mentioned seem to present not a few serious difficulties, from various sources, to the mind of even a grave and impartial inquirer. What then has given sanction to them? What obliges us to receive and admit them as Divine? Not one new doctrine in morals or theology is added to the general stock by them. If they were dropped from the Scriptures, our systems of divinity and morals would remain the same as they are now. Why then perplex our minds with these books, which present problems and paradoxes, some of which have never yet been satisfactorily solved? Why not leave them to the Jews, to be put with the Mishna and the Gemara, and to augment the Rabbinical store-house of wonders? Even the New Testament writers (as we shall see) have not once adverted to them; and if they did not pay any more regard to them, why should we consider and treat them as sacred?

In this manner many minds have thought and argued; and even some which are honest and upright, and to all appearance earnestly desirous of knowing the truth. For the scruples of such men I must always have respect. Even if I cannot regard their scruples as indicative of much knowledge concerning the matter that excites them, still, a conscientious pursuit of truth, and a readiness to receive it whenever good sound reasons for believing it are proffered, is a disposition of mind always entitled to respect, and has a claim to be treated with much Christian courtesy. There is a sentiment of Paul, which I would were oftener remembered and respected; this is, that we ought " to receive him that is *weak in the faith*, but not to doubtful disputations." I can easily suppose a sincere and earnest Christian, whose mind has never been duly enlightened in regard to the Canon of Scripture, to be in a doubting state with respect to some of the anonymous Old Testament books, while he heartily admits that the rest belong to a Divine revelation. So it was with Luther in regard to some books of the New Testament. His dispute with the Romanists about justification by faith alone, led him to regard the Epistle of James as spurious, yea, as even an *epistola straminea*, i. e. a strawy epistle. The Apocalypse he could not receive, because he thought there was "no Christ in it." So he threw these books into an *apocryphal* appendix. Yet, mistaken as he was, and poorly as he reasoned in this case, he was still a most hearty believer in the Divine word of God. The Scriptures were to him the supreme, the all-sufficient, the only rule of faith and practice.

So, with minds scantily informed in respect to the true basis of credibility in the Old Testament Canon, I can easily suppose other good men may act, in regard to some of the books in our Old Testament Canon; some which are never expressly quoted in the New Testament as Scripture, and which therefore may possibly be regarded, by one class of inquirers, as having never been duly authenticated. I know of some persons in this attitude of mind, for whom I cherish a high regard, and whose piety I should not think of calling in question. To them I would hope to be useful in the present investigation. I cannot agree with them in their views respecting the Old Testament; but I can look on them with fraternal feelings, and say in the most brotherly manner to them, Permit me, in this little work, ἀληθεύειν ἐν ἀγάπῃ.

Very different is the position of those who abjure the Old Testament *en masse;* who even cast it away with contumely, and will listen neither to Moses nor the Prophets. I must regard this as substantial unbelief. I apprehend it may be shown, that what they do is virtually to set aside the authority and express declarations of the Saviour and of his apostles. There are even some who would not consider this as *infidelity*. But while I am not fond of applying harsh and ungrateful epithets to any man or body of men whatever, I know not how to call the denying, or the designed evading, of the authority or the decision of Christ and of his apostles respecting the books of the Old Testament, any thing less than *unbelief*. It is not for me to examine and characterize the *motives* which lead to such an unbelief. In my opinion they belong to the cognizance of the Supreme, the Searcher of all hearts. Nor am I desirous of finding or believing grounds of making criminal charges against any one. This whole province I would leave, and most gladly do leave, to the prerogative of the supreme Judge. So much of the guilt of unbelief, where unbelief in reality exists, or where I may think it to exist, depends on the tone and temper and motives of the mind and heart, and on the light and means of information respectively possessed and enjoyed by different individuals, that I do not see how a human tribunal can take any adequate cognizance of such a matter, even if it possessed a right of cognizance. For one, I do not claim the right; nor do I concede it to others.

But when all this is said, and even conceded, there still remains a most formidable evil, fairly attached to and chargeable upon *unbelief*. If the Saviour and his apostles, for example, regarded and have treated the books of the Old Testament as of Divine authority and obligation, then it is an affair of the gravest nature to decide against them. Those who do not profess to be Christians, and who regard neither the Old Testament nor the New as of Divine authority, act consistently, to say the least, in rejecting the Old Testament as a revelation from God. For *unbelief* they too are accountable. If they are in the right as to their views and opinions, of course they will escape both guilt and punishment. But if they are verily in the wrong, and voluntarily shut their eyes against the true light which Heaven has kindled up to illuminate our darkened path, he who has said that unbelief is in his estimation a crime of the darkest hue in the catalogue of our sins, cannot be expected to omit a due cognizance of it, in his own proper time.

Having presented this matter in such a light it becomes me now to make the inquiry, Whether the writers of the New Testament do acknowledge and inculcate the authority and obligation of the Old Testament Scriptures? In other words, *Whether Christ and the apostles did appeal to the Scriptures as of Divine authority and obligation;* and *whether those Scriptures consisted of the same books which are now exhibited in our Old Testament Canon?* The way will then be prepared for coming to our final conclusion.

All early testimony, Jewish and Christian, exhibited independently of the New Testament, is accordant in regard to the nature and number of the Jewish sacred books. No one acquainted in any tolerable measure with the subject, will think of denying, that both Jews and Christians, at and after the earliest part of the Christian era, fully believed in the Divine authority and obligation of those books which belonged to the Jewish Canon. None will deny, that before this period the same belief pervaded the Jewish nation. We have only to ask then, at present, whether the highest court of appeal sanctions this decision; in other words, *whether Christ and the apostles, the authors of our religion, have sanctioned the Jewish views of the Hebrew Scriptures?*

In canvassing the testimony of Jewish and Christian witnesses, we have found occasion to look at the subject in a twofold light ; first, as having respect to *the Scriptures as a whole* or *one composite body* of writings ; and secondly, as having respect to *individual and particular works* which go to constitute the mass. The same method I shall still pursue, in the present investigation.

I ask the reader for no special deference, on the present occasion, to the lists of books contained in the creeds and confessions of Christian churches or Jewish synagogues, in later ages. These lists may indeed be correct. In the main I believe that they are. But we do not here defer to them as an *authority*. We make inquiry after the substantial grounds or reasons by which these lists of sacred books are supported, and their claims to confidence vindicated.

Our main object, moreover, is to inquire after a *matter of fact*. That matter is, What did Jesus and his apostles say respecting the Old Testament ? What constituted the Old Testament of their day, and in what manner have they appealed to it ?

It is needless to say, that the usual process of ascertaining facts in ancient times, must be resorted to on this occasion. We take nothing for granted, but what all reasonable men feel obliged to concede. We take for granted, after the preceding investigations, that there were Jewish Scriptures at the period in question ; that they were united together in a collection of books well known and defined ; that the Jews, one and all, (sceptics or heathenish persons excepted,) regarded these books as of Divine authority in all matters of faith and practice, spoke of them as such, appealed to them as such, and remained, and have continued down to the present hour (with the exceptions just noted) to remain, stedfast in the belief that such is the character of the books in question. So much will not be denied.

Did Christ, then, and his apostles, agree with the Jewish nation in regard to the matter before us ? If not, have they ever taught us the contrary ? Did they establish a new Hebrew Canon ? Or did they select one part of the Jewish Canon, and reject the rest ? Is there any conclusion to be drawn from their teaching and example, as to the duty of Christians in this matter ?

If now we wish to pursue our inquiries, with regard to these points, in a satisfactory way, we must do no violence to the laws of exegesis. We must search after evidence, in the same candid and dispassionate manner which we would approve of in the investigation of any and all matters of fact in ancient times. We are neither to force our own views upon the New Test. writers, nor do any violence to their representations in order to make them speak in our behalf, or in order that they should not testify against us. There is need of this caution. The principles by which it is justified, have so often been forgotten or violated, that there is great need of our keeping a watchful eye upon the whole process of investigation. And now to the work.

SECT. XVIII. *Appeals of a general nature, which are made to the Old Testament in the New.*

I NAME all those *general*, which refer to the *body* of Scripture, or to the Scripture as a *whole* considered in its collective capacity. A reference of such a nature may be made in a variety of ways, as the sequel will show. I have only to remark here, that throughout the appeals to testimony, the twofold object of the *authority* of the Scriptures and of the *books* of which it consists, go hand in hand, and need not, and should not, be separated from each other.

(1.) Let us examine the Scriptures, as arranged by the Jews under the usual *triplex* division. The Saviour says (Luke xxiv. 44) to his doubting disciples, "All things must be fulfilled concerning me, which are written in the *Law of Moses*, and the *Prophets*, and the *Psalms*." Now here is a distinct recognition of the threefold division of the Hebrew Scriptures, which is so expressly recognised in Sirach, by Philo, and by Josephus. It is impossible to entertain any reasonable doubt of this, considering the time and circumstances in which the words were uttered. And as we have already ascertained what books were included in this division, we of course must regard this as an appeal to the Jewish Canon, such as it now is. On any other ground than a definite and well-known collection of sacred books, the disciples could not have understood their Master, nor the Master have spoken with simplicity and in good faith.

There is one other thing directly and positively declared here, which most of the Neologists call in question, and in which Mr. Norton has expressed his unbelief; see p. 10 above. This is, that each of these divisions or parts of the Scripture is affirmed to contain *predictions respecting the Messiah*. Those who call in question the existence of *prophecy*, in the sense of *prediction*, and those who limit it to some few passages in one, or at most in two, of the Jewish divisions of Scripture, are placed by this passage in direct opposition to the Saviour. To suppose him to have said this merely in the way of *accommodation* to Jewish prejudices about the meaning of the Old Testament, is neither more nor less than to suppose him guilty of fraud. If we should call it *pious fraud*, this would not better the case, in the view of any ingenious and truth-loving mind. Or, as the only alternative, they must suppose the Saviour, like the Jews in general, to have either trifled with the meaning of the Scriptures, or to have been really ignorant of their true import. The responsibility of either or any of these assertions or suppositions, is what I would not desire to incur; and above all at the time when he, who is thus virtually accused of fraud or of ignorance, shall sit as my Judge, in a trial whose results are to last for eternity.

There is indeed one other way of escape; which is, by denying that Luke has correctly reported the words of Christ.

But as the New Testament is full of the same kind of words, from beginning to end, either the credibility of it throughout, in regard to this subject, must be rejected; or else it must come simply to this, that we are to believe only such parts and so much of it, as we may *a priori* judge to be probable and credible. This appears to be the exact position of Mr. Norton and many others. But I regard the entire rejection of it as more creditable to the understanding, and even to the heart, than this position ; for it virtually abjures faith in the testimony of past ages to such an extent, as must render all the past but a dark and troubled sea of elements eternally fluctuating, on which no one can ever launch with any good ground of hope that he may reach a safe and peaceful harbour. The unbelief that consistently sets aside the whole, shows a more manly and energetic attitude of mind ; and in my opinion, it is much more likely to be convinced at last of error, than he is who thinks that he is already a believer and is safe, while he virtually rejects from the Gospel all which makes it a Gospel, in distinction from the teachings of Socrates, of Plato, of Plutarch, of Cicero, and of Seneca.

I add only one remark, which is but a repetition of what has already been said. The names here given to the various divisions of the sacred books, (and which have already been explained,) must, from their very nature, indicate a *definite* and *well-known* collection of books ranked under each class ; for otherwise they could have no real significance to the disciples. When the civilian says, that the *Pandects* and *Novellæ* of Justinian have decided a certain point so or so, does any other civilian, or any body else who knows any thing of the works in question, entertain any doubt as to what and how many books or treatises are meant? When I speak of the works of Virgil at one time, and at another speak of the Bucolics, the Georgics, and the Eneid, am I not well and definitely understood by classical readers in both cases? The decision, however, of questions so easy and obvious as these, does not call for any enlargement on this topic.

(2.) Another mode of general reference to the Scriptures as a body, or as a collection of books fixed and definite, is by giving to the whole in union a general name, which usage has appropriated to them in order to distinguish them;

which name of course comprises within its import all the books that are thus united.

Such in particular is the word ἡ γραφή, or its plural αἱ γραφαί, corresponding exactly to our word *Scripture* and *Scriptures*, i. e. *the writing, the writings*. Every one sees what part the article plays here. It specificates and distinguishes the meaning of the word to which it applies from its common or generic signification, viz. *a writing*, i. e. any writing. THE *writing* is one which stands distinguished from other writings. The same also may be said of αἱ γραφαί, (plur.,) *the Scriptures*, i. e. the writings which are distinguished from all others. In the same manner the Moslem calls his Koran *the Scripture* (الكِتَابُ); indeed the word *Koran* itself has virtually the same meaning, viz. *the reading*, or *that which is to be read*. As to the singular γραφή, or the plural γραφαί, there is no appreciable difference in the meaning. The singular is employed merely with reference to the whole collection in its unity; the plural, in reference to the same, but as being made up of many parts. In like manner the Latins might and did say of a *letter*, for example, that it was *epistola* or *literæ*. Of course, in my references to the New Testament passages, I shall pay no regard to the *number*, whether singular or plural, of the noun which designates the Scriptures. In English we have to all intents and purposes the same idiom; for we say the *Scripture*, and the *Scriptures*, without any other distinction of meaning than the one already pointed out. Let us follow the New Testament in order.

Matt. xxii. 29, Jesus says to the Sadducees, " Ye do err, not knowing the Scriptures, nor the power of God." In other words, a knowledge of the Scriptures would save you from error, viz. in regard to the things of a future state. The same in Mark xii. 24.

Matt. xxvi. 54, Jesus had just said, that he could pray to his Father, and obtain more than twelve legions of angels to deliver him from the sufferings which were at hand; he then adds, " But how then could the Scriptures be fulfilled, that this must so be?" i. e. that he must so suffer. Of course this is a declaration, that what is *predicted* in the Old Testament respecting his sufferings and death, must of necessity have a fulfilment.

Matt. xxvi. 56, the writer is speaking of the apprehension of Jesus by the enraged multitude, and the violence done to him; he then adds, "Now all this took place, that the Scriptures of the prophets might be fulfilled." *Prophets*, in the language of the Jews, were, as we have seen, all the writers of the Old Testament, i. e. they supposed them all to be inspired, which is the true original idea of a prophet. Here, by the *prophets* is meant, those writers in the Bible who had predicted the sufferings of Christ. The same in Mark xiv. 49.

Mark xii. 10, "Have ye not read this Scripture? The stone which the builders rejected," &c., where Jesus quotes from the body of Scripture a particular passage (which he names *Scripture*, just as we now name such a quotation). The object is to show that the Scriptures had predicted what must be fulfilled.

Mark xv. 28, "The Scripture was fulfilled which says, He shall be numbered with the transgressors." If the fulfilment here is not predicated of a direct prediction, but the happening of an event of the like nature with one recorded in Scripture, still the reference to the authority of Scripture stands substantially on the same ground as if the prediction were more direct.

Luke iv. 21, Jesus, in the synagogue at Nazareth, had read a passage from Isa. lxi. 1, seq., which he applies (as a prediction) to himself, and then adds, "To-day, in your hearing, is this Scripture fulfilled." In other words, the predictions in the Old Testament have respect to him, and he it is who fulfils them. Of course, they are acknowledged as Divine.

Luke xxiv. 27, Jesus is addressing his wondering and incredulous disciples, after his resurrection: "Beginning from Moses and from all the Prophets, he explained to them the things concerning himself in all the Scriptures." Here are two recognisances of Scripture which are worthy of attention: (1.) Moses and all the Prophets. (2.) There are things respecting Christ in *all the Scriptures*.

Luke xxiv. 45, "Then opened he their minds to understand the Scriptures." The preceding verse speaks of the Law, the Prophets, and the Psalms. These, then, constitute the Scriptures, which appellation of course means in such a case the *whole of them;* for nothing short of this is designated by τάς γραφάς here.

John ii. 22, the disciples are said, after his resurrection, to have remembered the words of Jesus, (Destroy this temple, and in three days I will raise it up,) and then " they believed the Scripture ;" viz. the Scripture which predicts his death and resurrection.

John v. 39, Jesus bids the Jews to " Search the Scriptures, because in them they think they have eternal life, and these very Scriptures are those which testify of him." In other words, the Scriptures, i. e. the Old Testament, is the authority, which is to decide between him and the Jews in respect to his claims.

John x. 35, Jesus says to the Jews, "If it [the Law, which however is here used to designate the Scriptures in general] called them gods to whom the word of God came, and the Scripture cannot be broken," &c. Why cannot the Scripture be broken ? Plainly because it is the word of God. Is not this then of paramount and Divine authority ? And here *Scripture* stands for the whole Hebrew Bible, because the proposition plainly amounts to this, viz. that no part or portion of the Scripture can be broken.

John xiii. 18, " But [this takes place] that the Scripture might be fulfilled, He who eateth bread with me," &c. In other words, whatever is directly or indirectly foretold or prefigured in the Scripture, must needs be fulfilled.

John xvii. 12, None of the true disciples are to perish, but the son of perdition must perish, "that the Scripture might be fulfilled." That is, all the predictions of the Old Testament must have a completion.

John xix. 24, " That the Scripture might be fulfilled which saith, They divided my garments among themselves," &c. To the same purpose as the preceding quotation.

John xix. 36, The soldiers broke not the limbs of Jesus, "that the Scripture might be fulfilled, which saith, Not a bone of him shall be broken." The Scripture here is the injunction respecting the paschal lamb, the prototype of Jesus, Ex. xii. 46. But the reference to its *authority* is not the less, because the fulfilment appertains to a typical prediction. Nay, the case is even stronger than that of a direct prediction. It stands thus : Not only direct predictions must be fulfilled, but even indirect or typical ones. In other words, Nothing of the Old Testament Scriptures can fail.

John xix. 37, " Again another Scripture saith, They shall look on him whom they have pierced." The piercing of Jesus' side by one of the soldiers, is the occasion of this quotation. It is regarded as being a prediction of the Scripture, and therefore it must needs be fulfilled.

John xx. 9, " As yet they [the disciples] knew not the Scripture, that he must rise from the dead." Whatever the Scripture has determined must of course take place, is the tenor of the sentiment.

Acts i. 16, Peter says, in his address to the apostles, " Brethren, the Scripture must needs be fulfilled, which the Holy Ghost foretold by the mouth of David." This involves the necessity that the predictions should be accomplished, and the express idea of the inspiration of the writer of it by the Holy Spirit.

Acts viii. 35, Philip, beginning " with this Scripture, [Isa. liii. 7, seq.,] preached to him Jesus." That is, Philip showed to the eunuch that Christ is the subject of description in Isa. liii.

Acts xvii. 2, seq., Paul " as his custom was ... discoursed to them from the Scriptures, explaining [them], and setting forth that Christ must needs suffer and rise from the dead." In other words, the Messianic predictions in the Old Testament must be fulfilled.

Acts xvii. 11, the apostle praises the Berœans, not only because "they received the word with all readiness, but investigated the Scriptures daily, whether these things were so ;" i. e. they put the preaching of Paul to the test of the Old Test. Scriptures ; and they are called by him *more noble* for so doing.

Acts xviii. 24, Apollos is commended as an eloquent preacher, because " he was mighty in the Scriptures." If the Old Testament, as Mr. Norton avers, is a book utterly inconsistent with Christianity, how could Apollos be an excellent preacher from the circumstance of being uncommonly versed in it? Moreover it is said of him again, in ver. 28, that "he showed from the Scriptures that Jesus is the Christ."

Rom i. 2, Paul asserts that "the Gospel was before announced by the prophets in the Holy Scriptures."

In Rom. iv. 3, the same apostle appeals to "what the Scripture saith," in order to establish the doctrine of justification by faith. In Rom. ix. 17, he does the same thing in order to establish the Divine sovereignty: "For the Scripture saith to Pharaoh," &c. In Rom. x. 11, he makes the same appeal, "for the Scripture saith;" this he does in order to establish the certainty that the believer shall be rewarded. In Rom. xv. 4, he speaks of our possessing hope, "through the consolation of the Scripture." In Rom. xvi. 26, he speaks of the gospel as being made known to the Gentiles "by the prophetic Scriptures, according to the commandment of the eternal God unto obedience of the faith." And are these the books, then, which we are at liberty to pronounce inconsistent with the gospel?

In 1 Cor. xv. 3, Paul says that "Christ died for our sins, according to the Scriptures." And in ver. 4, that "He was buried, and rose again on the third day, according to the Scriptures." In Gal. iii. 8, he says, that "the Scripture.... before announced the gospel to Abraham, that in him all the nations should be blessed." In 1 Tim. v. 18, he appeals to Scripture as confirming the sentiment, that "the labourer is worthy of his hire."

James, in ii. 8, speaks of "the royal law," (Thou shalt love thy neighbour as thyself,) as being obligatory, because it is contained "in the Scripture." In ii. 23, he appeals to Scripture as confirming his doctrine of justification by faith. In iv. 5, he reproves those who think that the Scripture speaks κενῶς, i. e. to no purpose.

Peter refers to the Scripture as containing the revelation of a Saviour precious and all-sufficient, 1 Pet. ii. 6. In 2 Pet. iii. 16, he speaks of those who pervert the words of Paul to their own destruction, "as they do the other Scriptures;" i. e. the Old Test. Scriptures are put beside the writings of Paul, and are ranked with them.

Thus much under the single category of appeal to the Old Test. Scriptures by naming them as a whole, or as a collection of sacred writings under the distinctive appellation of ἡ γραφή or αἱ γραφαί, *the Scripture* or *the Scriptures*. In several of the passages, their inspiration is expressly declared; in all of them their paramount authority is openly and plainly assumed or avowed. It is impossible to call this in question, when the matter and manner of the appeal are fully taken into view.

(3.) Passages which directly declare, or plainly imply, the *inspiration* of the Old Test. writers.

2 Tim. iii. 14—17, "Do thou continue in the things that thou hast learned and believed: knowing from whom thou hast learned them, and that from childhood thou hast known the Holy Scriptures, which are able to make thee wise unto salvation, through faith in Christ Jesus. Πᾶσα γραφὴ θεόπνευστος, *every Scripture is inspired of God*, and is profitable for doctrine, for conviction, for correction, for instruction in righteousness; that the man of God may be perfect, thoroughly furnished unto every good work."

On this notable passage but few remarks are needed. (1.) Every Scripture, πασα γραφή, i. e. every constituent part or portion of the Scriptures, as the omission of the *article* of course implies, (not πᾶσα ἡ γραφή, *all the Scripture*, spoken of as merely a collective unity,) is *inspired of God.* Θεόπνευστος cannot mean less than this. If we might coin a new English word, to meet the Greek one here employed, we might render it *God-inspirited*, which would be altogether literal and exact. All attempts to fritter away this plain meaning are but vain. To appeal to the inspiration of heathen poets, and to the loose meaning of *inspired* among some of the Christian Fathers, is nothing to the purpose. What did *Paul* mean? is the question. And of this there can be no philological doubt. Even De Wette, with all his predominating incredulity, says of θεόπνευστος, that "it is an expression and idea which stands connected with πνεῦμα, lit. *breath*, since one regarded the energy of the Divine Spirit as causing the breath of life: and here it means *inspired, durchgeistet*, i. e. animated through and through by the Spirit, *geistvoll*, i. e. full of the Spirit." The *manner* in which the Spirit operated, is not here described by Paul, and must be learned, if learned at all, from other passages of Scripture. (2.) These Scriptures are not only ἱεραί, *holy, sacred*, but "they are able to make wise unto salvation," even that salvation which is "by faith in Christ Jesus." And is such a book, then, in *opposition* to Christianity? And must it be proscribed and rejected by an "enlightened Christian?" So Mr. Norton says; but Paul has presented the matter in a very different light.

(3.) " Every Scripture is profitable for doctrine, for conviction, for correction, for instruction in righteousness." How all this can be, in case the Old Testament is even *contrary* to the Gospel, and unworthy of our regard, is for those to explain who maintain the latter position. Then, again, "the man of God becomes perfect, and thoroughly furnished for every good work," by the use of these same Scriptures.*

No one who is acquainted with ancient critical and religious history, will venture to maintain that any other Scriptures than those of the Jews were then in general circulation, when Paul wrote the Second Epistle to Timothy. Of course, Paul has said all this of the Old Testament. More cannot be said by any one, and more need not be said.

The only alternative is to deny the genuineness of the epistle, or to reject the authority of Paul. Objections, I am aware, have of late often been made against the genuineness of the epistle; but they cannot stand before the tribunal of criticism. And as to rejecting the authority of Paul, I have only to say, that he who does this, raises the simple standard of infidelity, and enlists under it. It is not my present object to dispute with such.

2 Pet. i. 20, 21, "Knowing this first, that no prophecy is of one's own power of disclosure; for prophecy in time past was not introduced by the will of man, but holy men of God spake as they were moved by the Holy Ghost." I have translated ἰδίας ἐπιλύσεως by *one's power of disclosure*. This

* The most important point connected with this passage is here taken for granted, though it is a matter still in dispute, viz. whether the translation should be "every Scripture inspired by God is profitable," &c., or "all Scripture is inspired of God." The substantive verb *is* must be supplied somewhere; and the difficulty is in ascertaining its precise place in the sentence. It would be impossible in the compass of a note to present even the most meagre outline of the considerations advanced by the advocates of the rival interpretations. On the one side we refer to Dr. Pye Smith's Scripture Testimony to the Messiah; on the other, to a writer in the Congregational Magazine for 1838, p. 29, et seq. D.

locus vexatissimus, I am well aware, has been moulded into almost every shape, and made to mean a great variety of things. Among the rest, it has been made to patronize the doctrine, that no prophet understood or could explain what he himself, or at least his own words, meant! Of such an absurdity I say nothing. The plain sense is, that prophecy comes, not by the prophet's own power of disclosure, or of removing the veil from the future, but by the inspiration of the Holy Ghost. Let it be noted, that Peter employs the generic appellation προφητεία, (without the article,) *prophecy* in general, all that is prophetic in the Old Testament; and in the Jewish sense, every thing there is the work of prophets. The prophets were ὑπὸ πνεύματος ἁγίου φερόμενοι, *borne along, moved, influenced*, by the Holy Ghost. Thus does Peter exactly correspond with the θεόπνευστος of Paul.

In the preceding context Peter speaks of the *prophetic word*, i. e. the Old Test. Scriptures, as a "light shining in a dark place," and as something βεβαιότερον, *more stedfast, sure, more to be depended on*, than what the three disciples had seen and heard in the mount of transfiguration; at least such seems to be his sentiment, in the connexion in which his words stand. This is a very striking passage, and must be quite revolting to the feelings of Mr. Norton and those who sympathize with him.

In Heb. iii. 7, Paul cites a text of Scripture and says concerning it, "As the Holy Spirit saith." He does the same in Heb. x. 15, and introduces it by saying, "The Holy Spirit testifies to us."

In 1 Pet. i. 10—12 is a passage, which affirms that "respecting [gospel] salvation, the prophets have sought out and made diligent scrutiny, who prophesied respecting the grace that was to be revealed . . . To whom it was revealed, that not unto themselves, but unto us, they ministered the things which," &c. The idea of a revelation supernaturally made lies upon the very face of this representation.

Heb. i. 1 declares, that "God at sundry times and in divers manners spake to the fathers by the prophets." If GOD spake by them, then who shall be absolved from listening to what he said? If God spake by them, then they have not said what is contradictory to Christianity, or subversive of it.

In 1 Cor. ix. 9, 10, Paul, after quoting a passage from the Mosaic Law, forbidding to muzzle the ox which treadeth out the corn, adds, "Doth God care for oxen ? Or does he say this truly for our sakes ? *On our account it was written*, that he who plougheth should plough in hope, and he who reapeth should be a partaker in hope." On this I remark that the apostle says, (1.) That *God* says what is here quoted. (2.) That he says it mainly on our account ; and of course it follows that we are to read and profit by it.

In Rom. i. 1, Paul says, that " God before declared the gospel, by his prophets, in the Holy Scriptures." The authority of these Scriptures then consists in this, viz. that they contain the declarations of God.

But enough on the topic of *inspiration*. It is impossible, after acquiring a proper knowledge of what Philo and Josephus have unequivocally taught us in regard to the belief of the Jews in the inspiration of their Scriptures, to read the New Testament and overlook the fact, that every where and always the supreme authority of the sacred books is either directly asserted, or conceded by implication. Scripture is the supreme arbiter, in all cases where a decision is required. The validity of the Redeemer's mission, and his claims, are tried by it ; the doctrines which the apostles preached are tried by it ; every virtue either of morality or piety is sanctioned by it. It is impossible to doubt what the apostles and evangelists have taught, in respect to this subject, without at the same time assuming, that our own subjective views are to be the paramount authority, in all cases where authority is needed.

(4.) Under the head of miscellaneous recognitions of the authority of the Old Test. Scriptures, it were easy to produce texts almost without number. I must content myself, however, with a general exhibition of them, thus putting the reader in a condition easily to pursue this investigation in its minuter particulars, by giving him an index to the passages of the Old Testament which are cited or alluded to in the New.

MATTHEW.

i. 23—Isa. vii. 14.
ii. 6—Mic. v. 1.
ii. 15—Hos. xi. 1.
ii. 18—Jer. xxxi. 15.
iii. 3—Isa. xl. 3—5.
iv. 4—Deut. viii. 3.
iv. 6—Ps. xci. 11.
iv. 7—Deut. vi. 16.
iv. 10—Deut. vi. 13.
iv. 15, seq.—Isa. viii. 23; ix. 1.
v. 5—Ps. xxxvii. 11.
v. 21—Ex. xx. 13.
v. 27—Ex. xx. 14.
v. 31—Deut. xxiv. 1.
v. 33—Ex. xx. 7.
v. 38—Ex. xxi. 24; Lev. xxiv. 20.
v. 43—Lev. xix. 18.
viii. 4—Lev. xiv. 2, seq.
viii. 17—Isa. liii. 4.
ix. 13—Hos. vi. 6.
x. 35, 36—Mic. vii. 6.
xi. 5—Isa. xxix. 18, seq.; lxi. 1.
xi. 10—Mal. iii. 1.
xi. 14—Mal. iv. 5.
xii. 3—1 Sam. xxi. 6.
xii. 5—Num. xxviii. 9.
xii. 7—Hos. vi. 6.
xii. 18, seq.—Isa. xlii. 1, seq.
xii. 40—Jon. i. 17.
xii. 41—Jon. iii. 5, seq.
xii. 42—1 Kings x. 1.
xiii. 14, seq.—Isa. vi. 9, seq.
xiii. 35—Ps. lxxviii. 2.
xv. 4—Ex. xx. 12; Deut. v. 16.
xv. 8, 9—Isa. xxix. 13.
xix. 5—Gen. ii. 24.
xix. 7, 8—Deut. xxiv. 1.
xix. 18, seq.—Ex. xx. 12, seq.; Lev. xix.
xxi. 5—Zech. ix. 9.
xxi. 13—Isa. lvi. 7; Jer. vii.
xxi. 16—Ps. viii. 2.
xxi. 42—Ps. cxviii. 22.
xxi. 44—Isa. viii. 14, seq.
xxii. 24—Deut. xxv. 5.
xxii. 32—Ex. iii. 6.
xxii. 37—Deut. vi. 5.
xxii. 39—Lev. xix. 18.
xxii. 44—Ps. cx. 1.
xxiii. 35—Gen. iv. 8.
xxiii. 39—Ps. cxviii. 26.
xxiv. 15—Dan. ix. 27.
xxiv. 29—Isa. xiii. 10.
xxiv. 37, seq.—Gen. vii. 4, seq.
xxvi. 31—Zech. xiii. 7.
xxvii. 9—Zech. xi. 12, seq.
xxvii. 35—Ps. xxii. 18.
xxvii. 43—Ps. xxii. 8.
xxvii. 46—Ps. xxii. 1.

MARK.

i. 2—Mal. iii. 1.
i. 3—Isa. xl. 3.
i. 44—Lev. xiv. 2, seq.
ii. 25, 26—1 Sam. xxi. 6.
iv. 12—Isa. vi. 9.
vii. 6, 7—Isa. xxix. 13.
vii. 10—Ex. xx. 12.
ix. 14—Isa. lxvi. 44.
x. 4—Deut. xxiv. 1.
x. 7—Gen. ii. 24.
xi. 17—Isa. lvi. 7; Jer. vii. 11.
xii. 10, 11—Ps. cxviii. 22.
xii. 19—Deut. xxv. 5.
xii. 26—Ex. iii. 6.

SECT. XVIII. NEW TESTAMENT TO THE OLD.

xii. 29, seq.—Deut. vi. 4, seq.
xii. 31—Lev. xix. 18.
xii. 36—Ps. cx. 1.
xiii. 14—Dan. ix. 27.
xiii. 24—Isa. xiii. 9, seq.
xiv. 27—Zech. xiii. 7.
xv. 28—Isa. liii. 12.
xv. 34—Ps. xxii. 1.

LUKE.

i. 33—Dan. ii. 44.
i. 55—Gen. xvii. 19.
i. 73—Gen. xxii. 16.
ii. 21, 22—Lev. xii. 3, 4.
ii. 23—Ex. xiii. 2.
ii. 24—Lev. xii. 6.
iii. 4, seq.—Isa. xl. 3, seq.
iv. 4—Deut. viii. 3.
iv. 8—Deut. vi. 13.
iv. 10, 11—Ps. xci. 11.
iv. 12—Deut. vi. 16.
iv. 18, 19—Isa. lxi. 1, seq.
iv. 25, 26—1 Kings xvii. 1, 9.
iv. 27—2 Kings v. 14.
v. 14—Lev. xiv. 2—4.
vi. 3, 4—1 Sam. xxi. 6.
vii. 27—Mal. iii. 1.
x. 27—Deut. vi. 5; Lev. xix. 18.
x. 28—Lev. xviii. 5.
xi. 31—1 Kings x. 1.
xi. 51—Gen. iv. 8.
xiii. 35—Ps. cxviii. 26.
xvii. 27—Gen. vii. 7.
xvii. 29—Gen. xix. 15.
xvii. 32—Gen. xix. 26.
xviii. 20—Ex. xx. 12, seq.
xix. 46—Isa. lvi. 7: Jer. vii. 11.
xx. 17—Ps. cxviii. 22.
xx. 28—Deut. xxv. 5.

xx. 37—Ex. iii. 6.
xx. 42, 43—Ps. cx. 1.
xxii. 37—Isa. liii. 12.
xxiii. 30—Hos. x. 8.

JOHN.

i. 23—Isa. xl. 3.
i. 51—Gen. xxviii. 12.
ii. 17—Ps. lxix. 9.
iii. 14—Num. xxi. 8, 9.
vi. 31—Ps. lxxviii. 24.
vi. 45—Isa. liv. 13.
vii. 22—Lev. xii. 3.
vii. 38—Isa. lviii. 11.
vii. 42—Ps. lxxxix. 4; Mic. v. 1.
viii. 5—Lev. xx. 10.
viii. 17—Deut. xvii. 6.
x. 34—Ps. lxxxii. 6.
xii. 13—Ps. cxviii. 25, 26.
xii. 15—Zech. ix. 9.
xii. 34—Ps. cx. 4.
xii. 38—Isa. liii. 1.
xii. 40—Isa. vi. 9, 10.
xiii. 18—Ps. xli. 9.
xv. 25—Ps. xxxv. 19.
xvii. 12—Ps. cix. 8, 17.
xix. 24—Ps. xxii. 18.
xix. 28—Ps. lxix. 21.
xix. 36—Ex. xii. 46.
xix. 37—Zech. xii. 10.

ACTS.

i. 16, 20—Ps. lxix. 25; cix. 8.
ii. 16, seq.—Joel ii. 28, seq.
ii. 25—Ps. xvi. 8.
ii. 31—Ps. xvi. 10.
ii. 34—Ps. cx. 1.
iii. 22—Deut. xviii. 15.
iii. 25—Gen. xii. 3.
iv. 11—Ps. cxviii. 22.

iv. 25—Ps. ii. 1.
vii. 2—Gen. xii. 1.
vii. 6, 7—Gen. xv. 13, seq.
vii. 8—Gen. xvii. 10.
vii. 9—Gen. xxxvii. 28.
vii. 17—Ex. i. 7.
vii. 20—Ex. ii. 2.
vii. 24—Ex. ii. 11.
vii. 30—Ex. iii. 2.
vii. 37—Deut. xviii. 15.
vii. 38—Ex. xix. 3.
vii. 39—Ex. xxxii. 1.
vii. 42—Amos v. 25.
vii. 45—Josh. iii. 14.
vii. 46—2 Sam. vii. 1, seq.
vii. 48—Isa. lxvi. 1.
viii. 32—Isa. liii. 7.
x. 34—Deut. x. 17.
xiii. 17—Ex. i. 7; xii. 37, seq.
xiii. 18—Deut. i. 31.
xiii. 22—1 Sam. xvi. 13; Ps. lxxxix. 20.
xiii. 33—Ps. ii. 7.
xiii. 34—Isa. lv. 3.
xiii. 35—Ps. xvi. 10.
xii. 36—1 Kings ii. 10.
xii. 41—Hab. i. 5.
xii. 47—Isa. xlix. 6.
xv. 16—Amos ix. 11.
xxiii. 5—Ex. xxii. 28.
xxviii. 26—Isa. vi. 9, seq.

ROMANS.

i. 17—Hab. ii. 4.
ii. 6.—Prov. xxiv. 12.
ii. 11—Deut. x. 17.
ii. 24—Isa. lii. 5.
iii. 4—Ps. li. 4.
iii. 10—Ps. xiv. 1, seq.
iii. 13—Ps. v. 9; cxl. 3.
iii. 14—Ps. x. 7.
iii. 15—17—Isa. lix. 7, 8.
iii. 18—Ps. xxxvi. 1.
iv. 3—Gen. xv. 6.
iv. 6, seq.—Ps. xxxii. 1, seq.
iv. 11—Gen. xvii. 10.
iv. 17—Gen. xvii. 5.
iv. 18—Gen. xv. 5.
vii. 7—Ex. xx. 17.
viii. 36—Ps. xliv. 22.
ix. 7—Gen. xxi. 12.
ix. 9—Gen. xviii. 10.
ix. 12—Gen. xxv. 23.
ix. 13—Mal. i. 2, 3.
ix. 15—Ex. xxxiii. 19.
ix. 17—Ex. ix. 16.
ix. 20—Isa. xlv. 9.
ix. 21—Jer. xviii. 6.
ix. 25—Hos. ii. 23.
ix. 26—Hos. i. 10.
ix. 27, seq.—Isa. x. 22, seq.
ix. 29—Isa. i. 9.
ix. 33—Isa. viii. 14; xxviii. 16.
x. 5—Lev. xviii. 5.
x. 6, seq.—Deut. xxx. 12, seq.
x. 11—Isa. xxviii. 16.
x. 13—Joel ii. 32.
x. 15—Isa. lii. 7.
x. 16—Isa. liii. 1.
x. 18—Ps. xix. 4.
x. 19—Deut. xxxii. 21.
x. 20, seq.—Isa. lxv. 1, seq.
xi. 3—1 Kings xix. 10, 14.
xi. 3—1 Kings xix. 18.
xi. 8—Isa. xxix. 10; vi. 9.
xi. 9, seq.—Ps. lxix. 22, seq.
xi. 26—Isa. lix. 20.
xi. 27—Jer. xxxi. 33, seq.
xi. 34—Isa. xl. 13.
xi. 35—Job xli. 11.

SECT. XVIII. NEW TESTAMENT TO THE OLD. 311

xii. 9—Amos v. 15.
xii. 19—Deut. xxxii. 35.
xii. 20 — Prov. xxv. 21, seq.
xiii. 9—Ex. xx. 13, seq.
xiv. 11—Isa. xlv. 23.
xv. 3—Ps. lxix. 9.
xv. 9—Ps. xviii. 49.
xv. 10—Deut. xxxii. 43.
xv. 11—Ps. cxvii. 1.
xv. 12—Isa. xi. 10.
xv. 21—Isa. lii. 15.

1 CORINTHIANS.

i. 19—Isa. xxix. 14.
i. 20—Isa. xliv. 25.
i. 21—Jer. ix. 23.
ii. 9—Isa. lxiv. 4.
ii. 15—Isa. xl. 13.
iii. 19—Job v. 13.
iii. 20—Ps. xciv. 11.
v. 13—Deut. xvii. 7.
vi. 16—Gen. ii. 24.
ix. 9—Deut. xxv. 4.
ix. 13—Deut. xviii. 1.
x. 1—Ex. xiii. 21; xiv. 22.
x. 3, 4—Ex. xvi. 15; xvii. 6.
x. 7—Ex. xxxii. 6.
x. 8—Num. xxv. 1, 9.
x. 9—Ex. xvii. 2, 7; Num. xxi. 6.
x. 10—Num. xiv. 2, 27, 29.
x. 26—Ps. xxiv. 1.
xiv. 21—Isa. xxviii. 11.
xiv. 34—Gen. iii. 16.
xv. 3—Isa. liii. 8, 9; Ps. xxii.
xv. 4—Ps. xvi. 10.
xv. 25—Ps. cx. 1.
xv. 27—Ps. viii. 6.
xv. 32—Isa. xxii. 13.

xv. 45—Gen. ii. 7.
xv. 54, 55—Is. xxv. 8; Hos. xiii. 14.

2 CORINTHIANS.

iv. 13—Ps. cxvi. 10.
vi. 2—Isa. xlix. 8.
vi. 16—Lev. xxvi. 12.
vi. 17—Isa. lii. 11.
vi. 18—Jer. xxxi. 1, 9.
viii. 15—Ex. xvi. 18.
ix. 7—Ex. xxxv. 5.
ix. 9—Ps. cxii. 9.
ix. 10—Isa. lv. 10.
xi. 3—Gen. iii. 4.

GALATIANS.

ii. 16—Ps. cxliii. 2.
iii. 6—Gen. xv. 6.
iii. 8—Gen. xii. 3.
iii. 10—Deut. xxvii. 26.
iii. 11—Hab. ii. 4.
iii. 12—Lev. xviii. 5.
iii. 13—Deut. xxi. 23.
iii. 16—Gen. xvii. 7.
iii. 17—Ex. xii. 40, seq.
iv. 22—Gen. xxi. 2, 9.
iv. 27—Isa. liv. 1.
iv. 30—Gen. x. 12.
v. 14—Lev. xix. 18.

EPHESIANS.

ii. 17—Isa. lvii. 19.
iv. 8—Ps. lxviii. 18.
iv. 26—Ps. iv. 4.
iv. 30—Gen. ii. 23, seq.
vi. 2.—Ex. xx. 12.
vi. 9—Job xxxiv. 19.

PHILIPPIANS.

ii. 10—Isa. xlv. 23.

COLOSSIANS.

ii. 11—Deut. xxx. 6.
iii. 25—Job xxxiv. 19.

2 THESALONIANS.

ii. 4—Dan. xi. 36.
ii. 8—Isa. xi. 4.

1 TIMOTHY.

ii. 13—Gen. i. 27 ; ii. 18.
ii. 14—Gen. iii. 6.
ii. 18—Deut. xxv. 4 ; Lev. xix. 13.
vi. 7—Ps. xlix. 17.

2 TIMOTHY.

ii. 19—Num. xvi. 5.
iii. 8—Ex. vii. 11, 22.

HEBREWS.

i. 5—Ps. ii. 7.
i. 6—Ps. xcvii. 7.
i. 7—Ps. civ. 4.
i. 8—Ps. xlv. 6, seq.
i. 10, seq.—Is. xxxiv. 4 ; li. 6.
i. 13—Ps. cx. 1.
ii. 2—Deut. xxvii. 26.
ii. 6, seq.—Ps. viii. 4, seq.
ii. 12—Ps. xxii. 22.
ii. 13—Ps. xviii. 2.
ii. 13—Isa. viii. 18.
iii. 2—Num. xii. 7.
iii. 7—Ps. xcv. 7.
iii. 17—Num. xiv. 32—37.
iv. 3—Ps. xcv. 11.
iv. 4—Gen. ii. 2.
iv. 7—Ps. xcv. 7.
v. 4—1 Chron. xxiii. 13.
v. 5—Ps. ii. 7.
v. 6—Ps. cx. 4.
vi. 14—Gen. xxii. 16.
vii. 1—Gen. xiv. 18.
vii. 17, 21—Ps. cx. 4.
viii. 5—Ex. xxv. 40.
viii. 8, seq.—Jer. xxxi. 31, seq.
ix. 13—Lev. xvi. 14.
ix. 20—Ex. xxiv. 8.
x. 5, seq.—Ps. xl. 7, seq.
x. 12, 13—Ps. cx. 1.
x. 16, seq.—Jer. xxxi. 33, seq.
x. 28—Deut. xvii. 6.
x. 30—Deut. xxxii. 35.
x. 37, seq.—Hab. ii. 3, seq.
xi. 3—Gen. i. 1; Ps. xxxiii. 6.
xi. 4—Gen. iv. 4.
xi. 5—Gen. v. 24.
xi. 7—Gen. vi. 14—22.
xi. 8—Gen. xii. 1, 4.
xi. 13—Gen. xlvii. 9.
xi. 17—Gen. xxii. 1, seq.
xi. 18—Gen. xxi. 12.
xi. 20—Gen. xxvii. 27, seq.
xi. 21—Gen. xlviii. 16 ; xlvii. 31.
xi. 22—Gen. l. 24.
xi. 23—Ex. ii. 2.
xi. 28—Ex. xii. 11, seq.
xi. 29—Ex. xiv. 22.
xi. 30—Josh. vi. 20.
xi. 31—Josh. ii. 1.
xi. 32—Judg. vi. 11, seq.; iv. 14 ; xiv. 1, seq. ; xi. 1, seq. ; 1 Sam. vi. 13, seq. ; 1 Sam. iii. 19, seq.; Judg. xiv. 5, seq. ; Dan. vi. 16, seq.
xi. 34—Dan. iii. 20, seq.
xi. 35—2 Kings iv. 20.
xii. 5, seq.—Prov. iii. 11, seq.
xii. 9—Num. xxvii. 16.
xii. 12, seq.—Isa. xxxv. 3.

xii. 15—Deut. xxix. 18.
xii. 16—Gen. xxv. 31, seq.
xii. 18—Ex. xix. 12, seq.
xii. 20—Ex. xix. 13.
xii. 21—Deut. ix. 19.
xii. 26—Hag. ii. 6.
xii. 29—Deut. iv. 24.
xiii. 5—Josh. i. 5.
xiii. 6—Ps. cxviii. 6.
xiii. 11—Lev. iv. 11, seq. ; xvi. 27.
xiii. 14—Mic. ii. 10.

JAMES.

i. 19—Prov. xvii. 27.
ii. 1—Lev. xix. 15.
ii. 8—Lev. xix. 18.
ii. 11—Ex. xx. 13, seq.
ii. 21—Gen. xxii. 9, seq.
ii. 23—Gen. xv. 6.
ii. 25—Josh. ii. 1.
iv. 6—Prov. iii. 34.
v. 11—Job i. 20, seq.
v. 17, seq.—1 Ki. xvii. 1, seq.

1 PETER.

i. 16—Lev. xi. 44.
i. 24, seq.—Isa. xl. 6, seq.
ii. 3—Ps. xxxiv. 8.
ii. 4—Ps. cxviii. 22.
ii. 6—Isa. xxviii. 16.
ii. 7—Ps. cxviii. 22.
ii. 9—Ex. xix. 5, seq.
ii. 10—Hos. ii. 23.
ii. 17—Prov. xxiv. 21.
ii. 22—Isa. liii. 4, seq.
iii. 16—Gen. xviii. 12.
iii. 10, seq.—Ps. xxxiv. 12, seq.
iii. 14, seq.—Isa. viii. 12, seq.
iii. 20—Gen. vi. 13, seq.

iv. 8—Prov. x. 12.
iv. 18—Prov. xi. 31.
v. 5—Prov. iii. 34.
v. 7—Ps. lv. 22.

2 PETER.

ii. 5—Gen. vii. 23.
ii. 6—Gen. xix. 24, seq.
ii. 15, seq.—Num. xxii.
ii. 22—Prov. xxvi. 11.
iii. 4—Ezek. xii. 21, seq.
iii. 5, 6—Gen. ii. 6; vii. 21.
iii. 8—Ps. xc. 4.
iii. 10—Ps. cii. 26, seq.

1 JOHN.

i. 8—Prov. xx. 9.
iii. 5—Isa. liii. 4.
iii. 12—Gen. iv. 8.

JUDE.

5—Num. xiv. 35, seq.
7—Gen. xix.
11—Gen. iv. 5, seq. ; Num. xvi. 1, seq.

APOCALYPSE.

i. 6—Ex. xix. 6.
i. 7—Zech. xii. 10.
i. 14, 15—Dan. x. 5, 6 ; vii. 9 ; Ezek. i. 27 ; viii. 2.
ii. 14—Num. xxv. 1, 2 ; xxxi. 16.
ii. 20—1 Kings xvi. 31 ; 2 Kings ix. 7.
ii. 27—Ps. ii. 8, 9.
iii. 7—Isa. xxii. 22.
iii. 9—Isa. xlv. 14.
iii. 19—Prov. iii. ; xi. 12.
Chap. iv., v.—Ezek. i., ii. ; Isa. vi.

iv. 6—Ezek. i. 22; Ex. xxiv. 10.
v. 11—Dan. vii. 10.
vi. 8—Ezek. xiv. 21.
vi. 12—Isa. xxiv. 18—23; xxxiv. 4; Joel ii. 31.
vi. 14—Isa. xxxiv. 4.
vi. 15—Isa. ii. 19 21.
vi. 16—Hos. x. 8.
vii. 3—Ezek. ix. 4.
viii. 3—Lev. xvi. 12, 13.
ix. 3—Joel i. 6, seq.; ii. 4, seq.
ix. 14—comp. Dan. x. 13, 20.
ix. 20—Ps. cxv. 4; cxxxv. 15.
x. 2—Ezek. ii. 9, 10.
x. 3—Isa. xxi. 8.
x. 4—Dan. viii. 26; xii. 4–9.
x. 9—11—Ezek. ii. 8; iii. 3.
xi. 4, seq.—Zech. iv. 2—14.
xi. 5—2 Kings i. 9—12.
xi. 6—1 Kings xvii. 1; Ez. vii. 19, 20.
xi. 7—Dan. vii. 7, 8.
xi. 10—Esth. ix. 19, 22.
xi. 15, seq.—Dan. ii. 44; vii. 27.
xii. 1, seq.—Mic. iv. 9, 10; v. 2, 3.
xii. 5—Ps. ii. 9.
xii. 7—Dan. x. 13, 21; xi. 1; xii. 1.
xii. 10—Job i. 6, seq.; ii. 4, seq.; Zech. iii. 1.
xii. 14—Dan. vii. 25; xii. 7.
xiii. 1, seq.—Dan. vii. 3, seq.
xiii. 10—Gen. ix. 6.
xiii. 14—Dan. iii. 1, seq.
xiv. 8—Isa. li. 9; Jer. li. 8.
xiv. 10—Ps. lxxv. 8; Isa. li. 22; Jer. xxv. 15.
xiv. 14—Dan. vii. 13.
xiv. 15—Joel iii. 13.
xiv. 19, 20—Isa. lxiii. 1, seq.
xv. 3—Ex. xv. 1, seq.
xv. 4—Jer. x. 7; Isa. lxvi. 23.
xv. 8—Ex. xl. 34, seq.; 1 Kings viii. 11; Isa. vi. 4.
xvi. 2, seq.—Ex. ix. 8, seq.
xvi. 9—Dan. v. 22, seq.
xvi. 12—Isa. xi. 15, 16.
xvi. 19—Isa. li. 22; Jer. xxv. 15, 16.
xvii. 1—Jer. li. 13.
xvii. 3—Ezek. viii. 3.
xvii. 4—Jer. li. 7.
xvii. 12—Dan. vii. 20.
xvii. 15—Isa. viii. 7; Jer. xlvii. 2.
xviii. 2, seq.—Isa. xxi. 1–10; xiii. 21; xxxiv. 14, seq.; Jer. l. 39; li. 8.
xviii. 4—Isa. xlviii. 20; Jer. l. 8; li. 6, 45.
xviii. 6—Jer. l. 15, 29; Ps. cxxvii. 8.
xviii. 7, 8—Isa. xlvii. 7—9.
xviii. 11, seq.—Ezek. xxvii.; Isa. xxiii.
xviii. 18—Isa. xxxiv. 10.
xviii. 20—Isa. xliv. 23; xlix. 13; Jer. li. 48.
xviii. 21—Jer. li. 63, 64.
xviii. 22—Isa. xxiv. 8; Jer. vii. 34; xxv. 10.
xviii. 23—Isa. xxiii. 8.
xix. 2—Deut. xxxii. 43.
xix. 3—Isa. xxxiv. 10.
xix. 4—1 Chron. xvi. 36; Neh. v. 13.
xix. 6—Dan. ii. 44; vii. 27.
xix. 13—Isa. lxiii. 1, seq.

SECT. XVIII. NEW TESTAMENT TO THE OLD. 315

xix. 15—Ps. ii. 9 ; Isa. lxiii. 3.
xix. 17, 18—Ezek. xxxix. 17, 18.
xix. 20—Isa. xxx. 33 ; Dan. vii. 11, 26.
xx. 4—Dan. vii. 9, 22, 27.
xx. 8, seq.—Ezek. xxxviii. 1, seq.
xx. 11, 12—Dan. vii. 9, 10.
xxi. 1—Isa. lxv. 17 ; lxvi. 22.
xxi. 2, seq.—Ezek. xl.–xlviii.
xxi. 3—Ezek. xxxvii. 27.
xxi. 4—Isa. xxv. 8 ; xxxv. 10.
xxi. 5—Isa. xliii. 19.
xxi. 10—Ezek. xl. 2.
xxi. 11, seq.— Ezek. xlviii. 31, seq.
xxi. 15—Ezek. xl. 3.
xxi. 19, seq.—Isa. liv. 11, 12.
xxi. 23—Isa. xxiv. 23 ; lx. 19.
xxi. 24—Isa. lx. 3, seq. ; lxvi. 12.
xxii. 1, seq.—Ezek. xlvii. 1, 12 ; Zech. xiv. 8.
xxii. 3—Zech. xiv. 11.
xxii. 5—Isa. xxiv. 23 ; lx. 19.
xxii. 10—Dan. viii. 26 ; xii. 4.
xxii. 16—Isa. xi. 1, 10.
xxii. 17—Isa. lv. 1.
xxii. 19—Deut. iv. 2 ; xii. 32.*

Large as this list is of passages from the Old Testament which are cited or alluded to in the New, it is far from comprehending all of this nature, which the New Testament contains. The truth is, that there is not a page, nor even a paragraph of any considerable length, belonging to the New Testament, which does not bear the impress of the Old Testament upon it. What else is the so-called *idiom* of the Hebrew Greek of the New Testament, but an impression of this kind? It is indeed true, that some few peculiarities in the forms and grammatical structure of the Hebrew Greek, led in part to the bestowment of this appellation upon it. But after all, the *grammatical* departures from common Greek are now known and acknowledged to be but few; while the *lexical* ones arise mostly from the necessity of the case, (new *things* demanding either new *names*, or new meanings of old words, to designate them,) or else from the manner in which the kindred Hebrew verbs, &c. are employed in the Old Testament. In the latter case they help to exhibit the influence which the Old Testament has had upon the New throughout.

No one who has an intimate acquaintance with both Tes-

* For a list of quotations from the Old Testament in the New, and a full discussion of every point connected with them, the reader is referred to Davidson's Sacred Hermeneutics, chap. xi. pp. 334—515. D.

taments, in their original languages, can possibly fail to recognise the numberless transfers of the spirit and the modes of expression from the Old to the New. It is a thing to be *felt*, and not to be adequately described. It occurs so often, every where, and in respect to every thing, that one would not know where to begin, or where to end, such a description. No one must imagine, that the list of quotations or cases of allusion above conveys to him any really adequate view of the subject. The truth is, that it is no more than the mere beginning of such a view. But it presents to every reader, whether learned or unlearned, what is palpable and undeniable, and what must serve to convince a candid mind, that the New Testament writers every where lean upon, or stand closely connected with, the writers of the Old Testament.

It may be proper to remark, in order to prevent any misunderstanding on the part of the reader, that oftentimes he will find only some particular part of a verse in the New Testament which is referred to—some expression in that verse—the object of comparison between the New Testament and the Old: and so in respect to verses in the Old Testament which I have taken as being related to expressions in the New. If he does not at once see the point of comparison, (which may sometimes happen,) let him not forthwith conclude that there is none. Some mistakes I may have made, in recording so many quotations; for in a work so laborious as such a comparison, and trying to the patience, who might not make mistakes? It may be, that in some cases where I have supposed a reference to the Old Testament, it might not have been so in the mind of the writer. There is room, in a few cases, for difference of opinion with regard to such a matter. But, on the whole, I hope and trust the list will be found to be as accurate as could be reasonably demanded. Possibly there are a few instances, that should be struck from it; but should this be done, I have only to say, that *there are hundreds of expressions and thoughts, in the New Testament, modelled after the Old Testament, to which I have made no reference.* I have even stricken out not a few of Knapp's list of quotations, at the end of his Greek Testament, because I wished to retain none which did not seem to be palpable.

SECT. XVIII. NEW TESTAMENT TO THE OLD. 317

Among the several writers of the Gospels, the reader will perceive that there is not much difference in regard to the frequency of resort to the Old Testament, if one takes into view the comparative length of their productions. The book of Acts, the Epistles to the Romans and to the Hebrews, 1 Peter, and the Apocalypse, abound most in references to the Old Testament. Above all is the Apocalypse the most remarkable for this. While John has not made, in this book, a single quotation in the usual way of express appeal, he has, in more than *one hundred* cases, beyond all doubt, drawn his modes of expression and thought from the Old Test. Scriptures, using every part of them indiscriminately, but mostly the books of Isaiah, Ezekiel, Daniel, and Zechariah. Nearly *one fifth* part of all the references in the New Testament to the ancient Scriptures, belong to the Apocalypse. Thus much in the way of explanation.

After this general view of the subject, I proceed to make a few special remarks on the list above exhibited.

(1.) Many of the passages here noted, in the same manner as those before cited at length, have respect to Old Testament *prophecies* which are declared to have been fulfilled. An intelligent reader will easily perceive that this statement covers much ground. The New Testament writers make use of the formula ἵνα πληρώθῃ, (*that it might be fulfilled*, or *so that it was fulfilled*,) to a wide extent.* Not only *predictions*, in the proper and limited sense of the word, are said to be fulfilled, but also in cases where the type is answered by the appearance of the antitype (e. g. Christ our passover-lamb); and also in cases where the event related in the New Testament corresponds closely to the leading features of similar events related in the Old Testament. For an example of the last, we may appeal to Matt. ii. 15, where the statement is, that Jesus was carried away to Egypt, for the sake of avoiding the massacre at Bethlehem, in order that the Scripture might be fulfilled which saith, "Out of Egypt have I called my Son." Now if we turn to Hosea

---

* The Greek phrase in question never appears to have the meaning, *so that it was fulfilled*, but always, *that it might be fulfilled*. In other words, ἵνα has not the *ecbatic* sense attributed to it by Mr. Stuart after Tittmann, but the *telic* sense. Compare Sacred Hermeneutics, p. 473, et seq., where the topic is fully canvassed. D.

xi. 1, (the passage here cited,) we find it to run thus, "When Israel was a child, then I loved him, and called my son out of Egypt." Now here is a mere historical declaration respecting a past event, and nothing at all of prediction in the proper sense. The πλήρωσις, in this case, consists in the striking points of resemblance between the exile in Egypt and the deliverance from it, as it respects both of the parties in view. And so, of many other texts referred to in the New Testament.*

It is deeply to be regretted, that more narrow and confined views of this subject, (by which every *fulfilment*, πλήρωσις, was made to correspond with some real and direct prediction,) should have given occasion to boundless *allegorizing*, and to the making out of a *double sense* for the words of the ancient Scriptures, and to helping out the construction of supposed predictions, contained in simple historical narration, by inventing a ὑπόνοια or *occult sense* for the words of the narration. More enlarged views of the habitude of the Jews, in regard to the use which they made of the Old Testament, especially in respect to what they called a *fulfilment* of it, might have prevented all this. But now it will be a long time (so deep has the infection taken root) before the malady can be cured. But on this I cannot dwell.†

(2.) In every part of the New Testament, facts related in the Old Testament history are appealed to; not common and civil occurrences only, but miraculous ones. Such are the flood, the destruction of Sodom, the passage of the Red Sea, the manna of the desert, the feats of Samson, the miracles of Elijah and Elisha and others, the swallowing up of Jonah by the whale, the deliverance of Shadrach and Meshach and Abednego from the fiery furnace, the safety of Daniel in the lions' den, and other things of the like extraordinary nature. In a word, the whole of the Old Testament history, with all its extraordinary narrations, and all the miraculous events

---

* We have serious objections to Mr. Stuart's view of the passage quoted in Matt. ii. 15, and of similar quotations. See Sacred Hermeneutics, p. 488, et seq. D.

† The view taken by the writer of the verb πληρόω used in quotations from the Old Testament, and of a single and double sense connected with it, appears to be imperfect and incorrect. Compare Sacred Hermeneutics, p. 486, et seq. D.

which many of them imply, are every where appealed to, and are regarded by the Saviour and his apostles as absolute verities.

(3.) Principles and precepts inculcated by the gospel are every where established, or enforced, or illustrated, by an appeal to the Old Testament. There is a great variety here in the method of appeal, according to the object which the writer has in view. Sometimes it is made simply on the ground of the *authority* which is conceded to the Old Testament. Sometimes merely to *compare* ancient with recent things, and repel any accusation of novelty. Sometimes merely to *cast light* on any thing which may seem to be obscure. But in whatever way the appeal is made, there is still at the basis of it the idea of a standard authority—a tribunal before which causes are to be judged—in the Scriptures of the Old Testament. "All Scripture is inspired of God," is not a sentiment of Paul only, but it rules and reigns in every part and parcel of the New Testament.

(4.) In regard to the Epistle to the Hebrews, notwithstanding the writer has undertaken to show the superiority of the Gospel over the Law, the Divine origin of the Old Testament Scriptures and institutions is as fully acknowledged as in other parts of the New Testament, and the writer builds as much upon it. He has laboured every where to show, that the Jewish law and ritual were ordained, on the part of Heaven, as *introductory* to the Christian dispensation. The significance and importance of the ritual is confined mainly to this. "The Law was a shadow of *good things to come.*" So that, whether the author was Paul, or some other person, it is certain that here may be found the same opinion which Paul expressed, when he said, "The Law is our schoolmaster, to bring us to Christ." Why should it be any more inconsistent for the Godhead to make arrangements for the introduction of the gospel, by a series of preparatory measures, than it is to bring about many other things, and even extraordinary ones, in the like way? Our present life itself is but a preparatory arrangement for another.

(5.) There is something in the closing scene of Jesus' life, which is adapted strongly to impress our minds with the idea, that he gave the fullest credence and sanction to the Old Testament Scriptures. All the prominent circumstances of his sufferings and death are so arranged, that every one of them is the fulfilment of some portions of the ancient Scriptures. When he was disrobed, and the soldiers disputed about the possession of his garments, they cast lots to determine to whom the seamless coat should belong ; and all this in fulfilment, as the evangelist declares, (John xix. 24,) of the Scripture in Ps. xxii. 18. When his agony on the cross created an intense thirst, he disclosed this to the bystanders in order that the Scripture might be fulfilled (Ps. lxix. 21) which saith, "They gave me gall for my meat, and in my thirst they gave me vinegar to drink ;" John xix. 28, seq. The vinegar that was given him was mingled with gall, Matt. xxvii. 34. The demeanour of the populace and the priests, wagging their heads and saying, "He trusted in God ; let him deliver him now, if he will have him," is all specifically described in Ps. xxii. 7, 8. When agony beyond endurance forced from the expiring Saviour the bitter cry, "My God, my God, why hast thou forsaken me?" the words were chosen from the twenty-second Psalm, (ver. 1,) which contains a prophecy respecting his sufferings and death so strikingly descriptive and historical. His last dying breath came forth with the voice of prayer, "Father, into thy hands I commend my spirit ;" words taken from Ps. xxxi. 5. The soldiers, who brake the limbs of the malefactors that were crucified with Jesus, refrained from breaking his, seeing that he was already dead ; and all this (John xix. 36) in accordance with the symbolic and prophetic passover-lamb, not a bone of which was to be broken, Ex. xii. 46. One of the soldiers pierced his side with a spear, (John xix. 34, seq.,) and this was in fulfilment of a passage of Scripture in Zechariah, (xii. 10,) which says, "They shall look on him whom they have pierced." And can the evangelists and the Saviour thus appeal to the Scripture in confirmation and illustration of all these circumstances, and yet the Scripture contain no predictions respecting Christ, and no declarations on which we can rely? Can the Saviour himself, in his highest agony, and with his expiring breath, have expressed his feelings by quoting the language of a book unworthy of our credence and our confidence ?—But I desist, lest I should be thought to appeal more to feeling than to argument. Certain it is, that no book could be thus honoured by Jesus, in which he had not the highest and most entire confidence.

Sect. XIX. *Result.*

AND now, what shall we say to these things? The New Testament not only appeals to the Old in the way of illustration, and for the sake of comparison, but every where appeals to it as the word of God, as the testimony of his Holy Spirit, as the oracles of his prophets, as the rule of life, as the foundation of the spiritual building which Christ came to erect. Its predictions, its precepts, its narrations, are interwoven with every part of what apostles and evangelists have written. It is incorporated with the very material of religious thought, in the minds of all the New Test. writers. Even when they do not quote, and do not seem, as the hasty reader might suppose, at all to allude to the Old Testament, its ideas and its idioms are incorporated with all their productions. In the Apocalypse, John has not made one *formal* quotation of Scripture; yet no book of the New Testament, as has already been remarked, so abounds in and overflows with the spirit of the Old Testament, as this book. The writer had, if I may be allowed the expression, steeped himself in the ancient Scriptures, until he was thoroughly imbued with them. I know not how I can better express my views of the style of his production, than in this way. And so it is, indeed, with all the evangelists, with Paul, with Peter, and with James. It is impossible to conceal this, or withdraw it from sight. It is in vain to deny it before any candid reader. The most sophisticated reasoning cannot even make out an ingenious case to the contrary.

What shall we say, then? What can we say less than what the Saviour himself said to the Jews? "Had ye believed Moses, ye would have believed me; for he wrote of me. *But if ye believe not his* WRITINGS, *how shall ye believe my words?*" John v. 46, 47. It is in vain to make the effort to avoid this. The expedient to which Mr. Norton resorts, in substituting *spoke* for wrote, and *words* for writings, is one which shows the desperate nature of the cause which he is labouring to defend. On this ground, no declaration of Scripture any where, in any passage, on any subject, is exempt from arbitrary alteration, at the will and pleasure of every reader. Of course, the Scripture is not the rule of our faith, but our faith is the rule of Scripture. Much more ingenuous are those who come out at once and say, "The light within us is more perfect than the light without us, and much easier seen and apprehended; we know of no other supreme rule but this. Scripture itself must be tried by this test; and we accord to it our respect and regard only so far as we deem that its decisions agree with our own." They *say* this openly; while Mr. Norton only *acts* it, but will not venture to say it.

Why may we not ask, then, in the words of Jesus, "If ye believe not Moses' writings, how shall ye believe the words of him concerning whom Moses wrote?" He has decided that this cannot be. The authority of this decision rests not on my reasonings, but on his own words. He has said of the Old Testament Scriptures, that the sum of the whole is, that we should "love God with all the heart, and our neighbour as ourselves," Matt. xxii. 37, seq. "On these two commandments," moreover, for such are his words, "hang all the Law and the Prophets;" Matt. xxii. 40. That is, this is the very sum and substance of the Old Testament. And are these commands, then, to be regarded as nullities? Are these in their nature repealable? Can they be set aside? If not, then Jesus has sanctioned the books which contain them. If you deny this, then you charge him with prevarication, or with ignorance. I cannot believe him to be impeachable on either ground.

Did Jesus suspect or call in question the *moral* efficacy or influence of these writings? Let us listen to him, in the parable of Lazarus. The rich man in hell requests father Abraham that he would send Lazarus to his five brethren yet living, to warn them, so that they might not come into that place of torment. Abraham's reply is, "They have Moses and the prophets; let them hear them." The rich man still urges his request: "Nay," says he, "but if one went unto them from the dead, they would repent." And what does the father of the faithful, amid the glories of the upper world where no darkness is, answer? He says, "If they hear not Moses and the prophets, neither will they be persuaded, though one rose from the dead;" Luke xvi. 23, seq. The Old Test. Scriptures, in the estimation of Jesus, (for surely he does not put words into Abraham's mouth which he would not adopt as his own,) were more efficient in the moral instruction and conviction and conversion of men, than the rising of one from the dead would be, who should lay before them all the joys of the blessed and the torments of the damned.

Shall this book, then, be spurned away, and treated as a collection of fables, of barbarous maxims, and of trifling ritual ordinances? This is the question. It is this very question which lies between the declarations of the Saviour and his apostles on the one hand, and the scepticism of so-called Rationalists on the other. Whom shall we believe? There is no compromise in this case. He that is not for Christ is assuredly against him. He who rejects his authority on this point, virtually rejects it on all others. Christ was either in the right or in the wrong, as to the estimate which he put upon the Old Testament. It is impossible to doubt what that estimate was, after the evidence which has come before us. If he was in the right, then is the Old Testament a book of Divine authority—the ancient revelation of God. If he was in the wrong, then we can put no confidence in his teaching. He might be in the wrong, with respect to every command and opinion which he gave; and of consequence the whole system of Christianity is nothing more than an airy figure moving in the *mirage*, or one which floats along upon the splendid mists which surround it.

Sect. XX. *Conclusion.*

THE history of the Canon, from its inceptive state down to its completion, has been traced. We have seen, that when testimony and historical circumstances are fully taken into view, there is no good reason to doubt, that the scriptural Canon was completed during the reign of Artaxerxes,

i. e. during the time of Malachi, the last of the prophets. Somewhat more than 400 years old, then, were all the books of the Jewish Scriptures, in the time of Christ and of his apostles. The division of those books, with appropriate names for each portion, we can trace to nearly 200 years B. C., if not still higher. That division must have been definite and well known. No new books could be added, after it was completed, without the knowledge and concurrence of at least the priesthood among the Jews. That state of parties—Pharisee and Sadducee—who differed on the very point of exclusive Scripture authority, rendered it impossible for either party to augment or diminish the books of Scripture. The state of party can be traced back to a time beyond the period of the Maccabees, and probably the origin of it should be dated at a period not long after the closing of the Canon. We are of necessity compelled to admit, that the sacred books among the Jews have been unchangeable since that period. Sirachides, Philo, Josephus, the New Test. writers, know of no other scriptural books than those which we now have. The appeal to such books, in all their writings, is limited to these; for when Josephus comes to later history than what they contain, he tells us expressly, that the other books to which he appeals are entirely of a different character and credit from those which belong to the Old Test. Scriptures.

Besides, Josephus has told us *how many* books there were in the Hebrew Canon. We have traced these in quotations made by him, and Philo, and Sirachides, and the New Test. writers; and with still more certainty in the lists of individual books, by Melito, Origen, Gregory Nazianzen, Hilary, Athanasius, Jerome, Rufinus, the Talmud, and others. We find them to accord with our present Old Testament. There cannot be any doubt left, then, that the Jews of our Saviour's time did receive and regard these books as of Divine origin. And inasmuch as Christ and his apostles have never intimated, directly or indirectly, that the Jews were in an error with regard to this subject, what grounds have we for supposing that they were? Christ and his apostles every where quote, appeal to, and use the Jewish Scriptures, as of Divine and paramount authority and obligation.

What then of him who rejects them as a part of our present Scriptures? He follows not the example of Christ, or of his apostles. Nay, more ; he acts in direct opposition to their authority and example. In so doing, as far as in him lies, he repeals or abrogates the decisions of the Gospel. Mr. Norton has averred, that no enlightened person can be a Christian, and *admit* the claims made in behalf of the Jewish Scriptures. He has given his reasons for such an opinion. I have come to a very different conclusion, viz. that no enlightened person can well be deemed a Christian, who *rejects* the claims made in behalf of the Old Testament. I have given my reasons for it. If obedience and submission to the decisions of Christ and his apostles be an essential ingredient of Christianity, then is my conclusion inevitable, in case I have duly shown that Christ and his apostles did receive the Old Testament Scriptures as Divine and authoritative. If this be not fully shown, then must I despair of ever seeing any point established in sacred criticism, either in respect to facts or opinions. There is not a circumstance in all the history of true religion, appertaining to ancient times, that is capable of more absolute demonstration than this.

I have now done this part of my work, and must commit the whole to the judgment of the reader. I ask neither more nor less of him, than to scan the whole process of proof with a scrutinizing eye ; to weigh well the historical evidence, which we must receive, or else reject all ancient testimony ; and then to decide with candour, and without prejudice or partiality. I have a right to ask for so much, in respect to such a cause. It is no light matter what judgment we form on a subject of such high and holy import as this. It is a case in which direct demand is made upon us for submission and deference to Christ and his apostles ; and we cannot thrust it aside. The simple and ultimate question is, *Are we to admit their authority and example, or to gainsay the one, and shun an imitation of the other?*

SECT. XXI. *Remarks in regard to the conscientious scruples of those who have doubts and difficulties as to the authenticity of some Old Testament Books.*

It is one thing to reject the Old Testament *en masse*, without paying any deference to the declarations and opinions of Christ and the apostles ; it is another and very different one merely to doubt whether some two or three books of our present Old Testament belong properly to the Canon, or did belong to it in the time of our Saviour. The first class reject it on account of the many and (as they allege) incredible miracles which it relates ; on account of the imperfection and contradictions and incongruities to be found in its history ; because of the burdensome and trivial rites and ceremonies which it enjoins; because of the very imperfect morality in respect to some important matters which it inculcates ; and because of the violations of the law of love which it commands, and of the cruelty and spirit of revenge which it breathes forth. They find no other evidence of *prediction*, even in the leading prophets, than the shrewd conjectures of sagacious men about the future, or the patriotic hopes and expectations which are breathed forth in the language of impassioned poetry. The Old Testament is, with them, merely an undistinguishing *Collectaneum* of the remains of Jewish literature down to the time of Antiochus Epiphanes, styled sacred or holy because the subject of holy things so often comes into view, and because the *pragmatism** of the writers so often introduces the providence and decrees of the Godhead, in order to account for this and that event. And as to Christ and his apostles, they allege that every thing was done in the way of *accommodation* to Jewish views and feelings. These teachers did not mean to excite the jealousy or hatred of the Jews, by contradicting or opposing any of their capricious notions or superstitious conceits. Hence they often acted and spoke κατὰ συγκατάβασιν, or in the way of accommodation or con-

---

* I use this word in the usual German critical sense. Pragmatism, in a historian, would be any undertaking to account for certain facts. His simple business as a *historian* is to *relate* facts ; and so *pragmatism* and *pragmatic*, thus employed, become very significant.

descension to their countrymen. And the notions of the latter about the Scriptures were of the extreme kind, so that the former felt obliged to spare the mention of those things respecting these books, which would wound the feelings of the Jews.

To this class principally the preceding pages have been devoted. I cannot quit my subject, however, without saying a few things to the second class, i. e. to those who only doubt of some two or three books of the Old Testament, but believe in the canonical authority of the rest, and rely upon the ordinary considerations that are alleged in favour of it.

It seems hardly necessary to say, that this latter class may consist not only of sincere and earnest inquirers, but, as I would hope and trust, of sincere Christians. Enlightened ones they may also be, in respect to most other subjects of a religious nature; but in regard to this, I must think that they have taken but partial views of the matter.

If the Old Testament stands justly chargeable with all the things which are objected to it, by the first class above named, then indeed we might safely conclude that it is not a Divine book. If Christ and the apostles looked on the Hebrew Scriptures in that light in which some recent critics place them, how could they possibly refrain from advertising the Jews of the great error and superstition which they fostered? As public teachers, bound to be faithful and thorough, how could they acquiesce in such views of a book that contains, if we may trust Mr. Norton and others, many things unworthy of God, and subversive of his justice, his equity, and his compassion, not to speak of incongruities, and trifling rites and ceremonies. Above all, how could Jesus, and Paul, and Peter, and John, leave the Christian church to feel under obligation to hold such a book as the Old Testament sacred, even after they had renounced all allegiance to the rites and forms of the Mosaic Law? Certain it is, that Christ and his apostles combated and refuted many of the Jewish notions, both of a doctrinal and a practical nature. How came they to spare this substantial and fundamental error, (if it be an error,) not only without a word of correction and admonition, but even to do as the Jews did in respect to their Scriptures, i. e. to appeal to them as Divine and authoritative, and thus to encourage and persuade all their disciples to follow their example?

For myself I see no satisfactory way in which these questions can be answered. I must put them to the minds and consciences of all who profess to reverence Christianity as a religion from God, and I must leave them to make out an answer as best they may.

But to the scruples of some minds about this or that particular book—to doubts whether this or that was a part of the Canon sanctioned by Christ and the apostles—while, at the same time, there is a ready deference to their authority in all cases where persons in this state can see it to be clearly shown, it would be unreasonable and disrespectful not to pay some ready and cheerful attention. Luther rejected the Epistle of James and the Apocalypse from his Canon, as we have seen above; but Luther had no doubt of the Divine authority of the New Testament as a whole, with this exception. He also admitted the Old Testament to the same rank. Now some other Christian, in the like spirit, may admit the Law and the Prophets and the Psalms; but he might possibly reject Esther, Ecclesiastes, and Canticles; or at least he might deem it doubtful whether these books ought to be ranked with those. Of such an one I could easily say that I regarded him as a Christian, if his demeanour and his principles in other respects were such as become this character. If he had no dark spirit of scepticism as to the books of Scripture in general, or as to revelation in general, but accorded to it a sincere and hearty belief, then I could easily suppose, that his head was rather in fault than his heart, (if indeed he be in fault,) and I should feel it my duty rather to labour to enlighten his mind, than to reprove the state of his feelings.

With such I suppose myself, at present, to be concerned; and to them I must take the liberty to address a few considerations.

That there are peculiar difficulties in respect to the books just named, I confess myself often to have felt, as well as they. It is difficult to account for it, how the book of Esther could be written even by a pious Jew who was uninspired, and yet this book relates events of a most sur-

SECT. XXI. A PART OF THE OLD TESTAMENT. 329

prising nature—deliverances of the most extraordinary kind
—without one recognition of the hand of Providence here,
or even once mentioning the name of God. This is almost
the only book in the Old Testament, which has completely
escaped the charge by the Neologists of *pragmatism* on the
part of the writer. And besides this, some of the circumstances related in it are certainly peculiar. I have already mentioned them, (p. 159, seq.,) but I must beg leave
again to bring some of them into view, in the present connexion. That 75,000 Persians should have been killed by
the Jews in one day, apparently without any loss of life on
their part (Esth. ix. 16); that Haman should, by proclamation diffused all over the kingdom, give them nearly a year's
notice of the attack to be made upon them (Esth. iii. 7,
seq.); appears, I acknowledge, to present some historical
paradoxes of no easy and ready solution. And in view of
such matters, it would be natural for the doubters to whom
I now refer, to put back the question upon me, How do
you satisfy your own mind, that these things do not entitle
us to reject the book as not canonical?

I feel bound to meet this question, and am ready to do it,
so far as I may be able.

Let me say, then, first of all, that I do not regard the question respecting the canonical authority of this book, in the
same light, in all respects, as I should the question whether
the Pentateuch, the Psalms, or Isaiah, is canonical. The
book of Esther teaches us no doctrine, in a direct way; it
gives us expressly no moral precepts. If it were struck out
of the Canon to-day, not a single doctrine or ethical principle
would be changed, or be found lacking. It is in vain to say,
that all the books of Scripture are alike, or are alike profitable to us, although they may all be inspired. The exegesis
that can draw from 1 Chron. i.—ix.—which is a register of
names in a series of genealogies; or from Ezra ii. and Neh.
vii. (lists of those who returned from the captivity); as much
instruction and edification as from the ten commandments,
or from the history of the creation, or from many of the
Psalms, or the Proverbs, or the prophecies, may be consistent with piety, and sometimes may even spring from excessive notions about the inspiration of the Bible and of the
peculiarly holy nature of all its books. But intellect and

reason never can find any satisfaction in such interpretation of the Scriptures; if indeed it may be called interpretation, and not caricature. The Bible is a book that, we may take it for granted, was made to satisfy the intellect and enlightened reason, as well as devotional feeling. It is only when we misconceive of the design and object of any particular part of it, that it fails to satisfy the intellectual and rational demands of our nature.

I set it down as certain, that inasmuch as the Jewish dispensation itself was one of types and shadows—a preparation for good things to come—a schoolmaster to lead us unto Christ—and inasmuch as all that was in its nature ceremonial, ritual, temporary, appropriate only to the Jews as one and a peculiar nation, was to be superseded and abolished when Christ should come, so there might be parts, even many parts of the Old Testament, which would cease to have any more immediate importance and value, whenever a Christian revelation, by which the will of God is perfectly made known, should supervene. It has supervened; and that which once was perfectly adapted to the exigencies of the Jewish nation, and (although "a ministration of condemnation") was still glorious, (2 Cor. iii. 9,) "has now no glory by reason of the glory that excelleth," (ver. 10,) i. e. by reason of the Gospel.

But be it so, that this glory is now comparatively like that of the stars after the sun has made his appearance; yet in the twilight of Judaism the stars did shine, and the same stars still radiate light, although we may not easily discern it when we undertake to look for it by sun-light. There is not even a genealogy in the Old Testament which did not once possess importance. It settled all questions of inheritances; it marked the bounds of property; it designated the right to this or that privilege. There is not a narration in the Old Testament which had not once its use. Examine the story of Er and Onan, and of Judah's connexion with his daughter-in-law, Tamar; which surely is among the narrations that at first sight we should be inclined to spare, and even be prone to wonder, perhaps, how it came there. Yet in Matt. i. 3, we find the fruit of that unlawful connexion, Pharez and Zara, in the genealogical register of the evangelist. It is one link in counting the genealogy of Joseph from Abraham downwards. So it is, also, as to the story of the Levite and his concubine 'in Judg. xix. The minute account given of the journey of this couple, seems, at first, to be somewhat strange, and perhaps even revolting to our feelings, considering how we are taught by the gospel to regard concubinage. But still, the horrid murder committed upon the poor woman by forcing her to gratify the lusts of a multitude of men successively, was the direct cause of a civil war, in which the Benjamites, who had committed the crime in question, became nearly extinct. And so I might go on with all the narrations of particular occurrences—the family histories—contained in the Old Testament. A deep interest they once had to many. Admonition, too, may be drawn from most of them. It is with most or all of them, as Paul says it is with the ancient history of the Israelites in the desert, "These things were our ensamples, and they were written for our admonition, on whom the ends of the world have come;" 1 Cor. x. 11.

Who now will venture to say, that the histories of the Old Testament are not of a different tenor from any other that were ever written by any of the heathen nations? First of all, they are throughout of a *religious* cast. The Hebrews, whoever administers the government, are always under a *theocracy*. Providence guides, admonishes, rewards, and punishes. God is the all and in all. Then, secondly, the Hebrew historians have no favourite heroes, about whom romance throws its gorgeous vestments. The faults and follies of Abraham, Isaac, Jacob, Moses even, Saul, David, Solomon, Asa, Joash, Hezekiah, Josiah—and all whose history is minutely written, are not concealed. Here are no mythic and romantic personages—not any one even like the Cyrus of Xenophon. David and Solomon, at the very zenith of all that was splendid and commanding in royalty, in triumphs, in wisdom, in riches, in honours, are placed, at times, in attitudes that cover them with darkness and subject them to degradation. And is there nothing in all this practical acknowledgment of God's providence and retributive justice exhibited by the history of the Hebrews, nothing in the exposure of the crimes and vices of the most renowned kings and ethical philosophers, which is adapted to our instruction? Well may we say with Paul, "They serve for our admonition."*

When I read the Old Testament, then, and there meet with genealogies which have no concern with the Gentiles, and family histories that must have been particularly interesting only to family relatives; when I peruse all the detail of the Levitical rites and ceremonies, and all the architectural details of the tabernacle and the temple; or when I read predictions respecting Edom, and Moab, and the Ammonites, and the Philistines; if I am tempted to ask, for what purpose were these things recorded in a book of public and permanent instruction, I then ask myself how the Bible would have appeared to us, in regard to the matter of credibility, in case all such things had been omitted? The only answer I can make is, that it would have assumed a *mythic* appearance—like a selection and dressing up of persons and things in the way of romance. If all actors are paragons of piety or of wickedness; if all historical circumstances pertain only to choice events of a thrilling nature; if all prediction be only Messianic or eulogistic of the church; then would such a book wear the air of having been written by designing men, who meant to invest all personages and events with a costume splendid and attractive. As it is now, all looks like veritable reality. *Human nature* is, and continues to be, *human*. In some cases great virtues are conspicuous, not unmingled with faults; in others great

---

* Most instructive is it to compare the biographies written by moderns with those contained in the Old Testament. If a man be distinguished for great abilities that are mainly directed towards the good of his country, he is *extravagantly* praised as a hero, and his crimes are palliated or omitted. He is held up to admiration as a marvellous hero *throughout*. Of this we have a notable example in D'Aubigne's vindication of Oliver Cromwell, to say nothing of Carlyle's extravagant, undiscriminating eulogies. When a religious author and historian can say, as D'Aubigne does of the Protector's conduct in Ireland; "Should he employ a few weeks with the sacrifice of 5000 men, or several years, with the loss of perhaps 20,000? Having weighed every thing, he decided for the hand of iron. That hand is never amiable; but yet there are cases in which it is salutary." In further apologizing for cruel butcheries perpetrated by the hero, the historian says that Cromwell "followed the most skilful course to arrive at a prompt and universal pacification." So then it is right to do evil that good may come. It is *the most skilful course* to massacre thousands of human beings in order to arrive at a prompt pacification. It is high time that such one-sided biographies be eschewed. D.

vices, with occasional touches of alleviation by reason of social or patriotic qualities. In a word, the lawgiver commands; the historian relates circumstances interesting to himself, or to the times in which he lived, or useful to all, according to the nature of the case; the prophet predicts things near, first and principally, then things far distant, such as pertained to the Messianic times ; the genealogist gives in his register : the Psalmist pours out the language of devotion in the sweetest and most engaging manner; the lover of ethical proverbs records his discriminating thoughts ;—*and all this makes up a* HEBREW BIBLE. There is something in it to interest all, to allure all, to do good to all ; at least this was so at the time when it was written. How can I doubt that all this is a reality ? No farce is acted here. There is not a fictitious personage upon the stage. All is reality ; and such reality as early ages and the state of society would seem to have afforded. I become impressed more and more with the idea, that here is no imposture. If it were a description merely of the fortunate or blessed islands, of an Elysium, of the garden of the Hesperides, of some El Dorado ever hoped and wished for but never actually found— then my suspicions would be instinctively awakened. But now, as it actually is—how exceedingly different is the Old Testament from every thing of this kind !

If I allow, then, as I readily do, that many parts of the Old Testament have now but a very small and subordinate interest to me, in a doctrinal or ethical respect, yet am I far from saying, that those facts are of no value, much less that they have never been valuable. I have pointed out their value. They aid in the authentication of the book. They lead me to the persuasion, that what it describes is a reality and not romance. They show how God's chosen people lived, and thought, and acted, in public and in private life. They present human nature as it has been and is, and not simply draw a picture of what it would be in a state of perfection. Why may I not conclude, with the apostle Paul, that even now " all Scripture is profitable"?

But the Jewish dispensation has passed away, and all that was ritual, and ceremonial, and merely external, and temporary, and peculiar to one nation only, has gone with it. All Old Test. Scripture which is exclusively occupied with things of this nature, has ceased to have any other interest for us, than that which I have stated above. In this light we may and ought to regard it. Its day has gone by. But it has had its day, and its usefulness, and its interest. Be it that I must now look upon it as I do upon the burning of incense, and the sacrifice of goats and bullocks, and the washings and purifications of old; yet even all these had their use and significancy. Nay, are they not still symbolic, even to us, of the great atoning sacrifice, and of that purification of our minds which is required by the gospel?

In such a light would I place those parts of the Old Testament toward which the scorn of some, the severe satire of others, and the wonder and perplexity of many, are directed. Enough that they once had their usefulness and their interest in the then existing church; enough that they are still far from being altogether useless to us. I honour them as connected with a dispensation that was a type and shadow of the present. And while their light is now hardly seen, by reason of the sun which pours its flood of glory upon us, I call to mind, that when the ancient twilight was, they shone and twinkled in the sky, and gave sufficient light to guide the traveller on his way.

But let us return to the book of Esther. We have difficulties here; but are they invincible?

The fact that the feast of Purim has come down to us, from time almost immemorial, (clearly it was an ancient custom in the days of Philo and Josephus,) proves as certainly that the main events related in the book of Esther happened, as the declaration of Independence and the celebration of the fourth of July prove that we separated from Great Britain, and became an independent nation. And if such events, in the main, as the book of Esther relates, did actually happen, they were of the deepest interest to the Jewish nation. The book of Esther was an essential document to explain the feast of Purim. Hence the Jews have always had it read when that feast is kept. In this light, no one can well regard it as unimportant.

As to most of the circumstances respecting Ahasuerus's extravagancies and follies, there will be nothing improbable in the story, to any one who will read the history of Mohammed Aga Khan, not long since on a throne in the same country.

As to the fact, that Haman gave the Jews *eleven months'* warning of his assault, I have already discussed the subject in part, p. 160, seq., above. The thing looks improbable, at first. Yet when we read Esther iii., we see that Haman, like others of his time, was the slave of superstition, as well as cruelty. He must needs *cast lots*, in so great an affair, in order to hit upon the lucky day. In this way, an appeal to his gods must of course be made. "He who disposes of the lot" ordered it, that it should fall as late in the year as it could well be. Thus the Jews had time to prepare for the assault, or to remove from the country, at their option. Haman, although doubtless dissatisfied with the falling out of the lot, could not venture to change a matter thus solemnly determined by an appeal to his gods.

The number slain by the Jews remains—75,000. Extraordinary it doubtless is, and it must still appear to be so. But it is not impossible. Improbable, I would concede, it might appear to be, at first view; but, as I have stated before, if one calls to mind, that the Persian court was under the control of Mordecai and Esther; that the Jews were widely diffused at that time over the Persian empire; that the Persian magistracy aided them; and that a bitter hatred existed between the Jews and many of their neighbours, the improbability of the thing is greatly diminished. And with respect to the allegation that no Jews were killed or wounded in this terrible rencontre, it is true that no mention is made of any harm on the part of the Jews. But I do not deem this circumstance at all conclusive to prove that none was done. Luke, so circumstantial in his narrative of Christ's infancy, says not a word of the massacre at Bethlehem; nor does Josephus record it. The author of the book of Esther is wholly intent upon the victory and the deliverance of the Jews. The result of the encounter he relates, viz. the great loss and humiliation of Persian enemies. But how much it cost to achieve this victory, he does not relate. Had he been simply a historian professing to give a full account of matters, he would have told this part of the story. But as he is only showing why the feast of Purim is kept as a day of joy and gladness, it was hardly to his purpose to tell the story of Jews who might have been wounded or destroyed on this occasion. It is the main result only which he throws into prominent notice. And here he leaves the matter. We can scarcely doubt that many Jews were killed or wounded. But why need we discredit the historian as to what he has communicated, because he has not told this part of the story?

That the writer has said nothing of the providence of God, in the whole matter of deliverance from dangers so imminent, all, as I have acknowledged, will concede to be extraordinary, who are conversant with the Hebrew Scriptures. But it is almost as extraordinary, in case we suppose the writer to be *uninspired*, as it is if we regard him as inspired. It is without any parallel among the writings of the ancient Jews, whether sacred or not, Canticles only excepted. The confidence which Mordecai shows, (Esth. iv. 14,) that the Jews will experience " enlargement and deliverance" in some other way, if Esther should refuse her interposition, plainly shows, either that he had had some Divine monition of this, or else that he relied on God's promises to the fathers respecting their posterity. But why the writer does not plainly and openly recognise the hand of God, in all that happens, is still a difficulty that we know not well how to remove. Was the author a foreigner, I mean a Jew born and dwelling in a foreign land; then why, in case he wrote a book which he wished his heathen neighbours to read, did he not bring the doctrine of a special providence to view? Was he a native and an inhabitant of Palestine, how could he so depart from the manner of all the historians of his country? But as this difficulty presses almost as hardly upon the book, when considered as uninspired, as it does when we consider it as inspired, we do not seem to obtain any serious relief from our perplexity by denying the canonical authority of the book. There cannot be a moment's question, whether the author is a Jew, sympathizing in the highest degree with his nation, and fully believing in their title to precedence over heathen nations. These things lie upon the face of the whole narration. The impression of a special providence, which is made by the book, is a thing that admits of no doubt. What remains of difficulty is, a departure so marked from the usual style and manner of the Hebrew histories. We might conjecture various reasons for this; but what security could we give, that our conjectures would be well founded? Better to let the matter remain where it is, better to confess the difficulty and not make any attempt to conceal it, than to indulge in mere idle conjectures. Why can we not rest a matter about which we are in doubt, upon the authority of Christ and of the apostles, as to admitting the claims of the book before us to a place in the Canon? It was most surely in the Canon which they have sanctioned.

I cannot conclude my remarks on the book of Esther without saying, that nothing can be plainer than that, had the work been supposititious, the writer would beyond all doubt have been *pragmatic* in a more than usual degree, in order to deceive his readers by the guise of piety. The present character of the book proves, beyond all reasonable suspicion, that it is not supposititious.

We come next to COHELETH, or, as we name it after the fashion of the Greeks, ECCLESIASTES.

The ancient Jews doubted somewhat about admitting this book among those which might be indiscriminately read by all classes. Several of the later Jewish writers confess this, and variously state the reasons. In Vayyikra Rabba, § 28, f. 161, c. 2, it is said, "Our wise men were desirous to keep back (or conceal, לגנוז) the book of Coheleth, because they found in it words which might lead to heresy." The Talmud speaks of some "who found contradictions in it" סותתין זה את זה, *inclining this way and that*). Other Jewish writers have objected, that "it teaches the eternity of the world." But still, the party who admitted the book without scruple, have always been predominant, because, as the Talmud (Shabbath, fol. 30, c. 2) asserts, תחלתו וסופו דברי תורה, i. e. the beginning and end of it are the words of the Law. In other words, its main doctrine is accordant with the other Scriptures. On this basis the Jews have always remained, with the exception of individuals sceptically inclined. Some such have I seen among them, who maintained that the book teaches the doctrines of Epicurus.

Not exactly this, but not very unlike it, is the prevailing opinion of Neologists. The book was written, they say, by a sceptic; at least, by one who doubted or denied the immortality of the soul and a future retribution. By "the spirit's returning to God who gave it," (xii. 7,) they say, is meant only that God, who gave the natural breath or spirit, withdraws it and our death ensues. And all the declarations about *retribution*, they limit of course to the present world.

Of the justness and correctness of such an exegesis I am not persuaded. The book begins with the most emphatic declarations concerning the vanity and brevity of human life, and the unsatisfying nature of all earthly good. It exhibits the truth of this in the most vivid manner. It ends with the declaration, that the whole sum and conclusion of the matters discussed is this, viz. "Fear God, and keep his commandments; for this is the whole of man;" i. e. it is that for which man was created, and is his all for which he lives, or ought to live; Ecc. xii. 13, 14. This, which is the literal meaning of the Hebrew, is much stronger and more expressive than our common English version, "This is the whole *duty* of man." But why should men fear God and keep his commandments? The writer gives us the reason in the next and last verse of the book, "For God shall bring into judgment every work, with every secret thing, whether it be good, or whether it be evil." What can this mean, if it do not mean a *future* judgment? The writer often avers, in the body of his work, that in the present world the distinctions between virtue and vice oftentimes are not made, or are not discernible by us; and of course, that the retributions of virtue and vice are not made here. If not—where are they to be made? I do not see but one answer to this question; and that answer bids me to believe, that the writer had a *pious* intention in writing the book.

Herder, Eichhorn, and others, have supposed the book to be *dialogistic*, and that one of the colloquists is a sceptic. In this way they solve the apparently sceptical sentiments found in it. Others have supposed that Koheleth (קהלת) means *assembly*, and that the book is written as a representation of what passed in a company of ethical literati, in regard to the *summum bonum* of life. They compare it to the Arabic *Mecamath*, i. e. literary society. But with all this we may dispense. A dialogue cannot be carried through, without the greatest incongruity, in many cases; and the conflicting opinions of an assemblage of men is encumbered with the same difficulty. There is a more obvious and natural solution. The writer is one who had been through all stages of doubt in respect to the *chief good*, and the end of human life, and the doctrine of an overruling providence, and of retributive justice. He tells us in the most frank and impressive manner, the tenor and the drift of his cogitations on these various subjects, while he was in doubt. He tells us what he thought and said, in regard to them. In so doing, he has disclosed many a sceptical thought which passed through his mind. In all this, he has his eye upon those who are in that doubting state. He sympathizes with them, and lets himself down to their condition, so as to interest them and get their ear. Then he tells them in serious earnest of the vanity of human life, of the impossibility of escaping retribution, and distinctly lets them know, that the sum of all his thoughts and reflections, after passing through all the stages of doubt and perplexity, is, that "the whole of man [all in which he has any deep and lasting interest] is *to fear God and keep his commandments;*" and the ground of this conclusion is, that " all their actions, good or evil, will assuredly be brought into judgment."

I need not stop here to say how much this book has been misinterpreted by those, who had no true discernment of its real tenor and design. Perhaps no book in the Bible, if we except the Apocalypse, has suffered so much violence. All its sceptical declarations have been tortured, until they would confess thorough orthodoxy. Even the question which the doubter asks, (iii. 21,) in order to impress the idea that we have no certain knowledge of the future, viz. " Who knoweth whether the spirit of a man goeth upward, and the spirit of a beast downward?" (which assuredly must be the meaning of the original Hebrew)—this question has been turned into an argument to prove, that the spirit of a man does go upward! So our translators seem to have understood it; but so did not Luther and many others. There is nothing, in short, which stands in the way of this *spiritualizing* and *analogical* exegesis. It can make strenuous orthodoxy even out of Koheleth's doubts and sceptical musings. It can convert all the words of Job's occasional impatience and excitement into meekness and unqualified submission. In its crucible all ores are melted together, and seemingly sublimated so as to form but one purified and valuable substance.

When all is done and said, however, the understanding and the reason remain to be satisfied. Nothing will stand that does not compose these to peace. And why may we not be satisfied, that Koheleth has given us a picture of all the doubts and difficulties through which his mind had passed, and then subjoined the final result? In these times, we count those books very interesting and useful, in which writers give us faithful pictures of their former infidelity or scepticism, and then tell us that it was followed by an entire conviction of the truth and the power of the gospel. Two things are taught by this; the one, that scepticism never satisfies and quiets the mind; the other, that deliverance from it is the greatest of all good, as well as the highest duty. What forbade Koheleth to enter upon the like method of instruction? There is, and always has been, among reflecting and inquiring men, a class of minds to which such a book is admirably adapted. It enters into all their sympathies and views; it shows a familiar acquaintance with them all, and ability to appreciate them in a feeling manner; and finally it presents, in a strong and powerful light, the necessity and the duty of "fearing God and keeping his commandments." Had not this book been so much abused, as to its exegesis, by commentators and preachers who did not understand its plan, it might have been vastly more useful to the church. As matters now are, the violence done to it by interpreters revolts the candid and ingenuous mind, and turns many away from the book, because they are led to despair of obtaining any thing satisfactory from it. I would hope that the time is not far distant, when we shall have some more enlightened views of this production laid before our religious public, than have yet been presented. When this shall be done, I think the doubts of conscientious inquirers will be removed, and they will cheerfully accord to Koheleth a place in the Canon. Certain it is that the book had such a place in the time of Christ and the apostles. Whenever it shall be naturally interpreted, and the plan of it fully understood, objections to it must cease, except on the part of those who reject all revelation.

Last, but not least in point of difficulty, comes the book

of CANTICLES, or, as the Hebrews name it, the *Song of Songs*, i. e. the Most Excellent Song.

The history of what has befallen this book, and how it has been treated, would of itself occupy a volume of no inconsiderable extent. With one class, it is a book of a symbolic and mysterious nature, full of real *spirituality* under the images of fervent conjugal love. With another it is altogether *aphrodisiac* or *amatory*, like some of Horace's Odes, or Anacreon, or Tibullus, or Ovid's Art of Love. Others choose a kind of middle path, supposing the design is to commend chaste conjugal love, and to hold up in an attractive light the advantages of monogamy in distinction from polygamy. Each of these classes have much to say, in defence of their respective opinions. To canvass the subject at length, is out of question here. Only a few things that seem to be among the more important ones, can be discussed on the present occasion.

Amatory nearly all the German Neologists suppose it to be. And considered as such, the book, I suspect, has had more than its equal share of attention, in the way of illustrating its language and of unfolding its supposed amatory scenes. Young adventurers are very apt to choose this book as their theme. Ewald, Umbreit, Doepke, and others, put their hands to it while young; and they seem to have become rather shy of it since, as the book, on further consideration, seems not altogether so plain and obvious as they had once supposed. Those who regard it as a picture of chaste monogamic affection, are fewer, and are less able to make out, from the language of the book, the probability of such a meaning, than the preceding class. The scenery is *oriental*. One must do violence to his own mind to get away from the impression, that, if it is amatory at all, love is the subject as it exists in a harem, rather than in connexion with a single wife.

But, notwithstanding the confidence of not a few critics of late, I would ask, Is it, was it originally, designed to be regarded as *amatory?*

Herder, who seems rather to have taken the lead among the recent critics in Germany that favour the *amatory* exegesis, has boldly avowed his sentiments respecting it. "The whole book," he says, "is love, love. It begins with a kiss, and ends with a tender sigh." And so Eichhorn and many others, who have followed on in this train. Even in ancient times, the Jews had some difficulty with the contents of Canticles. Origen (Prol. ad Cant.) and Jerome (Præf. ad Ezech.) inform us, that the Jews of their time withheld this book, and also the beginning and ending of Ezekiel, and the first part of Genesis, from persons under thirty years of age, lest they should abuse them. Theodoret mentions, that in his day there were some who denied its spiritual meaning. Theodorus of Mopsuesta was condemned by the second Synod of Constantinople for saying, that "he was ashamed to read through the Canticles." In modern times, Clericus and Grotius avowed sentiments not unlike to those of Herder; and now this kind of exegesis has become the reigning fashion.

Were one to come to the reading of this book, without any previous knowledge of the habitudes of the Jews in connecting the conjugal relation and conjugal affection with religious subjects, and without any knowledge of the extent to which this is carried in the Eastern countries, I should doubt whether he would ever suspect the poem before us of being a *religious* one. The name of God, or any reference to him, does not once occur in the whole book. From beginning to end is apparently the language of love; and this without any explanation. Yet, after all, there is ground to doubt whether an interpretation that would convert the book into an Idyll, or an amatory Eclogue, is well grounded.

(1.) First of all—in what part of the Hebrew Bible can we find any composition of an analogous nature? All—every Psalm, every piece of history, every part of prophecy—has a *religious* aspect, and (the book of Esther perhaps excepted) is filled with *theocratic* views of things. How came there here to be such a solitary exception, so contrary to the genius and nature of the whole Hebrew Bible? It is passing strange, if real amatory Idylls are mingled with so much, all of which is of a serious and religious nature. If the author viewed his composition as being of an amatory nature, would he have sought a place for it among the *sacred* books? And subsequent redactors or editors—would they have ranked it here, in case they had regarded it in the same light? I can scarcely deem this credible. So different was the reverence of the Jews for their Scriptures from any mere approbation of an amatory poem as such, that I must believe that the insertion of Canticles among the *canonical* books, was the result of a full persuasion of its *spiritual* import. Had the case stood otherwise, why did they not introduce other secular works, as well as this, into the Canon? Nor is this estimate of the book a figment of allegorical exegesis, introduced by Philo, and spread far and wide by Origen. The book had a place in the Canon, at all events before the time of the Maccabees; so that the judgment of very ancient times, in the Jewish church, must have coincided with the judgment in later times, of a large portion of Christian interpreters.

(2.) It is now generally agreed, as Rosenmueller concedes, (Proem. ad Comm. II.,) that all the parts of this book are coherent and have a mutual relation, and that the same personages are introduced and continued as speakers through the whole. The tone of the language, the style, the idiom, the special formulas of expression, (such as adjuring by the does and the goats, &c.,) are of the same tenor throughout. From the same hand and mind the whole composition doubtless came, whoever the author was.

If now it is an *amatory* Eclogue, methinks there must be some plan, some progress, some *denouement*, that is not only appreciable by a critical reader, but discernible by an ordinary reader. Yet such a plan has never been developed, at least to any general satisfaction. One set of interpreters (even such men as Velthusen, C. F. Ammon, Lindemann, Umbreit, Michaelis, Jacobi) have endeavoured to make out from the book, that it consists of amatory epistles addressed by Solomon to a shepherd's beautiful wife; who retains, however, her fidelity and remains true to her husband. But how is this any less than to say, that Solomon's amatory effusions, designed for seduction, are incorporated with the Holy Scriptures? No refutation of this is needed. Others make the book a series of *epithalamia* on the marriage of Solomon with Pharaoh's daughter; which, as it was an open and palpable transgression of the law of Moses, does not much mend the matter. This seems to be kindred with the view which some recent critics (e. g. Lengerke) take of the 45th Psalm, viz. that it is an epithalamium on the marriage of Ahab with Jezebel, or (e. g. De Wette) of Xerxes with some Jewess! Ewald finds in the book a beautiful country girl, wandering in the pleasant fields of Engedi, seen, and forcibly carried off, by king Solomon, who attempts to seduce her by his amatory poetry. But what then are all the tender expressions of affection on the part of the woman, in i. 9—11; ii. 10—15; iii. 1—5, et al.? Bossuet found in the book a pastoral drama of seven acts. And these are not a tithe of the conceits which have been thrown out before the public, in regard to the work before us.

How difficult it is to make out any *plan* of an Eclogue, these perpetual changes and variations of opinion may serve to show. But let us go, for a moment, to the book itself. At the outset we find the fair one in the harem of the king's palace, exulting in the love of Solomon. Then (i. 7, seq.) we find her in the country tending flocks, and her lover a shepherd. But this shepherd has a domicile, whose beams are cedar, and the rafters fir (i. 17). Next, we find the lover leaping among the mountains, and skipping among the hills; ii. 8. Then the fair one has lost her lover, and she goes forth to seek him by night, and brings him back to the house of her mother; iii. 1, seq. Next Solomon is coming out of the wilderness, on a palankeen with sixty bearers; iii. 6, seq. Next he is with his beloved on Lebanon; iv. 8. Again she loses him, and goes out to seek him in the city, and is maltreated by the watch; v. 1, seq. Then we find him in the garden of spices, (vi. 1, seq.,) where she meets him, and they go to the harem, where are threescore queens, and fourscore concubines, and virgins without number, all of whom she excels, and they praise her beauty; vi. 8, &c. Throughout the whole, there is a mutual interchange of the language of passionate affection, rarely interrupted by any other speakers. A *drama* surely it is not, (although it has often been called so,) unless a colloquy in which there is no change of speakers is a drama. Besides, there is no plot, no denouement, no crisis. The whole book is neither more nor less than the seeming exchange of expressions of endearment, with localities and shifting of scenery adapted to call forth new and lively emotions.

Is it the custom, now, of any nation to write amatory eclogues in such a manner as this? If literally interpreted, the whole book, while it has some beauties of description, is still nothing less than a mass of incongruities, without plan, and without the accomplishment of any thing saving the outpourings of amorous desire.

It was on this ground, that Rosenmueller abandoned the literal exegesis, although he was nearly alone in doing so among the Neologists; Proem. III. I must confess for myself, that the words of the celebrated Rabbi, Aben Ezra, in the Pref. to his Comm. on this book, appear to me very just and striking: חלילה חלילה להיות שיר השירים בדברי חשק כי אם על
דרך משל ולולי גדל מעלותו לא נכתב בסוד כתבי הקדש ואין עליו מחלקת:
i. e. " Profanation ! profanation ! to place the Canticles among amatory compositions; but every thing is said in the way of allegory. And unless the dignity of it [the book] had been great, it had not been incorporated with the holy books. Nor is there any controversy respecting it." He means to say, that this was not, and could not be, fairly called in question. And why is he not in the right? " The universal genius and method of the sacred books," says Rosenmueller, " exclude the idea of admitting among them songs about the ordinary love of man and woman."

But is there any example in the other Scriptures of allegorizing as to *spiritual* things, by employing such language and such conceptions as are to be found in Canticles? I answer *yes*, without hesitation. This sort of imagery is frequent in the Old Testament, and in the New. Frequently are the Jews charged with " going a *whoring* after other gods;" Ex. xxxiv. 15, 16; Lev. xx. 5, 6; Num. xv. 39; Deut. xxxi. 16; 2 Chron. xxi. 13; Ps. lxxiii. 27; Ezek. vi. 9. Here the idea is, that they were affianced to the true God, and could not seek after idols without incurring the guilt of adultery. So God calls himself the *husband* of the Jews; Isa. liv. 5. The nation of Israel is his *bride;* Isa. lxii. 4, 5. In Isa. l. 1, Jehovah asks where is the bill of divorcement on his part, that Israel have departed from him. Jeremiah speaks of the *espousals* of Israel, when young, in the wilderness. In Jer. iii. 1—11, the prophet speaks of Israel as playing the harlot and committing adultery, in forsaking Jehovah. In Ezekiel, two long chapters (xvi., xxiii.) are occupied with carrying through the imagery drawn from such a connexion. Hosea (i.—iii.)

recognises the same principle, and carries out the imagery into much detail. These are merely specimens. Ps. xlv. presents the Mediator, the King of Zion, in the attitude of a husband to the church, and celebrates the union between the former and the latter. So in the New Testament this imagery is very familiar; see Matt. ix. 15; John iii. 29; Rev. xix. 7; xxi. 2. Especially consult 2 Cor. xi. 2, and Eph. v. 22—32, where the apostle has gone into much particularity as to the duties of the marriage relation, and then avows, that he "speaks concerning Christ and the church."

Such is the custom of the Hebrew writers and of the apostles. If now this imagery is so often employed, in all parts of the Bible, what forbids the idea, that there may be one short book in which it occupies an exclusive place, and is designed to symbolize the love that existed between God and his ancient people or the church, or rather, which ought to have existed on their part between God and his spiritually regenerated people, who have become one (in a spiritual sense) with him, and are for ever united to him? It cannot be shown, *a priori*, that this is even improbable.

Yet I would not wish to represent the case, in regard to Canticles, as different from what it really is. In other books these conjugal allusions and relations are only *occasional* and *local*, like other comparisons or similes introduced merely for the sake of illustration or of vivid representation; in Canticles they are sole and exclusive—the all in all. Nor is there even a single reference to simple spiritual things expressly given in the whole book. The reader finds not a hint, that he is to interpret the book in this way. It is this which constitutes the main strength of those who assert the book to be altogether amatory in its character.

I should feel more pressed by this circumstance, did I not know, that extensive usage of a similar nature exists, and has for a long period existed, in the oriental countries, e. g. among the Persians, the Turks, the Arabians, and the Hindoos. In the Musnavi of Jellaleddin, the poems of Jami, and above all in the odes of Hafiz, are many productions apparently of an amatory nature, which the Persians (there are some dissenters) regard as expressive of the intercourse of the soul with God. Hafiz, whose odes, as has been remarked, are sung to excite youth to pleasure, and chanted to remind the aged of the raptures of Divine love, was a Sufi devotee of the most strenuous cast. Hence his poetry is regarded as expressive of the longings of the soul after God, and of the enjoyment that results from communion with him. The loves of Megnoun and Leilah have been celebrated in the Arabic, the Persian, and the Turkish languages; yet with the understanding, in all cases, that these personages are mere allegorical characters—i. e. mere personifications of religious affection.

Mr. Lane, in his admirable work on the Modern Egyptians, has given us an opportunity of presenting this subject a little more *in extenso*, than I have yet done. While in Cairo he attended the religious exercises of the Dervishes of the highest order, on the birth-day of the prophet (Mohammed). Of course the devotional exercises of that day were designed to be of the very highest cast. A company of the leading Dervishes met, by moonlight, and after a variety of chants out of the Koran, they proceeded to the exercises thus described by Mr. Lane.

"I shall here give a translation of one of these *Moowesh'-shahhs*, which are very numerous, as a specimen of their style, from a book containing a number of these poems, which I have purchased during the present Moo'lid, from a durwee'sh who presides at many zikrs. He pointed out the following poem as one of those most common at zikrs, and as one which was sung at the zikr which I have begun to describe. I translate it verse for verse; and imitate the measure and system of rhyme of the original, with this difference only, that the first, third, and fifth lines of each stanza rhyme with each other in the original, but not in my translation.

> With love my heart is troubled;
> And mine eye-lid hind'reth sleep:
> My vitals are dissever'd;
> While with streaming tears I weep.
> My union seems far distant:
> Will my love e'er meet mine eye?
> Alas! Did not estrangement
> Draw my tears, I would not sigh.
>
> By dreary nights I'm wasted:
> Absence makes my hope expire:
> My tears, like pearls, are dropping;
> And my heart is wrapt in fire.
> Whose is like my condition?
> Scarcely know I remedy.
> Alas! Did not estrangement
> Draw my tears, I would not sigh

> O turtle-dove! acquaint me
> Wherefore thus dost thou lament?
> Art thou so stung by absence?
> Of thy wings deprived, and pent?
> He saith, 'Our griefs are equal:
> Worn away with love, I lie.'
> Alas! Did not estrangement
> Draw my tears, I would not sigh.
>
> O First and Everlasting!
> Show thy favour yet to me;
> Thy slave, Ahh'mad El-Bek'ree,*
> Hath no Lord excepting Thee.
> By Ta'-Ha',† the great Prophet!
> Do thou not his wish deny.
> Alas! Did not estrangement
> Draw my tears, I would not sigh.

I must translate a few more lines, to show more strongly the similarity of these songs to that of Solomon: and lest it should be thought that I have varied the expressions, I shall not attempt to translate them into verse. In the same collection of poems sung at zikrs is one which begins with these lines:

> O gazelle from among the gazelles of El-Yem'en!
> I am thy slave without cost:
> O thou small of age, and fresh of skin!
> O thou who art scarce past the time of drinking milk!

In the first of these verses, we have a comparison exactly agreeing with that in the concluding verse of Solomon's Song; for the word which, in our Bible, is translated a 'roe,' is used in Arabic as synonymous with *ghaza'l* (or a gazelle); and the mountains of El-Yem'en are 'the mountains of spices.'—This poem ends with the following lines:

> The phantom of thy form visited me in my slumber:
> I said, 'O phantom of slumber! who sent thee?'
> He said, 'He sent me whom thou knowest;
> He whose love occupies thee.'
> The beloved of my heart visited me in the darkness of night:
> I stood, to show him honour, until he sat down.
> I said, 'O thou my petition, and all my desire!
> Hast thou come at midnight, and not feared the watchmen?'
> He said to me, 'I feared; but, however, love
> Had taken from me my soul and my breath.'

Compare the above with the second and five following verses of the fifth chapter of Solomon's Song.—Finding that songs of this description are extremely numerous, and almost the only poems sung at zikrs; that they are composed for this purpose, and intended only to have a

---

* The author of the poem. The singer sometimes puts his own name in the place of this.

† *Ta'-Ha'* (as I have mentioned on a former occasion) is a name of the Arabian Prophet.

spiritual sense (though certainly not understood in such a sense by the generality of the vulgar*); I cannot entertain any doubt as to the design of Solomon's Song. The specimens which I have just given of the religious love-songs of the Moos'lims have not been selected in preference to others as most agreeing with that of Solomon; but as being in frequent use; and the former of the two, as having been sung at the zikr which I have begun to describe."

Such, then, is the custom of the Arabians, in their most sublimated devotions, and on occasions the most solemn. Who will deny that Mr. Lane has some good reason for saying, as he does, that "he cannot entertain any doubt of Solomon's Song."

Was it impossible, now, for the neighbours of the Arabians to have a similar custom, in their flights of highest devotion? From some of the deepest affections of our nature they drew their colouring, in order to portray the longings and the enjoyments of the soul. It will be allowed, on all hands, that no material for colouring could be of a more vivid nature. The *moral* tendency is the only draw-back in regard to the whole matter. On this I must say a few words more, and then leave the matter to the reader.

For one I feel obliged to say, that the state of feeling in our western world, which has been consequent on elevating the rank of women in society, and giving them a place among assemblages either for instruction or entertainment, stands in some measure opposed to the tenor of such a book as Canticles. As a book of amatory odes we might praise and admire it; for, in the original, it is much more delicate than our English version represents it to be. But we shrink instinctively from connecting amatory ideas and feelings with a devotional frame of mind. We find the temptation to dwell on the carnal imagery sometimes, perhaps often, leading us away from pure and spiritual devotion. This I believe to be the general—the all but universal feeling among us. I do not, I cannot disapprove of this feeling. I commend it. It shows what progress Christianity has made, in inspiring the mind with quick and powerful sensitiveness, in regard to a matter which is always fraught with danger, and

---

* As a proof of this, I may mention, that, since the above was written, I have found the last six of the lines here translated, with some slight alterations, inserted as a common love-song in a portion of the Thousand and One Nights, printed at Calcutta (vol. i. p. 425).

particularly to the young. Where promiscuous assemblage of the two sexes is so frequent as it is among us, nothing but a quick and high sense of delicacy could prevent the multiplied evils that might easily grow out of it. Our state of manners, our usages in regard to female privileges and companionship, render that kind of cautious feeling on the subject of amatory descriptions and allusions, necessary to us as a safeguard.

I take it for granted, that such a book as the Canticles presupposes a state of society which is far from the highest Christian refinement of manners. In the New Testament, such a book, i. e. one exclusively of such a tenor, would be an utter stranger. It could hardly be recognised as one of this collection. But when all this is said and conceded, it does not follow, that such a book as Canticles might not have found a place in the ancient Canon. Different — very different — was the state of the Jews in ancient times. Language that we could not now tolerate, above all could not tolerate in any company composed of both sexes, gave no offence to delicacy in the times of general simplicity and rude cultivation. It might be employed, then, much more unexceptionably among the ancient Hebrews than it can be among us. Certain it is, that the Old Test. Scriptures abundantly illustrate this position, by the not unfrequent expressions found in them, which we feel obliged to mollify in translating, but which, when first uttered, needed no such process. Every thing almost of this nature depends on the state and habitudes of a nation or people. Some things there are, which must always be indecent, at all times, and among all nations. But other things, e. g. phraseology, manner of dress, and all that may be classed under the ἀδιάφορα of morals, is mutable, and may be proper or improper *pro re nata*. Nor is this peculiar to the Old Testament. In 1 Cor. xi. 13, seq., Paul says that it is a shame for a man to wear long hair; that a woman must not pray unveiled in public assemblies; that women must wear their hair long in the way of ornament and covering; and the like. Is so much of this, now, as pertains merely to costume, or manner of wearing the hair, matter of perpetual obligation to all churches? Certainly not. And why? Because the things commanded or forbidden are among the ἀδιάφορα, i. e. things in themselves neither good nor evil, but still things that may be indecorous, if practised under certain circumstances and among a people of such usages as the Greeks. In public no woman could decently appear unveiled; a usage widely extant even now in Asia. For men to wear long hair, was an indication among the Greeks of an effeminate, imbecile character, who courted adornment like a female, and was probably one of the παθικοί. But in our country, the state of manners and customs is so different, that so far as decency of appearance is concerned, the matters of which the apostle here treats are things indifferent. In respect, however, to the *public praying* of females, the apostle, in the same epistle, becomes so impressed with the subject, when he comes to treat of the exercise of the gift of speaking with tongues in public, that he positively and plainly forbids the whole thing. "Let your women keep silence in the churches; for it is not permitted them to speak;" 1 Cor. xiv. 34. And so again in 1 Tim. ii. 11, 12, "Let the women learn silence with all subjection; but I suffer not a woman to teach, [i. e. in public, or to preach,] nor to usurp authority over the man, but to be in silence." Some have thought that these two passages are opposed or contradictory to the preceding. I do not understand them so. In the first passage, Paul is merely correcting abuses; and he so limits the public speaking of women, that, if done at all, it should be done with entire decorum. In the last two, he gives his opinion what ought to be and should be the established principle of the church, in regard to the matter of public female addresses. Of course, he must be understood as speaking in reference to *mixed* assemblies.

There are several things to be learned from cases of such a nature as this. First of all, that even Christianity, which is always watchful over the τὸ καλόν and τὸ πρέπον, may forbid things in certain circumstances, which are matters of perfect indifference in others. The like was the eating of meats that had been presented in the temple of idols; the circumcision of Christians standing in a peculiar relation to the Jews, e. g. of Timothy, &c. So there may be, and there are, some things which are *local* and *temporary* in the Gospel, as well as in the Law. Secondly, that which is not *malum in se* may be tolerated for a while, and regulated, even in cases where, in the sequel, it may be judged necessary or best entirely to forbid it. Such was the temporary toleration of the public addresses or prayers of women at Corinth, in promiscuous assemblies. The precept forbidding this, is of course not to be regarded as extending to exercises of this nature in assemblies exclusively female; but that it is designed to be a general and permanent precept, in regard to mixed assemblies, would seem to be plain from the reasoning of Paul when giving his grounds for such a precept; see 1 Tim. ii. 13, seq. The reasoning in this case is founded on a permanent state of things.

If now we find in the New Testament things about which certain directions are given, but which are plainly and evidently obligatory no longer than while certain circumstances exist; why may there not be some books in the Old Testament, once well adapted to the state of the Jews and useful to them, but which have now become obsolete by reason of the great changes which Christianity has wrought? All concede, that the Levitical rites and ceremonies are done away; that circumcision, and the passover, and sacrifices and oblations of every kind, are no longer obligatory. Of course all that part of the Old Testament which prescribes and regulates these things, is no longer a matter of *practical* moment to us, but only a portion of the history of God's former dealings with his church. We have no hesitation in adopting all this; especially after reading the Epistle to the Hebrews, the principal object of which is to show, that a new and better covenant than the old has been introduced, and one established on better promises and of a more liberal nature. But when we have gone thus far, is there any obstacle in the way of taking one more step? May there not have been some books, neither ritual nor politico-ecclesiastical, written for the time being and the circumstances then existing, and which were wisely adapted to do good in this state of things—which books, by the introduction of a better and more perfect system of religion, have become in a good measure obsolete, or no longer useful to us, because our circumstances, habits, manners, and modes of thinking, are so different from those of the Jews in their partially civilized state? I do not see how this question can be confidently answered in the negative.

Why may it not be, then, that the *Canticles* were written for Jewish pietists of a contemplative order, and somewhat of the temperament of the Essenes, i. e. able to control and keep in a state of entire subjection their animal passions? There were doubtless some Baxters and Thomas à Kempises among the Hebrews; we know that there were such men as could write the most devotional Psalms. Might it not have been customary among the Hebrews, so to speak of the marriage relation and its endearments, as not to excite in them the same feeling that it is apt to do among us, or at least not the same in degree? I must take it for granted that such was the case, when I call to mind how often Jehovah employs language of this kind, when addressing the Israelites. Nay more, I find the same thing, to some extent, even in the New Testament, on the part of Jesus and his apostles. It is clear that no indecency is intended; and equally clear, as it seems to me, that no improper feelings were excited by the language in question, in the minds of those who were originally addressed. But that time, those circumstances, that state of manners, and those usages, all of which contributed to render imagery of the kind in question harmless, and even useful—have all passed away. *Orientals* may read Hafiz's Odes, and the Loves of Megnoun and Leilah, or may sing as the Dervishes did when Mr. Lane heard them, and through the force of education appropriate to themselves religious nourishment from these elements. Why, then, should they be forbidden to them? Why might not the Jewish sacred writers provide for that class of devotees, who could be profited by this style of writing? The thing is neither impossible nor improbable. Every thing in this matter depends on education and custom. Is not the Bible so written as to offer something attractive to all classes of readers, to all kinds of taste that are not in themselves vicious? If so, why may not provision have been made to allure the class of the contemplative, the devotees in the East, and to attract the attention of even the Sufi and the Dervish?

Thus much, I think, may fairly be said in regard to the existence and canonical rank of such a work as the Canticles. But now as to the *Occidentals*—the western world who have been Christianized, and brought to a totally different state of manners. *Mixed* society in the East, is a thing that time out of mind has never been allowed and practised. Hence their freedom of language, in speaking of delicate matters. The restraints of the female sex were not felt, of course. Language assumed a fuller tone without offence, where only one sex was present. But among us, where both are present, (a matter which Christianity has brought about, unspeakably to the advantage of both sexes,) we cannot read or sing the Canticles with the same freedom as a company of monks or nuns could do. It is well. For one, I rejoice in this triumph of Christianity in prohibiting every thing, that may even seem to the unlearned or the passionate as adapted to excite unhallowed feelings. Innocent in themselves, with all the needful restraints and decorous limitations, some of these feelings may in themselves be. But we need no excitement, additional to what by nature we possess, to rouse them. It is not best to tamper with even a dubious matter. I have often heard it said by the friends of President Edwards, that he was peculiarly fond of the book of Canticles, and read and meditated much upon it. His character for piety was such, as entirely forbids the supposition that he was secretly nourishing his animal passions by this. Nay, I must believe that if he had found such to be the effect of his reading Canticles, he would at once have desisted. His example shows, then, what is possible, and what may be achieved by purified and exalted feeling. But as such men are not very rife in these days, and are not likely to be so, it is better for those who have not attained an elevated state of piety like his, to abstain, for the most part, from the book before us. The reason lies in our excitability, in consequence of our manners and our education. There is the same reason, for substance, why we should desist from this book, as there is why we should cease to hold obligatory the *local* and *temporal* in the New Testament. The book has had its day. I venture to believe, that many rejoiced in it and were made glad by it. But it was only twilight when it was written; it is now broad daylight. We who know and feel this, need not go back to the twilight, in order that we may see.

Still, there is yet an *oriental* world, and one that is to be converted to Christianity. Let the book stand for those, who have been trained to read Hafiz, and Meġnoun and Leilah, and to sing the odes of the Dervishes, with nothing but a spiritualized state of feeling, enjoy the pleasure of finding such a book in the Canon of Scripture. For us, men of occidental taste and habits, and of only ordinary growth in piety, (to say the best we well can,)—for us, (excepting the few that have reached the lofty heights of a Baxter or an Edwards,) who have a task difficult enough to keep our passions in due subjection even when we shun all the temptation and excitements that we can—it is the safer and better course to place the Canticles, as the Jews did, among the גנוזים or books withdrawn from ordinary use, and betake ourselves rather to the Psalms, and the Proverbs, and the Prophets, and the New Testament. Canticles, as a means of devotion—*doctrinal* it surely is not—is superseded for us by better means. This is reason enough, independently of the danger of being excited in an undue way, to prefer other parts of the Scripture. And all this brings no just reproach on Canticles, any more than the argument of Paul in his Epistle to the Hebrews, against all the rites and forms of the old dispensation, brings reproach on them while they lasted.

I am aware, that those Christians (and some such there are) who, because all the Bible was written by inspiration, hold it to be all alike valuable to us and obligatory upon us, and who read it *in course*, even through and through, in their families, (and perhaps in the pulpit,) with the best of intentions, will probably not receive these remarks with much approbation. Still, while I doubt not that they may mean right, I am fully persuaded that their practice is altogether wrong, or at least injudicious. What have we to do, in the way of Christian edification, with the details of building the tabernacle and temple; with the genealogies and lists of returning exiles; with all the prescriptions about offerings, libations, purifications, priests, &c., in the Levitical law; and with many a piece of family or individual history which developes nothing special of a religious nature? Even the prophecies against Egypt, Moab, Edom, Philistia, Tyre, Babylon, and Assyria, have but a subordinate interest for us. Why occupy our public or our family devotions with such parts of the Old Test. Scriptures? What moral and practical ideas would a family or a church obtain, from having Ezek. xl.—xlviii. read in course? General usage has decided all these questions, among the more intelligent Christians, and decided them rightly. I do not wish the decision to be revoked.

Nor is all this saying one word against the Canticles, or the other parts of Scripture to which reference has been made. I have already pointed out what use is to be made of such parts of Scripture, and what estimate is to be put upon them. I need not repeat here what I have already said. The whole thing lies in a very small compass. There was an ancient *preparatory* dispensation—a shadow of good things to come—many things were necessary to arrange and give it a successful trial; that dispensation has passed away, and has now comparatively "no glory by reason of the glory that excelleth;" and along with it have passed away all such parts of the Old Testament as were local and temporary—all which belonged merely to Judaism. Why can we not receive the simple truth, that the hand of God was in all these movements, and that the same hand has now introduced us to a much higher and better state, furnished us with better means of understanding truth, and of promoting our own personal piety?

Considerations such as these, and like to these, I would most heartily commend to those who are halting and doubting in regard to the book of Canticles. I do not perceive the need of such a state of mind. Certain it is, that the Canticles were a part of the Canon sanctioned by Christ and the apostles. Nothing as matter of fact in ancient criticism is more certain. It is of no use to deny this, or to make efforts to evade it. Better is it to meet it directly, and canvass the whole matter with an open and liberal and candid mind. If the *Orientals* still want such a book, let them use it, as the ancient Jews did. If the *Occidentals* can do better, on the whole, without making the use of it public and common, let them have the liberty of the Gospel. Our preachers, in general, have long since ceased to make it a text-book; families do not generally read it in their devotions; and if the remarks which I have made above are well founded, they are to be commended rather than blamed for this. The book has had its day in the *East*, or (if you insist upon it) is to have it there; in the *West*, it seems to me that it must continue to hold much the same place which general practice has assigned to it.

I cannot conclude these remarks without adding, as I have already hinted, that the perusal of the original makes much less impression on me of an exceptionable kind, than the perusal of our version. It is far more delicate, at least to my apprehension. It were easy to exhibit particulars, which would justify this statement. But I refrain because of the nature of the case. That there are many passages in this *pastoral*, if any must needs so call it, which are highly beautiful and tender and delicate, is quite certain. A heathen poet who had sung carnal love in like manner, would have doubtless been immortal among the Cythereans. But other passages, which are minutely descriptive of the person of the bride, oblige us to look well to the mastery of our feelings. It needs something of the tone of mind which a Sufi or a Dervish attains to by long and exclusive spiritualizing and meditation, or (which is much better) the elevation above all that is carnal of an Edwards or a Baxter or an Owen, in order to make any spiritual gain by the exercise. Something might be done to give the book a better dress than it has in our English version; but the general state of the case will remain as developed above. While I would say, with Aben Ezra, חלילה חלילה, to all profane rejection of the book, I think we may say with Virgil, on a somewhat different occasion, Procul, O procul, este profani!

Is it not strange that the mere *Elenchus Interpretum*, or list of commentators on this book, occupies more than twenty octavo pages in Rosenmueller's Commentary? And I presume he has not recorded any thing like the one half of them. Jews, Christian Fathers, Romanists, and Protestants, have all rushed upon this little book, by virtue, as it would seem, of some mysterious attraction. Yet the mystery does not probably lie very deep. Origen, as we might expect from his allegorical inclinations, wrote ten volumes of Comm. on Canticles. "As in other works of his," says Jerome, "he has surpassed all other expositors, in this he has outdone himself." "Here," says he on another occasion respecting Origen in this work, "here he sails *cum pleno velo*." We have also among these expositors an Ambrose, Gregory of

Nyssa, Theodoret, Cassiodorus, and many others. Among the Romanists there is no end of expositors. Poor monks! This book was converted into nectar and ambrosia to refresh and strengthen them in their mental revellings, and to compensate in some measure for the loss of realities. So they rushed by troops to the prey. Germans, (as we should expect,) Frenchmen not a few, (as we should spontaneously conjecture,) even Englishmen, although with some good degree of sobriety in most cases, and last of all the very Dutchmen, have revelled in this book; for what else shall I say of the matter of many of the commentaries that have been produced? There are, not improbably, a class of occasional readers of the Bible, who would sooner give up any book belonging to it than this. Their real reasons for this preference, they would not perhaps be fond of proclaiming.

Christianity, then, with that state of manners and society which it has introduced, has changed our relation to many things belonging to the Old Testament dispensation. All concede this, as to rites and forms and peculiarities of the Levitical worship and purifications. We have no temple at Jerusalem; no assemblages there to kill the passover, to celebrate sacred feasts, and to hear the Law once in seven years. We have it every sabbath, we may read it every day. It costs but a pittance to put it in our possession—the fruit of a single day's labour, at most, will accomplish this, for the poorer classes; while a pious Jew, to obtain the same privileges, must almost have expended a handsome little fortune. The consequence of all this is, a state of things and of manners exceedingly different from that of ancient times. It does not follow, that all which was permissible, or available, or useful then, is of course so now. Even some books, which are not conversant with Hebrew rites and forms, are not of course profitable to us, as they were, or at any rate might have been, to them. Why should we lay stress on these, and urge them into present usage, when little or no moral gain, comparatively, is to be made from them? I hesitate not for a moment to say, that we should not. Let them be—especially let the *Canticles* be—for *oriental* Christians, brought up very differently from us. I doubt not that many of them might find spiritual food, instead of poison, in them. At all events, we may consent to let a book stand where Christ and his apostles found it and left it, and against which they have no where testified, but, on the contrary, sanctioned it in connexion with other Old Testament books. It is safe for the doubting and wavering at least to let it alone. If they find that they cannot safely read it, they are bound to let it alone ; at least I should not hesitate in my own case.

All things considered, we may settle down, as it seems to me, in the conclusion, that the *Canticles* is a book rather to be regarded in the light of a *local* one, and adapted to *partial* usage, than as a book now, under the full light of the gospel, specially adapted to our use. It had its day. That its use was *religious,* I cannot doubt, from the company in which it is found, and the ordeal through which it has passed among the founders of Christianity. It may have still another day of usefulness among the Asiatics. Let us not disown it, or set it aside. But persons of timid consciences, who have an idea, that, since all parts of Scripture are inspired, they all must of course be *equally* useful, may be set free from this bondage. Are we to hold that the sketches of tabernacle and temple buildings, of ritual ordinances and customs, and catalogues of names and places, are as *edifying* as the Epistle to the Romans, or the Gospels, or the Psalms ? If we answer in the negative, then I would ask, whether, in other compositions, once adapted to the state of things then existing, there may not be a lack of former usefulness, since the light of the Gospel has become fully diffused ? As I have once said, I would say again, May not a star, that once shone brightly in the dim twilight, become no longer visible when the sun is shining in his strength ? But why should we deny that it has once shone, and that it is still a star ?

I have not undertaken to decide, exactly of what tenor the *spiritual* exegesis of Canticles should be. It is a question of no small difficulty. Does it refer to the *church* as a body ? Or is it to be applied to the converse of the soul with God, and the delight of communing with him ? If oriental analogy may speak, on this occasion, it would lift up its voice in favour of the latter. This I also prefer, because I can hardly regard the book of Canticles in the light of a series of *predictions* respecting a future Christian church. As far as what pertains to individuals, who are pious, is common to the church, whether Jewish or Christian, so far Canticles may be applied to the characteristics of the church, ancient or modern. But to me it seems better and firmer ground, to regard the Canticles as expressing the warm and earnest desire of the soul after God, in language borrowed from that which characterizes chaste affection between the sexes. But this is not the place to vindicate an opinion of this nature.*

SECT. XXII. *Use of the Old Testament under the Gospel Dispensation.*

THE most difficult and delicate part of my task remains. In many respects this is also the most important; for it is the *practical result* of all which has been hitherto laid before the reader and defended.

Where shall a Christian teacher or reader draw the line between what IS ABROGATED *in the Old Testament, by the coming of Christ and by the revelation of his will in the New Testament, and that which* REMAINS IN FULL FORCE, *and to which appeal may be made as being at the present time of Divine authority and obligation?*

If by this question is meant, a requisition to draw a boundary line between the two, which is always practically palpable, and always visible and plain even to the weakest eye, no intelligent and considerate man would undertake the task. The New Testament has passed sentence of abrogation on no specific book, or part of a book, as such, which is contained in the Old Testament. To its decision, viewed as designating this or that particular portion or book of the Old Testament as no longer having authority to decide matters pertaining to religion for us, we cannot appeal. All

* For a dissertation on the Song of Solomon unfriendly to its canonical position, and of course to its inspired authority, the reader may consult Dr. Pye Smith's Scripture Testimony to the Messiah, third edition, vol. i. p. 44, et seq., and Dr. Bennett's reply in the Congregational Magazine for 1838. D.

which it has done is to lay down and establish *general principles*, by the aid of which we must decide what still remains obligatory, and what is virtually repealed.

The ultimate appeal, then, is to understanding and reason; not in order to establish the *principles* in question, for Christ and his apostles have established them, but to make a discriminating and judicious use of these principles, in determining what still remains in full force. So does the Bible in respect to its interpretation. It narrates, it commands, it threatens, it promises, it encourages, it consoles, it holds out views of a future state of reward and punishment; but the language in which all this is done, is addressed to men in the usual way, and they are expected to give it a rational interpretation. The Bible teaches no system of hermeneutics; it instructs no one in the principles of rhetoric; it never descants on the use of figurative language; it never lays down any theory of exegesis which may serve as a certain guide to those who become acquainted with it. All these are presupposed to be understood or felt by the readers; and then it is expected of them, that by their discrimination and judgment, they should give a sound interpretation.

Exactly like to this is the case before us. The new dispensation is fully set forth in the New Testament. Its departures from the peculiarities of the Jewish religion, its true spiritual nature, its universality, its freedom from all pomp and rites and ceremonies, and (if the word had not been abused I might say, in a good sense) its *cosmopolitism*, stand in high relief upon the portico of the new temple which has been erected. On the very foundation stones of this temple are inscribed, in letters so plain that he who runneth may read: GOD IS A SPIRIT, AND THEY THAT WORSHIP HIM, MUST WORSHIP HIM IN SPIRIT AND IN TRUTH. On the next tier of foundation stones stands inscribed, in letters equally plain and prominent: THE FATHER SEEKETH SUCH WORSHIPPERS. On the third stands the inscription: THE HOUR IS COME WHEN NEITHER ON THE MOUNTAIN OF SAMARIA, NOR OF JERUSALEM, ARE MEN REQUIRED TO WORSHIP.

This last inscription contains the germ of all that I have or wish to say. The two former inscriptions were virtually engraved of old on the Jewish temple. But they were in the *Sanctum Sanctorum*, and common worshippers rather heard indistinctly of them, than saw them. On the temple of the new Jerusalem they stand, as I have said, in relief so high and prominent, that no worshipper who approaches can fail to see them, unless he shuts his eyes.

It is the third inscription which we are now called to read and interpret. Let us address ourselves to this grave and interesting task with becoming seriousness and candour.

All *social* religion, under the Mosaic code, centred in the temple at Jerusalem and its ordinances. The claims of the Samaritans to make their mountain the central point of all religious rites and services, was settled by the Saviour himself, in his conversation with the Samaritan woman, " Ye worship ye know not ... for salvation is of the Jews." We may therefore dismiss Mount Gerizim, and all its pretended services, from any further consideration.

To declare that *men should no longer worship the Father at Jerusalem*, is to declare that the whole system of Jewish social worship, with all its pomp, its rites and ceremonies, its sacrifices and oblations, is abrogated. What made the Jewish religion peculiar and appropriate only to one nation, was its *locality* and its *externals*. From its very nature the Jewish religion could belong only to one nation. Three times in each year were all the males of the nation to appear before God in Jerusalem. Once in seven years the whole population, men, women, and children, were to go up thither to hear the Law. How could Judaism be a practicable religion, except to a small nation within very circumscribed limits ? It was plainly impossible.

This solves the great problem contained in the question, Why was not the Jewish religion aggressive ? Why did not the pious part of the Hebrew community send missionaries to the heathen, and endeavour to convert them ? Jonah once preached abroad with signal success ; why did not the Jewish prophets repeat the experiment?

Without attempting to assign all the reasons which they had for abstaining from attempts of this nature, I merely remark, that the prophets could not fail of seeing, that an extensive prevalence of the Jewish religion would involve impossibilities. How could the Hindoos and the Chinese repair thrice in a year to Jerusalem ? How could the population of a world assemble in one small city, which never could have contained much over one hundred thousand inhabitants, if indeed so many can be supposed? The prophets knew, by circumstances such as these, that God did not design Judaism for a universal religion. Consequently they engaged in no foreign missionary enterprises, and never exhibited any special zeal for the conversion of the heathen.

We come, then, to the great question, which is the *nucleus* of the whole matter: *What is there in the Old Testament, which belongs to* JUDAISM *as such; and what is there which belongs to* THE NATURE OF TRUE RELIGION, *at all times, among all nations, and in all places?*

That which belongs merely to Judaism as such, is wholly abolished by the Gospel. WHAT BELONGS TO ALL NATIONS IS FULLY RETAINED. The proper application of these two simple principles is all that is necessary to a right understanding of this whole subject. The task needs, indeed, some good measure of discrimination and judgment. In some few cases it needs a more than ordinary knowledge of both the Jewish and the Christian religion. But in the main, the thing can be made intelligible to all; and it may fairly be considered as feasible for the mass of Christians even tolerably well instructed, to draw the lines of separation in most of the important cases.

The Jewish dispensation was *introductory*. To use the expressive language of Paul, "The Law was the shadow of good things to come, and was not the very image of those things." In the Epistle to the Hebrews, the substance of all that I aim at saying is fully exhibited. There we are most explicitly taught, that all the rites and ceremonies and sacrifices of the Jewish dispensation were utterly inefficient in themselves to remove the burden of sin from the conscience, or to cancel the guilt of the offender. *It is not possible that the blood of bulls and of goats should take away sin.* And again, "Sacrifice and the burnt-offerings and sin-offerings thou wouldest not, neither hadst pleasure therein." So even the prophets of old said to the formalists and the ritualists among the Jews. But there lay at the basis of all the rites and sacrifices of the old dispensation, an important principle, a prefiguration of the great and leading truth of the Gospel, viz. that *without the shedding of blood there is no remission of sin.* But that blood "which taketh away the sin of the world," was not the blood of bullocks and of goats, but "the blood of Christ, who, through the eternal Spirit, offered himself without spot to God, that he might purge our consciences from dead works, to serve the living God." Of this great atoning "sacrifice," all the victims slain at the altar of the Jewish dispensation were only *symbols* or *types*. The pious Jew, who presented the sacrifices in question, if he presented them with a penitent and believing mind, might obtain remission of his sins, even spiritual remission. Yet not by virtue merely of his sacrifices, but only by virtue of that which they symbolized. Even the impenitent Jew, who complied with the letter of the Mosaic law, might and did obtain *civil* and *ecclesiastical* remission. And this was all that any rites, ceremonies, or sacrifices could ever procure in themselves for any one.

That all this scheme of the Jewish ritual was, and was designed to be, *symbolic* and *typical* of a new and better state or dispensation, must be conceded, as it seems to me, by every candid mind. The utter *inefficacy* of all sacrifices of beasts to lighten the burdened conscience or to atone for sin, is a matter past all question. Then for what purpose did the Divine Being institute such a religion as that of Moses? No answer can be given to this question, which is reasonable and satisfactory, except it be, that *God designed all these things to be preparatory to another and better dispensation*. It is then, and only then, when we admit this, that any significancy or importance is attached to the Jewish religion, so far as all its externals are concerned. In every other point of view, it would be little more than solemn trifling. Mr. Norton, who denies the atonement of Christ, and all the prophetic anticipations of him and his sacrifice, must of course think very meanly of the Jewish religion. The contemptuous manner in which he repeatedly adverts to the Levitical ritual, shows clearly that such is the state of his feelings. Believing, as he undoubtedly does and should do, that no blood of bulls or of goats can take away sin, and acknowledging no symbolic and typical design in the Jewish offerings and sacrifices—what remains but to draw the conclusion, that the whole fabric was one reared merely by superstition? How different from this is the view of the thorough believer in God's ancient revelation! He sees in all the rites and forms of the temple, and all the purifications of temple-worshippers, the symbols of the all-important and distinguishing truths of the Gospel.

The way seems now to be prepared for further progress. Tabernacle and temple are no more. Jerusalem is no longer our spiritual metropolis. God's temple is every where, on the land and on the sea. The whole earth is its area, and its vaulted roof is the arch of heaven lighted up with its suns and stars. The sacrifices and oblations now accepted and required, are only a broken, contrite, grateful heart. No hyssop branch nor sprinkling priest has any office of lustration to perform. No priest is needed to sprinkle the altar with blood; no high priest to remove the veil and enter the most holy place. Christians are all *kings* and are all *priests* unto God, as to privileges and as to rank; whilst the peculiar offices of ancient kings and priests are no more connected with the church.

The high road, therefore, in which we are to travel, while searching out Old Test. ground, is plain and straight and broad. All in the Jewish Scriptures that pertains to rites and forms of worship, to sacrifices and oblations, to washings and purifications, to meats clean and unclean, to feasts annual or monthly, to circumcision and to the passover—all which is comprised within these, and all which are accidents or things attached to them or dependent upon them—*all of this is abrogated, is repealed.* It remains now only as the *history* of what is past, not the rule of action for the present or the future. And in this point of view, it will always be interesting to the pious reader. It will unfold to him, in what manner Divine Providence has been educating the human race; by what slow and cautious steps religion has advanced, and how utterly impossible it is for a religion that abounds in rites and forms to make much *effectual* progress any where, either among Jews or Gentiles; still more impossible that it should be a religion to convert the world. God had reserved that work for his own dear Son.

It is easy for us, in view of what we may see from our present stand-point, to account for it, that Paul rebuked so sharply the Galatian *Judaizers.* The whole system of Levitical rites and ordinances, compared with the truly Christian and spiritual service, he names *a bondage under the elements of the world.* That Christians, having once tasted the sweets of gospel-liberty, should turn back to these elements, rouses even his indignation. "How," says he in the strength of his displeasure—"how turn ye again to the weak and beggarly elements, whereunto ye desire to be in bondage?" The law, he tells them, was only "a schoolmaster to bring them unto Christ." And when they are introduced to him, he is the only master by whom they are to be guided.

All, then, which is merely *external* in religion, every thing pertaining to mere *manner* of worship, either as to preparation for it by ritual observances, or as to the costume in which it is offered, or the place where, or the manner in which it is offered, is all repealed. Along with this, too, must be classed all the statutes and ordinances of the Old Testament, which pertain merely to the form of the Jewish *ecclesiastical* and *civil* state. The substantial relations of individuals to the church of God and to the civil government, have indeed suffered no change, and never can be changed while the nature of man continues to be what it is. But the *manner* in which these relations are to be indicated or developed, is for the most part greatly changed by the Gospel.

We are not obliged to arrange our civil *government* after the model of the Jewish; and as to *priesthood*, in its distinctive character as offering sacrifices and prescribing external purifications, it is for ever done away. It is surprising to see how frequent mistakes are among writers even of the present day, in relation to this matter. A *priesthood*, in the literal sense, under the Christian dispensation, is out of all question. It is only in the *figurative* sense that Christians are priests, as well as kings; and, let it be noted well—they are *all* priests. There is no distinct order among them. A priest's business was to prepare and present offerings and sacrifices; to solve doubts and difficulties about ritual observances and concerning clean and unclean; but he was no religious teacher in the higher sense, no preacher, no public guide or exemplar in prayer, no minister of instruction with regard to the spiritual duties of devotion and piety in general. What has been said in the former part of this work in relation to priest and prophet, abundantly establishes all this. The PROPHETS were the only order of men, in ancient times, who can be compared with the ministers of the gospel. In all the New Testament, often as the various classes of officers in the church are mentioned or alluded to, such a class as *literal priests* never once occurs. The great High Priest has made an end for ever of all the rites of the priesthood, by offering up a sacrifice, in which all of this nature that could be needed, was consummated and fulfilled. All reasoning from the Levitical priesthood, then, to the Christian ministry, is out of question. It is without any foundation; and mistake and error are inevitable, where it is carried to any considerable extent.

All the arrangements in the Old Testament, which respect the investitures and forms of office, civil or ecclesiastical, among the Hebrews, are of no binding force upon us. All in their statutes and ordinances which respected merely the earthly Canaan as their land of promise, which related to their inheritances, their modes of acquiring or parting with property; all that pertained to dress, manners, customs, (not of an ethical nature,) houses, furniture, arts, occupations, and the like; in one word, all that belongs to the *external* and *physical*, whether of convenience or inconvenience; all this is done away, i. e. it is no longer binding on us. It has now become the *history* of what God's ancient people did, and how they demeaned themselves, and what were their outward circumstances; but not a rule of action for us, or an exemplar of the condition in which we must place ourselves.

I am aware that some difficult questions may be raised, in respect to the metes and bounds of political, civil, and ecclesiastical laws, ordinances, or arrangements. For example: Shall we have a *monarchy*, because the Jews had one? My answer to this would be, that Moses wished for no such thing; he merely made provision to regulate it, in case it should be established. Samuel opposed a monarchy; God himself severely reproved the Jews for desiring it; 1 Sam. viii. On the other hand; we cannot deny that David was set over the Jews as king, with special Divine approbation. But is a *republic* on this account unlawful?

One method of arguing, in this case, seems on the whole to be equally good with the other. In fact it is so; but then, neither mode exhibits the least force of argument. What the Jews did, or did not, in their civil and social capacity, is nothing to us, except as a matter of history. It may be very useful to us in the way of teaching us what consequences are connected with certain modes of government, or of administration, so that we may learn to imitate or avoid, as the case may require. Our *obligation* to follow them *politically*, amounts to nothing.

If this be correct, (as plainly it is,) can any more obligation, then, be shown to follow them *ecclesiastically?* I should answer this question almost as readily as the other. Their ecclesiastical state was so implicated and connected with their civil ordinances, that they could not be separated. Their government, whether under Judges, Kings, or Priests, was *theocratical*. The State was the Church, and the Church the State. All persons initiated into their civil community were initiated into their ecclesiastical one at the same time. Circumcision was the seal of admission to both. Hence all the males that were circumcised, were Jewish church-members, and at the same time Jewish citizens. (I do not take into view the slaves or servants, in this case.) As a matter of course, all *citizens* were *church-members.*

But can we carry over the analogy into Christian communities? It has been done. The Romish church virtually acknowledges the principle as obligatory. So does the English national church; so do the Lutheran churches generally in Europe. But would not the argument be equally valid, in respect to all the fasts, and feasts, and holidays, and sacrifices, and oblations, and purifications of the Hebrews? Surely it would; and so the Judaizers of Paul's day actually argued. But what was his reply? The Epistles to the Romans, Galatians, and Hebrews, answer this question.

Must we say, that *all* children are to be baptized, because the Jewish children were all circumcised? How then shall we make out the *all*, in this latter case? None but *male* children were circumcised. Then, again, all servants, i. e. slaves, were also to be circumcised. What becomes of the *analogy* then? It is out of question to maintain it; at least in any tolerably strict sense. Besides; what is plainer, than that the Jewish males and servants were all to be circumcised, in order that all might be ingrafted into the politico-ecclesiastical community? Every citizen was bound by religious as well as civil ordinances; and circumcision subjected him to both. But Christianity, adapted to all countries, times, and nations, of necessity gives up the idea of regulating the *forms* of government, and all that pertains to customs and manners in regard to things indifferent, or not of a moral nature. "The kingdom of Christ is NOT OF THIS WORLD." A body *politic*, in its view, is not of course a body *ecclesiastic*. Above all, we may say, the New Testament commits no power over the church as such, to the body politic. How could it? If it had so done, then Nero must have been *Pontifex Maximus* for the Christian church, in Paul's day. And not unlike to this, so far as *principle* is concerned, is the doctrine that kings and potentates are now the head of the church in Christian countries. Were even Jewish kings the head of the Jewish church, and because they were kings? I trust not. Where, then, is the present *right* of kings to such a place? They do not obtain any patent for this from the Jewish institutions. Most surely they do not find it in the New Testament. They obtain it only by virtue of *papal* example. Henry VIII. usurped the pope's place, and his heirs have inherited what he usurped. And what is the necessary consequence? It is that a Charles II. and a George IV. have been the supreme head of the national church of Great Britain. A consequence fitly joined with the arguments by which the whole matter is supported.

How unwary, too, are many excellent men, in contending for infant baptism, on the ground of the Jewish analogy of circumcision! Are *females* not proper subjects of baptism? And again, are a man's slaves to be all baptized because he is? Are they church-members of course when they are so baptized? Is there no difference between ingrafting into a *politico-ecclesiastical* community, and into one of which it is said, that "it is not of this world?" In short, numberless difficulties present themselves in our way, as soon as we begin to argue in such a manner as this.

The doctrine that a civil power is of course in some good

measure an *ecclesiastical* one, is merely an Old Testament and Jewish doctrine, not one which belongs to the New. It may, it does, suit well the ambitious and aggrandizing views of kings and potentates, to be placed at the head of the churches, to manage all their concerns, to have at their disposal all ecclesiastical places of profit and honour, and to direct matters in such a way, that all the measures of the churches shall tend to establish and secure their power and influence. Hence the eagerness with which they cleave to this arrangement, and their aversion to any interference with claims on their part of this nature. But the will and wishes of kings and princes and popes is one thing; the precepts and doctrines of the Great Head of the church are quite another.

Of all the analogical reasoning from the ancient dispensation to the new, that which respects the *rights* of kings and priests has been the most mischievous, and is the most fallacious. Constantine paved the way for all that has been assumed by civil potentates, since his time. The dark ages concentrated all power, civil and ecclesiastical, in the Roman pontiff. Luther, that morning-star of the Reformation, dissolved the spell of false *doctrine*, which laid to sleep the spiritual energies of all the churches. The *political* relations of the church, however, he never touched. He left her with as many popes as there were kings and petty princes in Germany, or elsewhere. Zuingli, and Calvin, and Knox understood this matter much better, but were able only partially to effect what they wished. Another Luther is needed in Europe; not merely to free the church from the spirit of rites and ceremonies, and penances and pilgrimages, and self-righteousness and formality, but to free it from all that domination which has no right to control it. Am I reproached with being *republican* in these views, and with proclaiming my own particular politics rather than the New Testament? My answer is, that I belong to a commonwealth, where "*all* are kings and priests;" to one also, "where there is neither Jew nor Greek, bond nor free, Barbarian nor Scythian," but where "all are one in Christ Jesus." I belong to a republic, one of whose fundamental laws is, that I "should call no man *Master* on earth." We are not forbidden to do this in a *civil* sense; such is no part of the Saviour's meaning. It is in a *religious* sense, that we are to acknowledge no supreme head of the church, except him who redeemed it.

It is true, I am a *republican* even in matters of civil government. But I am no bigot to this or to any other particular *form* of civil government. All governments cannot be alike in all respects, so long as nations differ so much from each other in cultivation, habits, and manners. I believe, too, that in general *the best government is that which is best administered.* I speak disparagingly of no monarchist, provided he is not a sycophant to those in power. But I do not envy him his opinions, and cannot gratulate him on the ground of his political relations.

But to my immediate object. All claims on the Old Testament for the support of civil domination over the spiritual kingdom of Christ, are futile. How can the king of one country be king over the Christian church, since this church belongs to *all* countries ? The claim is groundless; it is utterly without any good support. God speed, then, to the noble advocates of " the glorious liberty of the children of God," wherever they are or may be !

But I am losing myself in this interesting theme. Let us return, and see if there be not some additional considerations, that will help us to decide, in all cases of importance, what in the Old Testament is binding on us, and what is not.

Thus far we have gone upon the ground of specifying particulars, which are exempted from the category of perpetual obligation. Let us shift our position, and look at the matter from another point of view.

It is not difficult to lay down some simple and general principles ; and the application of them, in the main, is very easy. But in some cases, it requires indeed a nice discrimination, and an extensive acquaintance with both the old and new dispensation, in order to decide with any good degree of certainty. But these cases are not numerous, and will occasion no serious embarrassment to those who are intent upon their actual and practical duties.

I would lay it down, then, as a plain and palpable principle or maxim, in regard to the binding authority of the Old Testament, that *all in it of the nature of precept or doctrine, which concerns the* PERMANENT *relations of men to their God, their fellow beings, or themselves, stands unaltered and unrepealed by the Gospel.*

In view of such a principle the Saviour declared, that "heaven and earth should sooner pass away, than one jot or one tittle should pass from the Law, until all be fulfilled." True religion has always been, and always will be, *the love of God and man.* True religion always demanded, then, and always must demand, those duties which stand necessarily connected with the exhibition of love. To love God with all the heart, demands of us to reverence and obey him. To love our neighbour as ourselves, demands the performance of many duties connected with our relation to him. Now as to some of these duties, it is true that the *manner* of performing them may in some respects vary; but that manner, when not necessarily connected with the substance of the duty, is not a subject of prescription. The Jew, in order to pay his highest devotions and homage to God, must present his paschal lamb in the temple, and cause its blood to be sprinkled at the altar. But all that was external and ceremonial, in a word, all that pertained to the *manner* of paying his devotions and his homage, is now done away. And the same of every thing that concerns the manifestation of religious feeling, or of love to our neighbour. Whatever in the *manner* of any or all of the duties required of us, was Jewish, local, temporary, or dependent on, or modified by, time and place and external circumstances—all of this nature is no longer obligatory. We have only to inquire in every case, either of a doctrine or of a precept, what there is in it which pertained to time and place and external circumstances; and if we can find what that is, then so much of that precept or doctrine as pertains to the local or the temporary, is to be abstracted, when we appropriate either of these to our own use. The principle is plain; it is sound; it is beyond fair question. We are no more bound to look toward Jerusalem when we pray, as Daniel did, (vi. 10,) than we are to present our sacrifices and oblations there. The *duty* of prayer remains obligatory, because it depends on the permanent and unchanging relations of man to God; but the *manner* of it is not prescribed by any thing which the Old Testament (or even the New) contains.

How futile, then, are all appeals to *Jewish* altars and incense and priestly vestments, and pomp of worship, in order to justify and even to insist upon corresponding things in a Christian church! God has lighted up and adorned his own magnificent temple—even the whole earth. His altar is on every spot, where the sacrifice of a broken and contrite heart is offered. The sweet incense that he accepts is "the prayers of all the saints." How little do the advocates of all these externals seem to consider the true nature of that Being "who is a Spirit, and must be worshipped in spirit and in truth!"

Almost every where, through the Old Testament, lie scattered principles and precepts which are of a permanent and enduring nature. On the other hand, seldom can we find any extensive portions of these Scriptures which do not contain something that is merely local and temporary.

It is important to illustrate this; but it must be briefly done. I will select, as a specimen from the prophets, the brief work of Obadiah, consisting of only twenty-one verses. These are occupied with threatening evil to Edom, the old and bitter enemy of Israel. As the nation of the Edomites has been extinguished for more than 2000 years, it would seem that we had very little interest in such a book as this. Still, an attentive perusal of it will enable us to correct such a judgment. In that little book stands portrayed, in glowing colours, the doctrine of retribution for enmity and injury done to others. There stands too, in high relief, the sentiment that God is King of nations; that they are in his hands as clay in the hands of the potter; and that although he may delay, he will not remit, the claims of a just retribution. There, too, may comfort be found. The poor oppressed and injured Jews, who had been attacked with fury by the Edomites, when broken down and crushed to the dust by the Chaldean power, are cheered with the certain promise of deliverance from the Edomitish aggression, and with the assurance that Edom shall be trodden down and utterly unable to rise up any more against them. In short, God is King of nations; God will vindicate the cause of the oppressed; and "God is angry with the wicked every day." To attack and oppress the suffering and the humbled, is matter of high treason in his sight. We cannot exult over the calamities of others, without exposing ourselves to the righteous indignation of the supreme Judge of all.

Many other deductions might be made from this brief prophecy, which seems at first to promise so little that is interesting to us; but I have purposely confined myself only to those things which lie upon the very surface of the composition.

Once more; let us select a portion of Scripture, which is seemingly, or at first view, one of the most unpromising of all which the Old Testament exhibits. The last fifteen chapters of Exodus are occupied almost entirely with a sketch or plan of the tabernacle, its apparatus, and its appurtenances, and with an account of the manner in which the whole of this plan was carried into execution. A great portion is simple detail of architectural designs, and of the materials with which various things were to be constructed. What possible interest now can we have in all this?

If I may be permitted to answer this question, I would say, There are several points of view in which we may look at this with some interest. Does the architect take any interest in the *history* of his art? Here is rich material; and this in respect to things some 1500 years before the Christian era. Let him compare the whole with the remains of ancient art in Egypt. Does the historian, who relates the progress of invention in the arts, manufactures, luxuries, and conveniences of life, wish for a view of what existed at a most remote period, in each of these respects? Here he has ample material, in this sketch by Moses. Does the historian of the Hebrew nation wish to trace the progress of its improvements in the arts, and conveniences, and the luxuries of life? Here he has an important document. If there were no other uses than these of the document in question, they would be enough to make it very welcome to all the lovers of antiquity. But there are other important considerations still remaining.

For what purpose was such a magnificent and costly structure required? Was it that God dwells in temples made by hands? No, nothing of this. But still, when God reveals himself to men, and (so to speak) takes up his abode with them, he must do this in a manner worthy of his nature and of the occasion. Even idols had their magnificent temples. The true God is not to be placed below them. Under a dispensation where so much of the *external* was necessary, in order to meet the demands of the times and the ignorance of the people, God must be enthroned in a palace worthy as it were of his presence. An impression of his majesty and of his high and holy nature must be made, by such a use of externals as will command respect and homage. Nor is this all. God must be approached and worshipped, by a presentation of the best gifts, the most costly and precious offerings. The most valuable and costly substances are therefore put in requisition for his worship. Men are called upon to acknowledge him as the author and the rightful lord and proprietor of all that belongs to them, even of their most precious things. A *law dispensation* called in a special manner for veneration of the Law-giver, and sacred awe in his presence. The King and Lord of the Jewish nation deemed it proper to appear among them as their monarch, in his splendid and holy palace. God designed that the Israelites should feel his claims, and his perfect right, to the best which they could offer him. Nothing ordinary, common, valueless, impure, could be presented as material for his tabernacle, or to constitute the oblations and gifts there offered. The impression of all these arrangements upon the simple and untutored mind was salutary in a high degree, and filled it with a deferential respect which would check the spirit of disobedience. And from all may we not draw the inference, even at the present time, that men are bound not to withhold even their choicest substance and gifts, when the service of God requires them? Truly we may, and with good reason. God, whose temple is every where, does indeed no longer require us to rear magnificent edifices for his dwelling-place. But the spirit of tabernacle and temple building admonishes us, that churches should not be constructed so as to convey an idea of grudging and of avarice in the builders, or so as to inspire those who repair to them with disrespect or contempt. All should be done *decently*, as well as in order. Let the external not be at variance with the *internal*. Let both be such as becomes the nature of the worship and of the Being to whom it is paid. And this very consideration forbids all that is gaudy and finical, or fraught with mere display, and demands the simple, the chaste, the neat, the sober, the grave, the impressive.

And are these instructions, now, matters of no account? Is not the *practical* exhibition of them as striking and impressive as the mere abstract statement of the principles exhibited in them would be? Nay, is it not far more so? I understand, indeed, what is meant, when we are forbidden to approach our neighbour's house with hostile feelings, in the day of his calamity, or to exult over his misfortunes. But when Edom is held up before my eyes by Obadiah as having rushed upon the Jews, in the day of their humiliation by the power of Babylon; when the embittered enmity, the spirit of vengeance and of rapacity, and the unspeakable meanness of the Edomites, and their consequent punishment, is embodied and made palpable and held up to open view in this way; I am far more affected and even instructed by it, than I am by the abstract precept in question.

And when the splendid gifts of all who had a willing heart among the Jews are made, and the magnificent structure of the tabernacle is reared, and God descends in a shining cloud which fills and covers the building, and speaks from his awful sanctuary there, who wonders that even Moses was unable to enter in because of the excess of glory, or that all the people should fall prostrate on their faces and worship? And when we read all this, are we not as deeply impressed with a sense of the majesty of God, and of the reverence and obedience due to him, as we are with the simple declaration, that God is great, and greatly to be feared, and had in reverence by all who approach him? Whoever decides, that nothing is to be learned from even such narratives as these, decides hastily and without becoming consideration of the whole matter. Still, the instructions of the Gospel are more palpable and forcible; at least they are so to most minds.

May we not conclude, then, that fruit may be gathered from all parts of the Old Testament prophecy, and history, and even from the structure of sacred edifices? Are they not in some respects all "ensamples, written for our admonition, on whom the ends of the world have come?" I believe them to be so. I think Paul looked upon them in this light. And where is there now, in all the historical books of Scripture, any narrations from which something may not be learned? I do not say something *new*, but I mean to say, that some truth is taught, illustrated, or confirmed, which is a truth of permanent interest, at all times and in all places. Is not all the Jewish history *theocratical?* Is not all Hebrew prophecy *theocratical?* It is truly so; in prophecy and in history, God is all and in all. His providence, his retribution, his pleasure or displeasure, his hatred of sin, his love of justice and holiness, his supremacy, his requirements, are every where directly or indirectly taught. Even where nothing more than simple national or individual events are related, whether in history or in prophecy, there still lies in this, an account of the Divine dealings with men, or of the wickedness of the human heart, or of its penitence and obedience and holiness. There is always something to imitate, or something to be shunned. Even the most moderate intellect cannot fail to observe this.

It needs, I readily concede, some skill always in a successful manner to divest the kernel of its shell or its husk; more than some of those expositors have exhibited, who have the faculty of making one passage of Scripture just as fruitful as another, and even of deducing a whole system of theology from any given passage. But still, common sense and a moderate share of taste may suffice for the matter in question. The maxim of philosophizing civilians is, that *history is precept teaching by example.* If that is true of profane history, is it not more so of *sacred?* So, I must think, Paul believed and taught; and so we may believe and teach after him.

Then what a boundless variety is given to the themes of a skilful preacher! Without any double sense, or occult meaning, or forced allegory, or anagogical process, he can go any where in the wide field of Scripture, and find something that is useful and instructive. Such a preacher would be among the last to part with the Old Testament.

Thus far I have given mere hints; and these are all which time and place permit. I must not quit the subject, however, without adding a few more.

I have said, that rarely will one find any considerable portion of the Old Testament, where there is nothing in it of the *local* and *temporal* that must be abstracted, in order for us to reduce it to practice or present use. In the devotional Psalms even, there are references to places and modes of worship, which we must separate and distinguish from those sentiments by which we are now to be profited. The Psalms of complaint, of thanksgiving, of imprecation, and others, all have something which savours of time and place and circumstances. These we must omit; excepting that in the *exegesis* of the Psalm we must treat them as essential, but not in the practical use of it.

It is so with the Mosaic laws. Many, even most of them, have something attached to them or connected with them, which is *Jewish*, and therefore local and temporary. Even the *ten commandments* are not altogether an exception to this. When we are required to honour our father and mother, we are commanded to do what will always be a duty at all times, among all nations. But when the promise is added, that we *shall have long life in the land of Canaan*, in consequence of filial duty, this is a part which belonged only to the Jews. The promise to us, is a higher and a spiritual reward. The Gospel holds out no mere earthly promises other than what virtue generally holds out, by pointing us to the consequences which follow the practice of it.

I would say also, that " visiting the iniquity of the fathers upon the children, to the third and fourth generation,"(which is a part of another commandment,) has an *oriental* shape; for in the East, punishment for any high misdemeanor usually involved, as it still does, the whole of one's posterity in the same consequences which himself must suffer. What remains for us is, to regard the command as threatening severe and unmitigated punishment.

So I might go through the whole Pentateuch, yea, through all the historical and prophetical books, and apply the same principles with the like results. It does indeed require some good measure of sobriety, of discretion, and discrimination, always to make the separation between the local and temporal and the permanent, in a proper manner. And so it does rightly to appreciate the figurative language of Scripture, its metaphors and its allegories. The man whose mind is adequate to this task, may surely be fitted to perform the other. Indeed, most men of any tolerable education and of good common sense, can perform the task in question with little danger of erring, except in a few of the more difficult cases. To make the distinctions in question, is a matter, I may also remark, which really belongs to the *practical* commentaries upon the Scriptures; and some of them have in part performed it. But alas! how few of the authors of these have been distinguished for a profound critical and exegetical knowledge of the Scriptures! How few have satisfied the claims of the *reason* and *understanding* of men! Many of them abound in remarks full of pious feeling; and some of them show an extensive knowledge of Christian experience in matters of religion. But all this may be, without shedding any new light on the path of the ignorant and the inquiring. Pages, I had almost said volumes, of some of them may be read without meeting with any such light. The consequence of course is, that in many, perhaps in most cases, reading of this sort begins, after a while, to weary him who performs it, and he comes to it as to a task prescribed, rather than a privilege to be desired. It cannot be expected that such reading will be long practised. A commentary that would give us simply what is to be fairly learned from every part of the Old Testament, in respect to present duty, or as to doctrine, and which would do this throughout the Scriptures, is one of the things yet to be; for I cannot think that it now is. God is preparing men, I doubt not, for the accomplishment of such a work; one in which all the results of critical and exegetical study shall be embodied, and united with all that eminent Christian experience may suggest or teach. May such a work be hastened in its time!

Many good men, in treating of Old Test. matters, and explaining the contents of these books, seem to think that they are at liberty to pursue allegory and type and anagogical processes, to any extent that they please. A greater mistake can hardly be made, in so important a concern. The moment a reader or hearer gets possession of the idea, that a writer or preacher is merely addressing himself to his imagination and fancy, he ceases to give him his serious confidence. He may be amused—greatly amused, if we must concede it, by the ingenuity and vivid fancy of his interpreter; but after all he will with difficulty be brought to believe that the sacred writers addressed themselves to readers in the way of *amusement.* His first feeling, after a little of wonder or perhaps of admiration is over, is indifference. His next is uneasiness in reading or hearing things of this nature. It is well if the matter does not end in contempt of the whole.

I would that the Old Testament were employed oftentimes in quite a different way from that which is not uncommon in resorting to it. What can we say of those teachers, who find just as full and complete a revelation in the Old Testament of every Christian doctrine, as in the New ? For example; the doctrine of the *Trinity* is found as completely there, as in the New Testament. Yet the Saviour, in reference even to Moses, says, that "no man hath seen God at any time; the only begotten Son, who is in the bosom of the Father, *he hath declared him;*" John i. 18. Were the Jews *Trinitarians* before the coming of Christ ? I know of no satisfactory evidence of this fact. All the efforts to prove it have ended in mere appeals to *cabbalizing* Jews, who lived long after the New Testament was written. It is the light which the New Testament casts upon various passages of the Old, and that only, which enables us to bring the Old Testament to bear upon this doctrine. It remained for Christ to make the full revelation of this. It was only by the incarnation, that the Trinity of the Godhead was fully developed. And when the New Testament asserts, that this or that thing was done by Christ, or the Logos, under the ancient dispensation, or that this or that was spoken by him, it is only then that we come to a full knowledge of any specific nature, as it respects the Old Testament, concerning the *persons* of the Godhead. In this way, the Old Testament does indeed contribute important aid in making us acquainted with the doctrine of the Trinity.

Take another instance, in respect to the immortality of the soul and a future state. Paul says of Christ, that "he has abolished death, and *brought life and immortality to light through the gospel;*" 2 Tim. i. 10. But if all this was revealed and understood before the coming of Christ, on what can this assertion be grounded ? Not that the Hebrews were entirely ignorant, as many have asserted, of a future state. Were they inferior, in this respect, to their neighbours the Egyptians and the Greeks ? Not that some such men as Enoch, and Abraham, and David, and Isaiah, had no proper views of future rewards and punishments. The apostle explicitly asserts (Heb. xi.) that they had. But still, it was reserved for the Gospel to turn Jewish twilight into broad Christian day. It has done so. But in expounding the Bible under its influence, we must attribute no more to the Old Testament than belongs to it. The glory of the Gospel is not to be taken away, and given to a mere introductory dispensation. The ministration of the Law had indeed its glory; but the apostle assures us, that "it now has [comparatively] no glory, by reason of that which excelleth."

Let these and the like great principles be always kept in view. We need not become *Judaizers*, because we maintain the authenticity of the Old Testament. Its day has passed. But how could a Divine religion be revealed in it, and yet none of the principles inculcated by the Gospel be exhibited ? The thing was impossible. That we should love God supremely, and our neighbour as ourselves, was always taught—always urged. But a thousand things in respect to the detail of all the developments of these great principles, are different in the Old Testament from what is demanded by the New. Let us fully recognise this, and thank God for our better light. But our gratitude for the Gospel need not lead us to scepticism about the Jewish Scriptures, nor to any undervaluing of them. Very different must the state of our minds be which would lead us to do this, from that of Paul, who so often resorted to them in order to show that Jesus was the Christ. We should regard them in the light of a *preface* or of an *introduction* to the Gospel. Why should the book be admitted, and the preface, which explains the nature of it, be thrown away ?

It would be endless to particularize all the wrong uses which are made, even by many Christian ministers, of the Old Testament, and the violence often done to it in order to make it speak as men wish. It might be a profitable employment to present " the cry of injured texts," and plead their cause before an impartial tribunal. But my present object forbids me to enlarge upon this part of my subject.

I cannot well doubt, that not a few intelligent minds are

rendered somewhat averse to the Old Testament, on account of the many irrelevant appeals to it which are made both in and out of the pulpit, and the irrelevant quotations made from it. Books of such a peculiar nature as Job and Ecclesiastes, for example, are resorted to with as much confidence for *proof-texts*, as if they were all *preceptive*, and not an account of disputes and doubts about religious matters. Job xix. 25, seq., is constantly quoted, to show the patriarch's knowledge of a Messiah to come, and of the doctrine of the resurrection, notwithstanding the context and the tenor of the whole book are totally of a different nature.* The Psalms that breathe forth imprecations are appealed to by some, as justifying the spirit of vengeance under the Gospel, instead of being regarded as the expression of a peculiar state of mind in the writer, and of his imperfect knowledge with regard to the full spirit of forgiveness. Thanks for national blessings, and gratitude for individual deliverances from personal danger, are turned into expressions of gratitude for blessings purely spiritual, and for deliverances merely spiritual. There is indeed not much if any harm in this ; but still, it is on the whole better always to let the Bible speak just what it simply says, and no more. The practice of straining the construction of it in any way, gives rise to many improper liberties with it. Sceptics are always ready to take advantage of this ; and it is not best to give them occasion to exult over the weakness or the prejudices of its advocates.

I have hardly touched upon the subject of unlimited licence in the matter of *types* and *double sense* and *allegorical* exposition. The boundless liberties of this nature, which have been taken in days that are past, is too well known to need description. Every conspicuous person and thing has been regarded as a type of Christ, or of his church, until at last it comes to this, that all the ancient world existed and acted only in the capacity of types or foreshadowings of persons or events to come. All the articles of ornament

---

* The writer here settles the meaning of this much-canvassed passage in too summary a way. A great deal can be and has been said for the view he rejects, while as much unquestionably has been advanced in favour of the view he adopts. It would have been better, therefore, to have spoken of the passage with more caution and less confidence. D.

or furniture for the tabernacle and temple, were mere patterns of something that was to be attached to the new temple under the new dispensation. Even the trays, and bowls, and tongs, and snuffers, and candlesticks, bore a significant and not unimportant part, as it respected the Messianic times ; and of course all offices and duties, of priests and Levites and servitors, must have their proper significance. Any thing which befell Moses, or Joshua, or David, or other conspicuous personages, the story of which is found in the Old Testament, becomes, under such a process, and by virtue of a ὑπόνοια or *occult sense*, full of significance under the new order of things. Launched on a boundless ocean, and without chart or compass, the allegorists seem intent only upon rapid sailing ; it matters little in what direction.

Public taste has, some time since, begun to correct these extravagances. But every now and then the doubter of the ancient Scriptures meets with them still, and curls his lip in proud disdain. No wonder. " Si naturam furcâ expellas, usque recurret." Violence done to the understanding and to sober common sense, although it may be slow-footed, will be certain to avenge itself at last. If there is any book in all the world addressed to the sober reason and judgment of men, that book is the Bible. It is written by men, addressed to men, and designed for men. Of course it adopts a human and intelligible manner of address throughout. God has shown his paternal condescension to the weaknesses of men, in all this. The Scriptures, written in any other manner, could be of but little profit to us. And when we see methods of interpretation applied to them, which no other book will bear, and which would hold any one up to scorn if he should adopt them in explaining a Classic, how can it be expected, that the understanding and reason will not distrust them, and sooner or later be sure to revolt against them?

Among all the abuses of the Old Testament, none are more conspicuous than those which result from *sectarian* views and purposes. What a mere lump of wax does the Bible become in the hands of a zealous defender of sect, perfectly mouldable at his pleasure. No laws of language or of grammar stand in his way. The original intention of the writer of the Scripture is little or nothing to the purpose. The *occult* meaning is summoned to his aid; and this is always ready, at his bidding, to assume every possible form. Armed in this way, his antagonists are cut down by whole ranks at a blow, and the *standard* of sect waves speedily over that of the Bible.

Perhaps the *prophecies* suffer most of all from party spirit and narrow, partial views of exegesis. A popular writer, who is much more conspicuous for eloquence and imagination than for philology or discriminating powers of mind, rises up and proclaims great events at hand, or not far distant. The books of Daniel and the Apocalypse, above all, are thrown into the furnace, "heated seven times more than it is wont to be," and there comes out from the crucible a new and splendid metal, the result of wondrous combination and composition. The nations, the events, the ecclesiastical establishments, the heresies, of modern Christian countries, are all discovered in the reflection of this shining compound. Above all, the *successor of St. Peter* finds himself placed at the head of all the indications that are prophetic. It matters not whether a book is written to instruct a church, or to console one amidst the evils and sufferings of persecution; nor even whether it was addressed to the Babylonian Jews in exile; the same conspicuous personage, Peter's successor, and his attendants, fill all the foreground of every picture. The question as to the *edification* of those to whom the prophecies were *originally* addressed, has nothing to do with the exposition of the prophet's work. The only thing or personage that can fill the eye of a prophet, when he takes into view the new dispensation, must be the *pope*. No other beast of "seven heads and ten horns" ever made or could make its appearance; no other "scarlet beast, full of the names of blasphemy," has ever presented itself before the eyes of a prophetic seer; none other but she whom this beast bears, "the mother of harlots," has ever held in her hands the "cup of abominations" and been "drunk with the blood of saints." And then the partisan, in his overflowing zeal, would fain compel us to say, whether we can suppose that Daniel, or John, or any other prophet, was not a full-blooded Protestant? And such being the case, he wishes to know, whether such a prophet could ever think or prophesy concerning any other beast than the pope?

Such a use of the prophetic writings is what we are called to witness every day, even in these times, when the rage for type, and allegory, and double sense, and occult meaning, has in a very considerable measure abated. Protestants, not well furnished with other arms against the papacy, resort to this weapon, which is always ready at hand, and kept indeed tolerably well burnished by use. Alas! the misfortune is, that the weapon has two edges; and in its reverberating stroke, (for it is sure to make one,) cuts the assailant as deeply as he had wounded his antagonist. Another generation must pass before this battle will be over. And then, when time has shown, beyond contradiction, that all the calculations of prognosticators about the *times* designated in Daniel and the Apocalypse are clearly frustrated, confidence in such interpretations will vanish as a matter of course. The *pope* seen by John, and described by him! Then, in John's time, (i. e. about A. D. 68, when the Apocalypse was written,) there had, according to Rev. xvii. 10, *already been five popes* who were dead; one was then living and reigning; and one then to come, whose time would be short. And besides this—what a precious *consolation* to the poor bleeding and disconsolate churches of that period, to be told, that out of the bosom of that very church and religion which they so loved and honoured, would spring the most wicked, formidable, persecuting, and permanent enemy that the church had ever seen! *Consolation*, with a witness!

Sed manum—There is no end to abuses of this sort, whether of the Old Testament or of the New. Yet even the sacred cause of true Protestantism cannot defend them, or apologize for them. It must be true, that this cause invites to the use of no false armour; it asks for no pious fraud to support it. It regards the oracles of God as so immeasurably elevated above all human conceits or party feeling or effort, that it would scorn to employ means so little worthy of confidence as those in question.

I must say one word, before I lay down my pen, in respect to some GENERAL VIEWS of this great subject, viz. the use of the Old Testament.

There are not a few persons, who seem to feel, that if the Old Testament is a work of *inspiration*, it must stand on the same level with the New, and be equally obligatory. There is something of truth in this, and not a little of error. It is true, that whatever God has sanctioned is of Divine authority. It is true, at any rate in my apprehension it is, that the writers of the Old Testament "spake as they were moved by the Holy Ghost;" 2 Pet. i. 21. But then comes the all-important inquiry, *Did what they said have relation to the church Jewish, or the church Christian? Did it concern the Hebrew nation only for a time, and in their peculiar circumstances; or did it relate to the immutable principles of piety and sound morality?* God may give commands respecting things that are *temporary*, as well as those which are lasting. It is no derogation from his authority, or from the importance of the Old Testament, that temple, and priesthood, and sacrifices, and oblations, and purifications, and distinctions between clean and unclean, have passed away and are no more. And so all that was *peculiar* to the Hebrew nation and their particular condition has passed away. Our only difficulty consists in finding the boundaries between the *local* and *temporal* and the *permanent*. But there is one simple principle that covers all this ground. The main difficulty left is, the *application* of it in some of the nicer cases. The old maxim of the civilians, in regard to laws that are ancient, when the question arises, whether they are still in force, is, *Manente ratione, manet ipsa Lex;* i. e. *So long as the reason of the Law continues, the Law itself is in full force.* This is the compass to guide us, in traversing the whole ground from the beginning of Genesis to the end of Malachi. ALL THAT IS FOUNDED IN THE PERPETUAL RELATIONS OF MEN TO GOD, TO EACH OTHER, AND TO THEMSELVES, AND WHICH IS THE SUBJECT OF PRESCRIPTION, COMMAND, OR INSTRUCTION ON THE PART OF HEAVEN, IS PERMANENT.

But even in cases of this nature, whatever there is in any command or instruction, which concerns merely the *manner* of the thing, and not the essential nature of the duty, is no longer obligatory on us. We have a *new* and a *better* Testament than the ancient. In itself it is a sufficient guide. But we should thankfully accept whatever of confirmation or illustration of our Christian duties there is in the ancient Hebrew Scriptures. Even from the ten commandments, as we have seen, something in respect to the *manner* of promised reward, or of threatened punishment, is to be abated.

If any one now should demand of me to lay down a rule so precise and particular, that every reader of the Old Testament may judge with certainty in every possible case, what is local and temporary, and what is permanent, I can no more do this, than I could prescribe a rule in hermeneutics which would exempt all men from actual error in the interpretation of the figurative language of the Bible. The general principles that I have now developed are plain, practical, and certain in their result when rightly applied. The power to make such an application of them depends not on me, but on the gift of Heaven and the efforts of the inquiring to qualify themselves for the work. I can only speak my good wishes for inquirers; which are, that they may meet with desired success. Nothing but the want of skill or tact, stands in the way of acquiring that which they seek.

Of one thing I am fully persuaded, which is, that a proper use of the Old Testament will be made, in all cases, by no one who cleaves to the notion, that because the Hebrew Scriptures were inspired, they are therefore *absolutely* perfect. Such perfection belongs not to a prefatory or merely introductory dispensation. It is only a *relative* perfection that the Old Testament can claim; and this is comprised in the fact, that it answered the end for which it was given. It was given to the world, or to the Jewish nation, in its *minority*. It was given to "the heir, when he was under tutors and governors, and differed not from a servant, although he was lord of all." It seems difficult for some to believe that God has dealt with the world, as he does with each individual. There is a state of infancy, of childhood, of youth, of maturity, of old age. The same person is an actor in all these stages. And so it has been, and will be, with the world of mankind. The world has had its infancy, its childhood, its youth; it is slowly approaching its maturity. As to its *old age*, I trust it will be like the hoary head of him who is found in the way of righteousness—a crown of glory. Why now should any one insist that a revelation adapted to its minority should be as ample and complete in its requirements, as a revelation intended for its most perfect state? Divine Providence does not convert whole nations in a day from their sin and ignorance. Slow has always been the process and progress. One third or more of the time that the race of men have existed, they had no Bible. It was not until more than a thousand years after the composition of the Old Testament commenced, that it was completed. Why was it not all given at once? And why was not a revelation in writing given to the antediluvians? Why did not Enoch, Noah, Abraham, write one? Can any one answer these questions, except in the way in which I have already answered them? The race of man, as a whole, has all the different stages of development assigned to it.

Let us now proceed a step further. With the exception of such sins as were highly dishonourable to God and injurious to the welfare of men, the rules of duty were not in all cases strictly drawn. So our Saviour seems to have regarded the matter. When he reproached the Pharisees for the frequency of divorces which they allowed, and they appealed to Moses as sanctioning it, Jesus replied and said, "Moses, *because of the hardness of your hearts*, suffered you to put away your wives; but from the beginning it was not so;" Matt. xix. 8. I am well aware, that there are casuists at the present day, who think Moses to have judged very wrongly in this case. And so in regard to his permission of slavery, and some other things. We cannot reason, I allow, in all cases with entire certainty, as to what is allowable under the Gospel, because it was allowed under the old dispensation. Polygamy was allowable; and if concubinage was not, it was generally practised, and does seem to have been regarded as not forbidden, but only regulated. Slavery was allowed. Great latitude of divorce, at the will of the husband, (but not of the wife,) was allowed. Does the Gospel allow any of these? I know that some serious and well-meaning men are disposed to argue, that the Gospel allows of slavery. It is my opinion also, that where it has become a part of the constitution of any society of men, the Gospel does not require the whole system to be broken up and abandoned in a single day; for this might endanger the welfare of the whole. But I can never entertain a doubt, that the precepts and principles of the Gospel forbid the *making* of slaves. When it is required of us, that we should *love our neighbour as ourselves*; and in explanation of this it is also required, that we *should do to others whatever we would that others should do to us;* and when, with all this, it is expressly declared that *God has made of* ONE BLOOD *all the nations that dwell on all the face of the earth;* I understand this as settling all questions respecting any slavery, which is not the result of crime or a forfeiture of liberty by evil-doing, or of voluntary compact on the part of the slave.

Moses, then, did allow—the ancient dispensation did allow —of some things which are no longer permitted. In this an important principle is involved. The Old Testament morality, in respect to some points of *relative* duty, is behind that of the Gospel. Why, then, should we regard the Old Testament as exhibiting an absolute model of perfection, in its precepts and its doctrines? In some cases, most plainly this is not true. It needs discretion and judgment, then, to know how to argue properly from the Old Testament to the New. But why should the Old Testament be reproached for not having accomplished all which the Gospel has? Was it designed for such an end? Certainly it was not. Is it just matter of reproach, then, that while it is adapted to all the purposes which it was designed to subserve, it falls short of the higher mark which the Messianic legislation has reached? I trow not.

If preachers and teachers would but remember these plain and simple facts, they would be less troubled with that in the Old Testament which now presents them with difficulty. The Gospel is ever and always the *ultima ratio* in all matters of religion and morals. It is the supreme court, the highest tribunal. Whatever there is in the Old Testament, which falls short of this, or is at variance with this, is of course not obligatory on us. With certain states of society, and certain prejudices of men in regard to matters toward which they are naturally inclined, God has dealt more leniently in his ancient legislation, than in the Gospel. "The times of ignorance God winked at." But where light and knowledge abound, he will no longer do this.

If you ask, then, as many will doubtless be inclined to do, what test shall we apply in all cases to Old Testament precepts? My general answer would be, Apply to them the rules of the New Testament. Is it not certain, that the New

Testament is a *more perfect* rule of doctrine and of duty? What hinders us, then, from putting the Old Testament always to such a test? And if there be cases that are not specifically touched upon in the New Testament, which are brought to view in the Old, yet analogy may always guide us in inquiries of such a nature. The Spirit of New Testament doctrine, morality, modes of worship, (so far as modes are touched upon,) is always to be applied to judging of our obligations to the ancient Scriptures.

Will you ask me, then, 'Of what use is the Old Testament to us? If it is thus to be altogether subordinate and secondary, why not dismiss it from the lofty eminence of an authority?' I feel no difficulty, at least in satisfying myself, in relation to these questions. Is it of no advantage to be able to appeal to the ancient revelation in all cases of religious and moral precept or doctrine, and to find there the immutable principles of virtue and piety sanctioned, and thus to know that they are the same in every age? Is it no advantage to learn how God dealt with his ancient church for some 1500 and more years? Is there no advantage in having a *religious* history of the past, which is sketched by an unerring hand? a church history which has a Divine author? Is there no gain to the devout Christian, in seeing embodied in the Psalms and in the prophets, the workings of piety in the distinguished minds of ancient days? Is there no gain to the ethical teacher, in having before him the inexhaustible store of prudential and practical maxims in the book of Proverbs? Have Christian preachers no sympathies in common with the preachers, i. e. the prophets, of old? The New Testament gives us a precept, or teaches a doctrine; is it no satisfaction to find practical exhibitions of the precept, and confirmations of the doctrine, in the Old Testament? The Christian church is built upon the Jewish; not by destroying the foundations of the latter, but only by demolishing parts of the superstructure, in order to make the whole more perfect; and hast thou no holy curiosity to know what the ancient foundations were? In a word, the Old Testament teaches that God is all and in all, as well as the New; but from the Old Testament we learn, in a peculiar manner, that he may develope himself in a variety of ways, and that he has so done.

SECT. XXII. UNDER THE GOSPEL DISPENSATION. 391

True Christian liberality may be learned and enforced by considerations of this nature, as well as the duty of submission and obedience.

There are imperfections in the ancient system; but they are such as the nature of the case rendered necessary. They are in accordance with the principle of the slow and gradual amendment of the race of man. The record of our infancy and childhood, if it could be fully placed before us, would create a deep interest in the breast of every individual so far as his own story is concerned. Why, then, should the record of the church's infancy be spurned at, as though it was not deserving of our attention?

But I have said enough. It is time to withdraw my hand. And this I will do, as soon as I have said a few words on the general subject of charges made by Mr. Norton, against the *morality* and the *spirit* of the Old Testament writings.

It is not my object to enter at all into any discussion on these points. I have said, at the first, that I should leave these matters to be canvassed by others. Enough that I have shown the fact, that the Hebrew Scriptures were admitted as Divine and authoritative by Christ and his apostles. They must have had the same difficulties before their minds that we now have. But these did not hinder their forming an opinion in favour of the Divine origin and authority of the Hebrew Scriptures. How can the Old Testament be so vile a book as Mr. Norton represents it to be? Why have not Christians of every age been stumbled by it? And yet they have not. In some way or other, they have been brought to feel very differently from Mr. Norton in respect to it. Is it that they have had no sensitive consciences? no keen discernment of τὸ καλόν and τὸ πρεπόν? I trust not. Mr. Norton has scanned Old Testament matters in the light of New Testament revelation, and then passed sentence of condemnation upon the imperfect, because it is not perfect. Is this equitable dealing? Is it any proof that sacrifices and offerings were not Divinely authorized of old, because they are abolished now? Is it any satisfactory objection against this or that specific thing in the Old Testament, that the New has better arranged or modified it? Is it conclusive against the history or character of

David and other potentates, that they did things in war which were common in those days, but which the Gospel and a better state of things now forbid?

But I have done. Others will doubtless meet Mr. Norton on grounds of this nature which he has occupied. If they have enlightened and adequate views of the real difference between the Christian and the ancient dispensation, they need not fear the issue of the contest. How can we properly claim wisdom and light so superior to that of the founders of Christianity, as to reject the books which they have sanctioned? This is the direct, fair, and simple question. Let those affirm that we may make such a claim, who have made up their minds that we are not bound by their decision. I must believe, that the *disciple* is not above his MASTER.

One thing is plain from the present state of religious dispute among us; and this is, that the time has now come, when the advocates of revelation are to be separated from its opposers. How can two walk together unless they are agreed? I do not say, agreed in all the minutiæ—the detail of religious sentiments, but in respect to the very basis of all which is properly called Christianity. If there be no *revelation*, there is no Christianity; and if there be a New Testament and a Christian religion, then there is an Old Testament which is entitled to our high regard, our attentive study, and a listening ear.

It has become plain, that the battle which has been going on over most European ground for these forty or fifty years past, has at last come even to us, and we can no longer decline the contest. Unbelief in the Voltaire and the Thomas Paine style we have coped with, and in a measure gained the victory. But now it comes in the shape of philosophy, literature, criticism, philology, knowledge of antiquity, and the like. Hume's arguments against miracles, which some had thought to be dead and buried, have been *exhumed*, clothed with a new and splendid costume, and commended to the world by many among the most learned men in Europe. Before these, all revelation falls alike, both Old Testament and New. And if Mr. Norton remonstrates, as he does, against the sophistry of these arguments, yet he leaves us, after all, just where he found us. None of the

Old Testament, according to him, can be relied on. The New can be trusted only in cases where what is said agrees with our own view of things. This is honestly and plainly his simple position. I prefer to meet De Wette and Mr. Parker's views. We know where to find them. We cannot well mistake them.

Will it be taken in good part, (as it is meant,) if I say one word to another and different class of men? *Cum pace omnium*, I would say, Let those, now, who have stood aloof so long as to the matter of acquaintance with German productions, ask what is to be done with the contest in hand, in the shape that it has assumed. Have we not a right to expect from them, at least, that they will show their faith by their works? What I mean is, Have we not a right to expect that they will enter into the battle which is going on, clad with the panoply of days of yore, which they regard as the only trusty armour? For one, I will bid *God speed* to every stroke which they may strike in this way, provided it does any execution. It does not look well for them to shrink from the contest, after all that they have so long and often said to excite suspicion of others who have pursued a somewhat different course of study, and to cover their names with a kind of reproach. The time of trial for both parties (if they must be so named) has now come. No one will deny this. For myself, I shall with all my heart rejoice, if they show themselves ready and prepared to meet it. At least they have had sufficient time to make preparation; and the religious public have long since expected something to meet the allegations of Mr. Norton. In the mean while, I have had other engagements that must be met, and waited anxiously for some other and better advocate of revelation to make his appearance. I hope it will not be deemed a matter of reproach to me, that I have thought it important for defence, to find out if possible whence the armour of our assailants comes, and to meet them, if it may be, with arms adapted to new times and new methods of attack. I am indeed slow to believe, that we of the present day are bound to keep ourselves ignorant of the strength and resources of our assailants. The contest has truly become one, as I have said, PRO ARIS ET FOCIS. The question whether Christianity is to be the predominant religion of this country, or to yield to philosophic infidelity, is soon to be settled. Bowed down in some measure under the weight of years, and tottering under the long-continued pressure of bodily infirmities, I have still, perhaps most rashly, thrown myself into the arena of contest ; and there I mean to remain, so long as I can wield a weapon, however light, or lift up a prayer to the great Head of the church for the success of his cause. The standard under which I have enlisted waves aloft over the battle-ground, and bears the inscription in characters of light : CHRIST AND THE CHURCH ; THE NEW TESTAMENT AND THE OLD. I hope and trust in God that I shall never—never desert it.

APPENDIX.

CONTAINING AND EXHIBITING THE MOST IMPORTANT DOCUMENTS, EXCEPTING THE NEW TESTAMENT, TO SHOW WHAT WERE THE ANCIENT CANONICAL BOOKS OF THE HEBREWS.

No. I.

Prologue to the Wisdom of Sirach.*

Πολλῶν καὶ μεγάλων ἡμῖν διὰ τοῦ νόμου καὶ τῶν προφητῶν καὶ τῶν ἄλλων τῶν κατ' αὐτοὺς ἠκολουθηκότων δεδομένων, ὑπὲρ ὧν δέον ἐστὶν ἐπαινεῖν τὸν Ἰσραὴλ παιδείας καὶ σοφίας· καὶ ὡς οὐ μόνον αὐτοὺς τοὺς ἀναγινώσκοντας δέον ἐστὶν ἐπιστήμονας γίνεσθαι, ἀλλὰ καὶ τοῖς ἐκτὸς δύνασθαι τοὺς φιλομαθοῦντας χρησίμους εἶναι καὶ λέγοντας καὶ γράφοντας· ὁ πάππος μου Ἰησοῦς ἐπὶ πλεῖον ἑαυτὸν δοὺς εἴς τε τὴν τοῦ νόμου καὶ τῶν προφητῶν καὶ τῶν ἄλλων πατρίων βιβλίων ἀνάγνωσιν, καὶ ἐν τούτοις ἱκανὴν ἕξιν περιποιησάμενος, προήχθη καὶ αὐτὸς συγγράψαι τι τῶν εἰς παιδείαν καὶ σοφίαν ἀνηκόντων, ὅπως οἱ φιλομαθεῖς, καὶ τούτων ἔνοχοι γενόμενοι, πολλῷ μᾶλλον ἐπιπροσθῶσι διὰ τῆς ἐννόμου βιώσεως. Παρακέκλησθε οὖν μετ' εὐνοίας καὶ προσοχῆς τὴν ἀνάγνωσιν ποιεῖσθαι, καὶ συγγνώμην ἔχειν ἐφ' οἷς ἂν δοκῶμεν τῶν κατὰ τὴν ἑρμηνείαν πεφιλοπονημένων τισὶ τῶν λέξεων ἀδυναμεῖν, οὐ γὰρ ἰσοδυναμεῖ αὐτὰ ἐν ἑαυτοῖς ἑβραϊστὶ λεγόμενα, καὶ ὅταν μεταχθῇ εἰς ἑτέραν γλῶσσαν. Οὐ μόνον δὲ ταῦτα, ἀλλὰ καὶ αὐτὸς ὁ νόμος, καὶ αἱ προφητεῖαι, καὶ τὰ λοιπὰ τῶν βιβλίων οὐ μικρὰν ἔχει τὴν διαφορὰν ἐν ἑαυτοῖς λεγόμενα. Ἐν γὰρ τῷ ὀγδόῳ καὶ τριακοστῷ ἔτει ἐπὶ τοῦ Εὐεργέτου βασιλέως παραγενηθεὶς εἰς Αἴγυπτον καὶ συγχρονίσας, εὗρον οὐ μικρᾶς παιδείας ἀφόμοιον. Ἀναγκαιότατον

* This Prologue was probably written about 130 B. C. The Book itself probably about 180 B. C.

ἐξέμην αὐτὸς προσενέγκασθαι τινὰ σπουδὴν καὶ φιλοπονίαν τοῦ
μεθηρμονεῦσαι τήνδε τὴν βίβλον· πολλὴν γὰρ ἀγρυπνίαν καὶ
ἐπιστήμην προπενεγκάμενος ἐν τῷ διαστήματι τοῦ χρόνου πρὸς
τὸ ἐπὶ πέρας ἄγοντα τὸ βιβλίον ἐκδόσθαι, καὶ τοῖς ἐν τῇ παροι-
κίᾳ βουλομένοις φιλομαθεῖν, προκατασκευαζομένοις τὰ ἤδη ἐν
νόμῳ βιοτεύειν.

ENGLISH TRANSLATION. Since so many and important things have been imparted to us by *the Law, the Prophets, and other [works] of the like kind* which have followed, for which one must needs praise Israel on account of learning and wisdom; and inasmuch as not only those who read ought to be well-informed, but those who are devoted to learning should be able to profit, both in the way of speaking and writing, such as are foreigners; my grandfather, Jesus, having devoted himself very much to the reading of *the Law, the Prophets, and the other Books of his country*, and having acquired a good degree of experience in these things, was himself led on to compose something pertaining to instruction and wisdom, so that those desirous of learning, being in possession of these things, might grow much more by a life conformed to the Law.

Ye are invited, therefore, with good will and strict attention to make the perusal, and to take notice whenever we may seem to lack ability, in respect to any of the words which we have laboured to translate. For things in themselves the same, expressed in Hebrew, have not the same force when they are translated into another language. Not only so, but *the Law itself, and the Prophets, and the remaining Books* exhibit no small diversity among themselves as to the modes of expression.

When, in my thirty-eighth year, while Ptolemy Euergetes was king, I came to Egypt and took up my residence there, I found an exemplar of no small learning. I deemed it altogether necessary for myself to apply some diligence and industry to the interpretation of this book; for I expended much vigilance and study, during that interval of time, that, bringing to an end this book, I might publish it for those in a foreign country who wish to be learners, and so to regulate their habits as to live in conformity with the Law.

REMARKS. It seems somewhat remarkable, that this *grandson* of Sirachides, who appears not to have visited Egypt until he was thirty-eight years of age, should not have found a copy of his grandfather's book in Palestine; particularly since the latter assures us (l. 27) that he was an inhabitant or native of Jerusalem. The fact that he wrote in *Hebrew*, is enough to render this altogether probable; for the *Egyptian* Jews, if we may judge of them by the case of Philo, the greatest of them all, were moderate proficients in this sacred tongue. However, the fact that the *Wisdom of Sirach* had a currency, and probably some weight of authority in Egypt, falls in well with the history of the other apocryphal books. Egypt was the hot-bed in which nearly all of these somewhat sickly plants sprang up and were nurtured. This was natural. The Palestine Jews were rigid *Canonists*. Even the weight of character and learning which Sirachides possessed, could give his book no great currency and no authority there. There the Jews all partook of the spirit of their leaders ; and so it was out of question to add another book to the Canon. But the Egyptian Jews were far removed from the mother country. They had intercourse with Greek Schools, philosophers, and literati. Their views of *canonical* limits were probably less strictly defined, or at any rate less rigidly adhered to, than those of their Palestine brethren. So, while the grandson of Sirachides found no ἀφόμοιον, (as he calls it,) i. e. no *copy, exemplar*, or (as one might translate) *fac-simile* of his grandfather's work in his native land, he found one at Alexandria, where was more of a literary taste, and less of the feeling which dictated a rigid adherence to the views and traditions of the elders, זקנים.

For the rest, the translator well appreciates the difficulty of translating the Hebrew into Greek ; confesses his fear of occasional error, and begs for the indulgence of the reader, as well as for the exercise of his discrimination. He does not, therefore, lay claim to any inspiration on his part. But how is this matter in respect to the author of the book ? The reader, by referring to p. 224 above, will see, that while he omits making a direct claim to the office of a *prophet*, (which he doubtless knew would be controverted and denied,) he has still intended to be placed at the side of prophets, and take rank among the favourite disciples of Solomon. The whole work is an ambitious imitation of this king's writings. Even the πατέρων ὕμνος near the close, appears to have had its origin in the eulogy of Wisdom in Prov. viii. Moreover the book has many very fine sayings and sentiments in it. I doubt not that it was much better written in *Hebrew*, than it now appears to be in Greek ; and I fully accede to what the translator says about his inability adequately to express the Hebrew original in the Greek language. The Greek of his preface, at least, (which of course is all his own,) has so near an approach to barbarism in its idiom, in the disjointed connexion of the sentences, and in the use of some of the particles, (e. g. γάρ,) as to show that the writer expressed himself with much difficulty, and in the true style of a foreigner. And so it is with much of his translation. Still, it is *Hebrew-Greek*, and even better than some of the Septuagint. I have done my best to give the ideas of the *preface;* but I have been compelled to use some freedom in translating, in order to make the version bearable. Whether I have hit the exact shade of the original meaning in all cases, is of no importance to my present object. That part for which the whole is translated, is quite plain and intelligible.

I cannot refrain from asking here, If the Jews were so facile as to the admission of new books into the Canon, (e. g. Daniel, many of the Psalms, Jonah, &c.,) at a period so late as the Maccabæan times, how came it about, that the *Wisdom of Sirach*, written at Jerusalem and before these times, and making, as we have seen, no small claims on admission to an elevated place, was not even to be found in Palestine some fifty years after this, but was lighted upon only among the distant Egyptians? *Consistency* is a jewel of some value; and if so, why do not those confident neological critics, who so often hoist the standard on which is inscribed MACCABÆAN, and fight in earnest under this banner,—why do they not show us some good and satisfactory reason for the exclusion of such books as the Σοφία Σειράχ from the Palestine Canon, (and even the Jewish Egyptian one,) while books which they place far below this, now occupy, and for more than 1900 years (as they concede) have occupied a place among the sacred Scriptures of the Jews? The whole affair makes greatly against their confident assumptions.

I have only to remark, that in the first sentence of the Prologue, if προφητῶν be regarded as referring to *prophetical books*, (and so I have taken it,) then the ἄλλων which follows must also mean *other books*. I suppose the ἠκολουθηκότων, in this case, to refer to the order of arrangement in the Canon, which had been and still continued, (the appropriate sense of the Perf.,) rather than to the time of writing. *Prophets*, according to the Hebrew idiom, were all the writers of the Scriptures; so that προφητῶν, especially if compared with the preceding νόμον, would seem to mean the *books* so called, in the case before us. But still the participle ἀκολουθηκότων may appear rather to indicate *persons* who followed the so-called prophets, (also considered as persons,) if we look to the κατ' αὐτούς by which it is accompanied. So De Wette has taken it. I do not consider this construction, however, as being certain; for the gender of αὐτούς, if it refers to books, would in this case be regulated by its antecedent προφητῶν. In case *prophets* means persons, then the prophets, who were the authors of the books belonging to the Old Testament which bear their names, are meant, and *the others who have followed* must mean other writers of the Jewish Scriptures who lived after them. But this can be understood only as to the greater portion of them ; for Haggai, Zechariah, and in particular Malachi, have always been regarded by the Jews as among the latest writers in their Canon. Difficulties therefore lie in the way of De Wette's interpretation. Analogy with the passage in the second sentence—"the Law, the Prophets, and the other patrical books"—would rather plead for the interpretation which I have put upon the passage, notwithstanding the difficulty in respect to the participle ἀκαλουθηκότων.

Finally, τῶν ἄλλων πατρίων βιβλίων, with the definite article prefixed, and placed by the side of τοῦ νόμου and τῶν προφητῶν, which must in their very nature be *definite*, does beyond all reasonable doubt limit the *other books* in question here, to the complement or remainder of the books which made up the Holy Scriptures. The *triplex division*, therefore, as in later times, lies on the very face of this whole representation. The nature of the appeal takes it for granted, that this was well known, and would be universally understood. Of course, the usage of thus dividing the Scriptures must have been established for a considerable period, anterior to that in which the translator wrote, and anterior to the age of his grandfather.

No. II.

Passages in the Vita Contemplativa of Philo Judæus.—*Opp. II.* p. 475, *edit. Mangey.* (flor. A. D. 40.)

PHILO, in praising a contemplative life and in giving various examples of it, comes at last to the *Therapeutæ* or

Essenes, (== אסיא, *medici, healers,*) whose devotional practices he thus describes : Ἐν ἑκάστῃ δὲ οἰκίᾳ ἱερόν, ὃ καλεῖται σεμνεῖον καὶ μοναστήριον, ἐν ᾧ μονούμενοι τὰ τοῦ σεμνοῦ βίου μυστήρια τελοῦνται· μηδὲν εἰσκομίζοντες, μὴ ποτόν, μὴ σίτον, μηδέν τι τῶν ἄλλων ὅσα πρὸς τὰς τοῦ σώματος χρείας ἀναγκαῖα, ἀλλὰ νόμους, καὶ λόγια θεσπισθέντα διὰ προφητῶν, καὶ ὕμνους καὶ τὰ ἄλλα οἷς ἐπιστήμη καὶ εὐσέβεια συναύξονται καὶ τελειοῦνται. . . . . . Ἐντυγχάνοντες γὰρ τοῖς ἱεροῖς γράμμασι, φιλοσοφοῦσι τὴν πάτριον φιλοσοφίαν ἀλληγοροῦντες, ἐπειδὴ σύμβολα τὰ τῆς ῥητῆς ἑρμηνείας νομίζουσι φύσεως ἀποκεκρυμμένης, ἐν ὑπονοίαις δηλουμένης. Ἔστι δὲ αὐτοῖς καὶ συγγράμματα παλαιῶν ἀνδρῶν, οἳ τῆς αἱρέσεως ἀρχηγέται γενόμενοι πολλὰ μνημεῖα τῆς ἀλληγορουμένης ἰδέας ἀπέλιπον.

TRANSLATION. In every house is a sanctuary, which is called *sacred place* or *monastery*, in which, being alone, they perform the mysteries of a holy life; introducing nothing into it, neither drink, nor bread-corn, nor any of the other things which are necessary for the wants of the body, but *the laws, and oracles predicted by the prophets, and hymns and other* [*writings*] by which knowledge and piety are increased and perfected. . . . Addressing themselves to the sacred writings, they philosophize their country's philosophy, interpreting allegorically, inasmuch as they regard those things which admit a plain interpretation, as symbols of something that is hidden and is indicated merely by ὑπόνοια [i. e. an *under* or *secondary* meaning]. They have also writings of their elders, who, being leaders of the sect, left many monuments of their allegorical notions.

A doubt has been raised here, whether *hymns and other* [*writings*] *by which knowledge and piety are increased and perfected,* is meant to designate a portion of the Scriptures. I do not see that there is good room, however, for reasonable doubt. The intimate junction of these with the Law and the Prophets; the manner in which their contents are described; and above all, the express distinction between these books and others which were peculiar to the sect of the Essenes, and which were composed by the elders and leaders of the sect, make it quite plain that the *hymns and other writings* belonged to the Scriptures. Even if these circumstances did not decide the case, the fact that Philo, immediately after having mentioned these three classes of books, speaks of them as ἱερὰ γράμματα, *sacred writings*, decides the point. In the days of Philo, then, the Jewish Scriptures in the hands of the Therapeutæ consisted of three great divisions, in the same manner as we have seen in the book of Sirach. No intimation is any where given, that the Essenes had a different Canon from that of the other Jews. Indeed, all the knowledge we have of them would lead us to reject this idea. And as the sect was ancient, and rigidly adhered to the practices of their fathers, we may well draw the conclusion, that the *triplex* division of Scripture here described by Philo, had long existed in the usages of the Jewish nation.

No. III.

Passage from Josephus, contra Apionem, *Lib. I.* § 8. (Born A. D. 37.)

Οὐ γὰρ μυριάδες βιβλίων εἰσὶ παρ' ἡμῖν, ἀσυμφώνων καὶ μαχομένων· δύο δὲ μόνα πρὸς τοῖς εἴκοσι Βιβλία, τοῦ παντὸς ἔχοντα χρόνου τὴν ἀναγραφήν, τὰ δικαίως Θεῖα πεπιστευμένα. Καὶ τούτων πέντε μέν ἐστι τὰ Μωϋσέως, ἃ τούς τε νόμους περιέχει, καὶ τὴν -ῆς ἀνθρωπογονίας παράδοσιν μέχρι τῆς αὐτοῦ τελευτῆς. Οὗτος ὁ χρόνος ἀπολείπει τρισχιλίων ὀλίγον ἐτῶν. Ἀπὸ δὲ τῆς Μωϋσέως τελευτῆς μέχρι τῆς Ἀρταξέρξου τοῦ μετὰ Ξέρξην Περσῶν βασιλέως ἀρχῆς, [ἀρχῆς is omitted in Euseb.,] οἱ μετὰ Μωϋσῆν προφῆται τὰ κατ' αὐτοὺς πραχθέντα συνέγραψαν ἐν τρισὶ καὶ δέκα βιβλίοις. Αἱ δὲ λοιπαὶ τέσσαρες ὕμνους εἰς τὸν Θεὸν καὶ τοῖς ἀνθρώποις ὑποθήκας τοῦ βίου περιέχουσιν. Ἀπὸ δ' Ἀρταξέρξου μέχρι τοῦ καθ' ἡμᾶς χρόνου, γέγραπται μὲν ἕκαστα· πίστεως δὲ οὐχ ὁμοίας ἠξίωται τοῖς πρὸ αὐτῶν, διὰ τὸ μὴ γένεσθαι τὴν τῶν προφητῶν ἀκριβῆ διαδοχήν. Δῆλον δ' ἔστιν ἔργῳ πῶς ἡμεῖς τοῖς ἰδίοις γράμμασι πεπιστεύκαμεν, τοσούτου γὰρ αἰῶνος ἤδη παρῳχηκότος, οὔτε προσθεῖναί τις οὐδὲν, οὔτε ἀφελεῖν αὐτῶν, οὔτε μεταθεῖναι τετόλμηκεν. Πᾶσι δὲ συμφυτόν ἐστιν εὐθὺς ἐκ τῆς πρώτης γενέσεως Ἰουδαίοις, τὸ νομίζειν αὐτὰ Θεοῦ δόγματα, καὶ τούτοις ἐμμένειν, καὶ ὑπὲρ αὐτῶν εἰ δέοι θνήσκειν ἡδέως.

TRANSLATION. We have not a countless number of books, discordant and arrayed against each other; but only *two and twenty books*, containing the history of every age, which are justly accredited as divine [old editions of Josephus read merely, "which are justly accredited"—comes from Eusebius' transcript of Josephus in Ecc. Hist. III. 10]; and of these, *five* belong to Moses, which contain both the laws and the history of the generations of men until his death.

This period lacks but little of 3000 years. From the death of Moses, moreover, until the reign of Artaxerxes, [Euseb.—'from the death of Moses to that of Artaxerxes'—and so most of the Codices, omitting ἀρχῆς, *reign*,] king of the Persians after Xerxes, the prophets who followed Moses have described the things which were done during the age of each one respectively, in *thirteen* books. The remaining *four* contain hymns to God, and rules of life for men. From the time of Artaxerxes, moreover, until our present period, all occurrences have been written down; *but they are not regarded as entitled to the like credit with those which precede them, because there was no certain succession of prophets.* Fact has shown what confidence we place in our own writings. For although so many ages have passed away, no one has dared to add to them, nor to take any thing from, nor to make alterations. In all Jews it is implanted, even from their birth, to regard them as being the instructions of God, and to abide stedfastly by them, and if it be necessary, to die gladly for them.

Remarks on this passage are unnecessary, as they are so fully made in the preceding pages, viz. p. 208, seq. Of all the testimony among ancient writers about the Old Testament, this is unquestionably the most important. The intelligence, the connexions, the official character, and the integrity of Josephus, all conspire to render him worthy of the most entire credit. The matter is not one about which he could be in doubt, when he speaks the views and feelings of his countrymen. The latter part of his testimony makes it quite certain, that he did so speak; for he tells us explicitly what the views and feelings of the Jews had always been, in reference to their sacred books. To say as Herbst, many other Romanists, and some of the Neologists do, that Josephus only gives us his own *private* opinion, is saying what is contradicted by his own explicit statement. The appeal to the Talmud, rather than to him, to determine the *ancient* number of the sacred books, respectively contained in the division of the Prophets and of the Hagiography, is altogether uncritical and inadmissible. The admission of such an appeal by Neologists, in order to maintain their favourite views about the *lateness* of Daniel and the Chronicles, shows fully that the spirit of party and of prejudice is not by any means confined to the so-called Orthodox.

No. IV.

Testimony of Melito, bishop of Sardis, (flor. A. D. 170,) presented by Eusebius in his Historia Ecc. Lib. IV. c. 26.

Μελίτων Ὀνησίμῳ τῷ ἀδελφῷ χαίρειν· ἐπειδὴ πολλάκις ἠξίωσας σπουδῇ τῇ πρός τὸν λόγον χρώμενος γενέσθαι σοι ἐκλογάς, ἔκ τε τοῦ νόμου καὶ τῶν προφητῶν περὶ τοῦ Σωτῆρος καὶ πάσης τῆς πίστεως ἡμῶν· ἔτι δὲ καὶ μαθεῖν τὴν τῶν παλαιῶν βιβλίων ἐβουλήθης ἀκρίβειαν, πόσα τὸν ἀριθμὸν καὶ ὁποῖα τὴν τάξιν εἶεν, ἐσπούδασα τὸ τοιοῦτο πρᾶξαι, ἐπιστάμενός σου τὸ σπουδαῖον περὶ τὴν πίστιν, καὶ φιλομαθὲς περὶ τὸν λόγον· ὅτι τε μάλιστα πάντων πόθῳ τῷ πρὸς Θεὸν ταῦτα προκρίνεις, περὶ τῆς αἰωνίου σωτηρίας ἀγωνιζόμενος· ἀνελθὼν οὖν εἰς τὴν ἀνατολὴν, καὶ ἕως τοῦ τόπου γενόμενος ἔνθα ἐκηρύχθη καὶ ἐπράχθη, καὶ ἀκριβῶς μαθὼν τὰ τῆς παλαιᾶς διαθήκης βιβλία, ὑποτάξας ἔπεμψά σοι· ὧν ἔστι τὰ ὀνόματα· Μωϋσέως πέντε· Γένεσις, Ἔξοδος, Λευιτικὸν, Ἀριθμοὶ, Δευτερονόμιον. Ἰησοῦς Ναυῆ, Κριταὶ, Ῥοὺθ, Βασιλειῶν τέσσαρα, Παραλειπομένων δύο. Ψαλμῶν Δαβὶδ, Σολομῶντος Παροιμίαι ἡ καὶ Σοφία, Ἐκκλησιαστής, Ἆσμα Ἀσμάτων, Ἰώβ· Προφητῶν, Ἡσαΐου, Ἱερεμίου, τῶν δώδεκα ἐν μονοβίβλῳ, Δανιὴλ, Ἰεζεκιὴλ, Ἔσδρας· ἐξ ὧν καὶ τὰς ἐκλογὰς ἐποιησάμην, εἰς ἓξ βιβλία διελών.

TRANSLATION. Melito to Onesimus his brother, greeting. Since you have often requested, through the earnest desire that you cherish for the word [of God], that you might have a selection made for you from the Law and the Prophets, which has respect to our Saviour and the whole of our faith; and since moreover you have been desirous to obtain an accurate account of the *ancient books*, both as to their number and their order; I have taken pains to accomplish this, knowing your earnestness in respect to the faith, and your desire for instruction in regard to the word; and most of all, that you, while striving after eternal salvation, through desires after God, give a preference to these things. Making a journey therefore into the east, [Palestine,] and having arrived at the place where these things [i. e. scriptural events] were proclaimed and transacted, I there learned accurately the books of the Old Testament, which I here arrange and transmit to you. The names are as follows: The five books of Moses, Genesis, Exodus, Leviticus, Numbers, Deuteronomy. Then Joshua of Nun, Judges, Ruth, four books of Kings, two of Chronicles. The Psalms of David, the Proverbs of Solomon, (also called Wisdom,) Ecclesiastes, the Song of Songs, Job. Prophets: Isaiah, Jeremiah, the Twelve in one book, Daniel, Ezekiel, Ezra. From these I have made selections, distributing them into six books.

APPENDIX : ORIGEN.

Remarks on this passage, sufficiently copious, the reader will find on p. 239, seq. above. As the earliest Christian writer who has given us a list of the Old Test. books, and as a man of much learning and distinguished piety, his testimony deserves special consideration.

No. V.

Testimony of Origen, preserved in Eusebius' Hist. Ecc. Lib. IV. c. 26.

Τὸν μέν τοιγε πρῶτον ἐξηγούμενος Ψαλμὸν, ἔκθεσιν πεποίηται ('Ωριγένης) τοῦ τῶν ἱερῶν γραφῶν τῆς παλαιᾶς διαθήκης καταλόγον, ὧδέ πως γράφων κατὰ λέξιν· " οὐκ ἀγνοητέον δ' εἶναι τὰς ἐνδιαθήκους βίβλους, ὡς Ἑβραῖοι παραδιδόασιν, δύο καὶ εἴκοσι· ὅσος ὁ ἀριθμὸς τῶν παρ' αὐτοῖς στοιχείων ἐστίν." Εἶτα μετά τινα ἐπιφέρει λέγων· " εἰσὶ δὲ αἱ εἴκοσι δύο βίβλοι καθ' Ἑβραίους αἵδε· ἡ παρ' ἡμῖν Γένεσις ἐπιγεγραμμένη, παρὰ δὲ Ἑβραίοις ἀπὸ τῆς ἀρχῆς τῆς βίβλου Β ρ η σ ὶ θ, ὅπερ ἐστὶν ἐν ἀρχῇ· Ἔξοδος, Ο ὐ α λ ε σ μ ὼ θ, ὅπερ ἐστὶ ταῦτα τὰ ὀνόματα· Λευιτικὸν, Ο ὐ ϊ κ ρ ὰ, καὶ ἐκάλεσεν· Ἀριθμοὶ, Ἀ μ μ ε σ φ ε κ ω δ ε ί μ· Δευτερονόμιον, Ἔ λ λ ε ἀ δ δ ε β α ρ ὶ μ, οὗτοι οἱ λόγοι· Ἰησοῦς υἱὸς Ναυῆ, Ἰ ω σ ο ῦ ε β ὲ ν Ν ο ῦ ν· Κριταὶ, Ῥούθ, παρ' αὐτοῖς ἐν ἑνὶ, Σ ω φ ε τ ί μ· Βασιλειῶν πρώτη, δευτέρα, παρ' αὐτοῖς ἐν Σ α μ ο υ ή λ, ὁ θεόκλητος· Βασιλειῶν τρίτη, τετάρτη, ἐν ἑνὶ, Ο ὐ α μ μ έ λ ε χ Δ α β ί δ, ὅπερ ἐστὶ βασιλείετα Δαβίδ· Παραλειπομένων πρώτη, δευτέρα, ἐν ἑνὶ, Δ ι β ρ ή Ἀ ϊ α μ ὶ μ, ὅπερ ἐστὶ λόγοι ἡμερῶν· Ἔσδρας πρῶτος καὶ δεύτερος ἐν ἑνὶ, Ἐ ζ ρ ᾶ, ὅ ἐστι βοηθός· βίβλος Ψαλμῶν, Σ έ φ ε ρ Θ ι λ λ ί μ· Σολομῶντος Παροιμίαι, Μ ι σ λ ώ θ· Ἐκκλησιαστὴς, Κ ω έ λ ε θ· Ἄσμα Ἀσμάτων, Σ ὶ ρ ἀ σ σ ι ρ ί μ· Ἠσαΐας Ἰ ε σ α ϊ ά· Ἱερεμίας σὺν Θρήνοις καὶ τῇ Ἐπίστολῇ, ἐν ἑνὶ, Ἱ ε ρ ε μ ί α· Δανιήλ, Δ α ν ι ή λ. Ἰεζεκιήλ, Ἰ ε ζ ε κ ι ή λ· Ἰὼβ, Ἰ ώ β· Ἐσθὴρ, Ἐ σ θ ή ρ. Ἔξω δὲ τούτων ἐστὶ τὰ Μακκαβαϊκὰ, ἅπερ ἐπιγέγραπται Σ α ρ β ὴ θ σ α ρ β α ν ὲ ἔ λ.

TRANSLATION. In explaining the first Psalm, he [Origen] sets forth a catalogical view of the sacred books of the Old Testament; describing them in the following manner, " One must not be ignorant, that there are *twenty-two books* of the covenant, as the Hebrews reckon them; which is the number of letters in their alphabet." Then, after some remarks, he adds, " Moreover the *twenty-two books* of the Hebrews are these; the book entitled Genesis by us, but by the Hebrews *Bresith*, from the beginning of the book, for this means *in the beginning*; Exodus, *Oualesmoth*, i. e. these are the names; Leviticus, *Ouikra*, i. e. and he called; Numbers, *Ammesphekodim*; Deuteronomy, *Elle Haddebarim*, i. e. these are the words; Joshua the son of Nun, *Josue ben Noun;* Judges, Ruth, with them [the Hebrews] in one, *Sophetim;* Kings first and second, among them one, *Samouel*, the called of God; Kings third and fourth in one, *Ouammelech David*, i. e. the reign of David; Chronicles (or Supplement) first and second, in one, *Dibre Aiamim*, i. e. accounts of the times; Ezra first and second, in one, *Ezra*, which means *helper;* the book of Psalms, *Sepher Thillim;* the Proverbs of Solomon, *Misloth;* Ecclesiastes, *Koeleth;* the Song of Songs, *Sir Hassirim;* Isaiah, *Jesaia;* Jeremiah with Lamentations and the epistle, in one, *Jeremia;* Daniel, *Daniel;* Ezekiel, *Ieezkel;* Job, *Job ;* Esther, *Esther*. Besides these, there are the Maccabees, which are inscribed *Sarbeth Sarbene El*.

The names in *Italic* are the representatives of the Hebrew names of the books. Of the twenty-two books, said by Origen to belong to Hebrew Scriptures, he produces (as related by Eusebius) only twenty-*one*. But there can be no doubt that this is an error either in the copy of Eusebius, or of some of his transcribers. (See on this subject, p. 242, above.) The fact that Rufinus, in his translation of Origen, specifies the Twelve Minor Prophets, (in one book, as always in ancient times,) which are omitted in the catalogue above, and also the nature of the case, (since Origen has said that there are twenty-two books,) make it entirely clear that Origen's catalogue originally contained, or was intended to contain, the Prophets in question.

In respect to the MACCABEES, the Hebrew title which Origen has given it, (the first book only is meant,) shows that he was acquainted with the work in Hebrew; in which, no doubt, it was originally composed. So says Jerome: " Maccabæorum primum librum Hebraicum reperi. Secundus Græcus est; quod ex ipsâ quoque phrasi probari potest; i. e. The First Book of the Maccabees I found in Hebrew. The Second is Greek; which is evident from its phraseology." In Prol. Galeato. This is the reason why Origen speaks of it as being among the books of the Hebrews. But he expressly separates it from their *canonical* books: ἔξω δὲ τούτων, κ. τ. λ. To count upon Origen as *including* the Maccabees in his Canon, as Herbst does, is strange enough, after Origen himself has separated it by an ἔξω, i. e. *extrinsic*, *abroad, foreign.* In respect to the meaning of the Hebrew title, as given in the unskilful manner of Origen, who makes the Greek letters the representatives of it, not improbably it may be: *History of the Princes of the sons of God,* i. e. שרבת שרי בני אל, the first word being employed in its Aramæan sense; which would be no improbability, at the time when the book was written. Other explanations may be seen in Eichh. Einl. IV. p. 222 ; but they are less probable. The *princes* seem to be the Maccabæan leaders, and the *sons of God* means the party of the pious who clave to these leaders. There was another apocryphal book, also, extant probably in Hebrew, in Origen's day, namely, the Wisdom of Sirach. But he does not appear to have seen any thing but the *Greek* copy, when he wrote the catalogue above.

I would merely remark at the close, that Origen, from his long-continued critical study of the Scriptures, his enlightened views in relation to this subject, his integrity, and his long residence both in Egypt and in Palestine, must have fully known what the Jews in general, in both countries, thought in respect to their Canon. One difficulty only remains. This is, that Origen not only includes Lamentations with Jeremiah, but also an *epistle,* or rather *the epistle.* What is this? Is it the so-called Epistle of Jeremiah to the captives at Babylon, which constitutes one of the apocryphal books, and consists of seventy-three verses? So the Romanists affirm. But of this I must doubt; because no other ancient list of the sacred books has comprised this with Jeremiah and Lamentations, excepting such as appear to be copied from him. That Jeremiah wrote *letters* to the exiled Jews, is certain ; see Jer. xxix. That some of his predictions were written by Baruch separately, is plain from Jer. xxxvi. I cannot but feel, that some of the epistles named in the book of Jeremiah were added to it, at least in the copy which Origen had, in the way of an appendage, instead of being incorporated with the main body of the work. In the time of Jerome, the apocryphal Epistle of Jeremiah, as Herbst confesses, (Einl. p. 14,) was incorporated with Baruch, as a sixth chapter (and so oftentimes since); and yet of this Jerome says expressly, "Librum Baruch, qui apud Hebræos *nec legitur nec habetur,* prætermisimus, i. e. the book of Baruch, which the Hebrews *neither read nor possess*, we pass by." We must, therefore, either attribute error to Origen in respect to the *Epistle* in question, or explain it in some such way as I have done. The Council of Laodicea, as will be seen in the sequel, Hilary, also Cyrill of Jerusalem, Athanasius, and Synopsis Scripturæ, (in Opp. Athanas.,) all exhibit the same or the like difficulties, in regard to the component parts of Jeremiah, probably copying in this respect the representation of Origen. The disjointed and as it were fragmentary state of Jeremiah in ancient times, (witness the Septuagint Version,) is in all probability the basis of this peculiarity in some of the ancient lists of the scriptural books. The matter has not yet been fully cleared up; but the weight of testimony is altogether against the supposition of an *apocryphal* book being meant.

No. VI.

List of canonical Books as made out by the Council of Laodicea; (between A. D. 360—364.)

CAN. 59. Ὅτι οὐ δεῖ ἰδιωτικοὺς ψαλμοὺς λέγεσθαι ἐν τῇ ἐκκλησίᾳ, οὐδὲ ἀκανόνιστα βιβλία, ἀλλὰ μόνα τὰ κανονικὰ τῆς καινῆς καὶ παλαιᾶς διαθήκης. Can. 60. Ὅσα δεῖ βιβλία ἀναγινώσκεσθαι τῆς παλαιᾶς διαθήκης· ά, Γένεσις κόσμου. β', Ἔξοδος ἐξ Αἰγύπτου. γ', Λευιτικόν. δ', Ἀριθμοί. ἐ, Δευτερονόμιον. στ', Ἰησοῦς Ναυῆ. ζ', Κριταί. Ῥούθ. ἡ, Ἐσθήρ. θ', Βασιλειῶν ά, β'. ί, Βασιλειῶν γ', δ'. ιά, Παραλειπόμενα ά, β'. ιβ', Ἔσδρας, ά, β'. ιγ', βίβλος Ψαλμῶν ρν'. ιδ', Παροιμίαι Σαλομῶντος. ιέ, Ἐκκλησιαστής. ιστ', Ἄσμα Ἀσμάτων. ιζ', Ἰώβ. ιή, Δώδεκα προφῆται. ιθ', Ἡσαΐας. κ', Ἱερεμίας καὶ Βαροὺχ, Θρῆνοι καὶ Ἐπιστολαί. κά, Ἰεζεκιήλ. κβ', Δανιήλ.

TRANSLATION. Canon 59. Private Psalms must not be read in the church, nor uncanonical books, but only the canonical ones of the New and Old Testaments. Canon 60. The books of the Old Testament which ought to be read: (1.) Genesis of the world. (2.) Exodus from Egypt. (3.) Leviticus. (4.) Numbers. (5.) Deuteronomy. (6.) Joshua of Nun. (7.) Judges, Ruth. (8.) Esther. (9.) 1 Kings, first and second [1 and 2 Samuel]. (10.) 2 Kings, first and second. (11.) Chronicles, first and second. (12.) Ezra, first and second [i. e. Ezra and Nehemiah]. (13.) The book of Psalms, 150. (14.) Proverbs of Solomon. (15.) Ecclesiastes. (16.) Song of Songs. (17.) Job. (18.) Twelve Prophets. (19.) Isaiah. (20.) Jeremiah and Baruch, the Lamentations and the Epistles. (21.) Ezekiel. (22.) Daniel.

The Hagiography are here all put in junction together; Chronicles is joined with the historical books; Esther is placed before them; Job after the Hagiography; the twelve Prophets before the others; and Daniel along with them; as in our Bibles. But as this Council used the Septuagint, we cannot say with certainty that they followed any of the usual Hebrew copies in arrangement. How near they come to Origen, is plain from the peculiar alleged contents of the book of Jeremiah. Baruch and the (apocryphal?) Epistle both are included. These were probably now joined in one book, (as in Jerome's time,) and so they are here named. The solution of this phenomenon which appears most probable to me, I have already given in my remarks on the list of Origen.

No. VII.

Cyrill of Jerusalem, (flor. A. D. 350,) in Hierosol. Catechesis, IV. No. 33—36. Opp. p. 69, edit. Touttei.

Ἀναγίνωσκε τὰς θείας γραφάς, τάς εἴκοσι δύο βίβλους τῆς παλαιᾶς διαθήκης, τὰς ὑπὸ τῶν ἑβδομήκοντα δύο ἑρμηνευτῶν ἑρμηνευθείσας. —— — Τοῦ νόμου μὲν γὰρ εἰσιν αἱ Μωσέως πρῶται πέντε βίβλοι. —— ἑξῆς δὲ, Ἰησοῦς υἱὸς Ναυῆ, καὶ τῶν Κριτῶν μετὰ τῆς Ῥοὺθ βιβλίον ἕβδομον ἀριθμούμενον, τῶν δὲ λοιπῶν ἱστορικῶν βιβλίων, πρώτη καὶ δευτέρα τῶν Βασιλειῶν, μία παρ' Ἑβραίοις ἐστὶ βίβλος· μία δὲ καὶ ἡ τρίτη καὶ ἡ τετάρτη· ὁμοίως δὲ παρ' αὐτοῖς καὶ τῶν Παραλειπομένων ἡ πρώτη καὶ ἡ δευτέρα, μία τυγχάνει βίβλος, καὶ τοῦ Ἔσδρα ἡ πρώτη καὶ ἡ δευτέρα, μία λελόγισται· δωδεκάτη βίβλος ἡ Ἐσθήρ. καὶ τὰ μὲν ἱ σ τ ο ρ ι κ ὰ ταῦτα. τὰ δὲ σ τ ο ι χ η ρ ὰ τυγχάνει πέντε, Ἰὼβ, καὶ βίβλος Ψαλμῶν, καὶ Παροιμίαι, καὶ Ἐκκλησιαστής, καὶ Ἄσμα Ἀσμάτων, ἑπτακαιδέκατον βιβλίον· ἐπὶ δὲ τούτοις τὰ π ρ ο φ η τ ι κ ὰ πέντε· τῶν δώδεκα προφητῶν μία βίβλος, καὶ Ἡσαΐου μία, καὶ Ἰερεμίου μετὰ Βαροὺχ καὶ Θρήνων καὶ Ἐπιστολῆς· εἶτα Ἰεζεκιήλ· καὶ ἡ τοῦ Δανιὴλ εἰκοστηδευτέρα βίβλος τῆς παλαίας διαθήκης.

APPENDIX : GREGORY.   409

TRANSLATION. Make yourself well acquainted with the divine Scriptures, the twenty-two books of the Old Testament, which were translated by the seventy-two interpreters .... The first five books are of Moses, which is the Law .... Then comes Joshua of Nun ; Judges with Ruth, numbered the seventh book; of the remaining historical books, first and second of Kings [1 and 2 Sam.], one book among the Hebrews. One also is the third and fourth of Kings; with them also the Chronicles, first and second, are one book ; the first and second of Ezra [Ez. Neh.] are reckoned as one ; the twelfth book is Esther ; and these are the *historical* ones. The *poetical* books are five ; viz. Job, the book of Psalms, Proverbs, Ecclesiastes, and the Song of Songs, the seventeenth book. To these must be added five *prophetic* ones ; the twelve Prophets, one book ; one also of Isaiah ; of Jeremiah with Baruch, Lamentations, and the Epistle ; then Ezekiel ; and Daniel, the *twenty-second* book of the Old Testament.

Here is a different arrangement still, which is the same for the most part as in our present English Bibles. The only exception is, that the Minor Prophets are placed before the others. The books of the Hagiography, as described by Josephus, are here all associated and called στοιχηρά, i. e. measured, in metre, or poetic. The same difficulty also appears here, as in the Canon of the Laodicean Council, in respect to the constituent parts of Jeremiah. I have nothing more to say concerning this difficulty, than what I have already said. The list of books was evidently copied from the like source with the list of the Council, i. e. it was probably made out from Origen's Catalogue.

No. VIII.

Gregory Nazianzen, (flor. 370,) Opp. II. Carmina, XXXIII.

IN this 33d Carmen or sacred Ode, Gregory has undertaken, in accordance with the taste and fancy of the times, to throw the names of all the sacred books into measured verse. He thus proceeds with the Old Testament :

Ἱστορικαὶ μὲν εἰσι βίβλοι δυοκαίδεκα πᾶσαι,
Τῆς ἀρχαιοτέρης Ἐβραϊκῆς σοφίης.
Πρωτίστη Γένεσις, εἶτ᾽ Ἔξοδος, Λευιτικόντε,
Ἔπειτ᾽ Ἀριθμοί, εἶτα δεύτερος Νόμος.
Ἔπειτ᾽ Ἰησοῦς, καὶ Κριταί· Ῥοὺθ ὀγδόη·
Ἡ δὲ ἐνάτη δεκάτη τε βίβλοι, πράξεις Βασιλήων,
Καὶ Παραλειπόμεναι· ἔσχατον Ἔσδραν ἔχεις.

Αἱ δὲ στιχηραὶ πέντε, ὧν πρῶτός γε Ἰώβ,
Ἔπειτα Δαυίδ, εἶτα τρεῖς Σολομώντειαι,
Ἐκκλησιαστής, Ἄσμα, καὶ Παροιμίαι.
Καὶ πένθ' ὁμοίως πνεύματος προφητικοῦ·
Μίαν μέν εἰσιν ἐς γραφὴν οἱ δώδεκα,
Ὡσηέ, καὶ Ἀμώς, καὶ Μιχαίας ὁ τρίτος,
Ἔπειτ' Ἰωήλ, εἶτ' Ἰωνᾶς, Ἀβδίας,
Ναούμ τε, Ἀββακούμ τε, καὶ Σοφονίας,
Ἀγγαῖος, εἶτα Ζαχαρίας, Μαλαχίας·
Μία μὲν οἵδε. Δευτέρα δὲ Ἡσαΐας,
Ἔπειθ' ὁ κληθεὶς Ἱερεμίας ἐκ βρέφους,
Εἶτ' Ἰεζεκιήλ, καὶ Δανιήλου χάρις.
Ἀρχαίας μὲν ἔθηκα δύω καὶ εἴκοσι βίβλους,
Τοῖς τῶν Ἑβραίων γράμμασιν ἀντιθέτους.

TRANSLATION. All the historical books are twelve, of the ancient Hebrew wisdom. First Genesis, then Exodus, and Leviticus, then Numbers, then Deuteronomy. Then Joshua, and Judges; Ruth is the eighth; the ninth and tenth books are the acts of Kings; then Chronicles; the last is Ezra. There are *five* books in metre; the first of which is Job, then David, [Psalms,] three belong to Solomon, viz. Ecclesiastes, Canticles, Proverbs. In like manner there are *five* of the prophetic Spirit; twelve of these are comprised in one, viz. Hosea, Amos, Micah, then Joel, Jonah, Obadiah, Nahum, Habakkuk, Zephaniah, Haggai, Zechariah, and Malachi; these make the first. The second is Isaiah, then Jeremiah, who was called from the womb, Ezekiel, and the grace of Daniel. I have exhibited twenty-two books, corresponding with the twenty-two letters of the Hebrews.

It will be perceived, that in making out *twenty-two* books, Gregory has separated Ruth from Judges, and omitted Esther. The same omission we find in Athanasius, and in some other cases; but the testimony of Josephus, and of the feast of Purim, in behalf of the antiquity of this book, place it beyond our reach to call in question its place in the Canon. We have found the same omission in Melito, (p. 241, seq.,) but have supposed it to belong, in that case, merely to error in transcribing. In Melito and in Gregory, *Ezra* no doubt comprehends Nehemiah; for such was the usual custom of the ancients. But in Gregory, there is an evident *purpose* of omitting Esther; for he has separated Judges and Ruth, in order to make out the *twenty-two* books which are the usual number. It is difficult to say what was the inducement to this, unless it was, that the Greek copy

APPENDIX : ATHANASIUS.   411

of the Scriptures in his hands, embraced Esther with all the Alexandrine interpolations. No wonder he (having no acquaintance with the Hebrews) rejected it, if such were the case. Not a word in Gregory about any of the *apocryphal* books; and yet he entitles his Ode, περὶ τῶν γνησίων βιβλίων τῆς Θεοπνεύστου Γραφῆς, i. e. concerning the *genuine* books of the inspired Scriptures. Of course he regards books not named as not belonging to this category; and therefore he must have rejected the Apocrypha.

One other thing is worthy of note here, viz. that both Cyrill of Jerusalem and Gregory Nazianzen make a *triplex* division of the Scriptures; but not on Talmudic ground. They divide them into twelve *historical*, five *poetical*, and five *prophetical* books; for, on the ground of their ignorance of the true nature of Hebrew poetry, they never dreamed that the prophets were mostly *poetic*. Their division is not a bad one, inasmuch as it is built on the *matter* and *manner* of the books; with the exception of their error about the form of prophetic composition. It is substantially adopted in our English Bibles. Let the reader note well, in examining all these lists of the Old Testament Books, that not one of them joins Chronicles or Daniel with the Kethubim or Hagiography.

No. IX.

Athanasius of Alexandria, (flor. A. D. 326,) in an extract from his 37th festal Epistle, inserted in Opp. I. p. 961.

ATHANASIUS prefaces his list of Sacred Books by the following remarks:

"We fear lest, as Paul wrote to the Corinthians, a few of the simple may wander away from their simplicity and purity by reason of the craftiness of certain men, and finally may begin to take themselves to the books called *apocryphal*, being deceived by their likeness to the true books. I beseech you to bear with me, if I write to you reminding you of things already known, on account of the necessity and the edification of the church. Being about to do this, I shall employ, for the support of my undertaking, the formula of Luke the evangelist, saying as he did: Forasmuch as there are some who have undertaken to compose for themselves books called *apocryphal*, and to mingle these with the inspired Scripture, respecting which we have been fully persuaded, as eye-witnesses and ministers of the word from the beginning

have delivered to the Fathers, it seemed good to me also, being exhorted
thereto by my genuine brethren, and having made myself acquainted
with the subject, to set forth from the beginning and in due order the
canonical books which have been delivered to us, and believed to be
Divine; so that every one, if he is led away by deceit, may learn well
to know those who have seduced him, while he who remains pure may
rejoice in having this admonition again repeated.

"All the books of the Old Testament, then, are twenty-two; as many,
according to report, as the alphabetic letters of the Hebrews. In order
and name they are thus: First the Genesis, then Exodus, next Leviticus, after this Numbers, and finally Deuteronomy. In the sequel of
these are Joshua of Nun, and Judges, and after this Ruth; and then
follow the four books of Kings, and of these the first and second are
numbered as one, and the third and fourth likewise as one. After these
is the book of Psalms, then Proverbs, Ecclesiastes, Song of Songs;
then comes Job, and finally the Prophets. Twelve of these are reckoned as one book; then comes Isaiah, Jeremiah with Baruch and Lamentations and the Epistle, after these Ezekiel, and Daniel. Thus far
are set forth the books of the Old Testament."

I have deemed it unnecessary to transcribe the original
Greek here, as it is so exactly like the preceding lists, except in some trifling particulars. One of these is that
Athanasius places Job after the Kethubim, and next before
the Prophets. He also omits, as has before been remarked,
the book of Esther. That it is designed in him will be clear
from the passage which follows, and which he subjoins to
his catalogue of the New Test. books that follow those of
the Old Testament as given above. The concluding part
runs thus:

"These are the fountains of salvation, so that he who thirsts for
these oracles may be filled with them. By these only is the doctrine of
godliness taught. Let no one add to these, or take any thing from
them. By these our Lord confounded the Sadducees, saying, Ye do
err, not knowing the Scriptures. To the Jews he said, in the way of
exhortation, Search the Scriptures, for these are they which testify of
me. But for the sake of more accuracy, I have deemed it necessary
also to set forth in this writing, that there are other books besides these,
which are not canonical, designated by the Fathers to be read by those
who have recently joined us, and are desirous to be instructed in the
doctrine of piety; viz. the Wisdom of Solomon, the Wisdom of Sirach,
and *Esther*, and Judith, and Tobit, and (as we call it) the Apostolic
Doctrine, ($\delta\iota\delta\alpha\chi\dot{\eta}$ $\tau\hat{\omega}\nu$ $\dot{\alpha}\pi o\sigma\tau\acute{o}\lambda\omega\nu$,) and the Shepherd. Those, then,
being canonical, and these *being read*, let there be no mention even of
any apocryphal book. These are the inventions of heretics, who compose them at their pleasure, assigning and adding to them dates, so
that they may have the semblance of ancient books, and that by this
means they may find occasion to lead the simple into error."

APPENDIX: SYNOPSIS SCRIPTURÆ SACRÆ.   413

This remarkable passage places the books which we name *apocryphal*, in their position as estimated by the Fathers in general. They might be *read* in order to enlarge our Christian knowledge of religious things; but they were merely subordinate and secondary. The *canonical* books were separated from them by a wide distinction.

Athanasius evidently uses *apocryphal* in the sense of *spurious, worthless*, and not merely to designate books not publicly read, as some of the earlier Fathers used it. I get the impression from what he has said, in the last paragraph quoted from him, that he intends and expects the second class of books only to be read *in private*, by recent converts desirous of acquiring more enlarged religious knowledge; for how otherwise could he limit the reading to *new converts?* As he has expressly named *Esther* among these, I do not see how we can avoid the conclusion, that he positively rejected it from the proper Canon of the Old Testament. He makes twenty-two books, by separating Judges and Ruth, and omitting Esther. This is a peculiar circumstance, both in Gregory and Athanasius; but the reasons of it we can only conjecture, for we have no certain clue by which we can come to a proper historical knowledge of them. At all events, they can have no influence, (in the face of so much other testimony to the canonical rank of Esther,) in moving us to reject the book as they have done.

No. X.

SYNOPSIS SCRIPTURÆ SACRÆ, by an unknown writer of the times of Athanasius, attributed by some to him, and published in his Works, Vol. II. p. 126, seq.

THE Benedictine editors of Athanasius speak in exalted terms of the erudition and judgment of the writer of this Synopsis, whom they think not to be Athanasius. He has shown an accurate acquaintance with the holy books, and particularized each, by an extract from the commencement of each book, which he subjoins to the name of the book. To spare room, I omit the Greek original and the extracts, and give here the list of books, in his own language.

TRANSLATION. Genesis, Exodus, Leviticus, Numbers, Deuteronomy, Joshua the son of Nun, Judges, Ruth, 1 and 2 Kings [1 and 2 Samuel] reckoned as one book, 3 and 4 Kings numbered as one book, 1 and 2 Chronicles reckoned as one book, 1 and 2 Ezra [Ezra and Nehemiah] reckoned as one book, Psalter of David having 150 Psalms, Parables of Solomon, Ecclesiastes, Song of Songs, Job, Twelve Prophets, viz. Hosea, Amos, Micha, Joel, Obadiah, Jonah, Nahum, Habakkuk, Zephaniah, Haggai, Zechariah, Malachi, (these are comprised in one book,) Isaiah, Jeremiah, Ezekiel, Daniel. The canonical books of the Old Testament are *twenty-two*, equal in number to the Hebrew letters; for they have so many elementary signs.

Besides these are other books of the Old Testament, *which are not canonical* [inspired]; *and these are read only by catechumens;* viz. Wisdom of Solomon, Wisdom of Jesus the son of Sirach, Esther, Judith, Tobit. Thus many are the books of the Old Testament *not canonical.* Some of the ancients have affirmed Esther to be canonical among the Hebrews; and also that Ruth is joined with Judges and reckoned as one book. In this manner they make out the complement of twenty-two books.

The books of the Old Testament, canonical and uncanonical, are so many, and of such a kind.

It is easy to see, that this is little else than an exact copy, throughout, of the list of Athanasius. But the writer is more explicit. While he omits Esther in his list, he gives us an acccount of a different opinion, viz. in favour of inserting it. So he also notices the usual manner in which Ruth was united with Judges. He also tells us that *only the catechumens* read the uncanonical, i. e. uninspired books, which had been appended to the Old Testament. This seems of course to exclude the *public reading* of them, at least in the churches within his circle of knowledge.

Having completed his list, the writer proceeds to give a synopsis of the contents of each book; and when he has completed his summary of the *canonical* books, he again mentions that the others *are not read,* except in the limited manner already described; p. 168. It seems singular that no mention is here made of the Maccabees, Baruch, the additions to Daniel, Ezra, &c. Nothing can be clearer, however, than that Athanasius and the author of the Synopsis reject the idea of *inspiration*, in regard to what we now name *apocryphal* books. But at the close of his work the author of the Synopsis says, "The books of the Old Testament which are doubted ($ἀντιλεγόμενα$=denied) are Wisdom, Sirach, Esther, Judith, Tobit. With these also are

APPENDIX: EPIPHANIUS. 415

numbered Maccabees, four books, *Ptolemaici* (?), Psalms, Canticles, Susanna. These are the books of the Old Testament which are denied (ἀντιλεγόμενα)." As this is quite an enlargement of his previous list of uncanonical books, so it serves to show, that the latter class just mentioned did not attain even to the privilege of being allowed to the catechumens. An inauspicious passage to the Romish deutero-canon!

No. XI.

EPIPHANIUS, (flor. A. D. 368,) de Mensuris et Ponderibus, c. xxiii. Vol. II. p. 180, edit. Petav.

EPIPHANIUS has spoken in three different places respecting the Canon of the Old Testament; viz. in the passage named above, in Hæres. VIII., and Hæres. LXXVI. In the first two passages he gives a catalogue of the books. The most complete is the one here selected.

He prefaces his list with the following remarks : "The Hebrews have twenty-two letters; according to these they number their books, although they are in reality twenty-seven. But since with them five letters are double, making in fact twenty-seven, they contract them into twenty-two: and so the books which are twenty-seven are contracted into twenty-two." He then goes on to give a list of the books; which I copy here, because the curiosity of the Hebrew student will be gratified to learn how Epiphanius pronounced Hebrew, and in what way he represented it.

Πρώτη Βρισὴϑ, ἡ καλεῖται Γένεσις κόσμου· ἐλησιμὼϑ, ἡ Ἔξοδος τῶν υἱῶν Ἰσραὴλ ἐξ Αἰγύπτου· οὐδωϊεκρὰ, ἡ ἑρμηνεύεται Λευιτικόν· ἰουδαβὴρ, ἥ ἐστιν Ἀριϑμοί· ἐλλεδεβαρεὶμ, τὸ Δευτερονόμιον. Διησοῦ, ἡ τοῦ Ἰησοῦ τοῦ Ναυῆ· διὼβ, ἡ τοῦ Ἰώβ· διασοφϑεὶμ, ἡ τῶν Κριτῶν· διαρούϑ, ἡ τοῦ Ῥούϑ· σφερτελεὶμ, τὸ Ψαλτήριον· δεβρϊϊαμεὶμ, ἡ πρώτη τῶν Παραλειπομένων· δεβρϊϊαμεὶμ, Παραλειπομένων δευτέρα· δεμονὲλ, Βασιλειῶν πρώτη· δαδουδεμονὲλ, Βασιλειῶν δευτέρα· δμαλαχεὶ, Βασιλειῶν τρίτη· δμαλαχεὶ, Βασιλειῶν τετάρτη· δμεαλὼϑ, ἡ Παροιμιῶν· δεκωέλεϑ, Ἐκκλησιαστής· σιρασισεὶμ, τὸ Ἆισμα τῶν Ἀισμάτων·

δαθαριασαρὰ, τὸ Δωδεκαπρόφητον· ὀησαΐου, τοῦ προφήτου Ἠσαΐου· διερεμίου, ἡ τοῦ Ἱερεμίου· διεζεκιὴλ, ἡ τοῦ Ἰεζεκιήλ· διδανιὴλ, ἡ τοῦ Δανιήλ· διδέσδρα, ἡ τοῦ Ἔσδρα πρώτη· διδέσδρα, ἡ τοῦ Ἔσδρα δευτέρα· δεσθὴρ, ἡ τῆς Ἐσθήρ.

TRANSLATION. First Genesis, which is called Genesis of the world; Exodus, i. e. departure of the sons of Israel from Egypt; Leviticus, Numbers, Deuteronomy, Joshua of Nun, Job, Judges, Ruth, the Psalter, 1 and 2 Chronicles, 1 and 2 Kings [1 and 2 Samuel], 3 and 4 Kings, Proverbs, Ecclesiastes, Canticles, Minor Prophets, Isaiah, Jeremiah, Ezekiel, Daniel, 1 and 2 Ezra [Ezra and Nehemiah], Esther.

I have omitted in this version all the Hebrew names, and such words as are connected merely with the representation of them. Although Epiphanius was born and brought up in Palestine, and must have had some knowledge of the Hebrew language, the Hebrew names inserted in this list are but a sorry testimony to the accuracy of that knowledge. However, there is no doubt that he has suffered from transcribers; e. g. σιρασισείμ, for השירים, where -σειμ in Epiphanius's present text stands clearly for -ρειμ, by a mistake of copyists. The ει, here and elsewhere, represents the long Hhirêq in Hebrew. Peculiar is his prefixing the Aramæan ד to most of the names, which he writes δ, δα, δε, and even διδ, δια, and which means *of*, i. e. book *of* such or such a name. The name of Psalms, σφερτελείμ, = ספר תהלים. In some other cases, which I cannot here particularize, the Hebrew names are doubtless deformed by the ignorance of copyists; e. g. δεμουέλ = שמואל, δαδουδεμουέλ = David-Samuel? &c. But—to my direct object.

Epiphanius adds to the list translated above, after some remarks which we need not here repeat, "There is another little book, named *Kinoth*, which means the Lamentations of Jeremiah. The same, which exceeds the due number, is joined and united with Jeremiah." He then goes on, in the fashion of the day, to find corresponding *twenty-twos*, in a variety of things presented in the Scriptures.

We perceive that the list of Old Test. books is here complete; although the order is diverse from all others which have been presented. Job is placed, for example, after Joshua; but in his other list (Hæres. VIII. Tom. I. p. 19) he puts Job after Judges and Ruth. In the list above we have Judges, Ruth, Psalter, 1 and 2 Chronicles, Kings, &c.;

APPENDIX: COUNCIL OF HIPPO. 417

in the other list Judges, Ruth, Job, Psalter, Proverbs, &c. There are also other varieties. Altogether compared and considered, this Father appears to have been probably an honest, but yet a very hasty and blundering critic.

We must not omit what he says of the *deutero-canonical* books. It runs thus, "There are two other books *doubtful* among them, the *Wisdom of Sirach* and the *Wisdom of Solomon;* besides certain other books which are apocryphal." By this I understand Epiphanius to say, that the two books mentioned are *doubtful*, and the others clearly *uninspired*.

It will be seen by our next document, that the reception of the apocryphal books as deutero-canonical, had begun about this time to make some progress among the churches. There is no doubt that it had been gaining among the more unlearned and undiscerning, during most of the fourth century. Hence we are prepared for the first manifestation of it, in a public and a kind of authoritative way, in the manner announced by our next extract.

No. XII.

Extract from the Statuta of the COUNCIL OF HIPPO, A .D. 393. Mansi, Concil. Coll. III. p. 924.

THE XXXVI. Statutum runs thus : Ut præter Scripturas canonicas nihil in Ecclesia legatur sub nomine divinarum Scripturarum. Sunt autem canonicæ Scripturæ, Genesis, Exodus, Leviticus, Numeri, Deuteronomium, Jesu Nave, Judicum, Ruth, Regnorum libri quatuor, Paralipomenon libri duo, Job, Psalterium Davidicum, *Salomonis libri quinque*, duodecim libri Prophetarum, Esaias, Jeremias, Daniel, Ezechiel, *Tobias, Judith*, Hester, Hesdras libri duo, *Macchabæorum* libri duo.

This needs no translation. I have marked those books which are additions to all the catalogues hitherto exhibited. *The five books of Solomon* of course are Proverbs, Ecclesiastes, Canticles, the *Wisdom of Solomon*, and *Sirach*. Then we have Tobit, Judith, and 1 and 2 Maccabees. Here all the books are mingled together and stand under the category of *canonical*. There can be no doubt, that this Council meant so to decide.

No. XIII.

COUNCIL OF CARTHAGE, held A. D. 397. Extract from Cap. XLVII. of their decrees; Mansi III. p. 891.

This Council have repeated *totidem verbis* the list of the Council of Hippo, in No. XII., and doubtless consisted mostly of the same bishops. It is therefore unnecessary to repeat their words. On these two Councils the Romish church depend for the establishment of their *deutero-canon*. And yet even these do not reach the whole of it.

No. XIV.

Testimony of Jerome, extracted from his Prologus Galeatus;
(flor. A. D. 380.)

VIGINTI et duas litteras esse apud Hebræos, Syrorum quoque lingua et Chaldæorum testatur, quæ Hebrææ magna ex parte confinis est. Nam et ipsi viginti duo elementa habent, eodem sono et diversis characteribus.—Porro quinque litteræ duplices apud Hebræos sunt, Caph, Mem, Nun, Pe, Sade. Unde et quinque a plerisque libri duplices existimantur, *Samuel, Melachim, Dibre hajammim, Esdras, Jeremias* cum Cinoth, id est lamentationibus suis. Quomodo igitur viginti duo elementa sunt, per quæ scribimus hebraice omne quod loquimur, et eorum initiis vox humana comprehenditur; ita *viginti duo volumina* supputantur, quibus quasi litteris et exordiis in Dei doctrina, tenera adhuc et lactens viri justi eruditur infantia.

Primus apud eos liber vocatur *Beresith*, quem nos Genesin dicimus. Secundus *Veelle Semoth.* Tertius *Vajicra*, id est Leviticus. Quartus *Vajedabber*, quem Numeros vocamus. Quintus *Elle haddebarim*, qui Deuteronomium prænotatur. Hi sunt quinque libri Mosis, quos proprie *Thora*, id est Legem, appellant.

Secundum *Prophetarum* ordinem faciunt, et incipiunt ab Jesu filio Nave, qui apud eos *Josue Ben Nun* dicitur. Deinde subtexunt *Sophetim*, id est Judicum librum, et in eundem compingunt *Ruth*, quia in diebus Judicum facta ejus narratur historia. Tertius sequitur *Samuel*, quem nos Regum primum et secundum dicimus. Quartus *Melachim,* id est Regum, qui tertio et quarto Regum volumine continetur. Meliusque multo est Melachim, id est Regum, quam Melachoth, id est Regnorum, dicere : Non enim multarum gentium describit regna, sed unius Israelitici populi, qui tribubus duodecim continetur. Quintus est *Esaias.* Sextus *Jeremias.* Septimus *Ezechiel.* Octavus liber duodecim Prophetarum, qui apud illos vocatur *Thereasar.*

Tertius ordo *Hagiographa* possidet. Et primus liber incipit a *Job.* Secundus a David, quem quinque incisionibus et uno *Psalmorum* volumine comprehendunt. Tertius est *Solomon,* tres libros habens, Proverbia, quæ illi *Misle,* id est Parabolas, appellant : Quartus Ecclesiastes, id est *Coheleth.* Quintus Canticum Canticorum, quem titulo *Sir hassirim* prænotant. Sextus est *Daniel.* Septimus *Dibre hajammim,* id est Verba dierum, quod significantius Chronicon totius divinæ historiæ possumus appellare, qui liber apud nos Paralipomenon primus et secundus inscribitur. Octavus *Esdras:* qui et ipse similiter apud Græcos et Latinos in duos libros divisus est. Nonus *Esther.*

Atque ita fiunt pariter *Veteris Legis libri viginti duo,* id est, *Mosis* quinque, et *Prophetarum* octo, *Hagiographorum* novem.

Quanquam nonnulli *Ruth* et *Cinoth* inter Hagiographa scriptitent, et hos libros in suo putent numero supputandos, ac per hoc esse priscæ Legis libros *viginti quatuor* — —

Hic prologus scripturarum quasi galeatum principium omnibus libris, quos de Hebræo vertimus in Latinum, convenire potest: ut scire valeamus, quicquid extra hos est, inter *apocrypha* esse ponendum. Igitur *Sapientia,* quæ vulgo Salomonis inscribitur, et *Jesu filii Sirach* liber, et *Judith,* et *Tobias,* et *Pastor,* non sunt in Canone. *Macchabæorum primum* librum hebraicum reperi. *Secundus* græcus est, quod ex ipsa quoque phrasi probari potest.

It was my intention to subjoin a full *translation* of this, for the convenience of some readers; but my limits forbid. Indeed a translation of such plain Latin is in a good measure unnecessary. I subjoin, however, the substance of what Jerome has here said.

(1.) He has given, in words that cannot be misunderstood, a list of the *canonical* books, just as they are in our present English Bibles; the *Protestant* canon, and not the Romish. He has so designated the books by Hebrew names, represented in Latin letters, (printed above in *Italic*,) that there is no room for mistake. (2.) He has made the Rabbinic division, in the main, of the *Prophets* and the *Hagiography;* but still, he makes only twenty-two books, and of course includes Ruth and Lamentations among the *Prophets,* (as attached to Judges and Jeremiah,) which the Talmud throws into the *Kethubim,* and thus makes twenty-four books; see p. 233, seq., above, where this whole matter is discussed, and the testimony of Jerome adduced. (3.) The passage of his, exhibited above, concerning the books which we name *apocryphal,* runs thus:

> This prologue may serve as an introduction to all the books of Scripture, which we have translated from Hebrew into Latin; so that we may be able to know, that *whatever is beyond* (or *extrinsic to*) *these is to be put among the* APOCRYPHAL BOOKS. Wherefore *Wisdom*, commonly ascribed to Solomon, the book of *Jesus the son of Sirach*, and *Judith*, and *Tobit*, and the *Shepherd*, ARE NOT IN THE CANON. The First of Maccabees I have found written in Hebrew; the Second in Greek, which indeed is manifest from its phraseology.*

Now since we know that Jerome uses the word *canonical* as equivalent to *inspired;* and as he avers the so-called *deutero-canonical* books to be *not* canonical, of course he pronounces them to be UNINSPIRED. It is to be remembered, also, that Jerome says all this, some twenty or more years after the Councils of Hippo and Carthage had pronounced their decrees in favour of the canonical rank of most of these books. Jerome, who lived in the midst of the bishops that constituted these Councils, (on whose decision the Romish church in a great measure rely for the credit of their Deutero-Canon,) decides fearlessly against them, as does Rufinus also. The opinion of one such critic as Jerome, respecting this subject, which he fully under-

---

* It was my intention to add to this Appendix a chapter, in which the claims of the *Apocrypha* (as we call it) would be critically examined, and some brief view of the nature and object of the books respectively be subjoined. But as I understand that the publishers of this volume design, if they find encouragement, to print an *English edition of the Apocrypha*, for the use of such persons as have a desire to investigate these ancient records, and in such a way as to embrace something of the *literary history* of the Apocrypha, and particularly of its *claims to a place in the Canon,* I have thought it best to omit the addition named above.

stood, is worth more than that of scores of Hipponensian and Carthaginian Councils, respecting a matter which they did not understand. How can such matters be decided, without any of the critical and philological knowledge which is necessary to judge rightly?

No. XV.

HILARY of Poictiers, (flor. A. D. 254,) Prologus in Lib. Psalm.; § 15. Opp. p. 9.

I SHALL merely give a translation of this section; as it seems to be little more than a repetition of Origen's list.

The reason why the Hebrews make twenty-two books, is because their alphabet has so many letters. The books, according to the tradition of the ancients, are thus designated: There are *five* books of Moses. (6.) Joshua the son of Nun. (7.) Judges and Ruth. (8.) 1 and 2 Kings [1 and 2 Samuel]. (9.) 3 and 4 Kings. (10.) 1 and 2 Chronicles. (11.) Ezra. (12.) Psalms. (13.) Proverbs. (14.) Ecclesiastes. (15.) Canticles. (16.) Twelve Prophets. Isaiah, Jeremiah with the Lamentation and Epistle, Daniel, Ezekiel, Job, Esther. These complete the number of twenty-two books. To some it seems good to add Tobit and Judith, and thus make out twenty-four books, according to the number of the letters in the Greek alphabet.

We see how κατὰ πόδα Hilary has followed Origen, from whom he draws most copiously, in his remarks on the Psalms. It is unnecessary, therefore, to say any thing more than what has already been said, respecting the testimony of Origen. One thing, however, is worthy of note, as to the *order* of books. Job and Esther are here put last of all; the twelve Prophets before the others; and Daniel before Ezekiel. He has also disclosed a new project for enlarging the Scriptures, viz. taking in *Tobit* and *Judith*—the most *apocryphal* of all the apocraphies. This only shows what a floating affair this whole matter of the *deutero-canonical* books was, in those times. Nothing is fixed and stable. In short, it is most manifest that the churches had not yet been brought to a general consent, that these books should be admitted.

No. XVI.

RUFINUS, (flor. A. D. 390,) the distinguished friend and opponent of Jerome; Expos. in Symbol. Apost., ad calcem Opp. Cypriani, ed. Oxon. p. 26.

HE thus commences: "Those volumes which belong to the Old and New Testament, which are, in accordance with the tradition of our ancestors, believed to be inspired by the Holy Spirit, and have been handed down to the churches of Christ, it seems appropriate to designate in this place." After this he proceeds as follows:

Itaque Veteris Instrumenti primo omnium Moysis quinque libri sunt traditi—post hos Jesu Nave, et Judicum, simul cum Ruth; quatuor post haec Regnorum libri quos Hebræi duos numerant; Paralipomenon, qui dierum dicitur liber; et Esdræ libri duo, qui apud illos singuli computantur; et Hester. Prophetarum vero Esaias, Hieremias, Ezechiel, et Daniel; præterea XII. Prophetarum liber unus. Job quoque, et Psalmi David, singuli sunt libri; Salomonis vero tres.

The order then in Rufinus is thus: Pentateuch; Joshua; Judges with Ruth; 1 and 2 Samuel in one book, viz. 1 Kings; 1 and 2 Kings in another, viz. 2 Kings; Chronicles, comprising two books; Ezra [Ezra and Nehemiah]; Esther; Isaiah; Jeremiah; Ezekiel; Daniel; Twelve Prophets; Job; Psalms; Solomon, three books [viz. Proverbs, Ecclesiastes, Canticles]. Here we have the true order, as seems plain, of Josephus' Hebrew Scriptures. After completing the list of the New Testament books he goes on to say, "*These are the books which the Fathers have included within the Canon, by which they would establish the assertions of our faith.* One should know, however, that there are other books, *which are not canonical*, but which our ancestors called *ecclesiastical*; e. g. the *Wisdom of Solomon*, *of Sirach*, called by the Latins *Ecclesiasticus* . . . . *Of the same order* is the little book of *Tobit* and *Judith*, and the books of the *Maccabees.*" Nothing can be more decisive or discriminating than this; and in this Rufinus agrees with all the leading Fathers.

THE END.

www.ingramcontent.com/pod-product-compliance
Lightning Source LLC
Chambersburg PA
CBHW060911300426
44112CB00011B/1421